MARKETING AND THE COMPUTER

Edited by WROE ALDERSON and STANLEY J. SHAPIRO

THIS BOOK is a full length treatment of the subject of computer applications in the field of marketing. It presents the subject in a style suitable for marketing professionals who *do not* have formal training in management science and computer technology.

Marketing and the Computer shows how computer techniques can aid marketing executives faced with difficulties in three areas:

(1) the solution of problems, (2) the movement of goods and information, and (3) long-range planning.

Theoretical discussions of possible applications are combined with detailed individual case studies of the computer at work as a tool of marketing executives to show the relevance and benefits of computer techniques.

No book designed to help marketing executives solve problems can omit discussion of significant recent developments in the field. Therefore, such topics as Bayesian decision theory, civilian applications of military planning techniques, industrial dynamics, simulation, and inventory theory as well as the essential role played by computers in these techniques are emphasized.

of Finance and Commerce, University of Pennsylvania.

MARKETING
AND
THE COMPUTER

EDITORS:

Wroe Alderson

Professor of Marketing and Director of the Management Science Center
Wharton School of Commerce and Finance
University of Pennsylvania

Stanley J. Shapiro

Assistant Professor of Marketing
Wharton School of Commerce and Finance
University of Pennsylvania

PRENTICE-HALL, INC.

MARKETING

AND

THE COMPUTER

ENGLEWOOD CLIFFS, N.J.

PRENTICE-HALL INTERNATIONAL, INC., *London*
PRENTICE-HALL OF AUSTRALIA, PTY., LTD., *Sydney*
PRENTICE-HALL OF CANADA, LTD., *Toronto*
PRENTICE-HALL OF JAPAN, INC., *Tokyo*

MARKETING AND THE COMPUTER

WROE ALDERSON and STANLEY J. SHAPIRO, editors

Second printing......June, 1965

Library of Congress Catalog Card Number 63-7403

Printed in the United States of America

55713-C

INTRODUCTION

This book is an outgrowth of the senior editor's belief that marketing executives and students of marketing are not fully aware of possible computer applications in their field. Although computers are playing an important role in business, marketing executives have been slower than their counterparts in finance, accounting or production to make use of this new and valuable piece of equipment. This delay may be due to the marketing executive's fear of a strange and unfamiliar tool, a wide-spread belief that marketing problems do not lend themselves to computer-oriented management science techniques or the monopolization of existing computer facilities by executives from the other functional areas of the business. In any case, the present volume is designed to overcome fears that might exist, to reveal how computers can and are being used in marketing, and to show the very real value of such computer applications. Since the prospective audience for this book was clearly defined, each contributor has directed his remarks and shaped his presentation to meet the needs of present and potential marketing executives.

The structure of the book is elaborated upon at some length in the opening chapter. In summary, however, emphasis is placed on three major difficulties which plague a decision maker; lack of information, inability to draw meaningful conclusions from and to base operating decisions on adequate information of unquestioned accuracy, and uncertainty as to the consequences associated with possible future strategies or alternate plans. The first three of the volume's five sections contain materials which indicate ways of overcoming or dealing with these problems. The chapters in the first section review the related flows of goods and information and the computer's role in facilitating these flows. The chapters on the physical distribution system and on warehouse design point up the often neglected fact that electronic data processing has accounted for much of the recent progress in these areas. In the second section of the book, certain important considerations in decision making are set forth, and techniques used to solve a number of marketing problems are explained and illustrated. The authors contributing to the third section discuss a number of computer-based approaches to various aspects of business planning. Although the management scientist would find little with which he is unfamiliar, the techniques and the benefits associated with their use have not been extensively discussed in marketing literature.

Inclusion of case studies in the fourth section of the book seemed logical, since one of the volume's previously stated objectives was to show that computers are being used as well as talked about in marketing circles. Consequently, cases and related readings were solicited from organizations that employ computers in their marketing operations. The range and number of cases is not as extensive as was originally planned. Many of the firms known to be using computers were reluctant to submit information for fear that they would be endangering a competitive advantage. Nevertheless, when the case studies and the results of the survey conducted by McKinsey & Company are added to the examples of computer use found in the first three sections of the volume, a full range of pertinent computer applications in marketing is presented. The essential content of each case study or related reading is indicated by its title. This material can thus be used as supplementary reading when references are made to corresponding applications in the text. The range of material covered in each chapter and the discussion by more than one contributor of topics such as forecasting and inventory control made a more formal linking of text and cases impractical.

The fifth and final section of the volume contains readings which are not directly related to the decision-making problems and activities of marketing executives. Although such material is placed in an appendix, the editors do not consider a knowledge of marketing-oriented business games or of computers themselves to be of secondary or limited importance. The material on the characteristics and possible marketing applications of various types of computers should be especially helpful to marketing executives whose firms have not yet purchased computers or are planning additional acquisitions of such equipment.

The editors believe that the book has some additional uses not fully appreciated at the time this venture was first undertaken. In the first three sections, some of the most important research presently being conducted in marketing is discussed. A volume designed to acquaint marketing managers with recent developments of great significance might be expected to include a review of Bayesian decision theory, civilian applications of military planning techniques, Industrial Dynamics, simulation, and inventory theory. The most advanced thinking in the design of warehouses and physical distribution systems would also have to be considered. These same topics are treated in this volume in a way that gives present and potential executives a grasp of the essential aspects of such techniques and developments while omitting treatment of points of interest primarily to technical specialists.

In retrospect, this book's adequacy as a partial guide to significant research in marketing is not surprising, since the computer plays an essential role in the techniques mentioned above. The present volume, of course, does not contain all the material that would be found in a publication primarily concerned with new approaches to research in marketing. Many important developments, some of them computer-oriented, have not been reviewed because they fall beyond the scope of the volume.

The editors also consider the book a useful source of additional readings or supplementary material for formal courses in marketing management. If one shares the senior editor's view that the marketing manager is primarily a planner and problem solver and that a course in marketing management should be structured accordingly, the usefulness and relevance of a volume of supplementary material emphasizing these two functions need not be belabored. Marketing management courses which treat these topics but stress the marketing manager's need to determine his opportunities and to adapt to a changing environment, to arrange for inter and intra-departmental coordination, to manipulate successfully the elements of the marketing mix, and to decide upon an acceptable product line are more common. In such courses, the present volume may give an added dimension to a text coverage which must be, in large part, descriptive and hortatory.

The chapter by Dr. Hertz, for example, points up more vividly than is usually the case the danger of suboptimization and the need for coordination between the various functional areas of the business. The simulation approach in general, and the contribution of Mr. Weymar in particular, raises some doubts as to the usefulness of any functional division. Although the importance of goods handling and physical distribution in marketing is gaining increased recognition, the contributors to this book have gone considerably beyond the standard check list to show how the costs of storing and shipping merchandise can be reduced. Mr. Sevin's article points up the difficulty of measuring the productivity of marketing dollars and of intelligently allocating resources to the different components of a marketing mix or the various products in a product line.

The book also contains other material which deals with topics frequently covered in marketing management courses. The articles by Dr. Fabian, Dr. Baumol, and Dr. Kuehn provide marketing students and executives of limited mathematical training with the important aspects of certain management science and operations research techniques. Dr. Jay Greene and Mr. Børge M. Christensen show how critical path scheduling, a computer-based approach originally designed for military use, can overcome some of the difficulties of coordinating efforts in the introduction of new products. Forecasting problems, procedures, and techniques are discussed in the chapters by Mr. Abouchar and Dr. Fabian as well as in a number of cases. Mr. Halbert and Dr. Paul Green have considered certain aspects and applications of statistical decision theory, another topic which can only be touched upon in the conventional marketing management text.

As the preceding comments indicate, the editors are pleased with the results of their venture and of the quality of their specially commissioned contributions. We believe that the book does reveal how computers can aid the marketing manager in his data gathering, decision making, and planning activities. Another cause of satisfaction is the successful tailoring of the content of the various chapters to the intended audience. Each contributor was selected because of unquestioned technical mastery of the subject area in which he has written. Indeed, many of the authors are widely recognized as outstanding management scientists and Operations Research practitioners. Another criterion in selection, however, was the belief that these men would be able to convey clearly and meaningfully the aspects of their work of greatest interest to marketing executives. The completed manuscripts indicate that our preliminary judgments as to the competence and expository skills of the contributors were justified.

WROE ALDERSON
STANLEY J. SHAPIRO

ACKNOWLEDGMENTS

There is no doubt as to whom the editors of a volume of especially prepared material are most beholden. It is to the numerous contributors who have taken time from busy schedules to write on the topics about what they are knowledgeable. We especially appreciate the promptness with which chapters were submitted and the good spirit with which the authors responded to frequent urgings that all else be disregarded until manuscripts were completed.

It would be impossible to give full credit to everyone else from whom the editors obtained advice and assistance. Some individuals, however, seem especially deserving of public mention. Many authors received useful suggestions on first drafts of their material from businessmen who attended a Wharton School conference on *Marketing and the Computer* in June of 1961. Funds received from the Ford Foundation and made available by Dean Willis Winn of the Wharton School were used to defer the costs of the conference and the clerical work involved in editing this book. We wish to acknowledge Dean Winn's support of this venture and a number of other research projects now in progress. Thanks are also due to Dr. John Lubin of the Wharton School's Department of Geography and Industry for many suggestions as to possible contributors in subject areas where he is far more knowledgeable than are the editors. Finally, Chris Kentera's great patience, helpful suggestions and full cooperation deserve public recognition.

The unsung heroes of any book are those secretaries who painstakingly type and re-type manuscripts. In the present case, some of this work was done by Jacquelyn Lewis, Dora Nash and Molly Horowitz. The great bulk of the typing and all the secretarial work connected with this project was cheerfully and ably performed by Eva Reiff. Only those who have engaged in similar editorial projects will realize how indebted we are to Miss Reiff for her diligence and her unstinting efforts.

CONTENTS

PART IV: CASE STUDIES

PART V: APPENDICES

BIOGRAPHIES

Wroe Alderson is Professor of Marketing at the Wharton School of Business and Director of its Management Science Center. He is past president of the American Marketing Association and active in the Institute of Management Sciences. He was founder of the management consulting firm, Alderson Associates. His publications include *Marketing Behavior and Executive Action* and *Theory in Marketing* with Reavis Cox. He is also planning a book on problem solving in marketing.

Stanley J. Shapiro is an Assistant Professor of Marketing at the Wharton School of the University of Pennsylvania. He received an A.B. degree from Harvard College and earned his M.B.A. and Ph.D. at the University of Pennsylvania. Dr. Shapiro is to be co-editor with Reavis Cox and Wroe Alderson of the second edition of *Theory in Marketing*. He has done research in the areas of marketing history, metropolitan information systems, and livestock marketing.

Roger J. Abouchar has a broad background in computer and office equipment marketing. He is senior product planner in the Electronic Data Processing division of RCA. He has produced a number of definitive studies of the digital computer market and has formulated a number of projects utilizing the computer as a marketing and research development tool. Mr. Abouchar holds an M.B.A. degree in marketing from NYU.

Michael H. Halbert is a member of the advertising research staff at DuPont. He is a graduate of the University of Pennsylvania and has published a number of articles on marketing research and consumer behavior. He is associated with ORSA, the Institute of Management Sciences, the American Marketing Association, and the Society for Industrial and Applied Mathematics.

William H. Meserole is president and chief distribution system designer for the Ballinger-Meserole Company. He also has had extensive experience with the United States Army and with the Department of Commerce in designing warehouse systems. He is author of numerous books and articles on warehousing and distribution and is a member of the American Materials Handling Society and the American Marketing Association.

John F. Magee is Vice-President in Operations Research for Arthur D. Little, Inc. He has served as a consultant in marketing and advertising research, production planning, inventory control, transportation, communications, distribution cost analysis, and managerial controls. He is author of a number of articles on operations research and is a member of ORSA.

David Bendel Hertz is in charge of operations research for McKinsey and Company. He has had operations research experience with Arthur Anderson and

Company, RCA, and Celanese Corporation of America. At present, Dr. Hertz is vice-president of the Institute of Management Sciences and Associate Editor for Publications of the Operations Research Society of America. He is also author of *The Theory and Practice of Industrial Research* and other publications.

Robert S. Weinberg, a mathematician turned economist, is Manager, Market Research, IBM. He also served on a pioneering project dealing with the application of electronic computers to budgeting and logistics problems. He is a frequent contributor to the literature of economic forecasting and analysis, management planning and control, and operations research. He is author of the book *An Analytical Approach to Advertising* and a contributor to *Mathematical Models and Methods in Marketing* and the forthcoming *Planning Management Strategy.*

Patrick J. Robinson heads Integrated Operations Planning for Mobil Oil. Previously, he managed marketing and operations research for Imperial Oil and was in management consulting. He also taught university night school courses for eleven years. He holds degrees in mechanical and industrial engineering, accounting and business administration, and is active in TIMS, AIIE, and ORSA.

Tibor Fabian is Vice-President of Mathematica and Adjunct Associate Professor, University of Pennsylvania. He was formerly Director of Operations Research at Lybrand, Ross Bros. and Montgomery. He is secretary-treasurer of the Institute of Management Sciences and a member of ORSA. His research and writings cover applications of mathematical methods to business, industrial and technological problems.

Charles H. Sevin is a Vice-President of Alderson Associates, management consultants. He has extensive experience in the areas of long range planning, optimization of marketing profits through expenditure control, and product development. He is author of numerous articles on mathematical programing, distribution cost analysis, and control and channel management.

Borge M. Christensen is Manager of Special Systems in the Computer Department of General Electric. He was project leader of their Critical Path Planning and Scheduling Group. In addition to his years of engineering experience at General Electric, he has had marketing research and sales experience in southeast Asia. Mr. Christensen has also lectured extensively on CPM and PERT and is author of several articles on network model techniques.

Jay R. Greene is Manager of Merchandising, Del E. Webb Corporation. He has experience in business analysis, marketing research, and business systems with General Electric, as well as experience as an operations analyst with the General Analysis Corporation. His dissertation was entitled "A Computer Simulation of a Marketing Organization." He is author of several articles in the field of gaming and is co-author of a book on *Dynamic Management Decision Games.* He also has experience with operational games in executive training programs and university courses.

William Baumol is Professor of Economics at Princeton University, having taken his Ph.D. at the London School of Economics. Currently associated with *Mathematica*, he has had a number of years experience with the consulting firm of Alderson Associates. Among his publications are *Economic Dynamics; Economic Processes and Policies; Business Behavior; Value and Growth;* and *Economic Theory and Operations Analysis*.

William R. Dill is Associate Dean of the Graduate School of Industrial Administration, Carnegie Institute of Technology. He helped to develop the CIT Management Game and has explored its potential as a method of education and research. In addition to his work with management games, Professor Dill is author of numerous articles on group problem solving, business decision making, and management development.

Alfred A. Kuehn is Associate Professor at the Graduate School of Administration, Carnegie Institute of Technology and a consultant to the Market Research Corporation of America. His doctoral dissertation analyzed consumer brand choice as a probabilistic process. Dr. Kuehn is co-editor of *Quantitative Techniques in Marketing Analysis* (Irwin, 1962) and has published a variety of articles on advertising budgeting, merchandising strategy, business games, and the use of hueristic programing in the solution of marketing problems.

Ralph L. Day is Associate Professor of Marketing Administration at the University of Texas. Professor Day has worked with the management game while on the faculty of the Carnegie Institute of Technology, and also has a number of years experience in industrial marketing and retailing, and consulting experience in industrial economics and marketing research. He is author of *Marketing in Action: A Dynamic Business Decision Game* and a number of professional articles.

Edward L. Brink is presently Associate Professor of Marketing and Foreign Commerce at the Wharton School, University of Pennsylvania. In addition to many years of teaching experience, he has served as marketing research consultant in the areas of consumer behavior, promotion analysis, and research methodology. He is the author of numerous articles and the book *Promotion Management*, to be published in 1963.

F. Helmut Weymar teaches at the School of Industrial Management, Massachusetts Institute of Technology in the area of Industrial Dynamics. He previously served as Administrative Assistant in the Department of Electrical Engineering at M.I.T. He is currently in charge of a consumer market study for Minute Maid.

Paul. E. Green is engaged in marketing planning and marketing research activities for the DuPont Company. Dr. Green also teaches marketing at the Wharton School, University of Pennsylvania. He has had experience in operations research with Luken Steel Company and in marketing research with the Sun Oil Company, and also has contributed extensively to a number of articles in the area of marketing and business management.

Donald F. Blumberg is Associate Director, Business Planning, with the Diebold Group, Inc. He has had experience in planning, operations analysis, and large scale systems design for industry and the armed forces. As an army officer, and later as a civilian systems analyst, he was also responsible for systems analysis, and development of large scale military command control, intelligence, and planning systems.

Edwin Malcolm McPherson is an industrial market analyst and has advised manufacturers, insurance firms and government agencies in plant layout, equipment design systems, and marketing problems. He has served as consultant to the Small Business Commission for the state of Tennessee, and has participated in legislative activity involving business problems. Mr McPherson is author of a book on industrial economics and of articles on economics and computers.

Charles G. Cooper is Executive Vice-President of Computer Applications, Inc. Majoring in engineering and mathematics, Mr. Cooper has had experience as a logic-design engineer with IBM and with CEIR in computer services and programming. He was formerly assistant director of research and development at CEIR.

John R. Parks is a member of an operations research group at Monsanto Chemical Company. He has had previous experience as a research analyst in chemicals and calorimetric evaluation of radio-active materials. He is currently engaged in operations research analysis of various aspects of Monsanto's operations.

Lester H. Krone, since 1961, has been Associate Professor of Engineering Science on the faculty of Washington University. He has had experience in process development and served on the staff of Monsanto Chemical Company in applied mathematical research. There he was involved in studies of a number of phases of the company's operations.

Hans B. Thorelli is Professor of Business Administration, Graduate School of Business, University of Chicago. Dr. Thorelli was in charge of the group which designed the first advanced simulation of international business operations. He has had previous experience with the marketing service division of General Electric, and is the author of a number of articles on government and business, and economic development.

Samuel Zuckerkandel is manager of Marketing Development, Haveg Industries, Inc. He holds an M.A. in Economics and Marketing from the Wharton School, University of Pennsylvania, and is instructor in marketing at Drexel Institute. He has a number of years experience in marketing research and sales analysis.

Roger F. Burkhardt is director, SABRE, Operations for American Airlines. He has had many years of experience with American in reservation management and sales service training. Mr. Burkhardt holds an M.B.A. degree from the Graduate School of Business, Harvard University. He is former chairman of the Air Traffic

Conference reservations committee and a member of the Institute for Management Science.

W. R. Platt is a senior editor for computer applications in the Product Information Department of the National Cash Register Company. He majored in journalism at the University of Notre Dame and studied engineering at the Illinois Institute of Technology. Currently, he is chairman of the Dayton chapter of the Society of Technical Writers and Publishers.

Elmer R. McClay, prior to joining RCA as an administrator for industrial applications of electronic data processing equipment, served as a Naval Aviator. He has had extensive experience with RCA in systems development, product planning, and EDP installation. He is author of numerous reports and analyses of industrial application of EDP to aviation, banking, insurance, retailing, publishing, health insurance, manufacturing, and inventory control.

Mark E. Stern is Manager, IBM liaison to the Graduate School of Business Administration at NYU. He has previous experience with IBM in applied science, engineering, and marketing planning. Previously, he was an instructor in mathematics at Johns Hopkins University. Mr. Stern is also author of a number of papers on mathematics applied to computers.

Gerrit W. Van Schaick is manager of the Branch Offices and Traffic Division of American Cyanamid Company. His division is responsible for warehouse and packaging as well as branch offices and traffic. He holds an M.B.A. from Harvard and has had many years experience in distribution management.

Purnell H. Benson brings a varied background to his task of analyzing market audit data. He holds degrees in philosophy from Princeton University and in sociology from Harvard and the University of Chicago, where his fields of study included social psychology, methods of social research, and statistics. After ten years of teaching at Temple University and then Drew University, he turned to consulting in consumer and personnel research. He is the author of a book and research papers in psychology and sociology.

Edward A. Ide is president of the marketing research and consulting firm, IDE Associates. Prior to establishing his own firm, Mr. Ide was with the United States Bureau of Labor Statistics and with Alderson Associates, in statistical sampling and market analysis. While at Alderson Associates he had complete responsibility for planning and control of research and survey projects.

Richard F. Neuschel is a partner with McKinsey and Company. He has served as a consulting specialist in business organization, planning and control, and has worked in the automobile, petroleum, chemical, food processing, retailing, insurance, public utility, banking, and transportation industries. He is also author of the book *Management by System,* and numerous magazine articles on business subjects.

William F. Massy teaches at the Graduate School of Business, Stanford University. He took his Ph.D. in Industrial Economics at M.I.T. and was co-developer of their marketing game. He has also served as business consultant to a number of firms including Arthur D. Little and Dynatech Corporation. He is co-author of both *Quantitative Techniques in Marketing Analysis: Text and Readings* and *Planning in Marketing—A Selected Bibliography*.

Gerald B. Tallman is a member of the staff, School of Industrial Management, M.I.T. and a developer of their marketing game. He has served as a consultant to the Office of Price Administration and War Production Board and, presently, acts as a marketing consultant for Arthur D. Little. He is also the author of industrial development plans in Puerto Rico and in Tanganyika, and has written articles on marketing simulation and marketing games.

Arnold E. Amstutz is Assistant Professor of Marketing at the School of Industrial Management, M.I.T. He helped develop both the M.I.T. marketing game as well as the control and environmental simulation programs on which the game is based. Professor Amstutz has also directed a research project investigating the use of simulation techniques in analyzing consumer and industrial markets.

Man speaks; he gives names to objects in his environment; and then he goes around counting them. Advancing skill in handling numerical data is a major facet of intellectual and material progress. Man, the marketer, is first of all Man, the counter. Whether he keeps his score on clay tablets or magnetic tapes, the perennial questions of the market place are: "How many?" and "How much?"

There have been several remarkable turning points in the struggle to cope with numbers: the invention of zero and of decimal notation; census taking by the ancient Hebrews and Romans; the development of the Hollerith punch cards in the United States Bureau of Census; contributions to mathematics by Liebniz and Pascal and their dreams of mechanical computers. This book takes a narrower and more immediate view of the revolution in data handling. It is an attempt to assess the implications for marketing of the development of electronic data processing beginning about 1950.

MARKETING AND THE COMPUTER:

AN OVERVIEW

Marketing will be viewed in this discussion as a set of managed activities, a system of action in which information is employed to generate decisions. Adopting the viewpoint of the executive endeavoring to control the system, three issues arise as to how marketing management can be made more effective. These three issues correspond to three areas of opportunity for electronic data processing in marketing and provide the basic themes for the three parts of this book.

How can the vastly expanded capacity for data handling be used to improve the lot of the marketing executive? Or, starting with the problem rather than the tools, what are the essential difficulties facing the decision-maker, and how can electronic computers help in overcoming them? Here are the three principal possibilities treated by the contributors to this volume. (1) The executive has not been getting the information he needs. (2) He has had information more than enough but the weakness has been on the side of analysis, or the process of deriving decisions from data.

(3) Information and analysis are both quite adequate with respect to the problem of interpreting the past. This leaves the executive to cope with his main problem almost bare-handed, namely that of choosing among strategies governing future action and predicting their outcomes.

Electronic data processing is a promising resource, whichever of these difficulties turns out to be most fundamental. The case studies reported hereafter reflect some success in each of these areas for improving marketing decision. It is obvious that all three types of difficulty exist in marketing. Some decision makers are not getting the right information, or they do not get it fast enough, or it costs too much to obtain it by conventional means. Others possess mountains of data but lack the analytical processes for extracting meaningful conclusions and reliable guides to action. Still others are well equipped by information and analysis to deal with current emergencies in the marketing system but not for evaluating alternatives as to major modifications in the pattern of action. Deferring any judgment as to which of these difficulties is most fundamental, the threefold classification will provide a useful framework for the subsequent discussion of computer applications in marketing. This survey chapter will deal with information in marketing systems, analytical solutions of marketing problems, and games and simulation for prediction and planning.

INFORMATION IN MARKETING SYSTEMS

Information is visualized here from the standpoint of the executive endeavoring to manage or control the marketing system. The qualifying term "control information" might suffice to distinguish data gathered for this purpose. The flow of product information to trade buyers and consumers is only indirectly related to the present discussion. Control information or marketing intelligence comprises the data needed for management decisions. It tells the executive that the system is operating smoothly or that some disturbance in the system calls for adjustment to put it back in balance. Managing frequently means doing a little less of one thing or a little more of another, activating special procedures when circumstances arise which demand them, terminating an activity when the objective has been accomplished and instituting another when the time seems propitious. Control is exercised at many levels of primary and delegated authority. Control information comprises direct signals for action at each level together with less pointed and more voluminous data from which executive judgment can generate signals for action. The need for control information is extensive and diversified, serving many decision centers in any large marketing system.

The demand for information is a little like the demand for goods. Some aspects of the distribution of goods at least provide useful analogies in considering needs for control information. The utility of information depends on time, place and the form in which it is presented. Perhaps the best supported claim of electronic data processing for management attention is that it can increase the time utility for control information. By speeding up data handling, information is made available in time to influence marketing results as compared to evaluation after the fact. Several of the case studies reported deal with the problem of making feedback effective for current control and avoiding the overcorrection that often springs from delays in the transmission of signals.

Data handling also resembles goods handling in creating time utility by keeping items in inventory until needed. Ready access storage of information is scarcely less important than speedy processing. Frequently, the data in storage must be utilized together with a new item of information for an effective marketing decision. The historical background of relations with a given customer may be needed for the successful conclusion of a pending transaction. Devices such as magnetic tape have greatly increased capacity for storing data which may be needed in the future. The mechanisms for storage and retrieval by no means eliminate the problem of inventory management. There are inventory costs to be considered in storing information and decisions to be made as to the items to be kept or discarded.

When an operating period is completed, the immediate utility of the operating record may diminish rapidly and approach zero. Yet, the constant pressure for better forecasts may occasion deep regret for past records thrown away. It is impossible to foresee all the possible uses of information which appears relatively useless today. It is somewhat like the manager of a merchandise inventory who had to decide whether to scrap all obsolete items or hold them until they come back in style.

Effective use of data storage capacity in marketing requires some broad gauge planning leading to current decision rules. Rules concerning what to store might take account of the cost of restoring an item once discarded. Thus, documents might be removed from a file, if duplicates can readily be obtained when needed. The statistical history of a company's own marketing operations is not usually available elsewhere. Yet judicious choice of records to be retained would facilitate restoration of missing parts by estimation and interpolation. The historical basis for forecasting requires both length of perspective and depth of detail but source material need not be of the same intensity for all periods and all statistical series.

Place utility for control information should be interpreted in terms of actual presence at the points where decisions are to be made. It often happens that the data are available elsewhere in the system yet are never brought to bear at the decision point. It is odd but not unusual for an executive at the middle management level to be held responsible for profits and yet be denied information which is vital to that purpose. Computers make possible a running analysis of profit margins and marketing costs for each profit center but the exercise is futile unless the results are available to the manager. The opposite situation can also occur in which the responsible manager is deprived of data available piecemeal in the hands of his subordinates. Information management requires that data be accumulated or broken down on a pattern paralleling the organization of decision centers.

If time and place utility are essential with respect to the flow of information, the form in which it is provided is no less significant. Huge printouts of tabular data do not serve the needs of decision making but in fact discourage attempts at application. Some control programs highlight changes or deviations from trend in accordance with the principles of management by exception. A staff group may be responsible for pulling out the items requiring attention or the computer can be programmed for a selective printout of information deserving attention. The items so selected by either method are those which exceed pre-established limits and which indicate that the system is running out of control or not behaving as expected. In such a feedback system, it may be useful to distinguish the steady flow of operating data and the exceptional items which serve as signals for corrective action. It is the latter which may properly be called control information.

Another aspect of the form utility of information is whether it should be reported as absolute magnitudes or as relative figures. A general answer is that data should be reported in absolute form if the recipient is a staff man whose function is to manipulate it further while a line executive may prefer some set of ratios as a basis of action. The need of the latter is to see the new item of information in relation to other aspects of the operation he is managing. The mere fact that the company made a million dollars net profit last quarter is neither good nor bad in itself. Is the figure up or down from the previous quarter? The same quarter a year ago? How does it compare with previous quarters as a percentage of sales? As a percentage of investment? Was the result good as compared to other firms in the industry? Was it achieved without loss of market position or without injuring the outlook for future profits?

Such questions are multiplied when a marketing organization looks at sales and profit results by individual products, by sales territories, or by classes of customer. Which questions should be answered to reach a decision on appropriate corrective actions? A general answer again is that the executive who has to make a decision as to the allocation of his resources can use a figure most readily if it relates results to the resources under his control. The ratio of profits to investment will not help him very much, if he is not making decisions about investments. This figure may be just right for the treasurer's department but the Director of Marketing would do better with return per salesman, per dollar of advertising expenditure, or return on the total marketing budget under his control.

The somewhat shocking implication of these considerations is that the same raw data may have to be reported in various forms to the various decision centers in the company. The shock is inherent in the suggestion of further complications in the already difficult problem of communication among various departments or specialists in a company. Superficially, it might seem desirable to insist on a single common management language to promote understanding within the company. Actually, the real differences in needs for information and in the form in which they are prescribed will not go away just because management ignores them. A well known business executive has suggested that the post of intelligence officer be created in major companies and that this officer be responsible for managing an intelligence system which has to meet diverse demands. The electronic computer might finally come into its own in marketing as the primary working tool of such an intelligence officer.

Behind the facts reported to the various decision centers in a company or a marketing organization must lie a theory of how the organization operates. Behind the computer programming for this purpose, there should be some model of the operation as a feedback system and of the means whereby information is to be translated into action. To achieve this perspective on marketing is to realize the potential contribution to business now brought within reach by the advance of electronic computers. Without the systems approach to marketing, backed up by the capacity of the computer for rapid processing and for selective diversified outputs, information cannot really become effective in marketing decisions. Companies will go on being production-oriented or finance-oriented, lacking an adequate intelligence mechanism to orient them to the market.

The revolution in data handling has made possible a more centralized structure for the corporate decision making process. The key facts about market opportunity, production and distribution capability can be brought together in reaching strategic marketing decisions. The whole process of internal allocation of resources can then be made in such a way as to attain these strategic objectives. The main point of the preceding discussion is that this does not come about automatically by generating and processing a vast amount of data. The revolution in data processing opens new possibilities for detailed implementation of the marketing concept. The new approach will not become effective, however, until the intelligence system has been created and the organization structure appropriately modified. Only then can the computer supply the data to make the system work.

OPERATIONAL SOLUTIONS TO MARKETING PROBLEMS

A marketing problem may be said to arise when a marketing system or program is not operating according to expectations. A disturbance in the system is signaled either by failure to achieve the desired outputs or by the need for inputs in excess of what had been budgeted. The outputs that are deficient can be sales or profits over a recently completed operating period or conditions that were to be achieved by a certain date such as a percentage market share or a percentage of eligible retailers stocking an item for sale. The inputs which have had to be increased might be advertising expenditures, field salesman or promotional incentives to consumers and trade buyers.

There are other problems which begin to show up in some aspect of performance, although not signaled directly by changes in inputs and outputs. The marketing organization may be achieving its stated goals all too easily and the management problem may be that of raising the level of aspiration. A self-satisfied sales department like an overconfident football team may be in for trouble later on, even though it seems to be doing well today. In another type of situation, explosive tensions may be mounting in an organization because of conflict over ends or the means of carrying them out.

In all of these typical situations, some symptom is noted indicating that a problem may exist. Diagnostic investigation leads to a judgment that the symptoms are superficial or that there is a basic maladjustment in the system which ought to be remedied. Further consideration leads to a decision to seek a remedy immediately, or to delay action because some other problem is still more pressing or some expected event which relieves the pressure for remedial action is pending. Once a specific problem solving effort is undertaken, it may be defined as an attempt to reduce uncertainty to tolerable limits so that the responsible executive is willing to take action. Uncertainty in a marketing situation may arise either because of the lack of information about the issue at stake or because of a conflict of opinion among the various executives who will be involved in the proposed action. Thus a problem solving project should rest on an advance agreement as to the kind of information needed and how the information will be used in deciding the issue.

There are a number of relatively new ways of dealing with data to obtain marketing solutions. These methods are identified with such terms as operations research, management science, and mathematical economics. In general, these problem solving methods revolve around the idea of creating a model of the problem situation. A model is a statement of how the factors or variables in the situation are related to each other. There are now available some general models for recognized classes of problems. A general model may have to be made more specific to apply to a particular problem. Some of the general models are associated with such relatively new procedures as linear programming or queuing theory or with more traditional procedures such as multiple correlation or break-even analysis.

My intention in this chapter is not to apply these specific methods in marketing but rather to consider the educational problem of gaining acceptance of such methods by executives faced with marketing problems. In actual experience, it has turned out to be essential to give the decision making executive some conception of what the model means. He needs to know what variables are included, what relation among them has been assumed, and why the particular analytical procedure is expected to give him results he can act upon. It is not really too difficult to give an executive the kind of perspective he needs to have on linear programming. The difficulty lies in the rather severe requirements placed on the market research director or consultant who is attempting the explanation. He needs to have a thorough understanding of the technique under consideration, of the marketing problem to which it is to be applied, and he must also draw a sharp distinction between the substantive problem and the problem of communication to a given audience. The writer has seen such masters of exposition as William Baumol and Howard Raiffa present linear programming or Bayesian decision theory to groups of business executives without losing a man.

The real point which must be communicated is that problem solving always means identifying the relevant structure in the problem situation, quantifying the variables and arriving at a numerical solution. An appropriate model is one which reflects the relevant aspects of the problem situation and the appropriate solution procedure is one that develops the consequences of this problem structure with respect to the alternatives facing the executive. Attention should be concentrated always on the structure of the problem situation rather than on the mathematical equations or the various computational tools and techniques. The executive needs to feel comfortable with the picture of how the problem variables interact rather than be directly concerned with mathematical algorithms or computer programs.

It is convenient to designate some of the procedures and case studies presented in this book as analytical solutions. Yet they are not, for the most part, analytical in the mathematical sense. That is to say that the result is not ordinarily obtained in the form of a strict solution of mathematical equations. Rather, there is a large element of trial and error in this type of solution except that it is done systematically and very fast on the electronic computer. Many of the new methods with marketing applications such as linear programming and Monte Carlo are really trial and error, step by step, iterative solutions. The electronic computers deal primarily with the four fundamental arithmetical procedures of addition, subtraction, multiplication and division. If equations enter into the machine program, they are usually very simple. The reason that their handling exceeds the capacity of more conventional calculating facilities is that so many equations are involved and the sequence of operations may be governed by complex logical relationships.

There is a sense in which all of the solutions discussed in this part can be called analytical solutions. They are analytical for the system under study in the sense that given the system, the solution inevitably follows. Finding the source of the difficulty in a marketing system is something like diagnosing the factors in a case of human illness or the malfunctioning of a mechanism such as an automobile. At first, the symptoms might appear to be consistent with several different ailments. A series of tests gradually narrows the possibilities down or increases the probability that the cause of the trouble is of one specified type. In marketing even more than medicine, there always remains a margin for error. A decision must be made even though there is some remaining chance that diagnosis and treatment were wrong.

GAMES AND SIMULATION IN MARKETING

For purists in management science, there is doubtless a major distinction between games and simulation but not all purists would agree on what that distinction is. For marketing executives, it will suffice to think of the term games and simulation as embracing a wide range of helpful techniques which generally but not always mean the utilization of electronic computers. Some authorities would say that management games involve the participation of human beings as elements in the system which is to be simulated while complete system simulation does not. Actually, there are some borderline cases which do not fit into this two-way scheme so readily. It is probably more accurate to say that the general notion of games and simulation can be described as a spectrum or range of methods with varying degrees of human participation.

From the standpoint of management it is more important to consider what a game or a simulation does for the decision maker. The marketing executive obtains through these devices a better understanding of the system he is responsible for managing. These techniques are of assistance in the following ways: (1) they help him to classify his own conception or model of the way the marketing system works (2) they provide a means for evaluating interactions between competitors or between agencies cooperating in marketing such as a manufacturer and his distributors (3) they give the executive a feeling for how sensitive or responsible the market is to the various factors under his control (4) they predict the results to be expected from the operation of a complex system over successive periods of time, (5) they offer a laboratory for preliminary testing of various plans and alternative courses of action short of the ultimate test of actual operation.

The first use of simulation, namely that of helping the executive to develop his own model of the market, sounds as if he were using the electronic computer as a consultant. There is indeed some parallel to the advantages the executive obtains from describing his situation to a knowledgeable and sympathetic outsider. The creation of a model often starts with asking the executive to identify the significant factors in the marketing process and to describe the interactions among these factors. He may be asked to specify the response he would expect from certain inputs. A model, for example, is then created based on the information the executive has provided. When the executive is shown some of the results obtained by manipulation of this model, he may want to change some of his initial estimates or judgments. The model may become progressively more consistent and congenial internally as these modifications are made. This trial and error approach to a model that feels right is quite common. The point to be made here is that participation in this process is in itself a clarifying experience for the decision maker.

In its more refined version, this interplay between executive and model builder induces the executive to estimate the probable outcome for specified alternative courses of action. The model builder then attempts to obtain the information he will need to make better or more confident predictions. This is in contrast with procedures in which the analyst takes full responsibility for coming up with an improved forecast for such help as it may be for the decision maker. A method which, in effect, involves the executive in the search for better prediction is perhaps a better psychological preparation for taking final action. This procedure for starting with the subjective probability estimates of the decision maker and calculating the payoff to be expected is called the Bayesian approach and is treated more fully elsewhere in this book. The term simulation here simply implies that the payoffs are obtained by working through the consequences of the assumption put into the model. Simulation at this level is scarcely distinguishable from what was called system-analytic solutions in a preceding section.

The second use of a model simulated on a computer is that of dealing with the interactions among competitors or cooperators on a marketing system. This is an area of business games in which two or more human participants are specifying marketing strategies and programs or negotiating and carrying out cooperative arrangements. Business games have had a good deal of attention as means of testing for executive ability or as pedagogic devices for training for executive positions. A more basic use in the present context is for research into how decision makers actually behave in the competitive situations which have been built into the computer models. In one company, simulated competition among retailers reveals the fact that self-interest forced the retailer to react in a way that was contrary to the policies of his suppliers even though the persons playing the roles of retail competitors were executives of a supplier company. Simulation here provides information about a marketing system which could scarcely be obtained by other research methods. Their personal participation in the research also offers a vivid demonstration to the executives who have to cope with the problem.

Sensitivity analysis is a related type of systems research in which the conclusions sought deal with operating characteristics of the system. In this third use of simulation, the values of a given variable are set down representing the range over which it can be expected to vary. Simulation takes the form of calculating out the final results assuming first one of these values and then another. In one sense, the analyst may be said to be plotting the response function with respect to a given variable input. It may turn out that variations of this input in the relevant range make little difference for the outcome so that the decision maker can concentrate his attention elsewhere. In the longer run, this type of finding may lead to a major reconstruction of the marketing system and its feedback circuits to provide fewer but more sensitive controls.

The fourth use of simulation is for forecasting which depends on such complex considerations that the procedure cannot be expressed as a forecasting equation. Such forecasting, for example, might assume that new types of interaction arise when the system approaches limiting values or that new factors come into play at such a point. The model employed might be a growth model for the economy, for an industry, or for a company. In some instances, simulation might serve the purpose of carrying the model through a series of periods in which what happened in each period depended on the state of affairs at the beginning of the period. The type of model building and simulation which goes under the name of industrial dynamics is of this general character.

Finally, there is the fifth type of use which is that of testing out plans in the laboratory rather than in the market place. Strategic planning is in great need of such a testing instrument. One element of effective strategy is surprise which is obviously lost by field tests. If the plan has weaknesses in operation which were not foreseen, great damage can be done by introducing it into even a limited portion of the market. Live market tests are usually restricted to two or three variations in the plan of action. Many more may need to be tested to have any hope of approaching the optimum.

For this type of simulation, a plan might be defined as a schedule of inputs designed to produce a specified output. Simulation on computers can calculate the consequences for many different input schedules. Under some of the newer techniques, there is choice among alternatives at successive decision points. This is equivalent to searching among a much larger number of alternatives for the plan to be recommended. Something analogous to this process occurs in the planning procedure known as critical path scheduling.

Doubtless, great advances can be expected in using simulation as a tool of planning. The simulation might be set up to show progressive change in objectives and how the system might be expected to adjust to these changes. Progressive shifts in the market environment might also be introduced including increasing competition or more exacting consumer requirements. An organization operating in a dynamic environment resulting from advancing technology is likely to have conflicting internal drives, one toward adjustment and the other toward preserving the existing organizational structure. The ultimate simulation of marketing plans would deal with the way in which an organization might succeed in reorganizing itself to survive in a world of uncertainty.

PART I

THE COMPUTER

AND THE FLOW OF GOODS

AND INFORMATION

chapter one | *R. J. Abouchar*

This chapter will concentrate on the informational aspects of computer use. Though some may infer from the title that the computer gathers market information, it does not. It does, however, make practical the gathering of vast amounts of statistical and other types of marketing data that otherwise could not be processed due to sheer physical volume. Several cases are cited to indicate a number of ways in which computers are used in the handling and gathering of market information.

Generally speaking, all information in marketing and market research can be considered as qualitative or quantitative. Qualitative is used here to refer to information regarding a specific company, outlet or consumer and quantitative to overall numbers or figures on markets, economic levels, finite universes, etc. The former might be termed "micro" and the later "macro" information, in that one builds up to the other (to borrow terms currently used in computer programming). A computer is well equipped to operate on massive amounts of both types of information in order to synthesize and/or analyze the data gathered.

THE COMPUTER AND THE GATHERING

OF MARKET INFORMATION

A computer system can accomplish many things in the handling of market information. It can store, extract, compile, summarize, and sometimes aid in gathering information. It can print reports from information and report deviations from set norms. Its utility as a tool for the marketing man depends largely on how well he meets the challenge of the major prerequisite which is careful and deliberate planning.

The biggest problem in using the computer in marketing, particularly on the industrial level, is lack of market information. This type of information originates from primary or secondary sources outside of a company's own operations, and provides the input required by the computer. Primary sources, of course, constitute information from field surveys with published census and trade data accounting for the secondary sources. One can conclude that the results of computer operations can be no more reliable than the data used for input.

The first step in applying the computer to the informational process is to establish the gathering function, and the next (but no less important) is to select the data for processing. The latter includes selection of appropriate universes for market research, selection of pertinent indices for sales forecasting (where the computer can help to some degree), selection of data to be stored for immediate retrieval, etc. It is naïve to expect miracles of a computer, or to view it as a substitute for good judgment in the marketing process. Intelligently used, however, it can provide a dimension heretofore impossible.

No generalizations are possible regarding the use of a computer in any particular area of marketing. Much depends on the orientation of a company and its degree of sophistication with regard to Electronic Data Processing (EDP) as to whether a computer would be applied to a given problem. Most of what is covered in this chapter is not new and has no doubt been accomplished before in ways other than EDP. Throughout the examples it should be noted that a computer provides capabilities that have heretofore been possible but rarely on a practicable, working basis. The computer provides larger capacity, higher speed, greater accessibility, and many other features not previously available.

The examples, though isolated problem types, cover a broad spectrum of the informational process and are explored in varying degrees of depth. Discussion ranges, in this section, from the "bread and butter" job of sales statistics (certainly the most often encountered of the applications discussed) to the more advanced concept of information storage and retrieval. Some of these are treated briefly but are included to create a well rounded picture. All have a common thread running through them in that they treat of the informational aspect of marketing with emphasis on the means of gathering market data.

Naturally the approaches suggested here are more applicable in some industries than others and could not apply to all companies. Neither do they necessarily require use of a computer. The complexity and size of a given problem, among other things, will determine the appropriateness of a computer. It is hoped that some of the suggested uses may in turn stimulate a few ideas of how the same concepts could be applied to other segments and levels of business.

A brief review of the contents should help to tie the separate areas together. Sales statistics, as the most prevalent application in the informational aspects of computer usage in marketing, is discussed first. The statistics are produced as a byproduct of the accounting process. In this particular case, the computer is directly responsible for the creation of marketing information. All cases are not so simple, however, and the next area studied is the creation of a market file, which essentially represents an extension and broadening of the sales statistics function to superimpose customer oriented data onto a universe of potential users. This will create a qualitative representation of a market or markets for specific products by individual firms in machine language. The creation of such a file requires a considerable amount of outside data not available internally to the computer. It serves the main function of determining market penetration. To indicate the progress being made in specific areas with the introduction of automated market data gathering devices, two specialized cases are cited, each using a somewhat different technique to survey broadcast listenership. Beyond this, the handling of quantitative market statistics is covered from the standpoint of their use in sales forecasting and sales distribution. Here, the problem is not so much in gathering the data as in selecting pertinent indices. To conclude the picture, brief mention is made of the application of information storage and retrieval techniques as a basis for marketing information systems.

COMPILATION OF SALES STATISTICS, A FUNDAMENTAL SOURCE OF MARKETING INFORMATION

The basic information for reports analyzing sales and sales trends is produced as a byproduct of various accounting operations. As such, it can be generated by a computer. Depending upon the type of industry and product, the reporting of sales statistics can take many formats. Many of the statistics that can be developed will be oriented towards the marketing side of the business, whereas others will tend to be more useful to other departments. However, as a rule, the reports will tend to reveal marketing trends with heavy emphasis on distribution patterns. The following example illustrates the development of statistical information as an output of the accounting function.

A typical order processing application for a manufacturer selling to retail outlets on a national level would accomplish all the bookkeeping necessary to process a given order. The order is received at the computer in machine readable form; the computer allocates inventory, prices out items, prepares shipping data for warehouses, posts to an inventory file, posts to an accounts receivable file, prints the invoice, and posts sales data to the various statistical files (NOTE: The files in this case are stored on magnetic type since the use of a computer in the medium scale category is hypothesized for this problem). Accounts receivable collections are similarly processed on subsequent runs.

The important item to emphasize here, from the standpoint of market information, is the creation of the statistical files. Some of the data that is traditionally captured in sales statistics is as follows: Date of each sale; factory or plant; product classification; item-style; size; color; quantity; dollar value; customer; customer classification data (size, type of business, etc.); city; state; sales territory; country (if export); discounts or trade in allowance; salesman; commissions; price; cost; net profit. This is a fairly comprehensive list but the bulk of the data is created as a result of the bookkeeping function so that little in the way of additional outside data is required. Certainly this constitutes a "bread and butter" computer application.

Many extremely useful analyses relative to the marketing picture can then be generated at desired intervals. Once created, the sales statistics tape files will be used to process reports similar to the following general listing.

1. Individual product sales trends.
2. Geographic sales distribution.
   · Domestic by county, city, state, sales territory, etc.
   · International by country.
3. Customer sales analyses.
   · By specific important accounts.
   · By classes of trade or type of outlet (retail level).
   · By industry (industrial goods).
   · Other pertinent analyses dependent upon the type of product.
   · Analysis for customer activity, trends by specific customers, etc.
4. Report of individual sales representatives' activities (profitability, volume, etc.).
5. Costs of sales by customer and customer class.

Essentially this listing provides the fundamental analyses required to be made in extracting useful market data. Such data should be most sensitive to reactions in the market-place and is extremely helpful in making the tactical decisions required in any business. Although this job has been done by other methods, through utilization of a computer the time lag can be compressed so that reports are in the hands of management considerably faster. Instead of receiving interesting historic information, management can obtain data in time to act upon it.

The data generated as a result of compilation of sales statistics can be utilized (once it is refined to extract information of historic importance) for more long range, strategic decisions. This is accomplished by superimposing the extracted historic sales data over a constructed universe of potential users. Realistically, the concept must be limited to markets composed of industrial firms or middlemen such as retailers, wholesalers, and the like. Extension to include individual consumers appears to be too cumbersome for most applications. Also, the concept will not prove equally suitable to all industrial areas but is dependent upon the specific type of product being sold. Just how a market can be reconstructed on magnetic tape is demonstrated in the next section which constitutes the major portion of this chapter.

THE COMPUTER AS A STOREHOUSE OF QUALITATIVE MARKET INFORMATION

A computer system has excellent attributes to serve as a repository for information of a qualitative nature on individual users or potential users of a given product. This would be in the nature of "micro" information or facts regarding particular industrial firms, retail outlets or whatever class of user or distributor represents the market for a given product. The main problem is gathering the necessary information to construct such a file for computer manipulation.

Consider a file which will have in ready form all information on individual companies or dealers that represent virtually all prospects for a product. The simplest version is the mailing list on paper which merely has the name and address of a prospect. This can be either a list or in some mechanical form for reproduction, as a large number of individual plates. In some cases, the level of sophistication of the plates is raised by including some details of classification information which can be used for selectivity. Punched cards can further broaden the area of utilization of classification codes and also provide a means of storing a large amount of market information. However, punched cards become a problem as the volume of data increases due to time and processing costs. Such developments indicate the possible economic utilization of EDP to process the data. With a transition to EDP the amount of market information per record (whether it be an industrial user, dealer, retailer or wholesaler) can be increased economically many fold over the physical limitations inherent in punched card manipulation. One can readily visualize the correspondingly high order of qualitative data that can be maintained.

What kind of information should go into such a file? How may such data be obtained? What determines the extent of the universe of companies to be included in the file? What of file maintenance and updating? The answers and approaches will differ from industry to industry as will the value of the file. Volume of data is generally the major determinant as to whether or not a computer should be employed. This discussion will indicate in a general way the uses of a market file and the way it might be constructed, attempting to relate the concept to as broad a segment of business as possible by emphasizing the "common denominators" rather than the differences.

The first determination to be made is the selection of the universe and its appropriate parameters. This problem is definitely dependent on the type of goods produced. In many cases, a universe can be selected from a company's old files of customers (old customers no longer purchasing plus newly opened accounts can create a basic file). Such a file would be somewhat broader but practically analogous to a sales statistics arrangement. This will reveal to a company how well they are doing with their own accounts but will not reveal what type of coverage is being obtained from the total market of possible customers. A file of maximum utility must be broad enough in scope so that a positive approach can be taken—one that will pinpoint new prospects and attempt to determine competitive performance in specific industrial and geographic areas. The need, then, is for some outside directory or listing that will, in a large measure, provide a frame on which to hang a company's own sales. The number of potential customers would determine if a computer is required. Naturally, if the product is sold only to a specialized market that is limited in terms of individual users, for example museums (458 units in the U.S. in 1956), utilization of a computer becomes uneconomical. If, however, a company already has 10,000 customers with 30,000 additional prospects for a given product, then a computer could certainly be of use, as the total universe would number 40,000 companies. The figure, of course, could be lower depending on the amount of information desired per record.

Finding and selecting the right source of information pertinent to a given product line is of major importance. In some industrial segments directories exist in abundance. In other areas, they are scarce. In some cases one directory will provide complete information on a specific market. For instance, if the product is sold to banks alone, a listing as provided in Polk's or Rand McNally's bank directories would suffice. But if this hypothetical product is also sold to savings and loan associations, then it becomes necessary to broaden the file to include necessary data on these firms. If credit agencies such as finance companies are also possible customers, then they too should be added, and so on, ad infinitum. Finding one listing that will indicate all the customers for a given product is generally unlikely. However, through judicious combinations it is often possible to approach a very high degree of market coverage within the framework of the directories selected. Periodically, new customers outside the universe selected can be added to the main body of information. This raises one important point: the universe should be dynamic and not static: it should be ever expanding and changing, with businesses that cease to exist being dropped from the rolls.

Directories exist for companies which have fairly clear cut, rather finite, industrial markets. Insurance companies, metal working companies, petroleum producers, department stores, and any number of other businesses are subjects of directories offered by various publishers and associations. There are even directories of directories available which cover the complete spectrum of sources. If size is a criterion, there are directories covering the "top 500" industrial firms, 21,000 companies with net worth of $1,000,000 or more, a directory of the top 7,500 companies, and so on. Failing to find the appropriate market in the various directories, mailing lists may be purchased which could be utilized as a frame of reference. These, however, are of limited use unless augmented with classification data, which may have to be obtained as a result of a field survey.

Once selection of the sources is made, a means of converting data into form acceptable to the computer is required. The traditional means is to take the information from the printed page and put it in machine readable form such as punched cards or paper tape. Sometimes, however, this step can be saved as many companies selling directories also offer tabulating cards or magnetic tape reels containing selected data from the directory. Such machine media can be purchased and they provide the marketer a ready made universe against which to measure his penetration of the market. Other possibilities are still in the future, for example the use of an optical page reader which could convert prescribed data into digital form.

The preceding section discussed data from the myriad directories available but no reference has yet been made to the type of data that is needed in the file. This is the classification data which is the key to the whole project. Although there are variations from industry to industry, in most cases at least the following is necessary:

1. Account or serial number, usually in alphabetic sequence.
2. Name and address of firm.
3. Some indication of size.
   - Number of employees
   - Dollar volume
   - Deposits (if a bank)
   - Net assets
   - Revenues (public utilities, transportation companies, etc.)
4. Standard industrial classification code (a four digit code showing industry and product).
5. Geographic code (there is a standard eight digit code for this).
6. Data that is particularly pertinent to a given product line such as the following specifics:
   - Number of accounts
   - Number of warehouses
   - Number of outlets
   - Number of transactions
   - Net profits

   or any other data that may be obtained from secondary sources that could be used to further classify the companies. Often, the first five items mentioned are sufficient with the additional one being added as a refinement, provided the specific information is available and not too expensive to obtain. Depending upon the type of industry it is likely that the specific information is provided in the appropriate directory.

Once the framework is selected with appropriate classification data, the informational content as it applies to a particular business must be formulated. The most obvious means of providing this information is by superimposing selected sales statistics upon the universe of companies. This, however, yields facts concerning only your company's own sales. This portion of data will be the strongest and most complete as the data is generated internally and no outside source need be consulted. Even on such a limited scale, the file can be of considerable value in aiding the expansion of a company's coverage. Certainly this could be a first step in establishing the informational content.

In order to enlarge information content beyond the scope of a company's own sales, it is necessary to devise a means of obtaining data on competitive products. The availability of such material is a question that varies with the specific product. The type of information sought revolves about "who uses which model (type, make, etc.) of a given product." This phase requires market research to capture the facts that will reveal the story on each potential customer. The type of product will determine the approach and the information to be gathered. The stress in this discussion will be placed on industrial goods and, mainly, large industrial goods.

Among the reasons for limiting the scope to industrial goods is that too great a distribution of a mass item (to consumers for instance) precludes creation of the file by sheer weight of numbers. Also, as there is little homogeneity of population in industrial markets, the need for a company-by-company analysis becomes more apparent. Ideally, such a file would approach an inventory of the product in question in each company within the universe. This is practically impossible with prospects for success increasing in inverse proportion to the number of units of the product to be accounted for. However, the greater the number of units, the less need for complete coverage, due in general to vaster distribution. Conversely, the fewer the number sold, the greater the need for accounting for as many units as possible.

The actual physical gathering of the data represents the largest single part of the job and probably requires the greatest outlay in money. Some possible approaches are discussed. One means is via a written questionnaire, kept simple to increase response. The best that can be hoped for is a response of 50-60% after repeated mailings. If complete coverage of the universe is not required, then this method will probably prove completely satisfactory and not too expensive. Another means of data collection would be to utilize company salesmen who in making their rounds could well ascertain a customer's or potential customer's usage of a product. This method could be employed in cases where there is not too long a list of possible prospects. Also, it can provide salesmen with a reason for calling on a prospect in other than a sales capacity and, in addition, encourage him to call on other than his usual clientele. A balancing factor, however, is the time taken away from a sales representative's normal routine. Such a program must be phased in with a salesman's usual activities so as not to have a detrimental effect on sales.

There are still other ways of gathering the data. Often a telephone survey can be used provided the information sought is simple in nature. This could be handled through local branch offices if geographic coverage is sufficient. One drawback with this method is that the calls might be construed as promotional efforts which might in same cases be welcomed but may likewise inhibit the release of the data sought. A telephone survey could be conducted by an outside agency, thus removing the possibility of concern by the respondent that a sales pitch is being made. Many firms specialize in this type survey, some of which are equipped to handle more complex questions than others. Survey costs will vary according to the degree of complexity of the questionnaire. Telephone surveys provide an excellent means of gathering brief qualitative information in volume. Other information gathering services exist that will gather data in greater depth, but the costs per interview will tend to be high. The latter method might be used to survey a smaller universe in depth.

Various other possibilities exist but unfortunately there is no automated way of accomplishing this aspect of the fact gathering procedure. The means used are the traditional tools of market research requiring contact between and among human beings, in human language, via the written or spoken word. The only part a computer can play in this phase is generating a list of potential respondents with prior sorting by geographic area.

Data gathering as described here differs from market research in one sense: it attempts to broaden quantitative coverage thus reducing relatively the importance of the qualitative aspect of the data. In this respect the procedure more closely resembles a census than it does a sample in a formal market research study. The attempt is to study a selected universe in its entirety without benefit of sampling techniques. This distinction emphasizes the fact that one is creating a market information file not conducting a one shot market survey. Once the data is obtained initially, a means can generally be devised for updating, short of a full scale study. A full scale survey might be desirable periodically, even if a satisfactory means is available to collect data for updating the file on a continuing basis.

Now the question arises as to the type of information sought. As envisioned by the author, the search is for product information. It could be broader, of course, but it is assumed that what is desired is a picture of the current state of the market for a hypothetical product "A". The type of information desired includes the answers to the following concerning the product:

1. Who is using it?
2. How many is the customer using?
3. When did he first buy?
4. From whom did he purchase?
5. How is he using it (if there is a question in this regard)?
6. If possible, where is he using it? What plants, warehouses, branches, etc.?

This is a basic listing that could fit a broad category of industrial products. It would be up to an individual company to determine its own requirements beyond the items mentioned and include same among the data sought.

Once the information is gathered, the problem becomes one of matching one set of data with the other. In this case two magnetic tapes will be produced, one created from the classification data and the other from the field information. The product information must be superimposed on the classification data for each company in the file. At this point, the computer comes into play with its powerful capability for processing data. Each tape is then sorted in ascending sequence (note, the important element here is a file number assigned to each company, usually in alphabetic order) and then merged using the file number to key them in. Once the tapes have been merged and edited the master market file becomes a reality.

The success of such a file is predicated upon: (1) proper selection of the universe with parameters, if possible, beyond the current actual market size, thus allowing for potential expansion; (2) reliable classification data derived from the secondary source(s) selected as the universe; (3) useful results from the field portion of the study; (4) satisfactory reduction of the data for machine manipulation. Presuming the requisites are met satisfactorily, a constructed image of the market and potential market for a specific product should exist on magnetic tape which will include data on virtually every firm that is a prospective customer.

An intelligent analysis of the file will reveal competitive strengths in various markets, market penetration by segment and geographic area, extent of the market, and rate of market expansion. The file can be used to produce selective mailing lists for sales promotions in specified target markets. If further qualitative information is desired, a list of the specific type of user to be surveyed or a random listing can be generated. From the initial conception of a universe of companies with product usage data superimposed on the basic frame, the file could be expanded to include more sophisticated customer or market intelligence. Certainly, other possibilities exist for usage of such a synthesis of the market in non-mathematical terms.

MARKETING AREAS WHERE MECHANIZATION OF THE FACT GATHERING FUNCTION HAS PROVEN FEASIBLE

In some areas, it has been possible to automate the fact gathering process to a degree. This is possible due to the peculiar set of requirements and characteristics of the research involved. In one such case the purpose is to gather statistics on listenership to radio and TV broadcasts. Of course, general interest in this area is limited due to its specialized nature: however, the applications do point out how ingenuity can mechanize certain aspects of market data gathering of a continuing nature. In the following examples, the data originating object is either a radio or a television set. However, parallel concepts of gathering data from other types of source devices are in the process of development. The main function of these devices, however, is not in the fact gathering area though statistics produced serve as a useful byproduct. The cash register is one device that is capable of producing data for sales analysis by a computer. Various on-line (direct computer access) systems entering the market (airlines reservation, on-line banking, etc.) are capable of automating the data gathering function and providing data for review and analysis. These products, however, have bookkeeping and accounting as their primary function and since the information gathering aspect is of secondary importance, discussion will center on the two cases where the primary purpose is the gathering of marketing (research) information.

The A. C. Nielsen Company is well known in the field of large scale fact gathering. Nielsen offers to clients many services which produce vast amounts of statistical data that can be digested only through the use of computers. The company estimates that it punches approximately 2½ million cards every two months for its Food, Drug and Camera Index audits alone. Computers are used to process the data and produce all the cross tabulations necessary. The index measures goods moving off retailers' shelves and produces statistics by market, class of store, etc. Data is provided on movement of competitors' items and goods in stock as well. Nielsen's operations involve some 250 million statistical calculations daily. The value of computer handling can be recognized due to the myriad of cross analyses that can and must be made. It should be noted that Nielsen's use of computers is essentially an extension and broadening of these machines' utilization of punched card equipment employed since 1933. The bulk of this fact gathering process is carried on by hand in the company's Retail Index Division. Nielsen's auditors make the rounds of sample stores on a periodic basis. They generate statistics on some 8,000 products in more than 6,000 stores. Even given such a large bulk of data, this particular operation can only be handled on a manual basis with the auditors collecting the data and submitting it in hard copy form to Nielsen's checking department. There the reports are inspected and then passed on to other departments where the data is transferred from field form to punched cards for data processing by the firm's computers.

However, the main reason for citing the A. C. Nielsen Company is to demonstrate how some portion of the gathering process has been mechanized. The Broadcast Division of Nielsen is similar to the Retail Index Division, but instead of human auditors (who do the checking and counting at the retail outlets) the data is collected by a device called the "Audimeter." The electronic device codes an accurate record of every minute of TV and radio usage in each house in the sample. The data is recorded on 16 mm film which, when fully exposed, is mailed to the Nielsen Company. There the film is inspected electronically by a specially designed computer to ascertain its accuracy. If the accuracy requirements are met, the records are decoded and converted to tab cards by a number of Nielsen designed decoders. The tab cards are then sent to the data processing equipment and computer where the data is sorted, tabulated, and computed. Through this procedure the radio and TV ratings are evolved.

The utilization of EDP enables Nielsen to determine rural and urban listenership patterns, general viewing habits, average audience for programs, share of audience, cost per 1,000 homes reached, minute by minute audience, viewing frequency and composition of audience. The key, of course, to the research is the utilization of the "Audimeter" which automatically gathers the data for later manipulation by the computer. Unfortunately, the technique is limited in application and is not feasible for the major portion of market research work carried on. It is conceivable that mark sensed cards could be used for some aspects of consumer research but a higher degree of respondent cooperation and effort would be required.[1]

Another specialized system which measures TV audience is operated by American Research Bureau, Inc. The system differs from the Nielsen procedure in degree of mechanization in that the respondent effort is kept to a minimum. The ARBITRON is an electronic system that interrogates several hundred selected TV sets in seven major cities by means of small units attached to the sets. The system works on an instantaneous basis so that immediate results can be obtained to determine listenership at any given moment. The information is fed into a central computer system that prints out the results at high speed.

It should be stressed again that the computer does not actually perform the data gathering function; however, extensions to the basic computer can enable data to be fed to it in machine readable form on an auto-

---

[1] A. C. Nielsen, "The Statistic Seekers," *Management and Business Automation*, March 1961, pp. 28-32. (Copyright, OA Business Publications, Inc.)

matic or semi-automatic basis (in the case of the "Audimeter" the completed film must be mailed back to Nielsen bi-weekly). In both cases the mechanical approach has replaced, to a degree, various methods previously used that relied heavily on the vagaries of respondent cooperation such as the "diary" method, personal observation, and telephone surveys. Looking ahead, one can anticipate increased usage of computers tied in with communications devices to provide for the collection of vital market data for management decision making. For instance, in Japan, a large electrical manufacturer is developing a special purpose computer to determine audience concentration by collecting channel switching data from equipment in homes of the sample audience. This is being done for the largest advertising agency in Japan and bears some resemblance to the ARBITRON system.

USE OF THE COMPUTER TO PROCESS QUANTITATIVE INFORMATION

FORECASTING

Forecasting is in many respects an informational function. Forecasts require a background of information in order to provide a valid prognosis into the future. Past sales are one vital ingredient and probably the most important factor in any given forecast. Future sales are influenced by many factors outside the historic index of past selling rates. Other forces in the economy and even within a company tend to make themselves felt. The problem here is one of selecting these forces and measuring their influence to determine the effect on sales.

Any number of gross and fairly refined statistics are readily available in government and industrial publications. Some measure trends of an overall economic nature and others are more specific, relating to individual industries or even particular products. The problem for the computer, here, is not one of gathering the information, but that of selecting the appropriate set of indices which have varying degrees of influence on the sale of a product, measuring the influence, and determining the weight to be assigned to each.

It might be well, at this point, to mention some available statistics of a broad economic nature. Some are in index form and others provide data in absolute terms such as dollars, units, etc. Many can be broken down into more specific areas. The applicability of these general business indicators would vary from industry to industry.

Gross National Product; Corporate Profits; Plant and Equipment Expenditures; Industrial Production; Wholesale Prices; Consumer Prices; Employment; Personal Income; Installment Credit; Business Sales and Inventories; Retail Sales and Inventories; and such sensitive business indicators as: Building Contracts (Residential and Non-Residential), New Orders, Stock Prices (Industrials), New Incorporations, and Business Failures.

One can readily appreciate, with this fund of data and the availability of more specific industry statistics, the problem of choosing the factors. In the past, various methods have been employed, usually involving some arbitrary methods of selection and weighting of indices. These generally involved only the subjective viewpoint of an economic analyst with some guidance of management.

The strictly scientific approach to index selection would involve the employment of multiple correlation, a technique which has gained only limited business usage due to its complexity. The computer now opens up vast opportunities for its utilization and exploitation. However, the scientific approach by itself has limitations in that it does not consider the realities of a situation. In order to create a valid model, or mathematical replica of the factors that influence the sales forecast, what is required is an optimal blend of management judgment with the scientific application of multiple correlation techniques. The way such a mathematical model for the sales forecast is made is to have the individual responsible for building the model submit a rough approximation to the computer by selecting historic data of a number of the indices available. These selections are based on his, and management's, experience and feel for the problem built up over many years. This provides the computer a rough area to work in. The computer statistically cuts and selects from the rough data those particular indices which most closely resemble the sales pattern of the company or particular product. The resultant model produces a forecast which is compared to actual past sales and is projected forward.

Management can review the results and check the performance by actually withholding the previous year's sales from the computer input and examine the forecast produced by the model. If a large variation is present, then an entirely new set of indices can be tried or the combination of indices altered. Other modifications can be tested until the resulting model is in the estimate of management a good reflection of the marketplace for a particular product or products. Management is then in a position to test differing estimates of the indices utilized and come up with an appropriate approximation of sales under varying economic conditions. The flexibility of the computer allows alternate views of the economic situation to be assessed in order to determine the resulting effects on the sales of given products.

A sample of how the procedure would work is as follows: Assume that a large appliance maker desires to create a forecasting model. Through experience, he selects population, GNP, discretionary income, employment and new construction as having some influence on sales. He chooses the last six years as typical (1955-1960) and uses them as a historic pattern. The analysis inputs are: company sales for 1955-1959 (1960 is withheld to test the accuracy of the model) and historic levels for the same years of population, GNP, discretionary income, employment and construction. The forecast inputs are the 1960 level of population, GNP, discretionary income, employment and construction. In less than a minute, the computer will produce the sales forecast for 1960.[1]

It can readily be seen that effective use of the computer can utilize market data which has been available although could not be put to efficient use due to the complexity of the analytical procedure. Previously management has relied on the intuitive and arbitrary selection of the indices out of the mass of useable statistics. If multiple correlation were used in past years, it could be employed on only a limited number of indices and any variation would be well nigh economically prohibitive. The computer now presents an opportunity for a more complete utilization of marketing and economic statistics than was hitherto possible.

DISTRIBUTION ANALYSIS

Thus far in this section, discussion has emphasized a projection forward of sales. The same multiple correlation technique can be utilized to ascertain geographic market potentials and thus determine sales distribution patterns for a product. This technique could be likened to similar systems employed by the major computer manufacturers in making their election night predictions in the presidential contests. In that case, certain demographic factors were stressed. Prior voting patterns were studied and used to prepare a comprehensive analysis to project election trends. Weight and consideration were given to such things as regional variance, economic status of the voter, percent of unemployed and percent of urban vote.

The factors used in quantitative measures of geographic sales potential would generally consist of business activity and economic indices. These could be related to indicate potential or ideal distribution of a product. The selection of the indices and proper weighting of the factors is of major import. Instead of using arbitrary selection of several indices or choosing just a simple factor to reflect potential sales activity, one can utilize multiple correlation to analyze all seemingly significant indices.

There are any number of possible indices that can be employed in addition to sales data of particular industries. Some are general economic indices and others are good indicators of business activity and buying power. The applicability to various industries will vary depending on whether the

---

[1] "Computers Predict Sales," *Business Automation,* August 1961, pp. 20-24. (Copyright, OA Business Publications, Inc.)

product is an industrial or consumer good. Some of these quantitative measures of geographic markets are: Retail Sales; Population; Number of Businesses by Type or Size; Bank Deposits; Dwelling Units; Telephones; Employment; Income Tax Returns; and many others. In addition, many publishers and advertising agencies have built up their own economic indicators by combining some of the foregoing with other measures to create ready mixed sets of quantitative market indicators.

Through the use of a computer, multiple correlations become practical and the best set of indicators of potential can be selected scientifically. The constructed index can be used to optimize salespower coverage, delineate sales territories, establish sales quotas and, on the basis of results in test markets, predict sales distribution and rate of sale around the country for a newly introduced product.

STORAGE AND RETRIEVAL OF MARKETING INFORMATION

Up to now, the areas discussed have been decidedly within the present scope of computers. Just to round out the picture, a brief mention here of information storage and retrieval as it may apply to the field of marketing is in order. The bulk of this work has been carried on in the scientific areas. However, the same problem a scientist faces in undertaking a research and development project (searching for material on what has been accomplished and what is available in a given technical area) is faced by the market researcher when attempting to survey a new market. He must find out at the start what backlog of experience he can build on and what is available in the way of statistical data. This task generally calls for a great amount of searching and sifting of library data in order to find what is pertinent.

The same concepts of storage and retrieval of scientific data can be utilized to make market information more readily available. Current development of the concepts range from simple, relatively unsophisticated manual card handling devices all the way up to computer based systems. Even within the computer area the range is broad, running the gamut from digital to video to photo image recording of complete documents. Just which area will hold the greatest import for marketing is difficult to ascertain. The developments are coming along at an increasing rate and some thought should be given at this juncture to the types of data that may in the future be stored by some of the varied systems. Some of the discussion is strictly hypothetical at this point in time and certain activities will not be feasible until technological and systems breakthroughs occur. Such breakthroughs seem inevitable however, and management should be in a position to capitalize on them.

One aspect is the storage of abstracted documents which provide key identification data in digital form. A system of this type could store vast amounts of library data, completed market surveys and even statistical tables from government census and commerce publications. Certainly this could be an excellent starting place for embarking on a study of a given market. The researcher need not rely on his own experience in order to recall the type of information available. As envisioned, eventually the researcher need only consult the file and by describing his problem and its parameters will be provided with all references pertaining to the specified subject. Many problems must be faced before an adequate system, geared to the peculiar information requirements of the market researcher, can be considered a reality.

However, for the short term, using currently available computer techniques, the accumulation of data of a statistical nature is being facilitated by broader computer usage. Up to the present, data has been published in hard copy form by the Federal Government; however, commencing with the last decennial census, the Bureau of Census is making available the statistics in machine language on reels of magnetic tape at a much earlier date than the release of the published data. This action will enable the alert marketer to take advantage of more timely information and to analyze and summarize the statistics in a pattern to suit his particular requirements. It is expected that this development is only one example of a trend that will make data immediately available to computer analysis by bypassing the interim transition to hard copy.

chapter two | *Michael H. Halbert*

This chapter title contains three terms that are used rather frequently, but are not easily defined. *Information* is something we know, but how do we know what we know? If the answer depends entirely on introspection, then it can never be part of science, since science is a social, communicative activity. The definition appears even more obscure when we rephrase the question. How can you know what I know? The point of departure for our developing definition of information will be behavioral—you can know what I know by watching what I do.

The definition of *needs* is something that ordinary people as well as economists and psychologists have concerned themselves with for many years. A first attempt to define need usually includes the notion of desire or want. But it is clear that children, for example, often want things they don't need. Decision makers as well may want things they don't need and may need things they don't want. The distinction is more than a semantic quibble. When a want is satisfied, one usually feels happier. When a need

THE INFORMATION NEEDS

OF DECISION MAKERS

is met, one becomes more proficient in some class of behavior. Since this is a book about marketing management rather than about individual happiness, we shall concern ourselves with the informational needs of decision makers rather than their informational wants.

A *decision* maker is obviously someone who makes decisions. But what is a decision? Is a choice between white or rye a decision? If yes, is it only different from a twenty million dollar investment decision by the amount of money at stake? What about group decisions? There is no logical need to interpret *decision maker* as an individual. Committees also make decisions, and the entire committee may be viewed as a single functional unit. What are *its* information needs?

In order to investigate these needs of groups or of individuals, we must be able to discuss within some rational framework the decision-making structure and the effect of information on that structure. As will be seen later in the chapter, information may be classified according to the function it performs in the decision-making process. Let us start out with the rather broad definition of information in the decision-making context as follows: Two decision-making states differ in their informational content if the probabilities of choosing various alternative courses of action are different in one state from the other. This may seem too broad a definition since it ascribes all differences in behavior to differences in information content, and this definition will be constrained somewhat later in the chapter, but let us see where it will lead first.

As a basis for further discussion, let us analyze the decision-making structure and identify the following components and their interrelationships.

ALTERNATIVE COURSES OF ACTION

For a decision to be made, at least two alternatives must exist. That is, the decision maker must realistically have a choice. It is surprising how many executive committee meetings and executive conferences are concerned with situations in which no realistic alternative exists. The conferees may not like the course of action toward which circumstance impels them, but they have no choice. This is not a problem but a worry. In individual psychology, the extreme of this preoccupation with situations in which no alternative exists is called neurosis. To rephrase the definition of alternative courses of action with a bit more rigor, we can say that at least one requisite for a decision situation to exist is that the *a priori* distribution of the probability of choice of mutually exclusive action alternatives contains at least two nonzero elements. There has been a great deal of discussion, both in the professional literature and elsewhere, of the problem of defining alternative courses of action. They can be defined with a great deal of specificity. For example, in an advertising situation one might consider budget alternatives as: (a) next year we will spend one million dollars in advertising; (b) next year we will spend one million and ten dollars in advertising; (c) next year we will spend one million and twenty dollars in advertising; etc. Obviously, although these alternatives are mutually exclusive, they are defined with more precision than the situation really permits, since no advertising department or agency can control its expenditures to within ten dollars a year. One might, therefore, specify the alternatives as follows: (a) next year we will spend between one million dollars and one million and one hundred thousand dollars in advertising; (b) next year we will spend between one million and one hundred thousand dollars and one million and two hundred thousand dollars; etc. Although this set of alternatives may seem explicit to anyone not in advertising, it actually would offer only the merest guide. It says nothing about timing, media, shows, appeals, campaign, target audience, or the thousand and one other factors that enter into the design and execution of an advertising program.

One of the major problems in decision theory as well as in all business planning is the degree of specificity associated with the alternatives to be considered. It is usually easier to implement highly specific choices but more difficult to choose among them, and if one tries to be highly specific, the number of choices that "ought" to be considered becomes astronomically large.

VALUES

A decision structure requires, obviously, that there be some interest on the part of the decision maker in the various possible outcomes. This necessitates the investigation of values, and this investigation has been the most difficult area of all decision theory, operations research, and scientific management. Many formal models of decision making assume that there is a single outcome that is desired or a single measure that is to be maximized. Examples of models containing a single, highly valued outcome are often found in military operations research in which winning the battle, winning the war, or surviving an atomic attack is the outcome, the probability of whose attainment is to be maximized, and no realistic consideration is given to additional values that may be bound up with the major value. Examples of the second type of value are to be found most commonly in business management and operations research studies in which maximizing profit, net return or discounted cash flow, or minimizing unit cost, total expected inventory cost, shipping time, or customer delays, etc., are to be found. Partial recognition is given to the interrelationship of the values of various outcomes by the use of system constraints. For example, in military decisions the probability of winning a particular battle may be maximized subject to the constraint that no more than 50% of the commander's resources be destroyed. In business problems, one often sees a maximization of market share, for example, subject to a constraint of net profit or return on investment. Unfortunately, the method of constraints imposes a serious lack of realism on the value structure that it implicitly defines. If we take 15% return on investment as a constraint for market share maximization, this says that no amount of market share increase is to be considered if it yields only 14% return on investment, but that a market share increase of 11% at 20% return on investment is better than a 10% market share increase at 40% return on investment. One might as readily have turned the value rule the other way and decided to maximize return on investment subject to some constraint on market share increase. There is no known acceptable way of combining values for conflicting objectives. The question, "How much return on investment is equal to a 1% increase in market share?'', is a question whose answer lies in psychology rather than in decision theory, since it is basically a matter of the temperament of the management of the enterprise. How do they feel about current profit versus future growth? There is no *right* answer. Many serious mistakes in scientific problem solving and operations research have been made by being naïve about the interactions of values.

As was the case when we examined alternative courses of action, value situations may also be defined more or less explicitly. One may evaluate the success of a sales campaign in terms of the overall market share at the end of the year, or one may be as detailed as one likes in the evaluation by examining the market share month by month, sales territory by sales territory, and customer class by customer class. The latter procedure, obviously, gives a more detailed evaluation of how the sales campaign actually performed, but it also leads directly back into the problem of combining values. How much success with the large chain stores in the New York area will make up for how much failure with small independents in southern California?

EFFECTIVENESS

Once the alternatives available to the decision maker are defined, and the value measure somehow has been arrived at, to make a choice or a decision we need to establish the probability for any outcome given any particular choice.

In the decision matrix in Figure 1, we have illustrated a very simple

	Outcomes				
Alternative courses of action	O_1	O_2	O_3	Σ	
C_1	.3	.6	.1	1.0	
C_2	.4	.2	.4	1.0	
C_3	.4	.1	.5	1.0	
Value	.8	.6	.4		

Fig. 1. Decision matrix.

decision problem in which there are three mutually exclusive and exhaustive courses of action labeled C_1, C_2, and C_3. There are also only three relevant alternative outcomes of interest and these are labeled O_1, O_2, and O_3. The bottom row in the matrix shows the relative value of the three alternatives. It is conventional in this matrix to represent value by a number between 0 and 1 with 1 representing some sort of upper limit or maximum value. Thus Outcome 1 has a value of 0.8, Outcome 2 has a value of 0.6, and Outcome 3 has a value of 0.4. The numbers in the body of the table represent the probability of achieving the particular outcome by pursuing the particular course of action, or the relative efficiency. Thus the probability of achieving Outcome 1 by pursuing Course of Action 1 is 0.3. The probability of achieving Outcome 2 by pursuing Course of Action 3 is 0.1, etc. Each row sums to 1 since for any course of action pursued, some outcome must result. To evaluate this decision matrix, it is necessary only to compute the sum of the probability of occurrence times the value for each course of action for each of its possible outcomes. Symbolically, the value of Course of Action 1, $V(C_1)$ is equal to the probability of obtaining O_1 if Course of Action 1 is chosen (E_{11}) times the value of O_1, plus the probability of achieving Outcome 2 if Course of Action 1 is chosen (E_{12}) times the value of O_2, plus the probability of achieving Outcome 3 if Course of Action 1 is chosen (E_{13}) times the value of O_3. This can be written, of course, as $V(C_1) = \Sigma E_{1j} \cdot O_j$ (O_j is the value of the jth outcome). $V(C_1)$ equals $.3 \times .8 + .6 \times .6 + .1 \times .4 = .64$. $V(C_2)$ equals $.4 \times .8 + .2 \times .6 + .4 \times .4 = .60$. Similarly, $V(C_3)$ equals .58. This design rule would then lead our decision maker to pick Course of Action 1 since its total value equals .64, which is higher than the total value of either of the other two alternatives. This simplified example makes it appear trivially easy to make a decision once the three components (alternate courses of action, values, and efficiencies) have been established. But if we interpret this example as though it represented a real decision problem, we see some of the difficulties emerging. For simplicity's sake, let us assume that C_1 is to advertise entirely in television next year, C_2 is to advertise entirely in magazines, and C_3 is to spend our entire budget for radio advertising. O_1 may be considered a return on investment greater than 20%. O_2 may be a market share increase of at least 10%, and O_3 may be a maintenance of our brand awareness among consumers at least at its present level. Let us further assume that our marketing management has somehow established the relative values shown in Figure 1, that return on investment is twice as important as maintenance of brand awareness, and that market share increase falls halfway between the two in relative value. All we need then to make our decision is to fill in the nine numbers in the body of the matrix. These are the relative efficiencies, symbolized E_{ij}, but how in the world is anyone going to find out the probability of achieving at least a 10% increase in market share if we spend our entire advertising budget in print media (e.g., $E_{22} = 0.2$)? Much of the coming discussion of informational needs will center around the establishment of these relative efficiencies.

DECISION MAKING

With the foregoing model of the decision structure as a guide, we can distinguish four classes of information that are needed by decision makers. Each of these four will be considered in turn. With respect to the courses of action, one needs information that will specify them. With respect to the outcomes, one needs not only their specification but their value. As has been mentioned, this information is probably the most difficult to obtain but the most vital, since without it decision making is either impossible or trivial. The third class of information needed is the relative efficiency of each course of action for each outcome. The fourth informational class is the one containing the rules for making a decision given that you have the requisite information. In Figure 1, these rules are simply multiply and add certain numbers and pick the course of action with the highest value. In more complicated decision situations, more complicated rules are often necessary. Before the close of this chapter, we will discuss decision rules for determining decision rules.

COURSES OF ACTION

It may seem that whenever a decision maker has a decision (or choice or a problem), he automatically knows what alternatives are available to him. Yet very often the major contribution of careful decision analysis is to explore alternatives that have not previously been considered or that were not recognized as having been available. Much of the difference between a creative marketing manager and a pedestrian one is that the creative manager will think of courses of action for consideration and evaluation that do not occur to his less imaginative colleagues. Even in the case of a decision problem in which the alternatives are choices of single points along a continuum, it may not be obvious how to partition the continuum. For example, in grading students a department may use letter grades or may use numerical grades. Letter grades usually give the professor seven alternatives, A,B,C,D,E,F, or incomplete. Numerical grades (at least theoretically) give the professor 100 alternatives. Yet, why not carry numerical grades to the first decimal and thus increase the number of alternatives to one thousand or, as is often done in the lower grades in elementary school, allow only two alternatives, satisfactory and unsatisfactory. The problem of reliability often limits the number of alternatives. It is quite likely that there is no conceivable information available to a professor that would enable him to distinguish reliably between the grades of 97.6 and 97.7. It is even doubtful whether there can be reliable distinction between the grades of 80 and 85. Thus, the general acceptance of the letter grades seems consistent with the amount and accuracy of the information available to the professor.

As was mentioned earlier in the chapter, the accuracy of implementation is another constraint on the number of available courses of action. For example, since an advertising expenditure cannot be controlled to, let us say, closer than one thousand dollars accuracy, it would be useless to consider as realistically different alternatives the expenditure of one million and one thousand dollars compared to one million and two thousand dollars. Since even the assignment of alternatives within a single continuum, such as students' grades or advertising expenditures, is thus seen to pose some serious problems, the difficulties of identifying and defining the alternative courses of action when these are defined qualitatively as well as quantitatively tax the ability and imagination of the best researchers and executives. The executive's contribution to alternative courses of action comes from his complete familiarity and long experience in the particular content area. The researcher's contribution may be large precisely because he lacks the background. Many brilliant marketing strategies have resulted from serious consideration of naïve questions, such as "Why do we always sell through drug stores?" "Why shouldn't people be able to buy our products in supermarkets or from vending machines?" The researcher can also contribute by the application of logical analysis to the definition of the alternatives. They must, in fact, be logically exhaustive and mutually exclusive.

Executives may often feel, after carefully considering a set of alternatives, that the best thing to do is to postpone the decision. They may or may not realize that postponing a decision is taking a definite position and that doing nothing right now requires as much justification as the choice of any other alternative. In any discussion of value, we must mention lost opportunity costs. It may be *relatively* easy to determine how much it will cost to build a new factory or to introduce a new product. It is much more difficult to estimate the cost of not introducing a new product or of not expanding capacity. Yet, it has been said that companies must innovate or die since both production technology and marketing structures are changing with ever increasing rapidity. Even the decision not to make a decision may have as much effect on the organization's future as anything a more dramatic executive may do.

OUTCOMES

Information about the value of outcomes raises theoretical problems that are only beginning to be attacked with any rigor by management scientists. In the earlier discussion in this chapter, it was conveniently assumed that it was the decision maker's values that were relevant to the decision problem. In many organizations, a shipping clerk may make decisions about which order to ship next from this storeroom. A district manager may make decisions about refunds for returned merchandise in his territory. An art director in an advertising agency may make decisions about layout for a newspaper ad. Yet, it is obviously not the shipping clerk or district manager or art director whose values should determine the decisions. An explicit account of some of the ramifications of this problem may be found in Ackoff's article "Toward a Behavioral Theory of Communication," but we may here at least distinguish between the values of an individual as an individual and his values as a member of an organization.[1] In the latter sense, he represents the combined values of the stockholders (in the case of a corporation) and the collective values of some culture or subculture in the case of institutions or governments. Churchman in *Prediction and Optimal Decision Making* treats this aspect of value theory and many others with great insight.[2]

If the stockholders' values are to be the values used, what information is necessary and requisite about values, that is, what measurements of the stockholders are implied? These problems are avoided but sometimes with disastrous results by assuming some single measure for the system. This is often called "The Measure of Effectiveness," and it may be net profit or minimum cost for a particular operation, etc. Anyone who has ever attempted to establish values for a serious analysis of corporate decisions soon becomes aware of the difficulty of the problem and the frustration of the attempts to solve it. It is seldom that corporate executives will agree on an unambiguous, operationally defined single goal for corporate advertising. Many companies have written goals for their corporate image at least. These, however, are usually extremely vague and internally conflicting. In the introduction of a new consumer product the goals of the treasurer, the sales manager, and the production vice president may be far from identical. Far too small a proportion of the resources of a company are devoted to measuring and remeasuring the values of either the stockholders or that amorphous and ill-defined group known as management.

One of the major roles of market research as currently employed is to measure the values of customers and potential customers. It is interesting to note that two very different uses of computers contribute to the increased potential for measuring management and consumer values. The computer's ability to handle large quantities of data makes the possibility of routine sophisticated market research more feasible than in the past and the use of computers in management games provides an entree to

---

[1] Russel L. Ackoff, "Toward a Behavioral Theory of Communication", *Management Science,* Vol. 4, No. 3, April, 1958.

[2] C. West Churchman, *Prediction and Optimal Decision,* (Englewood Cliffs, N.J.: Prentice-Hall, Inc., 1961).

management value estimation that may provide a major forward step in the improvement of total decision making.

EFFICIENCY

Almost all of the professional interest in scientific decision making and in management science has been directed toward establishing efficiency. The role of models in operations research is primarily to answer the question, sometimes an extremely complicated and difficult question, "How likely is this particular outcome from this particular course of action?" It is true that the design of a model partially specifies the alternative courses of action by at least identifying the controllable variables and completely specifies the value system since almost all operations research models have a single decision rule which is to maximize (or minimize) some particular function.

In order to determine this required efficiency, it is necessary to describe the way the system under consideration actually works. This is what the model attempts to do. Some systems are easier to model than others. In general, production, financial, and distribution systems are easier to model than marketing, personnel, or public relations systems. The basic reason for this difficulty is that we understand people less than we understand machinery. It is only recently that serious, well-designed experimentation in the area of marketing, public opinion, and sociology has begun. The experiments are easy to conceive but extremely difficult and expensive to conduct. The information gained from them, however, is often well worth the cost, and, in at least one area (new product test marketing), some form of experimentation is now fairly well accepted.

Often the development of a model will specify the information required for its solution. Thus, some of the recent investigations of consumer behavior as related to market share have suggested that the probability of a customer switching from one brand to another is the crucial bit of information necessary for the evaluation of the effectiveness of one pricing strategy or advertising policy as compared to another. Although a great deal of market information has been collected in the past, very little individual brand switching data have been collected.

PLANNING

In our discussions so far, we have been analyzing the informational requirements for solving what may be called production problems (in the broadest sense of production). The alternatives under consideration in these decisions are usually the allocation of resources (either money, people, or productive facilities) toward the achievement of goals that directly relate to the output of the organization. In most business management problems, the attention is directed toward these types of goals. March and Simon call these decisions highly programmed, but to emphasize the difference between making decisions and deciding how to make decisions, we may call these decisions completely preprogrammed; that is, although there may be a choice among alternatives, the procedure for making the choice is completely specified.[1] Thus, the informational requirements and the accuracies of the information are also specified. Yet many problems that face management are not so easily and so neatly described. Decisions may be difficult, not only because the informational requirements are extreme, as in the cases we have been discussing, but they may also be difficult because there is no known or accepted method for choosing among the alternatives. This is perhaps most easily illustrated in the area of games and puzzles. When children play tick-tack-toe, the game retains its interest just because the child does not have an explicit decision rule, that is, a preprogrammed method of play. Very few adults enjoy playing tick-tack-toe because anyone familiar with the structure of the game can play it so that, while choices still need to be made, the rules for making them are completely known to both parties. The evidence of this triviality of the decision process is that computers have been programmed to play a perfect game of tick-tack-toe. There is some evidence that the game of chess may eventually also yield to an analysis of its strategy, so that "perfect" chess programs may be written and the prediction that the world chess master in 1970 will be a computer may be fulfilled. For a much more detailed analysis of preprogrammed games and their implications in sociology and political science, see *Fights, Games, and Debates* by Rapoport.[2] When one listens at committee meetings of management in a large company, it becomes apparent that much of the effort is devoted not only to making a decision but to determining the ground rules under which the decision will be made.

Going back to our original notion of a decision structure in which the alternative courses of action have to do with allocation of the organization's resources to achieve productive goals, we may distinguish a completely different *level of decision making* in which the alternative courses of action are rules for making decisions themselves. This obviously extends to a hierarchy of decision making structures, the output of each level being the rules or procedures for making decisions at the next lower level (Figure 2). If one views levels of management in this context, it is apparent that almost all of the routinized information collection and use

---

[1] James G. March, and Herbert A. Simon, *Organizations* (New York: John Wiley & Sons, Inc., 1958).

[2] Anatol Rapoport, *Fights, Games, and Debates* (Ann Arbor: University of Michigan Press, 1960).

is for making decisions at the lowest of these levels, the level we will call *production decisions*—sales information, accounting information, costs, prices, market share, inventories, etc.—this information is relevant primarily to production decisions. It is used to establish the effectiveness of

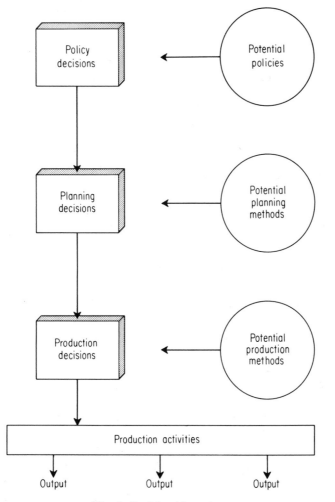

Fig. 2. Decision hierarchy.

various courses of action. These production decisions are characterized by having the values and the alternative courses of action more or less given or at least assumed with little investigation, and the major difficulty residing in the establishment of the relative effectiveness.

The next level in the hierarchy of decision making that we have proposed here will be provisionally called *planning decisions* since their purpose is to plan how to make production decisions. Very little of a company's effort is devoted to analysis and study of how planning decisions are made or ought to be made. At this level of decision making, the major difficulty lies in the area of value theory. Since little work has been done, it cannot yet be predicted how valuable adequate planning may be to the corporation of the future. Tick-tack-toe can be programmed for a computer, but the decision whether to play the game or not is reserved for the human operator. Similarly, given effective planning, many operating decisions can be assigned to the computer, leaving to the human manager the decisions at a higher level.

The whole history of organized behavior indicates that people's attention is usually concentrated at that level of decision making which is not yet preprogrammed but which appears to have the potential for preprogramming. It is thus interesting to estimate certain aspects of an individual's competence by seeing what kind of games he prefers to play. A third-grade student can solve long-division problems, but the decision rules involved during the course of the solution are by no means obvious to him. There are many adults for whom long division is extremely difficult, but its difficulty resides in their lack of skill in arithmetic rather than in their lack of knowledge of the decisions to be made in the course of long division. A refreshing example of this type of decision structure is available to anyone who will attempt to do a long-division problem using Roman numerals and not translating into the more familiar Arabic numbers in his head. During the second World War, the solution of cryptograms became largely preprogrammed with the ability to put frequency counts, syntactical structure, and other language variables into a computer routine for a cryptographic analysis. The availability of computer speed and computer flexibility exerts a tremendous pressure on management to make decisions at what has been called in this chapter the planning level, so as to improve decision making at the production level. As Churchman has said, the solution of the problems of present management will free future management to deal with the really important problems.[1] Thus the most important informational needs of decision makers turn out to be the needs for information about the decision-making process itself.

Industrial engineering has developed for most managements a useful set of techniques and approaches to the handling of physical material and its purchase, storage, and transportation. One of the results of the increased use of computers for management purposes is that some scientific discipline will have to develop as useful a set of techniques and approaches for the acquisition, storage, and use of information. One of the obvious

---

[1] C. West Churchman, "A Summing-Up", *Proceedings of the First International Conference on Operational Research,* Operations Research Society of America, Baltimore, 1957.

reasons why overhead costs per unit sold have been increasing while production costs per unit have been decreasing is that industrial engineering
is at present a more effective discipline than information engineering. It
is considered routine for companies to have a staff of purchasing agents
and a staff of product designers so that the exact requirements for raw
material can be specified and the most economical purchase can be made.
It is rare indeed for companies even to consider having information-pur-
chasing staffs or decision-planning groups so as to specify accurately and
purchase economically the information that the company needs for adequate performance. Viewing market research activities again as a purchase of information about consumers, we seldom find the degree of specificity in the information required of a market research study that we
find in the purchase of a raw material for production. The use of statistical design in the conduct of market research is a step in the direction of
more economical purchase of information, but this is a useless activity if
it is not accompanied by an equal increase in the accuracy with which the
informational needs are specified.

Very few manufacturing executives would attempt to keep a knowledge of production costs and inventories in their heads and not have them
recorded in some systematic way in the files. Yet very few marketing
executives keep well-organized, useful files of the information they need
to make marketing decisions. In fact, it is extremely unlikely that there
will even be high agreement among marketing executives as to what information is necessary, for example, in deciding how to price a new consumer product. Some of the recent work in simulating marketing systems
indicates that marketing decisions may be planable in the sense used in
this chapter if the marketing executives can sit down and get common
agreement about the structure of the market under consideration.[1] The
computer's requirement for specificity of language and logical adequacy
of structure is a major force in this direction. It is unlikely that a marketing executive will reach an optimal decision using an implicit model
in his head along with the information currently available in his files and
in his experience. It is equally unlikely that a competent machinist will
turn out a good product with no design or blueprints after collecting material in a casual stroll through an unmarked inventory. This is not intended to belittle the competence of marketing executives. The reason for
the lack of precision, structure, and planning in marketing decisions is not
due to laziness or incompetence on the part of marketing executives. It is
due to the difficulty and complexity of marketing problems. The usual
course of human activity is that when a system is poorly understood,
bright people with imagination and experience can do better than meticu-

---

[1] Kalman J. Cohen and Eric Rhenman: "The Role of Management Games in
Education and Research," *Management Science*, Vol. 7, No. 2, Jan., 1961.

lous plodders, who attempt to establish rules for systems they don't understand. But the second stage of behavior comes when the structure of the system is sufficiently understood and the information sufficiently adequate and accurate so that the imagination and experience of the intuitionist are no longer a match for the speed and precision that can be achieved by someone who knows the rules.

Many of the aspects of the practice of medicine are currently in this transition state from art to science. There have even been some serious attempts to use computer facilities in diagnosis and symptom interpretation. As management becomes more sophisticated in the analysis of its own function and in the specification of informational requirements for decision making, more and more operating decisions will become routine, more attention will be devoted to planning, and in the distant future even more effort will be devoted to policy making. As once hard tasks become easy, the impossible tasks become only hard and therefore challenging.

SCOPE OF THE CHAPTER

This chapter examines the activities of certain types of distribution facilities, and discusses the areas in which computers may be of aid. The kind of business examined is that of the middleman engaged in food distribution. There is no reason to suppose, however, that what applies to this group would not also apply to middlemen in other lines of trade.

The food merchants we shall discuss are the "common garden" variety of inventory carrying distribution centers; chain store facilities, retailer-owned cooperatives, voluntary group operators, and the so-called old line middlemen who have nothing but a sales relationship with their customers. The paperwork functions and tonnage-handling characteristics of these operators are so similar that when a computer is employable by one, it is employable by all. Not considered because of the unnecessary complications this would involve are brokers with and without stocks, stor-

WAREHOUSES AND COMPUTERS

age companies, field warehouses and other operators characterized either by narrow lines, consignment selling, or non-ownership of the goods.

The agencies that will be examined are usually distinguished by wide inventories, rapid turnover, ownership of the goods, delivery to customers, and back-haul from sources of supply. We propose to point out areas of research and day-to-day operations wherein the use of a computer by such distributors has become not only feasible but necessary because of the complexity of processing, by less sophisticated means, an ever-increasing amount of paperwork. We should point out, by way of eliminating the subject, that a computer might be programmed to undertake research into the relative value of possible new areas of operation being considered by a distributor. Moves to new markets, however, by such firms are so few as to be unimportant in this discussion. Growth by merger or absorption of other already established enterprises is much more common.

Also among the topics to be discussed are the effects of a site's size, shape, facilities, utilities, accesses, and topography on its suitability for the distributor's purposes. Certain design principles, construction and equipment requirements, are then mentioned. Finally, the applicability of a computer in a middleman's daily routine of receiving, storing, order-picking, and shipping will be considered. It should be emphasized that we are *not* discussing the various aspects of automation. The author views automation as separate and distinct from the use of a computer and as requiring heavy hardware which, while it may be activated by a computer, is different in design and intent. Microvolts do not handle tonnage.

For the sake of this discussion, we will define automation as the use of hardware which eliminates labor in a warehouse. The function of a computer, in contrast, is the accomplishment of what has been done manually by paperwork in the past. Consequently, we shall not deal extensively with the physics of distribution, even though, it is recognized that the computer can greatly facilitate the labor involved in warehouse operation.

THE GENERAL NATURE OF DISTRIBUTION BY MIDDLEMEN

Warehousing is one of the oldest of activities, and distributors have long been with us. Also, collecting things together for use when wanted is instinctive in some animals, such as the squirrel, jackdaw, and beaver. This activity, whether performed by instinct among animals, or intelligence among men, provides time and place utility. One attempts to have what may be needed on hand at the time of need.

The growth in the number and volume of goods distributed by middlemen has been phenomenal. At the beginning of this century, the food distributor handled less than two thousand items, and the typical firm had a volume of sales only a fraction of today's average. Work in the warehouse was performed by strong backs, and goods were handled piece-by-piece whether the task involved receiving, storing, order-picking, or shipping. The paperwork was also done manually. Generally, salesmen were used and selling was done from an extensive catalog. The orders were written out by hand in any sequence of invoice lines that suited the fancy of the merchant who placed the order. In the office, many copies of each order were prepared and sent to the numerous accounting and physical work stations. All of these copies had to be re-gathered and checked out before the order was shipped. Needless to say, this required a great deal of work by an office staff, and frequently, one whole floor, usually the first, of a five or six story warehouse was devoted to office space.

In contrast, many present-day distributors no longer employ salesmen. Conventional selling has been replaced by the mailing out and mailing back of a catalog or order form which describes the items fully. All the merchant has to do is to indicate the quantity wanted in the space provided. Characteristically, the smaller middlemen employ some form of punch card system which requires inventory tubs, sorters, tabulators, key-punches, etc. Larger wholesale distributors use similar but much more advanced high speed equipment. In the very largest operations, computers of varying degrees of sophistication are used. The changes that have taken place in equipment have been ones of degree not of kind. The early type of punch card machinery was the ancestor of the highly sophisticated computers presently employed.

The punch card machinery still used by small distributors operates in the following manner: The order is obtained as was stated; the cards are punched or pulled from the tubs; the invoice is printed on a tabulator; and this documentation is sent to the warehouse for action. The machinery also can indicate inventory conditions when this information is wanted, because the cards remaining in the tubs represent merchandise available for sale.

Today's large distributor, however, handles between five and six thousand items. He no longer finds it economically possible to prepare a card for each case, or to maintain the extensive tubs necessary to contain these cards. At the same time, his volume of sales has increased greatly, and so he maintains a larger inventory of each item as well as a broader line. Consequently, the clerical work and the time lag between the receipt of the order and the printing of the invoice would be too costly for a punch card method. Despite the efforts of the manufacturers of punch card machinery to keep pace with the users of their product, something more had to be developed for the large distributors. The computer meets this need since it is able to store and to process economically millions of facts. Without the computer, the cost of the paper work associated with increased sales and an ever-widening inventory would have placed an important limitation on the growth of the large wholesaling establishment.

DATA PROCESSING AND WAREHOUSE LAYOUT

As punch card machinery grew in sophistication, the distributor found it possible to reduce the cost of labor in the physical handling of the goods. In early days, goods had to be stored in "family groups," each group comprising a very few "fast-movers" and many "slow-movers." This required the order picker to cover a much greater distance than is now necessary in filling a typical order in the warehouse. The growing sophistication of punch card machinery has permitted the distributor to employ a "ton-mileage" or "frequency-of-visit" arrangement in his warehouse, by which the amount of walking or the turns of the wheel required of mechanical equipment has been greatly reduced. Consequently, despite the ever-burgeoning inventory, the rate of output per man hour has kept pace or even increased.

A ton-mileage or frequency-of-visit arrangement of goods completely disregards the family group arrangement and assigns goods to positions in the warehouse in accordance with their behavior as merchandise rather than their kind. A "slot"-system is used in which the warehouse is divided into a number of sections, each containing a given size of "slot" that will accommodate up to three weeks supply. Each section is situated in the warehouse as close to the input and output points as its sales volume justifies. With the introduction of the slot system, an additional number for each item, in addition to the catalog number, becomes necessary. This new number is the slot number or warehouse location. This slot number is carried on the punch cards, and a high speed sorter can sort the punch-cards from one array into another in a very short time. Subsequently, the cards can be run through the tabulator and the invoice produced in warehouse sequence. This basic system was developed some ten years ago, but as the punch card machinery advanced in usefulness and speed of operation, it began to emerge as a computer, and the slot system became widely used.

SELECTION OF A SITE

Preceding sections of this chapter have discussed in a general sense the operations of the large distributor and his growing use of tabulating machinery. In the following paragraphs, we shall deal with some of his specific problems, the first of which is the selection of a site.

As any firm grows from a pigmy to a giant, it outgrows its physical facilities, land and warehouse. A warehouse built two or three decades ago is no longer adaptable for the use of modern technology in distribution. Few distributors have been foresighted enough in the past to have purchased an excess of land on which they could expand their warehouse as sales volume increased. Two or three decades ago, the distributor was typically situated in the downtown part of the city, where land was too valuable to remain idle against a future need. Consequently, many distributors have been faced with the need for building their new larger plant somewhere else.

The selection of a new site is always a difficult problem. This site must be situated more or less centrally in the trade area; it must have rail facilities, accesses to highways, and utilities; it must be so shaped and sized as to suit the needs of the user. Moreover, the topographical and subsoil conditions must permit the economical construction of the warehouse.

Let us examine each of the factors in greater detail:

SIZE

Having been caught once with an inadequate plot, the distributor in search of a new site will be eager to assure himself of enough land. As a precautionary measure, he should be able to at least double his original construction on the new site and still have room for aprons, car parking, and truck parking on his own land. Use of this as a rule suggests that the land he purchases should be at least three times as large as his initial construction.

SHAPE

Even the smallest operation should have a plot at least 300 feet wide. Ideally, these 300 feet should extend between a highway and a railway line. This minimum width is arrived at as follows: There must be at least 70 feet for a truck apron, 50 feet for a covered truck dock, 30 feet for a front platform on which to assemble receipts and shipments, and at least 37 feet for a rail platform and rail spur. This would leave only 113 feet for merchandise, in stacks and aisles. Attention must now be drawn to an important rule of thumb. A warehouse becomes harder to organize for usefulness as it transcends a three-to-one proportion of length to width. Thus, a warehouse 113' wide x 339' long contains only some 38,300 feet which can be devoted to stacks and aisles. In such an area, there can be economically placed no more than 84,000 cases of groceries, worth an average of $5 a case, or a total of $420,000 worth of merchandise. This volume, turned over even at the optimum rate of fifteen times per year, will only support sales of approximately $6,000,000. For this reason, a plot of land suitable for a large operation must usually exceed six or eight acres. It is not easy to find a plot big enough in the location where wanted and with the characteristics needed that can be bought for a reasonable price.

TOPOGRAPHY

The topography of the land chosen must be suitable for low-cost construction. We cannot afford to move much earth in or out of the property because such action is costly. The level of the railroad spur is an important characteristic, because our floor must be from three to four feet higher than this level. By the time the topsoil has been removed and the sub-floor laid, some six or eight feet of fill usually must be introduced. This is true even if the subsoil conditions are such as to receive the foundations economically. Another important topographical consideration is the drainage of the entire plot and, particularly, of the shipping dock and rail siding.

UTILITIES

Utilities, such as electric power, water, and gas, must be present or brought in. Sewer facilities are not necessary, since septic tanks will meet the need of a warehouse and its associated office. There must be fire and police protection in the area. Also bus lines or other means of public transportation should be available to employees.

For the reasons given above, some distributors must search for years before they find a suitable site, and often they must pay an exorbitant price for the land they eventually purchase. Can the computer help in the selection of this site? No doubt a computer could be programmed and tortured into evaluating and stating some of the relative advantages of possible sites. Such an undertaking, however, does not appear to be either an economical or a proper use of a computer. Therefore, we must conclude that a computer can not contribute meaningfully to the selection of a specific site for a new warehouse.

WAREHOUSE DESIGN

A warehouse, or distribution center, is an expense item, not a money-making investment. But, although it will never make a penny of profit for a user, it may enable that user to save money which otherwise would be spent in the physical handling of goods. Therefore, the warehouse must be cannily designed to serve this end. Rules of thumb and experience have evolved the type of warehouse which can best utilize new methods of materials handling and techniques of operation. One rule of thumb, as we have seen, indicates that a warehouse should not be more than three times as long as it is wide. Other rules of thumb indicate a clear height in the warehouse of at least twenty feet and some inches. And common sense, rather than any rule, indicates that the column spacing should allow for maximum storage of pallets and racks. Little use can be made of space large enough for three quarters of a pallet.

The warehouse may be built of whatever materials are plentiful and cheap. One should bear in mind the common expression of warehouse character—"the best floor that the skill of man can design and lay, and the cheapest superstructure that will stay on the land for twenty years with reasonable maintenance." This statement requires some explanation. Goods are not handled today as they were twenty years ago, and it is a reasonable assumption that they will not be handled twenty years from now as they are today. Therefore, no warehouse should be an expensive monument built partially to enlarge the prestige of a firm or architect. Every warehouse will become an albatross around the neck of the succeeding generation of management in about twenty years. And when the firm that built the warehouse can no longer use it economically, the chances are that no other firm can either. Prospective purchasers will also want a warehouse better suited to the then prevailing methods of operation. We do not believe that a computer has anything to offer in the design of a warehouse.

WAREHOUSE EQUIPMENT

After it obtains a new warehouse suitable to its purposes and sized and shaped according to its needs, the operating firm must be prepared to spend a large sum of money in equipping the building. Machinery and equipment, such as pallets, racks, conveyors, lift tucks, warehouse carts, jacks, towlines (perhaps), dockboards, and other items, must be purchased before the new facility can be used economically. Experience indicates that between $1 and $1.25 per square foot would be the cost of such equipment.

The warehouse has now been designed, built, and equipped to perform the daily routine of receiving, storing, order-picking, and shipping, as well as to provide suitable security for the merchandise and adequate working conditions for the personnel employed.

DAILY ROUTINE

We have already discussed the slot system. Attention must now be focussed on physical layout. The determining factor in layout is whether one proposes to depend primarily upon conveyors or lift trucks. Our remarks will be limited to warehouses using lift trucks, since conveyor layouts are less common. Consequently, the appropriate rule of thumb specifies that the stacks and aisles should run at ninety degrees to the shipping dock, or at ninety degrees to the towline, if such be employed. To be sure, there is not always a choice, and a variety of factors may dictate a layout that would otherwise be undesirable.

The processes in the daily routine are receiving, storing, order-picking, and shipping. Although the computer has nothing to do with the physical performance of these functions, it can greatly facilitate them by preparing documents quickly and in the manner best suited for use by the men engaged in the physical work. As mentioned earlier, the computer will also permit the array and spatial placement of items in the inventory in accordance with their cost-making characteristics. These cost-making characteristics are velocity of movement, weight, bulk, and the variety in any one merchandise department. Fragility is no longer a factor of any importance because merchandise arrives at the warehouse well packaged and can be handled by lift trucks or, with minor exceptions, by a conveyor.

If we have arrayed our merchandise in space so that it can be stored and reached in a manner that minimizes man hours spent or turns of the wheel per work day, and if we have taken due account of the layout possibilities of stacks and aisles, we shall minimize labor costs. The computer's contributions to the achievement of this goal are the locational arrangement it facilitates and the speed and economy with which it performs an ever-increasing volume of paperwork. In addition to making possible the more useful layout of merchandise discussed earlier, the computer also keeps the record of the location of goods, of production per employee, of arriving goods, of shipments, of inventory, and of the time elements associated with these activities.

A LOOK AT THE FUTURE

Electronic machinery has come a long way since the days when "Hollerith" machines were first installed in the Census Bureau, and the first "Powers" machines were employed in accounting departments some fifty or more years ago. But the surface has not been scratched as to the future development of these machines. To employ the full potentialities of a computer, we must supplement it by hardware it can activate, which will handle the tonnage in any array and according to plan. As inventories become ever more complex and broader, as sales volume and the tonnage which a given firm must ship becomes ever larger in an unexpandable day, the ingenuity of man will permit computers to direct yet-to-be conceived machines. The result may be that virtually all the work associated with middleman distribution, both the paperwork functions and the tonnage handling, may be performed in a dark warehouse in which none but maintenance men will be needed.

chapter four | *John F. Magee*

The modern interest in physical distribution as a process is closely related to the changing role of the computer and associated information handling and communications facilities in the management of the physical flow of goods. The development of modern computing and data processing equipment has facilitated the consideration of physical distribution as an integrated process. At the same time, management of the physical distribution process has provided a field in which modern data processing techniques which were first applied in routine clerical cost-cutting efforts are now having a significant influence on the design of the total system, because of the flexibility, power and speed of the equipment available.

Modern data processing and communications equipment plays a significant, threefold role in physical distribution:

—As an aid or device in analysis of distribution techniques and design of the system;

—As a means for implementing more efficient decision rules used in control of the system;

THE COMPUTER AND THE PHYSICAL

DISTRIBUTION NETWORK

—As a means for shortening delays associated with information processing and thus improving the over-all reaction time of the system.

THE PHYSICAL DISTRIBUTION SYSTEM

A physical distribution system can be illustrated schematically, in simplified form, by Figure 1. This figure shows how a distribution system is made up of a series of inventory or stock points linked by operations. The stock points may in part be under the same roof—for example, inventories of material in varying stages of completion; the corresponding operations may be manufacturing operations—conversion of items withdrawn from one stock point into new items in another stock point.

The stock points may also be separated by considerable distances, such as central plant and field warehouses stocking finished goods. Here transportation is the operation separating individual stock points. Transportation in a field distribution system is much like a manufacturing operation inside a plant. In either case, material is taken out of one stock location and put into another in a different form. Transporting an item changes it, though perhaps not so strikingly as processing it in a manufacturing operation. Yet the utility to customers of a radio tube in a Chicago warehouse is quite different from that of a tube of the same specifications in Dallas.

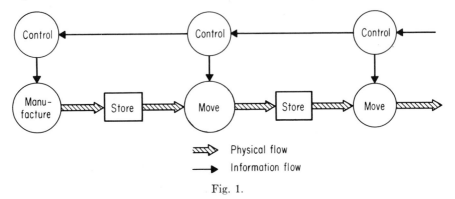

Fig. 1.

The physical product flow—operations transforming items in one stock location into those in another—is governed by a corresponding information flow, in the opposite direction. Customer or user orders place demands on the last stockkeeping stage. This stage, in turn, must follow some procedure to initiate the replenishment operation. This operation in turn draws on the preceding stock unit for the required material.

This highly simplified display of the interrelationship among stockkeeping units operations and information processing for an individual item can, in one's imagination, be compounded to represent the highly complex patterns of physical distribution, of material and information flow, which exist in the world today. These complexities arise in part from needs imposed by complex product lines, in part from efforts to balance production, transportation and marketing effectiveness, in part from regulation.

EQUIPMENT CAPABILITIES IN PHYSICAL DISTRIBUTION

Developments of modern information processing equipment have facilitated improvements in physical distribution in five key ways. These ways include improvements in data transmission, large-scale data storage, improved data display, effective real-time processing, and lowered cost per operation. Because of greater speed in data transmission, the distribution system manager now has greater flexibility in choice of alternatives. In the process illustrated in Figure 1, a time increment occurs at each one of the steps in the flow of information backward and flow of material forward from source to market. The flow of information back through each stage takes time. With high-speed data transmission, the time period required for sending key demand or reorder information required to stimulate material flow is potentially greatly shortened. This improvement permits greater flexibility in the choice of ways of accomplishing other tasks in the making of control decisions or in physical movement of material.

A few years ago, physical distribution systems were governed by the quality of information transmission service that could be provided by the United States mail, and more recently, the service that could be provided by teletype, roughly 75 bits per second. Now we may plan in terms of service that can be provided by voice-type circuits (1000-2000 bits per second) or by wide band circuits and microwave systems. Transmission capabilities are growing from the ability to send about 75 bits of information per second, up to the ability to send approximately 60,000 bits of information per second; and within a few years we will have capacities to transmit up to 5 million bits per second. In general, one finds that as the speed of the system goes up, the cost of the system goes up, but the cost per bit of information transmitted goes down. Thus, to capitalize on improvements in transmission capability, one does not attempt to hold the volume of transmitted data constant. Rather, he takes advantage of the lower cost per unit to increase the volume of data—for example, through more frequent reports—and thereby to improve efficiencies elsewhere.

The second significant improvement in capability is the present-day availability of large-scale data storage. One vital characteristic of an advanced information system for distribution control is the capability of pulling together a completed body of facts having to do with products, product movement, customer demand, and inventory conditions. Our ability to achieve this synthesis has been severely hampered in the past by, among other limitations, the unavailability of reasonably priced storage capacity. Some progress has been made. For example, a typical computer in 1954 had available to it 160,000 bits of information with a storage capacity of 4000 words. Today 600 million bits of information, though not yet a commercial commonplace, are available in some special systems.

A third important hardware development is increased data display capability. This includes plotters directly connected to computing facilities and, potentially of great importance, the equivalent of television displays directly connected to computing equipment. The possible benefits in the use of displays of information to increase understanding of the situation and to aid in action planning are now being explored in military command and control systems.

A fourth development is the reality today of real-time data processing —the ability to handle transactions immediately as they occur in a continuous stream instead of waiting for them to be batched together in a reasonable work load for later entry into a computer or a data processing system built around punch card machines. Real-time processing also implies capability for prompt, on-the-spot handling of unusual or emergency situations. Real-time data processing requires superior speed, now available, superior storage, also available, and the ability to move information over large distances with relative ease, and we can now accomplish this. Interruptibility—the ability for the data processing system to stop what it is doing temporarily and do something else, and then go back to the first thing—and reliability are essential; modern computers developed for critical defense requirements demonstrate these characteristics. Modern real-time reservations and space control systems, such as the American Airlines SABRE System, are examples of nation-wide real-time distribution control systems in commercial use.

Finally, the cost per unit of processing information in modern systems is falling rapidly. For example, it has been estimated that the average cost of performing an arithmetic operation in installed data processing facilities in the United States dropped by roughly 60% in the year from 1960 to 1961. Here also, the drop in cost per operation is accompanied by an increase in total cost; the cost advantage is obtained not by direct savings in processing cost but by using lower unit processing cost to achieve more sophisticated forecasting, improved control rules, and greater centralization and flexibility in distribution control.

PHYSICAL DISTRIBUTION ANALYSIS

The computer plays its first key role in the physical distribution system as a device for quantitative analysis and as a means for efficient collection and organization of facts about the business. The design of physical distribution systems depends significantly on quantitative study, first, because the proper choice of a physical distribution plan in the circumstances of any particular organization depends not merely on theory or generalizations but on quantitative facts, costs, times, characteristics of the market and customers, product line characteristics, statistics of demand.

In the second place, physical distribution decisions require a reconciliation or balancing of partly conflicting objectives of a business: low production cost, even flow of product, low transportation paperwork costs, prompt response to market needs—

The production man would like to operate under a level work load with long product runs and minimum disruption. The salesman would like to take selling and promotional action with the comforting knowledge that any demand he might generate would be met, on the spot and without delay. The treasurer would like to keep to a minimum the use of funds to finance plant capacity, inventories, warehouses, and equipment.

This balancing act poses difficulties for businesses whose thinking and organization often emphasize traditional functions. Physical distribution is a process in which no function has a dominant interest.

Physical distribution systems are so complex that there is no single elegant technique for organizing all aspects of a physical distribution study. However, theoretical studies in the last decade have contributed greatly to conceptual understanding and technical apparatus available for studies.

SOME ISSUES AND APPROACHES

Some of the significant issues to which quantitative studies employing modern computing facilities can make a contribution include:

INVENTORY INVESTMENT

How much should be invested in inventory of a particular item at a given location? This question has been covered extensively elsewhere.[1] It is sufficient to note, as shown in Figure 2, that one element of the inventory investment (cycle stock) depends on the size of replenishment shipment —a balance of order handling and shipping costs against the cost of holding stock, including the cost of capital. Another element of the inventory investment (safety stock) depends on policies with respect to capital investment and reliability of service, and on the variability of demand, the size of error characteristic of the inventory control forecasts.

The period over which the forecast error or demand variability must be measured is the response time or lead time of the replenishment system. Consider, for example, a field warehouse. Its lead time is the time needed for it to make a replenishment order, time to process the order, communications time to the source of supply, perhaps the factory, time for the supply source to make up and load the order, time in transit, plus the fixed time interval, if any, between replenishment orders. For exam-

---

[1] John F. Magee, "Guides to Inventory Policy," *Harvard Business Review,* Jan.-Feb., Mar.-Apr. and May-June, 1956.

See also John F. Magee, *Production Planning and Inventory Control* (New York: McGraw-Hill, 1958).

ple, if the warehouse is on a biweekly reporting or reordering cycle, the two weeks must be added to the time for paperwork, communications and transportation.

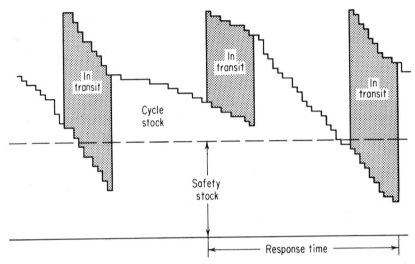

Fig. 2. Characteristic distribution inventory pattern.

Quantitative analysis of inventory control systems has contributed substantially, (1) in the identification of the system characteristics and costs that must be measured and the policies that must be made explicit, (2) in the use of inventory control theory to set up means for analyzing demand and making routine replenishment decisions automatically, consistent with policies, and (3) in the development of new techniques such as exponential smoothing for the routine forecasting required in distribution system management.[2]

The application of forecasting techniques illustrates the power of modern computing facilities in physical distribution. Before the day of the computer, the role of short-term forecasting in physical distribution control often went unrecognized. Where a formal forecast method was used, the clerical labor of repetitive forecasting generally limited the method employed to a crude device, perhaps a simple average over time, infrequently revised. The power of computers on one hand has stimulated extensive research into techniques for repetitive, controllable short-term forecasting. On the other hand, the costs of storing and processing lengthy

[2] Robert G. Brown, *Statistical Forecasting for Inventory Control* (New York: McGraw-Hill, 1959).

Holt, Modigliani, Muth and Simon, *Planning Production, Inventories and Work Force* (Englewood Cliffs, N.J.: Prentice-Hall, Inc., 1960).

records have led to development of methods such as exponential smoothing to reduce record maintenance requirements.

There are clearly interactions between these two elements of inventory. For example, we may lengthen the review period in a field warehouse to cut the number of reports, and thus save paperwork and increase the size of replenishment orders for transportation economy. This may, for example, permit shipment in carload lots at carload rates; lengthening the review cycle, however, lengthens the time period over which demand must be forecast, and characteristically increases the inventory investment needed to protect order service. Introduction of the inventory control problem serves to indicate that inventory control theory is fundamental to physical distribution studies and to point out the relationship between inventory investment and the response time or lead time and the time elements that make it up.

CHANGING THE LEAD TIME

The principal elements of response or lead time are identified in Figure 3 as reorder period, processing time, communications time, assembly and

LEAD TIME ELEMENT

REORDER PERIOD. .MORE FREQUENT REORDER. .TRANSMITTAL OF DEMAND ORDER-BY-ORDER. .

PROCESSING TIME. . .EDP-BOOKKEEPING. . .ROUTINE DECISION RULES, USING COMPUTERS. . . .

REAL TIME PROCESSING. . . . . .COMMUNICATIONS TIME. . . . . . .TELETYPEWRITER . . . .

HIGH CAPACITY DATA CHANNELS. . . .MATERIAL HANDLING TIME. . . .UNITIZED HANDLING. . . .

AUTOMATIC WAREHOUSING. . . .TRANSPORTATION TIME. . . .DIRECT DOOR-DOOR HANDLING . . .

AIR SHIPMENT. . . . .

Fig. 3. Lead time and components and some reduction possibilities.

loading time, and transportation time. Figure 3 also indicates some of the ways in which the various elements may be speeded up—usually at a cost. For example, we can reorder or report sales from a field warehouse more frequently, daily instead of biweekly; and in the extreme, by customer order. We can use mail, air mail, teletype, or a high-speed data channel like microwave or AT&T's TELPAK. Assembly and loading time may be cut by material handling aids, unitized handling, or possibly mechanized computer-controlled warehousing. The modern alternatives in transportation and the time and cost characteristics of these are reasonably familiar.[3] It is noteworthy how many new technical developments can be brought to bear on the physical distribution process, how each new possibility, if treated in isolation, will tend to increase the cost of the system, how important it is to analyze the characteristics of each new alternative in the light of the response system as a whole.

Analysis is necessary to measure the time characteristics and costs of the available alternatives, as well as to determine the relationship among well-balanced alternatives and between response time and system operating cost.

A significant advantage of response or lead time reduction is reduction in required inventory. Inventory investment, as noted before, at a given service level, depends on demand variability over the lead time. This variability depends, in turn, on the length of the lead time. For example,

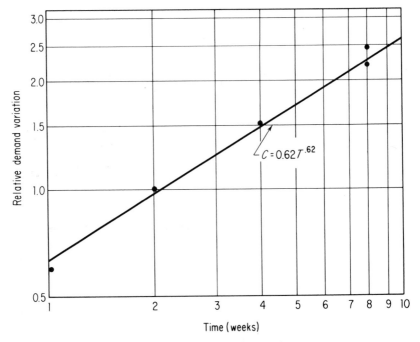

Fig. 4. Demand variation vs. time.

Figure 4 shows the observed relationship between lead time and relative size of demand variability for one particular product line. It conforms to the general form of relationship we have observed:

$$\sigma_{s,t} = At^{\alpha} \tag{1}$$

---

[3] "Management of the Physical-Distribution Function," *AMA Management Report,* Number 49, 1960.

where $\sigma_{s,t}$ is the standard deviation of demand vs. forecast, observed over time t.

The data in Figure 4 yields a value for α of .62. In some theoretical work, a value of α is arbitrarily assumed, sometimes $\alpha = .5$, sometimes $\alpha = 1.0$. In any real investigation, analysis is necessary to estimate the functional dependence of demand variability on lead time, and if it corresponds to (1), to estimate the value of A and α.

When $\alpha = .5$, the standard deviation of demand vs. forecast—the "forecast error"—changes in proportion to the square root of the lead time. Doubling the lead time will require, as a consequence, a 40% increase in inventories to protect against forecast error to maintain the same effectiveness of service. When α is near 1.0, the "forecast error" increases or decreases in proportion to the lead time. Thus, the larger the number α may be in any case, the more significance will lead time changes have on inventory requirements.

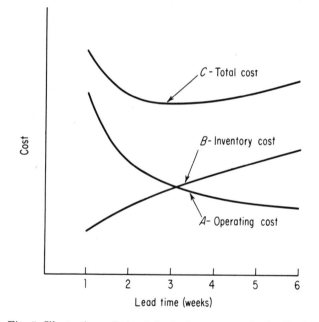

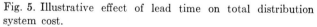

Fig. 5. Illustrative effect of lead time on total distribution system cost.

Figure 5 illustrates the balance required between operating cost of the response system and inventory investment. As the lead time increases, operating cost may be reduced (Curve A) while the cost of supporting inventory investment increases (Curve B), leading to an operating point with minimum total cost (Curve C). Since the position of Curve B depends on the cost of capital assessed against inventories and on service policies, the minimum-cost operating method is clearly dependent on managerial policy.

Quantitative analysis is necessary to measure and state this dependence and to indicate the consequences of policy change. Modern data processing systems provide, at least potentially, the means for monitoring and analyzing the dependence of forecast error on lead time.

THE NUMBER OF FIELD WAREHOUSES

Both operating costs and investment affected by the replenishment time will depend on the number of points being replenished. The minimum number of distribution points—plants, terminals and warehouses from which product is distributed to a customer—will depend on the geographical distribution of product, the acceptable time to deliver an order to a customer, the percentage of the market to be reached in a given time, and the speed of transportation from distribution point to a customer. For example, the following table shows the result of a study of the percentage of the U.S. consumer market that can now be reached by truck in a given time from receipt of order at the stated number of distribution points.

Share of Consumer Market Reached, Compared with Time to Reach,
Number of Distribution Points

	Distribution Points			
	5	25	50	100
Time				
1 day	33%	90%	95%	99%
2 days	85	99	100	100

These figures have obviously been affected by improvements in transportation techniques and facilities. Many firms, however, are operating distribution systems designed 20-30 years ago, which do not take advantage of recent major advances in transportation—for example, improvement of trucks and road systems.

The table of market service vs. time and number of distribution points must be worked out for the particular product line, taking into account its particular market structure. For example, in one case demand was found to be roughly proportional to population concentration, with 18 states accounting for 70% of demand. In another case, demand is highly concentrated on the West Coast and in a belt from the Great Lakes east, with 73% of demand concentrated in 10 states. Analysis of the present and anticipated pattern of demand is critical in distribution system design.

Subject to restrictions on service and on testing the price of changing these restrictions, analysis is needed to investigate the economic effects of varying the number of field distribution points. The principal cost elements of concern are:

1. Facilities cost: The operating cost of a warehouse including data processing and communication cost, as a function of its normal or design size, can generally be approximated by

$$C = a + bX$$

and thus, warehousing cost for the system,

$$C_w = aN + bS \tag{2}$$

where N is the number of warehouses and S is demand in total.

2. Transportation cost: Within a given mode of transport, transportation cost from plant to field distribution point may be affected only in a minor way by the number of distribution points. Outbound transportation from distribution point to customer may follow the form

$$C_{T0} = kN^{-\beta} \tag{3}$$

where N is the number of warehouses and β depends on the uniformity of market density. (If the market were perfectly uniformly distributed, β would equal .5.)

3. Inventory cost: When distribution point territories are combined, demand variability and thus inventory requirements combine in a complex way. The exact pattern is dependent on the cross-correlation of demand among areas. In practice, the variability of demand over a given fixed time interval, as a function of "area" or average demand rate, can be represented as

$$\sigma_{s,d} = gD^\alpha \tag{4}$$

where D is the total average demand and α may generally take on values between .6 and .9. In this relationship, as well, the value of α in a specific case will influence the relative cost of more or fewer stock points. A computer system with power to analyze the statistical characteristics of demand is a valuable system design and monitoring tool.

Clearly, the costs will depend on the modes of operation—for example, degree of warehouse mechanization, type of transportation used, type of communication and data processing system, etc. Thus, the cost balance and economy of operating more or fewer distribution points must be studied in relation to the replenishment system used.

Even at this level of complexity, in the physical distribution study, it is clear that one must deal with a host of alternatives: in policies—for example, policies with respect to capital cost, service standards; in operating modes—for example, transportation medium, communication and data processing technique; and in extensiveness—for example, the number of distribution points. These alternatives interact; service standards affect relative economy of operating modes, the choice of operating mode influences the cost of expanding or contracting the number of distribution outlets. This condition cries for quantitative analysis to explore these alternatives, subject to the particular statistical characteristics of the market and cost characteristics of the business.

IMPACT OF THE PRODUCT LINE

So far, we have considered physical distribution alternatives as if we are dealing with a single item while at the same time we are examining alternatives for distribution of the product line as a whole. In most businesses, however, we find a product line in which demand is highly concentrated in a few items while most items account for only a modest proportion of sales, as illustrated in Figure 6. The top curve in Figure 6

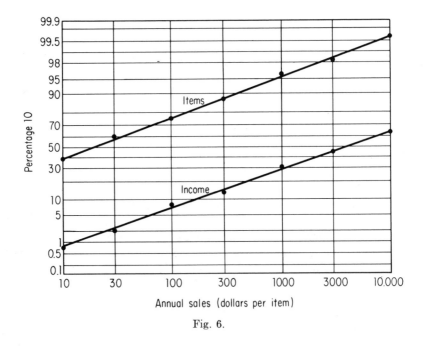

Fig. 6.

indicates the fraction of total items (vertical axis) with annual sales equal to or less than the amount shown on the horizontal scale. The lower curve indicates the fraction of total demand indicated by these items. We find this pattern, the lognormal distribution, to be characteristic of most product lines, though the slope (the standard ratio) may vary.[4] This product demand distribution leads to the relationship shown in Figure 7, which

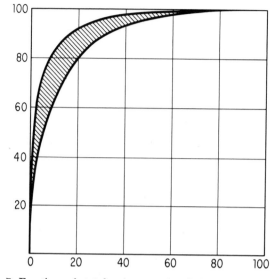

Fig. 7. Fraction of total sales accounted for by fraction of total items.

illustrates the characteristically high degree of concentration of demand among a small percent of the items in the line.

Other significant characteristics of the product line will also show wide differences. For example, inventory requirements usually do not increase in strict proportion to item demand. Thus the cost balance underlying the choice of system will depend on the level of demand of the item in question. Figure 8 illustrates some of the alternatives available; we may use programming methods such as the transportation and transshipment models[5] to study alternate routings for items in the product line, and to define the breakpoints, or conditions which define the boundary between those items to be distributed one way, for example, direct plant-to-customer, and those to be handled another way, for example, stocked in regional warehouses.

PLANNING FOR THE FUTURE

Up to this point we have considered the problems of distribution systems planning as if the planning were static, as if we could make our plans

[4] Brown, Robert G., *op. cit.*

[5] James C. Hetrick "Mathematical Models in Capital Budgeting," *Harvard Business Review*, Jan.-Feb., 1961, Appendix, p. 58 ff.

to meet a static (and presumably well-known) market requirement. In many cases, this is a reasonable assumption; the anticipated rate of change of the market is low enough and the ability to modify the distribu-

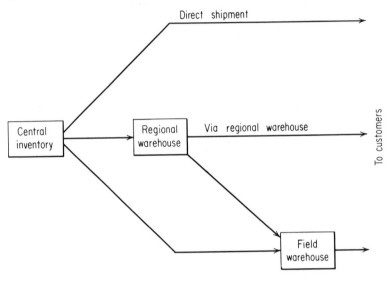

Fig. 8.

tion system great enough so that a static view is useful. In many other circumstances, however, we must take a dynamic view of the distribution system,

1. Because change in the system may be expensive and laborious
2. Because anticipated future needs may be inconsistent with present needs
3. Because we may not be able to see the future too clearly.

Under these circumstances we may want to give up some immediate advantage in order to be in a better position either to have a system better suited to the future as we anticipate it, without expensive changes, or to be in a more flexible position to deal with the future as it unfolds.

In these problems quantitative analysis with the aid of computing facilities can be of great value in working out the consequences of alternative systems under various possible market conditions. A series of solutions under alternative conditions is hypothesized for various future points in time.

DATA PROCESSING AS A FUNCTION IN PHYSICAL DISTRIBUTION

Now let us examine the functional operations of a distribution information system. The information system is concerned with planning of production, finished goods and in-process inventory control, transportation and traffic, warehousing, order processing, credit, and customer services. The distribution information system is itself a subsystem in a total company information and intelligence system. The distribution information system cannot, or should not, be considered independently of, for example, the market analysis system, the accounting system, and other systems relying on much of the same basic raw material.

In order to accomplish these basic functional operations, there are two basic information system designs in common use. Both of these variations are concerned with the processing of orders and the production of invoices; they have been termed the "backboard" system and the "clay pigeon" system. In the "backboard" system, as shown in Figure 9, all orders are

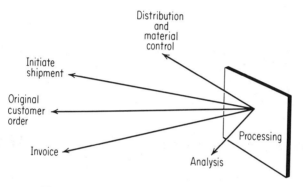

Fig. 9. The "backboard" information system.

funneled from wherever they may originate in the marketing territory to some common point for processing. The invoicing and shipping papers are produced and issued from this single common point. The purposes of this method are 1) to take advantage of the cost decreases possible from centralized large-scale data processing, 2) to achieve and maintain rigorous control of the type of information developed, the accuracy and usability of the information being increased through centralized operation.

The "clay pigeon" system, as illustrated in Figure 10, uses a different concept: when an order comes to some intermediate point, invoicing and shipping papers are produced; a reasonable facsimile or extract of information from this order is then transmitted to a central point. More information is produced and from that point on this information filters to the various other interested elements of the company. The proponents of the "clay pigeon" system are usually to be found in the sales organizations. The basis for their preference is often the theory that the closer one stays to the customer in processing his order, the less are the risks of error and inappropriate action in credit, in customer service, and in handling the order. This is not the type of argument that in general can be resolved on

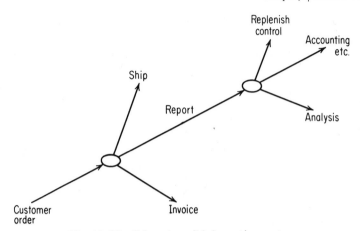

Fig. 10. The "clay pigeon" information system.

general or even objective grounds. Each type of system has as its objective obtaining the right amount of control and sending the right information to the customer, to the plant, to the distribution point, to the field force, and to various types of management.

THE ELEMENTS OF THE DISTRIBUTION INFORMATION SYSTEM

If we look more closely inside the functional blocks of the distribution information system, the elements indicated by the term "control" in Figure 1, we see certain common essential elements no matter how the system is laid out. In concept, the control elements appear on inspection somewhat as shown in Figure 11.

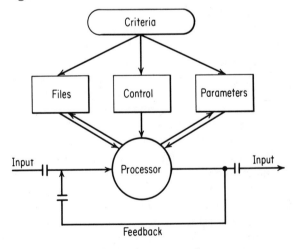

Fig. 11. Information system elements.

Information flows into a processor and this processor can be a department of human clerks or it can be a machine or set of machines. The control is the source of data that indicate to the processor how the input information will be handled, what reports will be produced, what data will not be transmitted, how these reports will be developed, and so on. The control may be systems and procedures; it may be programs; it may be verbal instructions. However, it is usually some combination of those factors. This control actually determines in detail how the processing is done. Information then comes out. There are criteria set up which tell one first of all what information should come out, and, secondly, where. From this output of information presumably we feed back information into the processor again and improve, confirm, or modify the processing of information.

The processor, in operating on the input data such as a customer order, will draw on files available to it. These may be status files, for example an inventory balance, or historical record files, such as the customer's ordering pattern. The processor typically will revise some or all of the files in the course of processing the input. More specifically, the order may be used to produce a new inventory balance or a new demand forecast.

The output of the processor and the modification of files the processor makes will be governed by parameters or control numbers in the system. These are somewhat different from the control process. These may include, for example, the smoothing constant to be used in the forecasting procedure, or the cost to be assigned against funds invested in inventory for replenishment decisions. These parameters may be modified from time to time by application of outside management criteria, or they may be modified directly within the system as a processing result. A system with the capability for modifying its own parameters as a result of its own operation demonstrates elementary learning capability, vital for long-term efficiency.

Filters are indicated by pairs of bars; these may be filters on output, filters on feedback, filters on input. These may be termed censoring devices or discrimination. Examination of a typical tabulating room or clerical department in a business will demonstrate that an enormous volume of paper is used and data produced. The presence of filters implies that much of it may not be necessary and is eliminated.

Mathematical and statistical methods, such as those described previously in this chapter, may be used to formulate the control procedures, including the procedures for "learning" through modification of parameters. These methods may be used to set parameter values and to analyze the operation of the system as a whole as an aid to establishment of management criteria. The purpose of the system is to handle three tasks on a continuous basis: to produce information to operate on a day-to-day basis, to produce information to make decisions, and finally to measure performance.

QUESTIONS FOR REVIEW OF THE DISTRIBUTION INFORMATION SYSTEM

The potential role of the computer in physical distribution control has directed management attention at the effectiveness of the information subsystem. A number of key questions are useful in testing the effectiveness of information processing in the physical distribution system.

First, is the system working too hard to process the routine, that is, to get invoices out or to get shipping papers produced? Do routine functions absorb system capacity? On the other hand, is the system prepared and does it have capacity to process the unexpected?

Does the distribution information system make effective use of a common body of facts, within itself and together with other activities in the firm, or is it a case of everyone for himself? Is the system capable of providing required information to the other elements of the business that link with physical distribution, so that everybody is using the same data on which to base analyses and action?

Is the distribution information system perceptive? Is it able to detect long-term trends or the beginning of trends that will ultimately affect the business significantly?

Have cost reductions and techniques of cost control been used with discrimination? As has been noted several times before, apparent economy in one element in the distribution system, especially an element as significant as the distribution information system, may enforce high-cost practices or added capital investment elsewhere.

Finally, is the distribution information system responsive? Very seldom can an executive face a day in management with certainty as to the questions he must meet and the information he will require. More often he must say, "I have a problem; I want to assemble the facts that are needed to solve this problem."

The distribution information system should have the capability to get at those facts even though the time is not the standard reporting date and the facts needed are not drawn from the standard reports.

Marketing decisions have a fundamental influence on the design and operating cost of the physical distribution system. Indeed, the pressure for physical distribution improvement under which many companies are turning to modern computing equipment for help springs largely from marketing actions. These actions include particularly:

1. Expansion of the product line. In many product lines, in both consumer and industrial products, introduction of style differences, new packaging concepts and products with more specific uses have

led to vastly expanded product lines. Examples include typewriters, paper, lamp bulbs and home appliances. Substitution of three items for one, even with a resulting 50% increase in demand, may generate a 25-60% increase in *unit* distribution cost.

2. Use of service as a competitive weapon. Increased speed and reliability of service have tended to force expansion of field stock items and investment levels. The same objectives may be achieved in part by system redesign, to achieve greater responsiveness.

Advances in information handling technology—symbolized by the internally programmed computer—open up new means in a properly designed physical distribution system to meet the needs of marketing.

Even in the smallest of businesses, the interrelationship of functional activities must be recognized if the business is to survive and prosper. In a small business, a single executive makes the day-to-day decisions and develops the longer range ideas and plans which will spell the success or failure of the business over the years. In doing so, he can often keep in mind such factors as production schedules, customer requirements, prices, legal problems, banking relationships, inventories, and competitive activity. The possibility of maintaining a clear view of all these factors rapidly diminishes with increasing size. Indeed, it is sometimes surprising that business ventures have sufficient stamina to withstand the difficulties which automatically stem from lack of coordination, conflicting policies, and the pursuit of contradictory goals by different functional areas. Often the sales department places maximum emphasis upon price and ability to deliver on demand in its selling efforts, while the production activity is stressing quality and custom performance. Conversely, the sales department stresses

INFORMATION FLOWS AND THE

COORDINATION OF

BUSINESS FUNCTIONS

production according to customer needs, while manufacturing is developing mass production machinery, long production runs and high inventory. Such conflicts are an obvious result of differing *short run* objectives within the various functional areas of a business. In the small business, the top executive often combines many of the functions in his own person. He keeps within his own mind the information storage, the estimates of joint consequences, and the formulas for compromise which make coordinated decisions possible. If his information, estimates or formulas are faulty, then the probability that his business will be a success is correspondingly reduced.

What holds for the small business man is true with even more force for the large business—with one mitigating circumstance. The large business often has a greater lease on life through the possession of greater resources and can live through more mistakes of miscoordination than can the small. In a sense, the consequences of such mistakes take longer to manifest themselves. On the other hand, if enough of them are made—whether in information storage and transmission, in the estimating of the consequences of decisions, or in the formulas for compromise—the large business will be as badly off as the small, and with much more unfortunate effects upon the whole economic community.

No one would deny that marketing decisions are part of the crucial apparatus of running a successful business. Prices, number and kind of products, customer services, advertising and promotion—decisions in each of these areas will affect the long term market position and health of the business. The sales and marketing executives see themselves primarily as facing the customer directly and as determining the share of market and volume of business done in each product through the stimulation of customer demand. It should also be clear that they are helping to determine production schedules, inventories, cash in the bank *and* profits. In fact, subtle and unrecognized as the influence may be, these other areas have influence on the share of market the sales executives are able to obtain, on the prices they set, and on the profit the company earns. In dealing with marketing decisions, one courts disaster if he ignores requirements of coordination with other functions. Modern methods of analysis and the advent of computers have made the competitive potential and the competitive requirement of coordination necessary for long run survival.

COST AND REVENUES — THE CONSEQUENCES OF DECISION MAKING

The development of information in a form which will allow for estimating future consequences of decisions is crucial to modern management. What is the character of these estimates? As far as the executive is concerned, they must tell him what costs he may expect to incur and what revenues he may expect to receive as a result of the particular decision. In essence, he would like to know the immediate and long term effect on profits of a decision to establish a certain price, to hire a certain number of new salesmen, to open a new warehouse, to drop a line of products, and so on. It is not enough, however, to know only the narrow consequences of the decision. The lowering of the price on product A may be estimated to yield a given increase in sales volume for A along with a certain amount of additional profits on that product. If there are other related products involved, it will also be necessary (for "good" decision making) to know what will be the effect of the new price on *their* sales and profits. One must know whether additional inventories of A will have to be carried, the cost consequences thereof, and the effect of the additional demand for A on the production schedules for other products.

As far as decision making is concerned, the business man keeps records of past activities in order to improve the accuracy with which he can estimate the future consequences of his actions. Therefore, the way in which he has collected and maintained information in the past will influence his ability to make "good" decisions in the future. One of the most significant results of the installation of analytical methods and computers may be the effects on data processing for decision making. The information storage, handling, and transmittal systems within an organization are completely revamped, and the computer automatically changes the way decisions *can* be made. In contrast, if the *proper* information required for "good" decision making is already being collected, stored, and transmitted to the right people, the decision making process will be subject to little or no instantaneous improvement.

As a rule, the business man is engaged in a series of relatively continuous decision making processes. Year in and year out, he will ordinarily make decisions on a regular and periodic basis about inventories. He will also decide on the size of the labor force, on specific production schedules, on advertising budgets, on promotions and many other matters. From time to time, he will make what may be called "one-shot" decisions. Such decisions might be to build a new plant, to acquire another business, to add a product line, to change the organization structure, or to liquidate the business. Although there is no hard and fast rule in assigning decisions to either the continuous or the sporadic category, most businesses usually have to make both kinds of decisions. Important differences exist in the processes involved in determining the alternatives, in estimating the long run consequences, and in working out what appears to be the best course of action in the two cases.

In the first instance, where the decisions are continuous and are made on a regular basis, emphasis must be placed on the collection, storage and analysis of past information to give a clue as to the consequences of changing the decision process. When a decision to be made is of a type which has not been made in the past and which is not likely to be made again for some time in the future (for example, the building of the first central warehousing facility for a business operation), the consequences of various specific decisions can be estimated in detail but nothing is known for sure of the consequences of employing alternate methods of making such decisions. So-called "simulation" techniques have been devised to get around the difficulty of few decisions and long time periods for viewing their consequences. In essence, these kinds of decisions change the basic design characteristics of the business. The continuous decisions, on the other hand, adjust the operating characteristics for greater or lesser efficiency on a day to day, week to week, or month to month basis.

Thus, we must subject the *methods* whereby we make decisions to analysis and scrutiny. In fact, one of the greatest advantages associated with approaches making use of the newly available computational tools is their capability for using changes in methodology and examining quickly the consequences of such changes. In the installation of an inventory control system, it is possible to examine the changed level of inventory, the relative change in customer service, and the number of production orders or purchase orders placed within comparatively short periods of time after a new decision process is first used. Note that it is not the decisions themselves which are critical to the future health of the business, but rather the decision making methods. Perhaps the best analogy to use is that of a poker game. The rules of poker are relatively simple, and virtually anyone can play. However, even following the rules, one can make decisions as to betting, taking cards, etc. in many different ways. One player may make all his decisions strictly on the basis of hunch without any knowledge of the relationship of one kind of hand to another in terms of the odds on getting such a hand. Another player may know the odds involved and use them in addition to his psychological judgments in making decisions. Although the first player might from time to time be lucky and win in some games, it appears obvious that a superior decision making process on the part of the second player would usually win out. The same thing holds true in the competitive business world. Each of the actions taken by business will have some smaller or larger effect on the outside world and will affect virtually all the internal activities as well. If we know enough about these effects, we can establish the best decision making processes to give us the best chance of "winning" (although there is no guarantee that we would achieve the "optimum" results).

This type of knowledge has another very important result. When decisions of the one-shot variety are made, as noted previously, they involve changing the design characteristics of the business operation. In any process, it is much more likely that one will be able to estimate the consequences of design changes if one knows the present operating characteristics in the greatest possible detail. It is exactly this kind of knowledge that provides for the best simulation of future activities under the new procedures. Therefore, the internal application of continuous improved decision making methods will have far reaching results with respect to the ability to make better long run, one-shot decisions.

No matter how large, bureaucratic, or impersonal an organization becomes, the decisions described above hinge upon and are reflected in the behavior of individuals. This is plainly seen in the small business where an executive maintains intimate contact with all the functions the business fulfills. Although the location of decision making authority in the large business is not as clear, the need for coordination of the behavior of those working in different functional areas becomes even clearer. Also, the method of coordination establishes the pattern for future decision making and problem solving in the organization.

The best way to assure gradual deterioration of competitive posture and erosion of the ability to meet the requirements of the future is to attempt to maintain the same behavioral attitude towards problems and toward decision making as has existed in the past. It is only with the introduction of new methods and new ways of facing the unknown future that the business can be assured of decision making strength. The introduction of analytical and quantitative methodology, the use of computers, and the development of the necessary interconnections between the functional operations of a business enables us to meet today's problems and today's competition. More important, it prepares the foundations for problem solving in the longer range future. A number of streams of information which flow between functional centers must be carefully coordinated if the value of these devices is to be fully realized.

COORDINATION — MAJOR INFORMATION FLOWS

LONG RANGE FORECASTING

There is a thread of information which runs throughout a business, generally from the top down, which concerns the views of the business's decision makers concerning a long range future. There is no way to avoid having such an attitude and most of the "single shot" decisions are made in terms of some sort of a long range forecast. This forecast may well be simply that the businessman has no way of foretelling what will happen, and, therefore, assumes he knows absolutely nothing about the long range future. This is certainly a valid approach and will lead to very specific consequences in decision making. Another approach often used is to assume that the long range future will be very much like the present or the immediate past. Or, if trends are involved, one may assume that the trends will continue as they have for some specific past period. All of these are perfectly legitimate ways of laying out the future so as to be able to make decisions today. The important thing to recognize in terms of the institution of new devices and new methods of decision making in a business is that each functional area must periodically make decisions on the basis of a long term view. If one department of a business makes decisions on the assumption that the long term future is a blank, and another department assumes that the future will be precisely like the present, the resulting decisions are likely to conflict and perhaps even to nullify each other as far as profitable results are concerned. The information which the business uses in forecasting the long range future must be coordinated and the specific forecasts of the outlook dovetailed sufficiently so that joint effective decision making is possible.

Active long range forecasting is certainly a requirement of modern competitive business. In this connection, one must not be misled by the term "forecasting." Forecasts which are a single estimate of some future

state of economic affairs are almost certain to be incorrect. If such an estimate turns out to be correct, this is probably a coincidence. There are
several reasons why forecasts will inevitably be incorrect. These include
the inherent errors in the data which are used to make them up and, per-

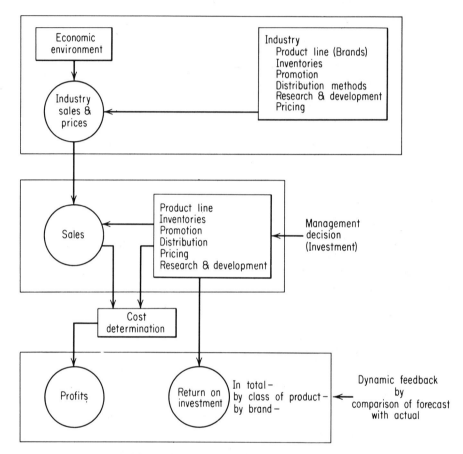

Fig. 1. Coordination of business functions.

haps more importantly, the fact that they are estimates of conditions
which exist in an "organized complex" of activities in which one action
brings an (unknown) counteraction. These socio-economic systems of organized complexity have stability and predictability in many senses, but
not in the same way that physical systems ordinarily do. It is exactly the
characteristics of stability which the proper long range forecasting information flows attempt to describe. These stability characteristics should
be described in terms of probabilities that a given estimate of a future
state of affairs is likely to be wrong. With probability forecasting, a busi-

nessman is enabled to take current action with specific knowledge of risks defined through consideration of alternative forecasts.

SHORT RANGE FORECASTING

Long range forecasting provides the setting within which the various functional activities of a business are carried out. Short range forecasting triggers specific day-to-day and continuous action on the part of the components of such an organization. As with long range forecasting, a specific prediction as to the likely state of affairs tomorrow, next week, or next month will determine the kinds of decisions that are made in many areas of a company's activity. For example, a prediction that next week will be a period of intense sales demand may lead to many specific decisions, such as increasing inventories, increasing labor force, adding work shifts, and expediting purchase orders. Obviously, if the production department is acting on the basis of one short range forecast and the sales department on the basis of another, wires will almost surely get crossed and the ultimate profit of the firm will be reduced.

The same set of events, however, can be forecast in different ways with differing values for various specific uses in the firm. For example, sales may be forecast at one level for inventory purposes and another for promotional purposes. Both these forecasts may be entirely correct for the uses to which they are put. One may state that sales will be no less than such and such a value with a specific probability, while the other may state that sales will be no greater than some amount, again with some specified probability. Both forecasts are of the same set of events, but they differ in actual values and, of course, in use. For given kinds of decision making, it is likely that there will be kinds of forecasts which are particularly efficient. What appears necessary is not a single forecast nor the same forecast being used throughout the enterprise, but rather the coordination of the function of forecasting and the flow of information relating to forecasts throughout the firm.

COST INFORMATION

The objective to be attained by using computers in marketing is improved decision making through the ability to tap, to analyze, and to apply in better ways crucial information about the firm. No information could be more important than that pertaining to costs. In some sense, there is no decision, marketing or otherwise, which does not hinge on a knowledge of costs. Yet, many management information systems do not normally develop those cost data which are necessary for good decisions. For example, in knowing costs in a coordinated way throughout the functional and operating divisions of a business, one virtually has already made a series of important decisions. Profit performance by product line, by product line and geographic markets, by sales territory, by type of outlet, among others, can only be determined by a knowledge of costs. Decisions relative to such things as customer service, new product introduction, and promotional campaigns are shaped by the kind of cost information available to marketing, engineering, and production personnel. Such information is thus one of the key kinds of knowledge which enables a business to operate in a coordinated fashion, provided that the various functional areas have carefully defined and measured their costs. In many areas, profitable decision making requires detailed and clear understanding of the opportunity costs available not only on a departmental or divisional basis, but to the entire business.

ALLOCATING RESOURCES

If a business is to be operated in a coordinated fashion, the manner of allocating specific resources to specific tasks must be developed with considerable care. If the same resource (say, a machine) is assigned to several tasks at once through lack of coordination, then confusion, lost production and probably higher costs will ensue. However, many more subtle problems than this exist in the area of resource allocation. Proper information systems must be developed to ensure balanced use of resources, and to prevent production bottlenecks, stock-outs in inventory, low turnover rates, and poor utilization. Coordination of production facilities with a marketing plan is possible only when careful consideration has been given to the balancing problem. For example, one can consider current and future customer demands by product and by geographic location in the light of alternate production sources. Utilizing knowledge of costs, fixed facility costs are determined for each production plan, and through the use of various decision making models, variable costs can be minimized within each fixed cost program. Very often, under such coordinating procedures, one can find considerable areas for saving in variable costs. Alternately, with possibly small increases in variable costs, large reductions in fixed costs are possible. If such information is made available to all segments of the firm, the organization will acquire new knowledge with respect to the real meaning of the resources at its disposal and gradually begin to be able to plan the use of those resources in more and more profitable ways. Thus, one more important thread of information which is required for the coordinating process is for each major decision making center to know how each resource is to be employed.

ACTIVITY SEQUENCING

In addition to knowing how the various resources are to be used, the order in which things are done must also be known. Furthermore, there are many activities in which order cannot be changed if an operation is to be successful. For example, if we are considering a special promotion which requires new packaging, the promotion cannot be effective if the new packages and the product in those packages are not ready before an advertising campaign is launched. As a rule, specific information is required at specific times by specific individuals in carrying out tasks similar to these. It is also very helpful in coordinating business functions to lay out critical paths for information flows and events which are associated with such regularly occurring events as the implementation of major advertising campaigns, the preparation of catalogues, the introduction of new products, and the phasing out of old products. Much of this can be done with the help of computers. More importantly, much of it must be done in order to prepare the way for the use of computers. The more the decision makers in the various departments of a business know about who is going to do what at what time and how much it is going to cost, the more closely coordinated will the functions of that business be.

ACQUIRING RESOURCES

If we have developed the flow of forecast information about the longer range and shorter range future, if we know a good deal about the costs of alternative actions, if we understand the role of each piece of equipment and of each person, we will have advanced a long way down the road to having a coordinated operation. The culmination of such a coordinated plan is rather clear knowledge of the resources needed in the future and the time they will be needed. Thus, the next and perhaps inevitable step in the information flows which tie a business together is that relating to the acquisition of resources. Resources may be materials, equipment, personnel, money, marketing and advertising devices, media, and ideas. Resources generally cost money and are usually intended to serve a specific purpose. Unwanted resources; resources which are acquired before they are needed, thereby tying up the firm's energy and capital; resources which do not perform as they were originally intended: all serve to drain away potential profits. Therefore, we must coordinate the acquisition of resources within the framework of the needs of the firm and its ability to utilize and pay for the items involved.

PERFORMANCE EVALUATION

All of the information streams mentioned above combine to provide business management with an ability to examine the "possible." More specifically what we have been talking about are methods of examining or looking at the consequences of alternate ways of operating or making decisions within a business enterprise. Given this ability, we can proceed to determine not only what the business ought to do, but whether what it has done comes close to achieving what it could have done. In this way, we can evaluate the performance of the various functional activities of the business, of the various individuals, and of the business as a whole. It is possible to put together the information available from forecasting, cost determination, resource allocation, activity sequencing, and resource acquisition into a comprehensive picture that will tell us which departments have done as well or better than seemed feasible, which divisions and individuals have improved performance or have shown themselves unable to operate as satisfactorily as they ought, and which products have performed in accordance with expectations and possibilities. Given such evaluations, business management can operate so as to change in the future what is "possible" and therefore what is likely to happen.

COORDINATION — DECISION AREAS

The ultimate reason for coordinating business functions is to make decisions in every area which will help the firm toward greater profits, rather than hinder it by conflicting with decisions or activities in some other part of the operation. The flows of information affecting such decisions cut across departmental lines and serve as the net which keeps the various functions from operating independently. Indeed, it is because functional areas cannot operate as profitably independently as they can in a single enterprise that we have the modern business entity. To summarize these thoughts on the need for and ways of coordinating business functions we shall examine some specific decision areas briefly and discuss the pervasive effects of decisions made in them.

In order to provide for adequate coordination of the functions of a business in making decisions, one must first understand the fundamental questions which these decisions raise. Then, it will be possible to collect quantitative data and qualitative information, and to choose the type of analyses required to determine the ramifications throughout the firm of alternative courses of action. It will be essential to review constantly the results of coordinated plans of action, once these are implemented. This requires the measurement of significant relationships between the goals of the firm and its economic and technological characteristics. The remainder of this book will outline types of models and specific approaches to many of the problems we are discussing. The cases included will indicate many of the detailed implications of specific decision procedures. These initial remarks are intended to raise a series of questions in order to emphasize not only the desirability, but the essentiality of coordination. As analysis, improved information systems, and decision procedures are gradually implemented in the firm, one's ability to determine the relationships among the objectives which are considered significant will improve continually.

Let us list the major decision areas and indicate how decisions in each of these areas raise questions with respect to all the others.

MAJOR DECISION AREAS

1. Promotion and advertising
2. Production and production scheduling
3. Distribution and customer service
4. Products, lines and plans
5. Pricing
6. Investment in new plant and equipment
7. Investment in acquisitions
8. Research in new products and new marketing concepts

As we noted earlier, each major decision area involves revenue and cost effects which must be spelled out in detail. Answers to decision making questions cannot properly be determined in one area independently of the others. Forecasting, for example, must provide a sound basis for an understanding of the likely position of markets and products in the future. It, in turn, will include and be based on much market research from beginning to end. We shall outline the basic questions which confront the particular function and indicate subsidiary questions which must be answered to give an aggressive and profitable result. We shall also mention some quantitative data which are relevant to the particular decision making activity, although this procedure is not intended to be comprehensive.

PROMOTION AND ADVERTISING

The basic question with respect to promotion and advertising concerns the total size of the promotional and advertising budget and the means by which it should be distributed among products, among brands, by media, by regional markets, and by types of activity. To answer this question, we need to know the relationship between the firm's total promotion and its sales in the various industries in which it may be a factor. Further, we must know the share of advertising and the share of sales by type of product for the industry and within the enterprise, as well as sales and promotional shares by individual products within the company. These questions are simply the starting point for a coordinated attack on this particular problem.

In addition, it is necessary that we understand the manufacturing and distribution cost effects of any changes in sales induced by a particular promotion. We must take into account the fact that increased sales and production of different products in different areas may influence costs in many different ways. From a strategic point of view, we need to understand the feedback effects of the company's promotional policies relative to the industry's response to these policies. We all know that the successful innovator is often emulated (with greater or lesser success) by others in a particular industry. This is true whether the actions originally taken pertain to advertising, promotion, pricing, product development, or plant expansion. Thus, an intensified advertising program is likely to induce competitors to follow suit. What are the effects of such advertising programs on the firm's sales, once other firms in the industry have reacted with programs of their own? From an economic point of view, we would like to have the promotional resources expended in such a way that the last dollar spent on each activity is equally profitable. Thus, the success of the overall program will depend on the media used, and the skill in which advertising is employed in developing specific marketing strategies and in estimating or forecasting their relative net profit contributions. The need for coordinated information in problems such as these cannot be overestimated. The basic problem as it affects decision makers is often misunderstood and the use of computers to aid decision making is only in its infancy. It is the objective of the cases and models described in this book to lay out tasks for future improvements.

PRODUCTION AND PRODUCTION SCHEDULING

In terms of production and production scheduling, the basic questions here relate to how much of each type of product should be produced, where it should be produced, and when. The adjustment of production to forecasts and actual orders is, of course, related to promotional decisions and pricing policy. Among the significant questions is the effect on our costs and thereby on net profits of changing product mix at a particular plant or location. The kind of data that is necessary to provide genuine answers to these questions is a forecast of sales by type of product for at least each year for several years ahead. Part of this forecast certainly involves estimates of realized prices in the future for each of the product categories. We need to determine the direct or marginal costs for each of the major products and to have some reasonable understanding of the problem of joint costs where we manufacture more than one product in a plant. Programming models such as those described by Baumol in an ensuing chapter are of considerable assistance in reaching answers to these questions.

DISTRIBUTION AND CUSTOMER SCHEDULING

Closely related to the production and production scheduling problem is that of inventory distribution and customer service. We need to determine where and in what quantities we wish to stock each of our products and the types of service we are prepared to offer and stand behind for our customers. If we choose to offer 24 hour service, this will be a major factor in inventory determination and our net profit picture. We also need to determine what we plan to do when actual inventory departs from our expected or intended stocks. Where should the adjustments in production and stocks be made and how may these adjustments be facilitated by decisions in the area of promotion and pricing policies?

The distribution system of the company will have a geographical structure and a hierarchical structure. Decisions to change either of these will influence investments, in the case of warehouses or local distribution points, or promotional activities, in the case of determinations as to the channels to be employed and the services offered. A number of related questions will be constantly under investigation. Given the regional demand patterns for various products, where should warehouses, facilities, and distributorships be located? What is the best size of these operations? How large a territory should they serve? Should the company directly control distributorships, at least those serving larger markets? If not, what margin allowed distributors produces the greatest net profit for the company? A large amount of coordinated data is essential to a proper set of answers to these questions. We need to know carrying costs at each distribution level, throughput costs, transportation costs in and out of distribution points, distributors' and retailers' margins by products and by market areas, and the ultimate cost of customer service. None of these costs should be considered fixed and immutable. This is an important aspect to the dynamic operation of a modern business. It is, in fact, because we can change costs or ultimate sales that we make changes in our business's operating characteristics. Therefore, when the problems mentioned above come under consideration, attention should be given to possibilities of making changes which will affect costs and thereby net profitability.

PRODUCTS AND PRODUCT LINES

Most firms neglect the problem of deciding on adequate and proper variety. The question here is: what is the optimal number of different brands, packages, or other types of variety we can offer to the consumer? This is related to a number of other questions which must be specifically answered, such as how products should be categorized and how these categories should be broken down. This problem of categorization is of extreme importance to advertising and promotional policies and raises an immediate subsidiary question. What is the relative importance of the physiological bases (such as taste, shape, and feel) and the psychological bases (which may be largely shaped by advertising and promotion) to product preference? There are many situations in which advertising's pull is far more important than any degree of physical differentiation that might exist. Promotional activity is required if only to inform the public of some slight differentiation of the product on which the psychological preference may be based. The relative merits of increased advertising on existing products versus the introduction of products that are new in either a physiological or psychological sense needs to be carefully assessed. Intertwined with this problem and the area of pricing, the question of the number of brands required to reach markets composed of consumers of different income levels is almost certain to arise in the consumer products industry. In the capital goods area, the question of relative price-quality considerations is of equal importance.

PRICING

We have already mentioned the effect of price levels on the results of decisions in other areas. Briefly, the significant pricing question involves the appropriate level and structure of prices for the various categories of products and, possibly, of brands within these products. It is necessary to know how price concessions can be used to introduce or to reinforce products in the market. We have already mentioned the possible use of price adjustments to bring inventories into balance with demand—some imbalance must occur from time to time despite the very best forecasting estimates. Although price concessions are not the only means of rationalizing inventories, they certainly can be considered as an alternative. Immediately on serious consideration of price decisions, questions arise as to how changes in the level of prices will affect demand for the specific product changed and for all other products. It is also necessary to relate the promotional effects to the prices consumers are willing to pay. Our data requirements for doing an adequate job in the area of pricing include price and consumption data for all the company's products with due allowance being made for whatever geographic price structures exist. As far as possible, comparable data for competitors' products should also be obtained.

INVESTMENT DECISIONS

The analysis required to answer questions as to investment in current products, new products, or in the acquisition of new businesses, clearly necessitates adequate answers to all the other questions previously raised. Among other things, we need to answer the questions of when, where, and how capacity for old or new products should be expanded or contracted. Such questions are an outgrowth of questions in production, pricing, sales and other decision areas. In the ordinary day to day situation, plant capacities are more or less fixed. To answer questions as to what future capacity should be, we develop programs for altering this capacity in a simulated way and determine the expected profits from various programs of plant expansion or contraction. This hypothetical plant may involve new plant or equipment or the acquisition of existing firms, along with new products to be added to the line. Products outside of the firm's experience, of course, require detailed and separate study and not a mere extension of questions raised in the production and inventory areas. In research and development decision making, we are concerned with the question of the addition of new products, the modification of existing products, and the elimination of undesirable products. Decisions in these areas require a clear understanding of market position, costs, and net profitability.

The profitable ordering of practical economic decisions in the business world requires a careful coordination of all elements of the business operation. The increasing interdependence and complexity of marketing decisions leaves the era of the "independent" brilliant salesman behind. The use of increased knowledge of the effect of business decisions in one area on activities in another, and the development of computer programs which will boil large masses of data down to understandable and realistic terms present an opportunity in marketing as well as a challenge to management. It will not be easy to meet this challenge, since new habits will have to be learned and many experiments undertaken to determine ways of operating in a changed environment. But competition will force on all business an increasing rational usage of the tools which are now at hand.

Figure 1 (see page 86) summarizes the requirements for continuing coordination in managerial decision making. From an overall forecast by industry, we move to share of markets where management decides how and when to make its investment in resources and production and promotion, and thence to the ultimate net result which is a return on the stockholder's investment. Ours is not necessarily an easy world for those who manage and make decisions. The marketing executive must recognize that all the things which happen in a business affect the marketing function and that his decisions, in turn, affect the remainder of the company. The manager must also recognize that there are no fixed and final answers. Continual change in the economic environment and in the dynamic organization within a business must lead to adaptive decision making on virtually a day to day basis. The remainder of this book will attempt to illustrate ways of approaching the specific questions we have raised in this chapter.

PART II

THE COMPUTER AND PROBLEM SOLVING

chapter one | *Robert S. Weinberg*

It is not easy to forecast what progress will be made in the application of scientific techniques to market planning during the next decade. It appears obvious, however, that within this period many new quantitative methods will be used to develop more meaningful marketing plans. Although the new techniques and the extent to which they will be employed cannot yet be predicted, one point is already clear: by the end of the next decade, the computer will become one of the marketing man's most powerful tools. In fact, I am surprised, considering the progress that has been made in computer development during the last decade, that the computer is not presently a basic tool of the marketing manager. This lag in the acceptance of computer applications in the area of marketing does not reflect the inability of the computer industry to produce "hardware" useful to marketing management, but rather marketing management's inability to develop appropriate marketing applications. This condition should change quite dramatically during the next five to ten years.

MANAGEMENT SCIENCE AND

MARKETING STRATEGY

This prediction should not frighten marketing executives. Since business is becoming more competitive, the risks incurred in making the wrong marketing decision are becoming prohibitively expensive, almost fatal. The lead times necessary to plan and to implement major marketing programs are becoming longer, and the factors that must be considered and analyzed in deriving a sound marketing strategy are becoming more numerous and more complex. Marketing management can no longer afford a hit and miss strategy. Fortunately, this change in business environment has been accompanied by two other changes:

1. Computers have become increasingly available both to the large and small business. Larger companies have their own computers; smaller companies can buy blocks of computer time from data centers or can bring their problems to various service bureaus.
2. The data necessary for sound marketing conclusions are becoming

increasingly available from government, trade associations, and internal sources within a company.

Thus, we have computers; we have data; the missing link is a doctrine that will allow us to formulate basic marketing problems in a "machineable form." The following comments attempt to fill this missing link and to develop a doctrine of "Management Science and Marketing Strategy." I will discuss some of the problems encountered in developing marketing strategy and some of the new quantitative techniques available for handling these problems. I shall be concerned with the strategic problems normally facing top management.

NATURE OF MANAGEMENT SCIENCE

The field of management science is, for all practical purposes, a postwar development. The quantitative techniques developed within the military operations research groups during World War II were gradually adapted as useful tools for industrial planning. New tools were developed and new methods evolved as extensions of the earlier techniques. The Institute of Management Sciences was founded in 1954 and its journal, *Management Science,* was first published in October 1954.

Although the use of quantitative techniques to study military or business operations is a recent development, it is interesting to note that Thomas Edison directed an antisubmarine warfare project for the Navy during World War I. One might even consider St. Augustine, who lived from 354 A.D. to 430 A.D., as the first policy maker to be approached by a management scientist offering the solution to his problems. While I cannot find any mention of management science in St. Augustine's writing, the following passage appears: "The good Christian should beware the mathematicians and all those who make empty prophecies. The danger already exists that the mathematicians have made a covenant with the devil to darken the spirit and to confine man in the bonds of hell."

It would be useful to start our discussion with some appropriate definition of the term "management science." Recently, I reviewed the literature and jotted down the first dozen definitions I could find. These definitions are as follows:

1. The application of established research methods to "get behind" the superficial complexities of an industrial problem to the fundamentally simple, the basic idea, that makes it "tick."
2. The application of established research methods to provide the executive with objective quantitative guidance for management decisions.
3. The application of scientific methods to policy problems.

4. The application of research-minded people to operating problems of a large organization.
5. A scientific method of providing executive departments with a quantitative basis for decisions regarding the operations under their control.
6. Scientific (or quantitative) common sense.
7. The science of decision.
8. The application of the basic scientific methods of measurement, classification, comparison, and correlation to the selection of means for attaining, with the least expenditure in effort and time, the maximum operational effect which could be extracted from the available or potentially available resources in personnel and material.
9. What management scientists *do.*
10. What management scientists *think they do.*
11. What management scientists *would like to do.*
12. Management science is at present undefined but, in time, will become defined by the subject matter appearing in *Management Science, Management Technology, Operations Research,* and other publications.

From this it becomes apparent that we may have as many definitions of management science as there are practitioners. Although I do not want to add to this confusion, for the purposes of discussion, I would like to define management science as follows:

Management science offers a scientific method of providing executives with an analytical and objective quantitative basis for decisions. Management science research is applied research, and the output of such a research project must be of direct aid or use to the business executive. The three primary problems facing the management scientist are as follows:

1. To study as objectively and as precisely as possible the particular operations of the business.
2. Through the use of accepted analytical techniques (generally employed for the first time), (a) to uncover weaknesses in the business operation which could not be otherwise detected, and (b) to discover ways in which the company's operations may be made more effective.
3. To predict the results of contemplated changes in the company's operations or the results which may be expected if the company's operations are not changed.

Management science is a method or approach to management problem solving. It is not a new field or discipline. The tools of management science are particularly useful in analyzing marketing problems in changing business environments. Quite often we find that our old approaches—rules of thumb and approximate estimating procedures—work quite well until the business environment changes. In the face of these changes, we discover all too late that our former estimating and analytical procedures are weak.

It is impossible to discuss management science without considering the functions of management. Traditional management texts list three steps in the process of management. These steps are (1) the establishment of objectives, (2) the direction of efforts to attain these objectives, and (3) the measurement of the results achieved. For purposes of analysis, we can extend these steps into five management actions: (1) developing corporate objectives, (2) selecting among the strategic alternatives available for attaining these objectives, (3) estimating the resources required to support the alternatives that have been selected, (4) allocating corporate resources to specific projects, (5) developing timing patterns, that is, the precise time in which specific actions should be taken.

To carry out these five actions, we need three kinds of quantitative measurements: (1) measurements that will allow us to measure our performance, that is, to compare our actual against planned performance; (2) measurements that will let us diagnose our problems, measurements that will indicate present difficulties, factors requiring more careful attention, and future potential trouble spots; (3) measurements that will allow us to predict the future, i.e., various anticipatory indices.

THE COMPLEXITY OF BUSINESS DECISIONS

Let us consider the decision problem somewhat abstractly. When we speak of business decisions, we are concerned with the evaluation of alternatives and the selection from these alternatives, of the course of action that promises us the greatest advantage. Assume that management is considering the possibility of using four advertising media, and the question is which media should be used. As shown in Figure 1, there are 16 possibilities to evaluate in this example. Management can decide to use all four media, *A, B, C,* and *D.* Management can decide to use any 3 of the media. Management can decide to use any 2 or just 1 of the media, or none of the media at all. We would like to know our future market position under each of these conditions. This is comparatively an easy task. We have 4 media; there are 16 possible go, no-go decisions.

Now, let's complicate matters. Examine Figure 2. If we had 10 media to consider, we would have slightly over 1,000 combinations; with 20 media we would have slightly over a million, and with 30 media, over a billion combinations. With 50 media there are one quadrillion, one hundred twenty-five trillion, eight hundred ninety-nine billion, nine hundred six million, eight hundred forty-two thousand, and six hundred twenty-four possibilities. And, mind you, this is just to examine every combination of using or not using each of 50 media.

THE NUMBER OF POSSIBLE "GO - NO GO" ALTERNATIVES, THE FOUR MEDIA CASE

POSSIBLE ALTERNATIVES	MEDIA "A"	MEDIA "B"	MEDIA "C"	MEDIA "D"
1 EMPLOY ALL OF THE MEDIA	+	+	+	+
2 EMPLOY ANY 3 OF THE MEDIA	+	+	+	0
3	0	+	+	+
4	+	+	0	+
5	+	0	+	+
6 EMPLOY ANY 2 OF THE MEDIA	+	+	0	0
7	0	+	+	0
8	0	0	+	+
9	+	0	+	0
10	0	+	0	+
11	+	0	0	+
12 EMPLOY ANY 1 OF THE MEDIA	+	0	0	0
13	0	+	0	0
14	0	0	+	0
15	0	0	0	+
16 EMPLOY NONE OF THE MEDIA	0	0	0	0

+ = EMPLOY MEDIA
0 = DO NOT EMPLOY MEDIA

Fig. 1.

Only rarely, however, is management going to ask the question, should we or shouldn't we. They will want to know how much, so let's add this factor. Figure 3 shows the combinatorial jungle that arises when we consider additional choice alternatives. When we have four media and two choice alternatives, we have the 16 possibilities noted on Figure 1. Now, suppose we were asked, should we spend more on these media, should we spend less on these media, or should we spend the same amount of money on these media? With three choice alternatives, the 16 combinations jump to 81. If we had 20 such alternatives for four media, we would have 160,000 possibilities; with 100 choice allocations with the four media, a billion possibilities. Now if we were to have 10 media, the go, no-go decisions, as we indicated above, would be 1,024—three alternatives, 59,049—and if we consider one hundred possible expenditure levels, we will have to consider one hundred quintillion possible combinations.

NUMBER OF POSSIBLE "GO NO-GO" DECISION ALTERNATIVES WITH "N" MEDIA

Number of Possible Decision Alternatives	Number of Possible "Go No-Go" Decisions	Number of Possible Decision Alternatives	Number of Possible "Go No-Go" Decisions	Number of Possible Decision Alternatives	Number of Possible "Go No-Go" Decisions
1	2	21	2,097,152	36	68,719,476,736
2	4	22	4,194,304	37	137,438,953,472
3	8	23	8,388,608	38	274,877,906,944
4	16	24	16,777,216	39	549,755,813,888
5	32	25	33,554,432	40	1,099,511,627,776
6	64	26	67,108,864	41	2,199,023,255,552
7	128	27	134,217,728	42	4,398,046,511,104
8	256	28	268,435,456	43	8,796,093,022,208
9	512	29	536,870,912	44	17,592,186,044,416
10	1,024	30	1,073,741,824	45	35,184,372,088,832
11	2,048	31	2,147,483,648	46	70,368,744,177,664
12	4,096	32	4,294,967,296	47	140,737,488,355,328
13	8,192	33	8,589,934,592	48	281,474,976,710,656
14	16,384	34	17,179,869,184	49	562,949,953,421,312
15	32,768	35	34,359,738,368	50	1,125,899,906,842,624
16	65,536				
17	131,072				
18	262,144				
19	524,288				
20	1,048,576			100 approx.	1.26765×10^{30}

Fig. 2.

THE COMBINATORIAL JUNGLE

A	ONE MEDIA	TWO MEDIA	THREE MEDIA	FOUR MEDIA
2	2	4	8	16
3	3	9	27	81
4	4	16	64	256
5	5	25	125	625
10	10	100	1 000	10 000
15	15	225	3 375	50 625
20	20	400	8 000	160 000
25	25	625	15 625	390 625
50	50	2 500	125 000	6 250 000
75	75	5 625	421 875	31 640 625
100	100	10 000	1 000 000	100 000 000

A	FIVE MEDIA	SIX MEDIA	EIGHT MEDIA	TEN MEDIA
2	32	64	256	1 024
3	243	729	6 561	59 049
4	1 024	4 096	65 536	1 048 576
5	3 125	15 625	390 625	9 765 625
10	100 000	1 000 000	100 000 000	10 000 000 000
15	759 375	11 390 625	2 562 890 625	576 650 390 625
20	3 200 000	64 000 000	25 600 000 000	10 240 000 000 000
25	9 765 625	244 140 625	152 587 890 625	95 367 431 640 625
50	312 500 000	15 625 000 000	39 062 500 000 000	97 656 250 000 000 000
75	2 373 046 875	177 978 515 625	1 001 129 150 390 625	5 631 351 470 947 265 625
100	10 000 000 000	1 000 000 000 000	10 000 000 000 000 000	100 000 000 000 000 000 000

Fig. 3.

105

A hundred quintillion is an amazing number. If we had 10 different media alternatives, and we wanted to decide how much to spend on each, and we were willing to allow one of a hundred possible expenditure levels, and wanted to literally search each combination, we would have to look at a hundred quintillion possibilities. If we were to punch one IBM card for each possibility, we could construct 113,140 piles from the earth to the sun. If we wanted to be a bit more creative and try something a little less boring, we could construct eleven hundred and thirty-three piles from the earth to each planet of the solar system; and if the piles should fall over and cover the earth evenly, we would have the surface area of the earth covered with two and a quarter inches of IBM cards.

I have used this example to demonstrate that, as a practical matter, it is impossible to examine every combination in evaluating decision alternatives. There are just too many combinations. Consequently, one might doubt that there is a solution to the selection or allocation problem. Maybe, we should just continue to apply our judgment or react on impulse, particularly if we have been successful in doing this in the past. I think there is a solution, and the solution lies in the development of a series of mathematical models describing the environmental factors affecting the corporation. Our purpose in building these mathematical models is to understand the way in which the business operates and the precise interrelationship between the factors that will influence our success or failure in attaining our ultimate objectives.

THE BUSINESS AND ITS ENVIRONMENTS

Consider some specific examples graphically illustrating a business within its four operating environments. I have tried to keep this somewhat general and at the same time be sufficiently specific so that I would not be guilty of a familiar management science shortcoming—developing a set of tools and then looking for a problem on which to use them. If we think about it, every business without regard to its size, and in many respects without regard to its industry, operates simultaneously in four different environments: (1) an economic and industry environment, (2) a competitive environment, (3) an internal or operating environment, and (4) an institutional environment. One of the major problems facing management is to select the course of action that maximizes the business's position in all environments simultaneously. Consider this problem for the moment.

A company's net profits are dependent upon not less than five sets of factors:

1. The level of general economic activity insofar as it affects total industry sales.

2. The level of total industry sales, a share of which will represent company sales.

3. The actions of the company's competitors, insofar as they will determine what share of the total industry market the company will capture.

4. The actions of the company itself, insofar as they meet the actions of its competitors and insofar as they affect the company's profit-sales relation.

5. The structure of tax rates, insofar as they determine that fraction of gross profits which will be available after taxes (i.e., the company's net profits after taxes).

Consider first the effect of the economy on the industry. For purposes of illustration, Figure 4 shows the interrelation between industry sales

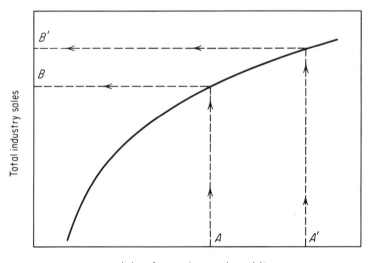

Index of general economic activity

Fig. 4.

and general economic activity. The horizontal axis shows some measure of economic conditions. This could be the level of disposable personal income, the FRB Index of Industrial Production, personal consumption expenditures, producers' durable equipment expenditures, or any other appropriate general economic activity index applicable to your business. The vertical axis shows total industry sales. When economic activity is at level A, total industry sales will be at level B. If economic activity were to be increased from A to A', total industry sales would increase from B to B'. Although I have sketched this diagram quite simply for purposes of illustration, the analysis of the company's economic and industry environment involves problems in economic forecasting and analysis; in market research and analysis; and in the other problem areas shown in Table One.

TABLE ONE

Major Problem Areas Related to a Company's Economic Environment

A.   Economic Forecasting and Analysis

1. Long-Term Forecasting
2. Short-Term Forecasting
3. Forecasting the Level of General Economic Activity
4. Forecasting Specific Industry Trends
5. Forecasting Technological Change and Displacement

B.   Market Research and Analysis

1. Consumer Survey Techniques
2. Industrial Survey Techniques
3. Motivation Research (Psychological Analyses)
4. Consumer Budget Studies (Statistical Analyses)
5. Industrial Purchasing Policies
6. Community Response Patterns

C.   New Product Development

1. Capital Requirements for New Product Developments
2. The Development of Joint and Complementary Products
3. Estimating the Demand for, and Distribution Channels for New Products
4. Development of New Product "Prototypes" of "Functional Least Common Denominators"
5. Acquiring New Products or Product Lines Through Mergers

D.   New Market and Customer Development

1. The "Economics" of Geographic Expansion
2. Measuring New Market Potential
3. The Analysis of "Latent" Demand
4. Acquiring New Markets through Mergers
5. Input-Output Analyses for Industrial Market Analysis

Since there is little a company can do to influence the level of general economic activity, its total industry sales are determined by factors over which the company has either no or, at best, only partial control. The company can, however, in the long run, change the industry in which it is operating in one of two ways: (1) by developing new products that fall into other industries, or (2) by finding new customers.[1] When we consider these alternatives, we must engage in economic and forecasting analysis

---

[1] For a more complete discussion of this problem, see pp. 154-163 of my paper, "Multiple Factor Break-Even Analysis: The Application of Operations Research Techniques to a Basic Problem of Management Planning and Control," *Operations Research,* April 1956, Vol. 4, No. 2, pp. 152-185.

and find the problems of long-term forecasting very different from those of short-term forecasting. Predicting the level of general economic activity as compared to the level of specific industry trends requires nothing less than forecasting technological change and the rate at which new generations of technology will replace older generations. In new product development, we must estimate the capital and resources required to develop new products, as well as decide whether proposed products fit into the existing line and are compatible with the existing mode of distribution. We must also decide how to acquire our new products—through development or through merger and acquisition. Similarly, when we consider new market and customer development, we have problems of economic and geographic expansion—where should we market, in the states, regionally, internationally? We have problems of measuring new market potential and of analyzing the latent demand for products that don't yet exist but will be introduced in the future.

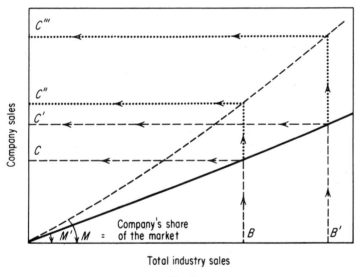

Fig. 5.

Figure 5 illustrates the second environment in which the company operates, the competitive environment. Here we are concerned with the interrelation between total industry sales and the company's own sales. Given the company's competitive position or share of market (in the case M) and given total industry sales B and B', we see the company sales will be C and C'. If the company is able to increase the share of market from M to M', their sales would increase from C to C'' and from C' to C'''.

As shown in Table Two, in analyzing the company's competitive environment, we are concerned with problems of marketing and promotional strategy, pricing policies, the collection and evaluation of economic intelligence regarding the operations of competitors, and the planning of long-term competitive strategy. Note that the problem of deciding upon

TABLE TWO

Major Problem Areas Related to a Company's Competitive Environment

A.   Advertising and Sales Promotion Strategy

   1.   The Determination of "Optimal" Advertising and Sales Promotion Expenditure Levels
   2.   The Allocation of Advertising and Sales Promotion Expenditure Effort
     a) to media
     b) to market
   3.   Determining Advertising and Sales Promotion Effectiveness
   4.   "Optimal" Distribution of Sales (and Salesman's Effort

B.   Pricing Policies

   1.   The Impact of Price upon Demand
   2.   The Impact of Competitor's Price Competition on Company Sales
   3.   The Interrelation between Cost and Price (Profit)

C.   The Collection and Evaluation of "Economic Intelligence" Regarding Competitor's Operations

   1.   The Evaluation of Data and Information Sources
     a) government
     b) trade association
     c) customers and salesmen
     d) published reports
   2.   Mathematical Models for "Intelligence Assessment"
   3.   The Determination of the "Behavior Patterns" of the Firm's Competitors

D.   Planning Long-Term Competitive Strategy

   1.   The Derivation of Long-Term Market Penetration Models
   2.   The Development of Long-Term Competitive Objectives
   3.   The Comparison of Various Alternatives Long-Range Competitive Postures

long-term competitive strategy differs from that of choosing a short-term competitive strategy. In the long run, the company has more freedom and more possibilities from which to choose.

The environment that we are probably all most familiar with and most used to working with is the internal or operating environment. We can represent this environment, as shown in Figure 6, by the interrelation between company sales and company profits before taxes. Given a level of sales C, the company profits will be D. If the company, through a cost reduction program, were to eliminate or reduce its fixed costs, the profits would increase from D to D' and the break-even point would decline from X to X'. In analyzing the company's internal or operating environment, we are concerned with all of the problem areas shown in Table Three.

In reviewing the application of management science techniques to the analysis of business problems, we find that the internal operating environment is the most studied environment and is probably the area in which the most immediate pay-off will occur. This is the setting in which we

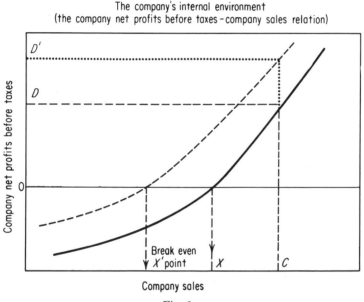

The company's internal environment
(the company net profits before taxes – company sales relation)

Fig. 6.

consider the production process, the distribution process, the financial process, and the planning and control process—the very heart of the business itself. In the production process we are concerned with such problems as production control scheduling, inventory control, "make or buy" policies, and the analysis of the factors with a determining influence on industrial productivity. In the case of the distribution process, interest is focussed on optimum warehousing, optimum transportation policy, the best channels of distribution, the control of administrative general selling expenditures, the best sales and marketing organization, and the best plant location. In the case of the financial process, the determination of working capital requirements, the problems of capital budgeting, the use of mathematical models in budgeting, the estimating or derivation of capital output ratios and, of course, the financial evaluation of merger and related policy opportunities are reviewed. But, again, we can represent the *net results* of our ability to function in each of these areas by Figure 6, admittedly a gross simplification.

The fourth environment is the one that is most difficult to build into a model. This is the company's institutional environment. Here we are

TABLE THREE

Major Problem Areas Related to a Company's Internal or Operating Environment

A. The Production Process

    1. Production Control
    2. Production Scheduling
    3. Inventory Control
    4. "Make" or "Buy" (Integration) Policy
    5. The Analysis of the Factors which Influence and Determine Industrial Productivity

B. The Distribution Process

    1. "Optimal" Warehousing Policy
    2. "Optimal" Transportation Policy ("Optimal" Routing) and Medium
    3. "Optimal" Channels of Distribution
    4. The Control of Administrative, General, and Selling Expenditures
    5. "Optimal" Sales Organizations
    6. "Optimal" Plant Location

C. The Financial Process

    1. The Determination of Working Capital Requirements
    2. Capital Budgeting
    3. Activity Accounting
    4. Mathematical Models for Budgeting
    5. Capital-Output Ratios (Analysis)
    6. The Financial Aspects of Merger Policies

D. The Planning and Control Process

    1. "Strategic" Operations Research Models
    2. The Management Decision Process
    3. Mathematical Models of the Firm
    4. An Analysis of Communication Flows Within the Firm

concerned with constraints, or limitations on the company's choice of action that are imposed outside the company or that represent limitations of company policy. These include government regulations, industry practices, business policies, and the limitations or desires of the financial community. Such factors represent constraints on the business's choice of action in its other operating environments. Figure 7 shows one major institutional factor (the corporate income tax) and the interrelation between the company's profits before taxes and company net profits after taxes. The company's pre-tax profits are D, the post-tax profits will be E. If pre-tax increases from D to D', post-tax will increase from E to E'.

THE NET PROFITS COMPLEX

The four basic environmental relations outlined above may be combined to derive the company's general economic activity—net profits complex (the E-P^* Complex). As discussed above, the company's ultimate profits

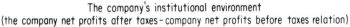

The company's institutional environment
(the company net profits after taxes-company net profits before taxes relation)

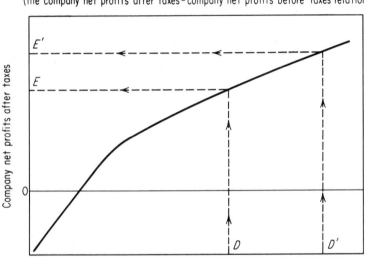

Company net profits before taxes

Fig. 7.

will be determined by the *interactions* between various economic, industry, competitive, internal, and institutional factors. The E-P^* Complex provides a logical quantitative basis for studying these interactions and their impact on the company's ultimate profits.

Figure 8 shows a typical E-P^* Complex derived by combining the four individual environmental relations shown in Figures 1 through 4. Figure 8 is divided into four quadrants:

II	III
I	IV

Table Four shows how these quadrants are filled to derive the company's E-P^* Complex. Each of the individual environmental relations is plotted in its logical order following the sequence discussed above. The four relations are arranged in such a sequence that the "output" of one relation becomes the "input" of the next relation (i.e., the dependent or endogenous variable of one relation becomes the independent or exogenous variable of the next relation). The shaded areas on Table Four show the common axes which serve as the linkages between the individual relations.

The company's general economic activity - net profits complex

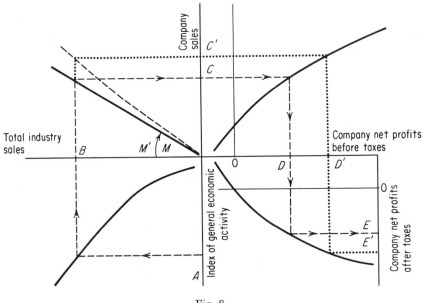

Fig. 8.

Consider Figure 8. The arrows on the heavy broken reference lines show that the following sequence of interrelations holds:

1. When general economic activity is at a level A, total industry sales will be B.
2. When total industry sales are at a level B, and the company's share of the market is M (i.e., the heavy solid C-I Relation) company sales will be C.
3. When company sales are at a level C, company net profits before taxes will be D.
4. When company net profits before taxes are at a level D, company net profits after taxes will be E.

From the above analysis, it is clear that the company's P^*-E Complex may be employed to determine the impact of any change or combination of changes in general economic activity, total industry sales, the company's share of the market, the company's cost structure, or the structure of taxes on the company's net profits after taxes. Therefore, the P^*-C Complex provides a framework within which the company's long-term advertising expenditure strategy may be developed.

The Derivation of the Company's General Economic Activity - Net Profits Complex

E - P* Complex Quadrant	Environmental Relation Represented	Information Plotted Along the Axes	
		Vertical Axis	Horizontal Axis
I (lower-left hand) quadrant	Economic Environment, the total industry - sales - general economic activity (I-E) Relation (Figure One)	Index of general economic activity (E)	Total industry sales (I)
II (upper-left hand) quadrant	Competitive Environment, the company sales - total industry sales (C-I) Relation (Figure Two)	Company sales (C)	Total industry sales (I)
III (upper-right hand) quadrant	Internal Environment, the company net profits before taxes - company sales (P-C) Relation (Figure Three)	Company sales (C)	Company net profits before taxes (P)
IV (lower-right hand) quadrant	Institutional Environment, the company net profits after taxes net profits before taxes (P*-P) Relation (Figure Four)	Company net profits after taxes (P*)	Company net profits before taxes (P)

Table 4.

Consider the second example shown in Figure 5. Assume the same level of general economic activity and of total industry sales, A and B respectively. Also assume the same P-C and P^*-P Relations. Further assume that the company was able to increase its share of the market M to M' and is now operating under the improved C-I Relation (the thin broken line). It will be noted (following the dotted reference lines) that company sales increase from C to C'; company net profits after taxes increase from E to E'.

The above example shows the contribution to ultimate profits of an increase in the company's share of the market, assuming that such an increase was accomplished without changing the company's cost structure or P-C Relation. In actual practice, however, such a situation is unlikely. The actions required to increase the company's share of the market will require the expenditure of expansionary funds (i.e., advertising, sales promotion, new customer development, new market development and related expenditures). These expenditures will weaken the company's P-C Relation causing it to move upward and to the left. Unless this shift in the P-C Relation is offset by a corresponding shift in the opposite direction introduced by a reduction in some other cost factor, *an improvement in the C-I Relation will generally be accomplished at the expense of a weakened P-C Relation. The key question in formulating an optimal competitive strategy is that of determining the most profitable trade-off between an improved C-I Relation vs. a weakened P-C Relation.*

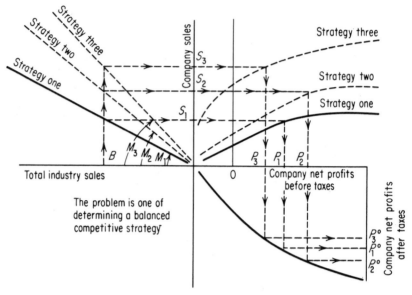

Fig. 9.

Figure 9 illustrates the major problem encountered in developing a balanced (optimal) competitive strategy. It shows the second, third, and fourth quadrants of the company's P^*-E Complex. In the present example, it is assumed that for the expected future level of general economic activity the corresponding expected future level of total industry sales will be B.

The problem facing the company's planners is that of determining the marketing strategy which yields an optimal share of the market, i.e., the share of the market which maximizes the company's ultimate profits.

In the present example, the company has three alternative plans reflecting marketing strategies, one, two, and three. The first plan, strategy one, assumes the company desires to maintain its current share of the market (M'). The second plan, strategy two, is designed to increase the company's share of the market from M' to M''. This improvement in the company's C-I Relation required an increase in the company's expansionary expenditures and a corresponding weakening of the company's P-C Relation. The third plan, strategy three, is designed to increase the company's share of the market from M' to M'''. In order to accomplish such a major improvement in its C-I Relation, the company must increase its expansionary expenditures substantially. This sharp increase in such expenditures seriously weakens the company's *P-C* Relation.

The net result of the improved *C-I* Relation and weakened *P-C* Relation on the company's ultimate profits is clearly shown on Figure 9.

If the company adopts strategy one, its share of the market will be *M'*, its sales *S'*, its net profits before taxes *P'*, and its net profits after taxes *P'**. If the company adopts strategy two, its share of the market will increase to *M''*, its sales to *S''*, and its net profits before and after taxes to *P''* and *P''** respectively. If the company adopts strategy three, its share of the market will increase to *M'''* and its sales to *S'''*, but its net profits will *decline* to *P'''* and *P'''**.

From the above, it is clear that while the company could attain a share of the market as high as *M'''*, it would not be profitable to do so. It would cost the company more to attain this larger market share than it could expect to gain in the form of profits originating from its increased sales. If the company elects to follow strategy one and maintain its current share of the market (*M'*), it is foregoing the increased profits it could expect under strategy two. Strategy two maximizes the company's profits.

MODELS AND COMPUTER-ORIENTED CONTROL SYSTEMS

Figures 10 and 11 illustrate how the model building technique can be employed to measure the value of effective control of advertising and

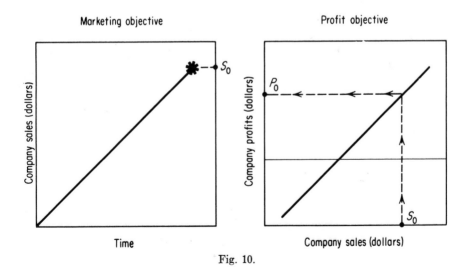

Fig. 10.

sales promotion expenditures. As part of the planning process, company planners will develop two objectives: (1) a marketing objective, and (2) a profit objective. The marketing objective will be stated in terms of cumulated sales during some time period (i.e., the planning period). The left-hand panel of Figure 10 illustrates a typical marketing objective; the company plans to attain a cumulated sales objective of S_0 dollars by the end of the planning period. The solid line shows the desired (planned) cumulated sales curve. The right-hand panel of Figure 10 illustrates the company's profit objective in terms of a profits-sales relation. Note that when company sales are S_0, company profits will be P_0.

The value of effective control

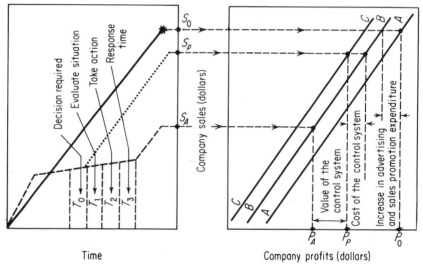

Fig. 11.

The two individual interrelated planning objectives shown in Figure 10 may be combined as shown in Figure 11. Following the broken lines, we note that if the company meets its marketing and profit objectives its sales will be S_0 and its profits will be P_0. The solid curve shown in the left-hand panel represents *planned* cumulated sales expressed as a function of lapsed time. In reality, the *actual* cumulated sales will rarely follow the planned sales curve exactly, but, as shown by the heavy broken curve, will tend to fluctuate about it.

Assume that the company's initial planning assumptions did not anticipate a new marketing campaign by a major competitor, and that as a result of this campaign the company's sales fell considerably below its planned marketing objectives. At first, the company was unaware of the impact of its competitor's campaign and it was not until time period T_0 passed that the company's management realized that they must change their market plan and revise their market and profit objectives. The company had to spend a time period T_1 evaluating the situation and developing a new counter-strategy. Time T_2 was required to implement the new strategy. Time T_3 was required before the market responded to the company's new counter-campaign.

The company's new campaign required substantial increases in advertising and sales promotion expenditures (moving the company's profits-sales relation from position A to position B), but as a result of these expenditures, the company's rate of sales increased reaching a level S_A (sales, actual) by the end of the planning period. The company's actual profits would then be P_A. The difference between P_0 (the profit objective) and P_A (actual profit) would most likely mean a new sales manager.

Now assume that the company could develop a computer-oriented market data information system (i.e., a short-term planning and control model) which would process and evaluate marketing data on a real time basis. If all other factors remain unchanged, except that the time necessary to realize that a decision is required (T_0) and the time spent in evaluating the situation (T_1) are reduced substantially, the company's sales recovery will occur sooner, and by the end of the planning period its sales would be S_P (sales, *possible*). Maintaining this market data information system will require an additional marketing research and analysis expenditure which will further shift the company's profits-sales relation from B to C. Note, however, that this increase in expenditures will be more than offset by the increased sales resulting from the company's new ability to assess more rapidly the market situation and revise its marketing strategy accordingly. The dollar value of the new control system may be measured in terms of the difference between the company's actual profits P_A and its possible profits P_P. This example shows how we can use an analytical model to consider the interaction between several variables.

THE DESIRABILITY OF NEW MARKETS UNDER CHANGED CONDITIONS

This problem is one of general interest to growth companies who are entering new markets. Visualize, if you will, the hypothetical but, I hope, realistic example. The company under analysis, as part of its long-term growth objective, anticipates entering a new market *seven* time periods hence. The company has in its research and project development programs money allocated to develop and announce this new product at that time. But something has happened. One of the company's competitors announces that it, too, plans to enter this market *five* time periods from now. The company's management faces a decision. They have prepared the following estimates: (1) an estimate of total market potential; (2) an estimate of the rate at which their competitor can be expected to penetrate the market; (3) an estimate of the rate at which the company could penetrate the market; (4) an estimate of the time in which competition will enter the market; and (5) an estimate of the time at which they will enter the market.

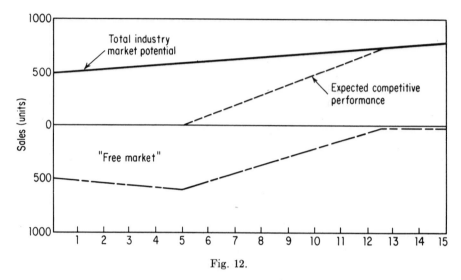

Fig. 12.

Consider Figure 12. The upper curve shows the total industry market potential. The company estimates an immediate potential of five hundred units and a modest growth rate paralleling economic growth thereafter. The company expects competition to enter the market during the fifth time period and to penetrate the market at a rate shown by the expected competitive performance curve. The lower portion of Figure 12 shows the "free market," that is, the market remaining for the company and any other competitors after the initial competitor enters the market. Note that from the current to the fifth time period the lower graph represents a mirror image of the upper graph. If the company does not enter the market, and their competitor is the only market entry, the market will be saturated midway between the twelfth and thirteenth time period. As we indicated above, the company expects to enter the market during the seventh time period. Since the company is already familiar with the market, its management expects that they will be able to penetrate the market at a rate somewhat faster than their competition.

Figure 13 superimposes the company's expected performance on the market curves shown in Figure 12. Figure 13 also shows a combined market penetration curve, that is, a curve representing the arithmetic sum of the expected company performance curve and the expected competitive performance curve. Note that the combined market penetration curve reaches a saturation point midway between the eighth and ninth time period. From this time on the company and its competitors will be competing for the normal growth increment in the market, the shaded area under the total market potential curve. At the time market saturation is reached, a total of 680 units will have been sold. The company sales would be 320 units and competitive sales would be 360 units. The company would attain a 47.1% share of market.

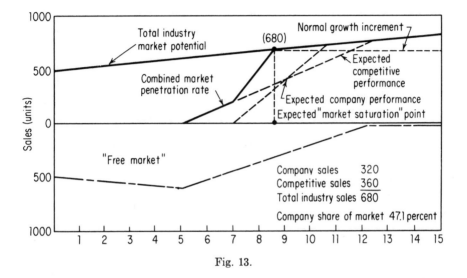

Fig. 13.

For purposes of analysis, assume that the company and its competitor will divide the growth increment market (the shaded portion below the potential market curve) proportionately to the market share the two companies hold at the time the market saturation point was reached (midway between the 8th and 9th time period). In Figure 13 you will note that the company can increase its market share by shortening its announcement schedule. If the company could announce its new product during the current time period, or within the next two time periods, they would be announcing their product from three to five time periods ahead of competition and under the assumptions outlined above could attain virtually one hundred per cent of the market. The company's management faces an important decision. Should they accelerate their research and product development effort to bring the new product into being in time for an earlier announcement? If the company can accelerate its efforts along these lines to meet an earlier announcement date, it can increase its total sales for this new product. To do this, however, the company would have to increase its research and product development expenditures. The problem is one of balancing the expected increase in sales against the increased costs of accelerating the product program.

Figure 14 shows the interrelation between unit sales and profits, excluding research and product development costs. This curve shows the level of profits the company could expect, expressed as a function of ex-

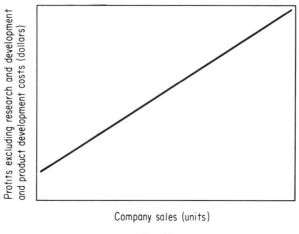

Company sales (units)

Fig. 14.

pected unit sales. It assumes no research or product development costs.

Figure 15 shows the interrelation between required research and product development expenditures and the product's desired availability date.

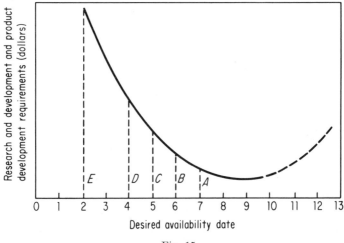

Fig. 15.

Note that the longer the company is willing to wait, the lower the research and product development costs required to put the first product model on the production line. The company originally planned to spend *A dollars* and to have the product available for announcement during the seventh time period. If the company was willing to accelerate its research and product development programs spending *B dollars,* they could have the

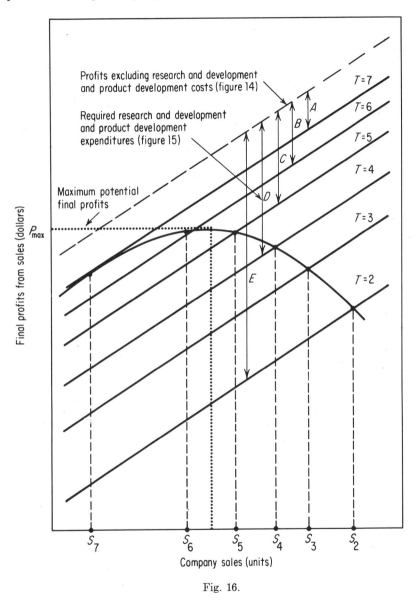

Fig. 16.

product available for announcement during the sixth time period. For *C* and *D dollars* in research and product development effort, the company could have the product ready for announcement during the fifth and fourth time interval, respectively. If the company was willing to initiate an around-the-clock crash program and spend E *dollars*, they could have the product ready for announcement during the second time period. It would be impossible for the company to have the product ready for announcement during the current or the first time period. The costs would be infinite.

Figure 15 illustrates the increased costs of maintaining a highly accelerated research and product development effort. Figure 13 shows that the longer we wait prior to announcing the new product, the smaller our share of market. Figure 15 showed the increased cost of accelerating the announcement schedule. The problem is one of determining the optimum trade-off between increased research and product development costs as opposed to a decreased share of market.

Figure 16 is a graphic representation of the optimization process. This figure was derived by combining the data in Figures 14 and 15. The broken curve corresponds to profits *excluding* the research and development costs curve shown in Figure 14. The six solid curves represent final profits curves for each of six announcement date assumptions, announcement in the second through the seventh time periods. These curves have been designated $T = 2$, announcement in the second time period; through $T = 7$, announcement during the seventh time period. Note that curve $T = 7$ is equal to the profits *excluding* research and product development cost *minus* A dollars in research and product development costs. Similarly, curve $T = 6$ represents the profits excluding research and development and product costs minus B dollars. The family of final profits from sales curves was computed by subtracting the appropriate research and product development expenditure requirement levels (Figure 15) from profit figures making no allowance for these costs (Figure 14).

Extending the analysis outlined in our discussion of Figure 13, we can compute the expected market shares and corresponding total unit sales forecasts associated with each product announcement date, from the second through the seventh time period. These estimates are plotted along the unit sales axis on Figure 16 and are designated S_2 through S_7. A curve is drawn through the intersection of each final profit curve and the corresponding total unit sales projection; for example, a point is plotted on the intersection of sales level S_2, and final profit from sales curve $T = 2$. The curve drawn through these intersection points represents a projection of the net interrelation between unit sales and total profits for various product announcement dates.

Note by tracing the broken line parallel to the horizontal axis that the company's final profits from sales would be maximized if the company planned to announce their product between the 5th and 6th time period. If the company delays announcement beyond this point, the gain in the form of reduced research and product development cost will be offset by the shrinkage in the company's total sales. Conversely, if the company decides to accelerate their announcement date, the corresponding sales increases (i.e., the level of sales at S_2 through S_5) will be offset by the increase in research and product development expenditures from C to E dollars. If the company tries to enter before the 5th time period, it will increase its sales but will spend more money to attain these sales than the incremental profit generated from the increased sales warranted. Similarly, if the company waits to enter the market beyond the 6th period, its total cost will be lower and more favorable but it will have lost too large a share of the market to competition.

THE USES OF MATHEMATICAL MODELS

One of the difficulties that the management of American industry faces today in a changing marketing and competitive environment is its tendency to view each problem as a completely independent event. We are not relating our specific problems to an overall framework. As we have seen, the problem is one of balancing your operations within each environment. For example, how much are you willing to trade off in a weakened sales profit relation for an improved competitive relation. When we attempt to build a model of a business or a Management Science model of a specific business problem, we are really trying to quantify the relationships between the various pertinent factors and to apply logic and common sense to the solution of business problems.

Another powerful advantage that we gain through the use of mathematical models is a process that mathematicians call invertibility. Mathematical models are strange sausage meat machines. We can put the sausage in one end, run the machine backwards, and take the live pig out the other end. A mathematical model may (assuming we have preserved its invertibility) be "run" forward or backward. That is, we can estimate the resources required to carry out a given level of marketing activity, or conversely, given the availability of resources, we can estimate the level of marketing activity that can be sustained.

The invertibility principle is particularly useful in analyzing the resources required to attain a given competitive position. Consider the following example. In developing a marketing strategy you must consider the actions and counter-actions of your competitors, as well as your own actions. This will require that you estimate your competitor's marketing and/or product development expenditures. These estimates may, of course, be subject to wide error.

Using the mathematical model you can reformulate the competitive assessment problem as follows. Starting with an initial estimate of competitive marketing and/or product development expenditures, the model can be used to calculate the level of company expenditures required to attain your marketing objective in the face of the competitive expenditures estimated above. This would be a forward solution. The invertibility principle will allow you to check the consistency of your planning as follows.

Given your desired marketing objective, your present marketing position, your marketing and/or product development budget, and the historical interrelation between your relative market position and marketing and/or product development expenditures, you may calculate backward through the model to determine the implied level of competitive expenditures that would be consistent with your actions and objectives.

You can check the consistency of your planned action by comparing the implied level of competitive expenditures derived from the planning model with the corresponding estimates of competitive expenditures generated from the best available intelligence. Your plan would be consistent if the implied level of competitive expenditures derived from the planning model was approximately equal to the competitive expenditure estimates that you would derive from the best available intelligence.

The use of mathematical models and similar tools of management science as a basis for management planning and control may be regarded by some as "nothing more than some long-hair gadget or impractical academic exercise." This attitude is in part the fault of "impractical" model builders who lose sight of the fact that the mathematical model is a means to an end—not the end itself. The validity of the method, however, is not disproved by the errors of some individuals who claim to follow the method.

Another cause of skepticism is the fact that the mathematical model builder uses terms and techniques with which the average man is unfamiliar and therefore suspicious. This, however, is a weakness common to any specialized field. The model builder simply employs a unique "shorthand" (developed from the fields of mathematics, statistics, and econometrics) that enables him to do a difficult job better than it has ever been done before. The layman may not always understand this shorthand, but he can understand and evaluate the results and that is what counts.

The validity of the mathematical model technique for management planning and control is no longer a matter of speculation. When properly employed, it does work . . . and in so doing, it offers five significant advantages:

> First, the model constitutes a well-defined statement of the problem at hand. As such, it enables us to state and to employ all our a priori information on this problem. The model assists the planner in reaching a conclusion; it does not provide nor is it intended to provide a final judgment-free mechanical answer.

Second, the model renders *explicit* the assumptions on the basis of which the investigation or analysis proceeds. Management's basic assumptions are incorporated into the model itself.

Third, the model makes it possible, if it is possible at all, to orient research to answer specific questions of policy.

Fourth, the model—when fully formulated—serves to determine the statistical techniques which ought to be employed so that (a) there will be no inherent contradictions in procedure and (b) estimates will be consistent and will have known error probabilities as well as desirable properties.

Fifth, once estimates have been made using a mathematical model, management finds it easier to understand and to interpret the full significance of these estimates—in terms of the overall company and its environment.

A FINAL NOTE

In the preceding sections, I have discussed some of the new tools that will be available to the marketing executive during the next five to ten years. The application of the scientific method, whether it be called operations research, management science, or ordinary quantitative common sense, is here to stay. Mathematical models will never replace marketing judgment, but they can be fruitfully employed to narrow down the range over which marketing decisions must be made on the basis of judgment alone. In the future, our marketing plans and strategies will be far more scientifically and objectively derived. With this challenge there also comes the responsibility of using these new tools wisely. There are no panaceas or "cure-all" formulas, but these new techniques will allow the marketing community to use all available information to develop more realistic and efficient marketing plans.

chapter two | *Patrick J. Robinson*

This chapter is intended to discuss some potentially controversial topics in a provocative yet constructive manner. Students of business or businessmen looking for discussions of fundamentals should recognize a four-fold purpose in the material:

1. To establish the importance of considering marketing problems in proper perspective with the general interests of the firm as a whole. So-called "sub-optimization" is the big pitfall here.

2. To emphasize the importance of moving from the usual symptomatic expressions of problems to their underlying causes and to a consideration of what may be done in a practical sense to improve performance. The danger of solving "the wrong problem" is the point at issue here.

3. To suggest that high-speed computing and data-handling aids should be regarded as potentially profitable aids to problem-solving only when properly applied as a means to a valid end. Electronic aids them-

THE DEVELOPMENT

OF FEASIBLE GOALS

AND SUITABLE STRATEGIES

selves are no substitutes for proper problem formulation and the exercise of sound judgment and experience. The possibility of losing touch with reality under mountains of data is no longer remote. There are far too many costly examples of this happening in business today.

4. To demonstrate that practical representations or "models" of activities may take many forms (including graphs, maps, equations, tabulations of customer buying behavior). But to be of value as reliable predictors of probable business performance for alternative strategies, these representations must be as much a product of the business administrator and his people as of the business researcher or planner. Co-responsibility and realism are the keynotes here. Any realistic model can be explained in unambiguous terms in plain language. The acid test of utility is whether it is designed to give answers to irreverent but direct "so what?" questions that can be translated directly into business plans and action.

THE NEED FOR PROPER PERSPECTIVE

The business analyst or researcher must have a workable understanding of the aims and objectives of interest to management before he undertakes a quantitative analysis of any significant aspect of marketing operations. A general indoctrination in the firm, or training and experience in marketing and modern business practices is not sufficient. Although such grounding can be of substantial value, it must be augmented by adequate knowledge of the specific operations under study. Effective quantitative evaluation requires that all key factors be identified and viewed in their proper perspective. This is true despite the difficulties encountered in attempting such a task. Management frequently characterizes problems primarily by symptoms recognized in the course of administering operations. These symptoms provide important clues but they may not reveal the fundamental relationships which must be uncovered before an adequate analysis can be completed.

At this point, a word of caution is in order. At the beginning of a problem-solving project, all concerned should seek the best possible "meeting of the minds" and recognize practical limitations on their collective efforts. Unless this initial step is taken, the real problem may not be solved or even recognized. Even worse, the study may provide misleading results which might go undetected until they have become a basis for incorrect action. However eager he may be to turn in a rapidly prepared piece of impressive staff work, the researcher must not neglect adequate analytical procedures. Sometimes, a guideline or check list of procedures can prove invaluable to those patient enough to employ a systematic approach to setting up problems and identifying desired ends. If such an approach is used, the most appropriate problem-solving technique may be selected in an orderly and appropriate fashion. In the initial stage, the researcher must decide whether or not the problem appears to lend itself to the use of specific computerized techniques. The probable virtues as well as the time requirements of each possible method of study must be considered.

One must also view the business in proper perspective in relation to its markets, its competition and its resources. Peter Drucker has written that the primary purpose of any business enterprise is "the creation of customers." He and many others feel that the marketing activity of the business represents the mainstay of the entire operation, and is fundamentally the "object of the exercise." Others tell us how very complex marketing activities are, and how difficult or even impossible it is to quantify many of the qualitative elements in marketing. The unquestioned importance of marketing and the difficulty of constructing adequate analytical tools makes it imperative that the goals of the operation and the range of possible alternatives be fully specified *before* employing such techniques. A step by step approach to business problem-solving in marketing is outlined in the following discussion and accompanying case illustration. Its use should present the intuitive business administrator and the scientific business researcher from drawing conclusions on the basis of inadequate evidence.

 If this geometric display of lines is thought of as "in formation" What does it tell us of recognizable value? Does it answer our irreverent "so what" question?

 By applying a different viewpoint we see a cube which may reveal something important that was previously obscure. Perspective can lead to insight; and insight to profitable action.

Fig. 1.

Figure 1 is intended to illustrate that frequently the proper perspective, using available knowledge, enables one to gain a realistic and meaningful view of what might otherwise be a mass of confusing or apparently useless information.

FEASIBILITY — THE "WALK AROUND THE PARK"

An adequate statement (or re-statement) of a problem can be obtained only if all concerned agree on the differences between symptom and causes. Although one must limit the complexity of the problem, all the significant aspects of the situation have to be recognized. The experienced analyst or professional planner attempts to bound the problem within reasonable limits. This should not prevent him from considering factors which may not at first have seemed relevant. It may be helpful to enumerate the following steps as a generalized guide to determining the pertinent aspects of a typical business problem. Of course, some steps may only have to be carried out periodically since many of the assumptions and objectives obtained in connection with each project may remain valid for other projects conducted at a later date. Generally, the order and scope of steps required are these:

1. Obtain a realistic definition of the objectives of the firm and/or the operations under review. A knowledge of the products and services the firm provides may prove insufficient. Any related areas of operation in the firm should be considered, as should trends and pending policy shifts or diversification plans.

2. Determine the full range and flexibility of existing activities and identify all key physical facilities and other resources, both human and material. The nature and extent of limitations on all potentially signifi-

cant items should be gauged. An awareness of limitations leads to an appreciation of practical constraints which restrict scope, timing and flexibility.

3. Assess the span of control exercised by those directing operations, and determine the ways in which such control is governed and limited by financial, legal, planning or other considerations. The importance of this step justifies the great degree of effort and tact necessary to obtain such insights. As a rule, management must confine its efforts to the region of the firm's operation over which it exercises effective control. Note the use of the phrase "effective control" here. Frequently, formal organizational charts do not define adequately what an individual or group may with propriety cover under customary administrative practices. It is quite possible for the span and degree of authority to be either greater or less than might at first seem likely from an inspection of formal charts or position descriptions. Whatever the case, it is essential to recognize these fundamental business "facts of life."

4. Discover the measures of performance or criteria of success in use in the firm, or potentially applicable to its operations, and any practical guides as to their ranges or permissible limits and cutoffs. Here it is important to identify not only which measures of criteria might be considered for the given project, but also which individuals or groups concerned favor one or other of these essentially conflicting aims—and why. Look also for any available comparisons of results with previous predictions and identify recognized benchmarks within and outside the company. What have been the apparently key considerations in relevant, prior decisions? The availability and usage of industry standards or published comparisons may also be of value.

A simple illustration of this concept is presented in Figure 2. This may appear self-explanatory in concept, but its full significance deserves special emphasis. Likely, few students of business, and not many businessmen themselves, ever take adequate time to ponder and challenge some of the fundamental assumptions (as well as "folklore" or "sacred cows") concerning "the object of the exercise." How often do we hear someone calling forcefully for more profits, greater market share, lower costs or improved rates of return on funds employed? Is it safe to assume these advocates really mean simply what they seem to say? Add to this the impassioned appeals for improved customer, stockholder, government, and employee relations; and the desired aims of the company become extremely diverse. In practice, different departmental "types" tend to adopt and to sponsor distinctly different aims as being the "real reason we are in business." Seldom does a company's executive body fail to represent less than several of these essentially non-interchangeable and conflicting goals. Ideally, this may lead to a balanced "optimum compromise" approach to problems. Alternatively, it may result in wasteful discord and indecision.

To emphasize this fundamental problem, we should consider the genuine difficulties which can arise if any single objective is stressed at the expense of all others (whether consciously or unconsciously).

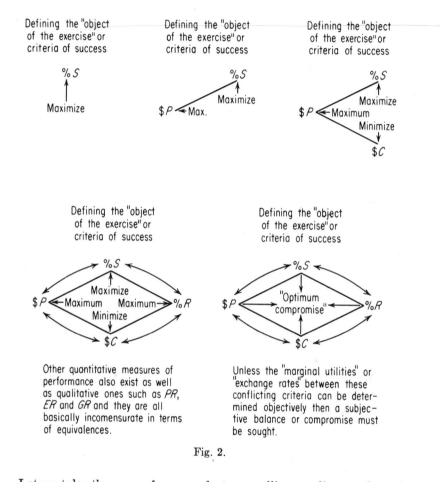

Fig. 2.

Let us take the case of a manufacturer selling appliances through a chain of stores. If sales were declining owing to aggressive competition, and if the market share were regarded as the desired performance measure, then an effective-seeming, yet ruinous strategy could develop. The company might achieve maximum market position by a "give away" program of low prices, special services and very superior quality product and packaging. Clearly, profits could become losses (despite great volume increases) and return on funds could fall or disappear.

Similarly total dollar profits, or percent return, or total dollar cost might be employed as a single key to failure by following a specific path beyond a reasonable limit. All too often, such limits are not established unless real trouble has appeared forcing recognition of other considerations and a change of emphasis.

To further illustrate this, consider profit as a single performance measure. If profit maximization alone is pursued, then a heavy borrowing and investment program might be set up for all possible new appliance ventures that bring in more than they cost to operate. High unit profit sales lines could be added, extra services eliminated, product quality and merchandising cut; all to fatten profits (at least in the short run). This policy may produce more dollars than before, but may also lose markets, reduce returns and irreparably damage public or government relations. This process can go unrecognized until too late.

One more example of the many possibilities is centered on cost minimization. This is usually not the same as profit maximization—especially over a period of many months or years. Here in fact lies a major pitfall of some elaborate mathematical models and computerized programs. They are really not "optimizing," as their staff and line exponents would lead one to expect, but rather use a single "objective function" to do everything possible to raise profits or lower costs (implicitly to the exclusion of all else). The questions that might be dealt with relatively easily *before* a model is built can be very difficult and upsetting after a great deal of effort and time has been expended. In fact, dangerous rationalizing may result from an attempt to avoid starting over, or undertaking fundamental revisions. If this happens, everyone may become the loser, and intellectual honesty can become hopelessly compromised. It is far better to face up to these issues late and salvage what may be useful, than to go on burying past oversights in problem definition or model building. Of course, a tolerant and understanding environment can be a great help in the early stages of employing new methods. But it is far better to use such latitude and understanding to really get the problem "out on the table" in a thorough beginning than in a patched-up ending.

Going beyond Figure 2 (which provides a relatively simple illustration), one may visualize Figure 3 as providing the greater range and inter-relationships between a number of primary and secondary performance measures or management controls. Figure 3 includes everything in Figure 2, and goes substantially beyond to suggest other familiar (and also unfamiliar and probably hard to measure) criteria. This is not to suggest that all or even most of these are useful guides, but rather that an appropriate mixture should be identified for the business after comprehensive management review.

5. Enumerate the available symptoms for the problem in hand and identify the unanswered questions and the apparent problem areas. Add

potentially helpful information from similar cases elsewhere (e.g. past experience and literature searches). Whenever possible, it is useful to note known successful approaches or solution methods that have applied to such cases in the past. These may include the use of "canned" computer routines as well as various established Operations Research and Management Science tools.

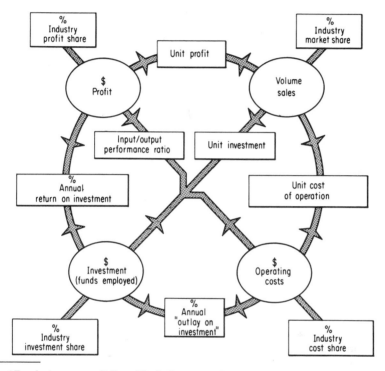

* Four basic measures: Dollars of Profit, Investment, Cost, and Sales Volume may be related to each other and to comparable industry statistics, to provide management with selected ratios as guides to performance and opportunities. Some of these ratios are commonplace; others are seldom available but are illustrated for completeness. Proper selection among such indicators and following their stock fluctuations and trends are essential for effective management control of operations and evaluation of alternatives.

Fig. 3.*

6. Consider apparently feasible alternative modes of current operation and/or future investment as guides to enumerating research and development goals and specifying possible attractive activities for expanded or diversified operations. Such a procedure should not be limited to new product appraisals. It applies with equal relevance to such possibilities as new business systems, and innovations in selling methods.

7. Evaluate problems in measurement and precision which appear likely to influence observations or distort evidence from company or external sources. One must be especially careful to avoid attributing un-

warranted preciseness to estimates that are nothing more than relatively crude approximations. Limitations on the representativeness of data effectively reduce the reliability and validity of inferences which may be drawn for useful generalization. One should determine the maximum amount of precision justified for all factors which are being taken into account. This is similar to the problem of determining the area of a lot if one knows the length to the nearest foot. If one is content to use this measure, then one should measure the width also to the nearest foot to obtain a reasonable indication of the area. But this requires rounding the answer to the appropriate number of significant figures (e.g. $121 \times 92 = 11,000$ sq. ft., *not* $11,132$ sq. ft.). If greater or less accuracy in area is required, one should measure the lot accordingly. Furthermore, when precision is spoken of in measurement, one enters the entire field of mathematical statistics, including statistical "confidence limits" for all the results or outputs of interest in studies. Modern measuring devices and analytical techniques are refined and practical, but they are best employed by qualified practitioners.

8. Decouple the activity under study from surrounding and related activities. If one is considering only a small portion of the entire business, one should intelligently appraise what may be best for this activity while not overlooking the problems and hazards of sub-optimization. When a physicist studies a problem of very large scope, he frequently subdivides it into smaller and more manageable parts. He first seeks so-called "weak links" or regions in which the interaction effects between activities will be either negligible or quite small. This approach to analysis permits a modular attack so that after a number of pieces have been studied they can be reassembled analytically and still provide meaningful and coherent results in terms of the overall interests of the company. In early operations research work and pre-operations research analytic studies, a failure to recognize this frequently resulted in a "best" policy being indicated which in point of fact was either the worst or at least an undesirable policy in the overall interests of the concern.

9. Assemble a rough-cut, order-of-magnitude representation or model of the operations under review. It may even be possible to perform certain rough-cut, order-of-magnitude manipulative tests or experiments on this model to indicate the sensitivity of the outputs of interest to changes in various key factors or assumptions. This can give some notion as to where comparatively great precision must be employed and where a simplifying assumption to ignore a factor or take only relatively crude readings can be made. At this point, one may find the "solution space" reduced to the vanishing point. If too many restrictions have been imposed, there may not remain any feasible mode of operation. If this is the case, some constraints must be relaxed in order that decisions can be made and feasible operating policies adopted. If the solution space is relatively very

small, the problem may be revealed as technically "trivial" with only one remaining course of action defined in the problem-formulation stage. Figure 4 depicts this bounding concept in an elementary example built in the form of a graphic model.

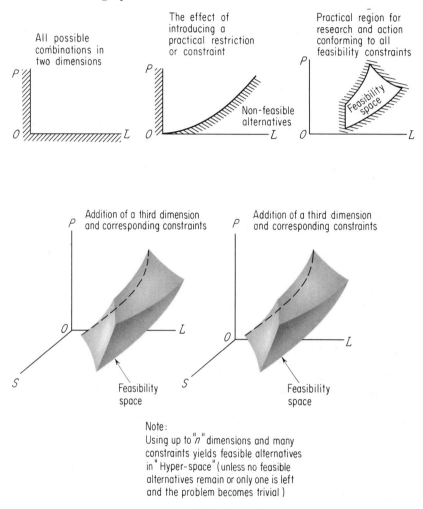

Fig. 4.

Once one has gone through this so-called "walk around the park" stage of problem definition (and if possible rough-cut analysis), one should be in a good position to report back to the management initiating the project. It is essential to obtain clear-cut agreement on just what may be done, how long it should take, who should be involved, how it should be tackled, and whether in fact the possible gains or knowledge that may be achieved justify the effort and cost.

At this stage, another word of caution. It may not be possible to assign a rough order-of-magnitude estimate of the value of the project in terms of likely gains. Some studies are designed to assess existing operations and one may find that the operation is already performing in a desirable manner. Before any study is undertaken, management must realize that one possible outcome may be simple reassurance that present practices are "near-optimum." Even if this should be the case, prior agreement should be reached that such assurance would justify the study as "cheap insurance." On the other hand, when the need for new policies is demonstrated, the results speak for themselves in terms of the economic incentives for such changes.

To illustrate the foregoing examples and suggested procedures for effective problem-solving and planning, there follows a condensed case which further illustrates these concepts and the method of identifying feasible goals and suitable strategies.

A MARKETING STRATEGY CASE ILLUSTRATION

Marketing executives were concerned with one phase of the company's operation which had been losing ground to competition for some years until "something new had to be done." Although the volume of sales had been growing, the industry growth rate had been much faster. As a consequence, the company's share of the market had declined an estimated 20% in about five years. Unfortunately, lack of reliable industry statistics had concealed this situation until company sales began leveling off and special studies and surveys revealed recent trends. The studies also revealed that total industry potential had finally reached saturation and only a nominal continuing growth was likely in the future. Company sales growth had slowed under sustained competitive pressure and would soon decline if the loss in market position continued.

In an effort to combat this adverse sales performance and possibly to reverse the trend, a series of strategic planning discussions took place. The surveys and other information obtained from customers and trade channels indicated a number of competitive practices which were contributing to the relative decline in sales. In the course of the discussion, it became clear that most of these practices could be successfully combatted—but, at a price. It then became necessary to consider the profit implications as well as the expected sales benefits of expensive countermoves. Pertinent investment requirements were also identified. Certain capital outlays would yield sales improvements but they could not all be undertaken at an equally attractive expected rate of return on the funds employed.

The discussions essentially focused attention on the first major symptom—declining market share; and on the various remedial steps that might be feasible provided they could be "justified." Justification could be measured in terms of improved market share, change in total dollars profit or expected percentage return on funds employed. An "optimum compromise" between these three criteria was needed since no single standard would balance the different desires of management and no one course of action was consistent with all three conflicting objectives. Al-

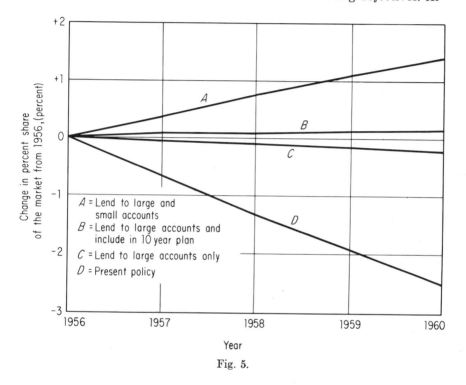

Fig. 5.

though these objectives lacked a satisfactory common denominator, an assumed floor or minimum could be established for each one. Such action, however, did not resolve the question of how to measure a "best" course of action. The feasible alternatives of interest to management had to be identified.

A thorough exchange of views revealed that there were probably four clearly different strategies that straddled the range of feasible moves. The "continue as is" alternatives was one of these four. The other three adequately covered the major alternatives. Minor variations were agreed on as falling between and might be interpolated if necessary. After identifying the feasible alternatives (which essentially bounded the so-called feasibility space), it was agreed that each of the four alternatives would be projected in terms of probable performance as measured by the three

criteria (market share, dollars profit, percent return on funds). The final
presentation of expected results would then be exhibited graphically for
management to compare the probable behaviors of the four strategies as
measured by their expected impact, over the next four years, on each of
the criteria. The graphic summaries of results were dramatic.

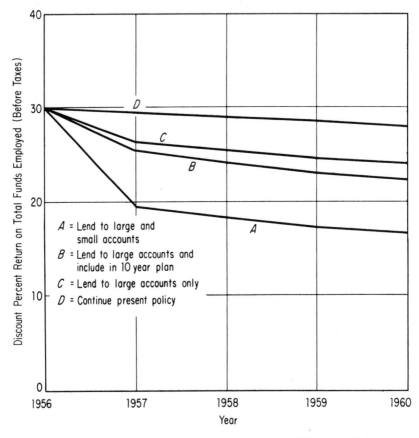

Fig. 6. Return on investment of business with different policies.

In one display (Figure 5), Policy A was "best" and Policy D "worst"
in terms of projected market position. In contrast (Figure 6), their positions were reversed as gauged by expected return on investment. Finally
(Figure 7), Policy D was more profitable in the near future; but A became more profitable in subsequent years. Furthermore, both policies
were exceeded in profitability throughout the four year projection by
Policies B and C. Thus, no single strategy was dominant as measured
by all three criteria. Furthermore, the projections showed that a really
significant change in performance would likely result from adopting any

one strategy versus any other. Clearly, the consequences of the decision were not likely to be trivial or insignificant.

From this description, one might question the adequacy of such a set of charts. Instead of a clear cut definitive answer, management was receiving an aid to decisions depicting a whole range of probable consequences. The knowledgeable researcher, however, could hardly attempt to

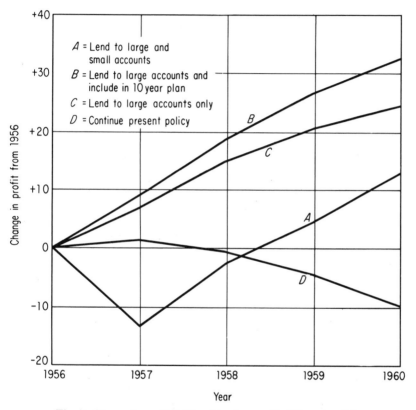

Fig. 7. Change in profitability of business with different policies.

do more. As with other projects, the manager must still exercise judgment and experience. He has the responsibility and must decide on the best available guides. In this instance, the range of uncertainty was narrowed and attention was focused on exercising skill and judgment in weighing alternatives and risks. Management liked the approach and based decisions upon the research findings. Furthermore, the performance results that later occurred were in keeping with the predictions.

On two subsequent occasions, related projects were requested and carried through similar steps. In all cases, management found it desirable to evaluate subjectively the graphed results of the analyses which were

regarded as well completed staff work. It was not feasible for management to specify in advance how much emphasis or marginal substitut-
ability one performance measure had in terms of another. The conflicts
between criteria were best resolved by careful weighing at the time of
decision. Everyone agreed that a new and important perspective was
achieved when the expected results were available for examination.

Undoubtedly, in some instances, one may obtain marginal utilities or
equivalences between measures at the beginning of a project. However,
failing this, it is better to employ several standards rather than to design
one arbitrary compromise measure as a basis for planning.

In the foregoing case, no one measure could have yielded a realistic
perspective, and each criterion alone would have suggested a different
answer both as to range of choice and performance. It was the business
researchers' responsibility not to usurp the business administrators' responsibility by "jumping to conclusions" or by over-simplifying either
the problem or the results of the study.

CONCLUSIONS

Any serious student of business or experienced businessman will be able
to absorb the notions outlined in this chapter and the accompanying figures illustrating such concepts as "feasibility space." This may be likened to picturing the real environment within which a firm operates. It
is not an unconstrained or theoretically tidy world. There are many dimensions and restrictions which may not at first appear obvious or even
easy to define. But today, the opportunities and aids are numerous and
careful efforts can prove both challenging and rewarding.

Once one delineates the region of feasibility, it is essential to identify
the objectives considered most desirable as measured by some single
agreed on scale (such as profits) or some compromise or balance between
several conflicting criteria. Whatever the objectives, they must be sought
within the confines of the feasibility space so that realistic targets or goals
can be established and overall strategies and detailed tactics planned.

Since various means may be devised to achieve the desired ends, each
alternative strategy should be carefully formulated. Its uses of scarce resources, its timing, and its likely degree of success may then be gauged
in terms of the expected impact on the one or more measures of performance or goals selected previously. It is in the formulation of such strategies
(and the tactical details involved) that a particular amount of care must
be exercised to cover an adequate range of alternatives. Of course, if only
one course of action appears feasible, then the solution may have been
obtained in the problem formulation stage. In this situation (or one with
a vanishing feasibility space), a realistic re-appraisal and relaxation of

constraints may reveal additional possibilities or previously unrecognized opportunities.

In some instances, the use of advanced mathematical models and modern automatic computing equipment can permit so-called integrated optimization models to be built. If enough is known about the feasibility space and the objective function, it may be possible to search for "optimum" policies or strategies. In this way, a "best" plan may be derived and the penalties that occur by departures from this plan may be explored. Such procedures permit exploring for key factors by sensitivity analysis. This is a powerful approach when properly exploited (possibly using exotic new tools such as parametric linear programming and the decomposition technique for very large systems). The expected influence of changes in key assumptions or objectives can be pre-tested in terms of changes in the end results being predicted.

A variation in strategy may appear justified because only a nominal penalty is involved. Alternatively, if a less desirable strategy must be adopted, one can appreciate what it will cost versus any other basis. In any event, the suitability of the strategy under review will depend on more than the quantitative evaluations that prove possible. Equally important are the critical, subjective judgments that experienced managers bring to bear in making the final decisions, once they are aware of the predicted probable outcomes and risks for the various alternatives.

chapter three | *Tibor Fabian*

The objective of this paper is to provide an introduction for laymen to the mathematics used in the formulation and solution of business problems by operations researchers and management scientists. In order to permit more than a capsule treatment of each subject yet less than a book, the following rules will be observed:

1. Only such mathematical approaches will be considered which apply to managerial problems that lie within the responsibility of the chief marketing executive of a business enterprise;
2. Only such management problems will be included which are or can become subject to routine administrative systems.

The first limitation on scope immediately indicates that there is more to mathematics in management than is described in this paper. Several functional areas, such as production management, procurement, financial

MATHEMATICAL APPROACHES TO

MARKETING PROBLEMS

management, controllership, etc., provide fields in which mathematical approaches have proved successful. To date, the marketing area lags behind the others in the application of mathematical techniques—and for that matter the use of computers.

The second limitation on scope constrains the interest of the paper to administrative type problems or those which conceivably could be reduced to such problems if they were approached with the tools recommended here. Once the problems are resolved, through the process of "model building," "solution of the model" and "testing of the solution," the routine of the system can be performed by an electronic computer, a punched card system, a manual system, or some combination. The result is a "real time administrative system" which prepares the necessary documents that trigger events, exercise control, and report on performance.

Mathematics used in the following areas will be investigated:

Sales Forecasting
Marketing Logistics
Allocation of Advertising Budget

The mathematical aspects of these marketing problems are referred to as "model building." Briefly, this implies that the assumptions of the problems are explicitly stated and statements are quantitative or mathematical. Variables are identified; constraints are made explicit. Since the mathematical statements are normally based on research of facts, we may refer to the mathematical approach as *quantified experience*. This is in contrast with traditional approaches to management problems, which, at their best, can be identified only as *codified experience*. There are significant merits associated with the model building approach. It can be taught; it can be enlarged upon; it is objective: if the results are used by different persons, the outcome is likely to be similar.

The mathematical model is the beginning of a rigorous approach to a marketing problem. The model presents the analyst's conception of the problem from which a numerical solution is derived. The path from this to a management system usually is lengthy and involves the following steps:

1. Data collection and analysis to determine the constants (parameters) of a problem.
2. Test computations to measure the expected results and to evaluate the new approach before costly implementation.
3. System design for repetitive application of the solution.
4. Choice of hardware (computers, office equipment, data transmission equipment) which results in a system compatible with, or capable of being integrated into, company operations.
5. Computer programming and manpower training.
6. Debugging of the new system.
7. Transition to and operation of the new system.

This detailed checklist is presented here for three reasons: (1) to indicate that the mathematical model of the marketing problem has to be compatible with aspects of implementation; (2) to warn of the possible shortcomings in the process of implementation which might reflect on the mathematical or quantitative approach; (3) cost considerations.

As to the first of the points, if the analytical study of a management problem is to result in a "real time" operating system, mathematical solution has to be compatible with the capability of computational facilities or any other element of the system. Complex mathematical computations, or the computation of solutions to large scale problems, could defy computers altogether. In some cases, the computational results cannot be produced by the time they are required. Similarly, the timely collection and transmission of large volumes of data may not be possible. Also, it may not be worth developing a complex administrative system based on an elaborate mathematical model if the data lack the desired accuracy.

The final pragmatic judgment as to the value of mathematics depends on the success of implementation. A host of problems with little relevance to the mathematics normally arises during implementation. The tasks of data collection, programming, choice of hardware, etc., are not mathematical, and problems associated with these aspects of systems work should not reflect upon the rightness or wrongness of the mathematics used. Yet they frequently do. This may explain why some simple and not quite correct, but adequately implemented, mathematical models were judged good, while correct models of a problem were judged wrong where the implementation lacked success.

Finally, the process of implementation of a mathematical solution requires the analysis of the economics of the new system. Correct solutions, or "better" solutions, may depend on the use of costly computing and/or data transmission equipment and staff. The price tag of the resultant system may be too high to be paid for by the resulting benefits.

After this cautionary introduction, we may discuss mathematical considerations of specific systems in marketing.

SALES FORECASTING

A standard problem of marketing is the prediction of product sales. Each level of the marketing channel requires a sales forecast, and possibly a good one. At the level of original planning, a good one-time analysis of the market structure requiring detailed information on behavior of demand for the product, the nature of competitive supply, and the availability and price of production factors is needed. Elaborate individual market studies are usually associated with initial plans. Once the production and marketing of the product are under way, a gross annual forecast of sales is normally used for budgetary planning and control. This gross forecast may be broken down by quarters or months, and further by sales regions. Finally, the day-to-day logistics of marketing requires a continuous look ahead in order to keep the channels of supply sufficiently full to meet the customer's requirements, but not so full as to result in unnecessary capital tie-up in inventories, added cost of rented warehouse space, and return of outdated merchandise.

The needs of each of these three administrative tasks for a forecast can be met wholly or partly by mathematical developments of the recent past. These developments do not create perfect forecasts; indeed, it is not even claimed that a forecast so obtained will be much more accurate most of the time than forecasts attained by guesswork. The following should, however, serve at least as a strong recommendation for their use:

1. If the analytical procedure recommended for the first of the three approaches is applied, a deep and useful understanding of the forces operating on a product's market can result. If the procedure is successful and is to be applied repetitively, a data collection system can be devised and routine computations can be programmed for a computer.

2. The forecasting procedures used here to illustrate forecasting for the second and third types of administrative needs can be programmed for high speed electronic computers, and the sales forecasts for a large number of products can be prepared routinely at a relatively small computational cost. Furthermore, routine forecasts can be combined within the computer to create various types of reports; such as a continuous check on fulfillment of regional sales quotas, production plans and schedules for the transportation department, etc. The last approach discussed here can be made part of a real-time, integrated administrative system with the use of a computer as the central data processing unit. Such a system could incorporate the bookkeeping, billing, production scheduling and inventory control aspects of paperwork, or as much of it as is economical.

ECONOMETRIC ANALYSIS

Econometrics or econometric analysis is a branch of economics concerned with the statistical verification of economic theories. Econometric analysis deals with theories concerning the national economy, and also deals with theories of the markets of specific products or product lines. In this latter aspect and as a research tool for product planning, pricing, and promotion of products, it is of interest to us.

It is difficult to describe econometrics to those who are unfamiliar with the term. In addition to statistical testing, econometrics ultimately deals with economic assumptions about market behavior of buyers and sellers. These are assumptions concerning the characteristics of demand and of supply. Normally, economic assumptions as to the elasticity of demand with respect to price or advertising expenditure make little impression on practical people who are accustomed to dealing with and interpreting facts according to their own criteria. For these people, assumptions stated in quantitative terms are usually not only suspicious but are considered downright impractical. For that matter, all of mathematics in management systems falls under the same judgment. Instead of arguing the point, I will give a brief explanation to illustrate econometric analysis, and the reader can form his own opinion.

Let us suppose that we wish to analyze the market of an agricultural product to arrive at conclusions concerning the pricing policy and the forecast of sales over a year.

The amount of this product grown usually depends on last year's price. The higher last year's price, other things being equal, the more acreage will be allotted for growing this product. This quantity also depends on last year's price of all other agricultural products which compete with this one for acreage. Finally, random elements, such as rainfall, temperature, blight, etc., will affect the supply this year.

Let us assume that the product is perishable and inventories are held by growers or distributors. Otherwise, the inventory change for the last two years also would influence the acreage allotted for this year. We then postulate that $Q(t)$, the crop supply available for harvest in year t, is a function of the above elements in the following manner:

$$Q(t) = aP(t - 1) + bC(t - 1) + eW + f$$

Where

P is the price of the product in year $t - 1$

C is the price of the product in $t - 1$ that competes for the acreage

W is a measure of the weather, say a temperature-rainfall index

f is a random variable which stands for all other unexplained factors

a, b and e are constants whose value remains to be determined.

The quantity offered on the market, $X^s(t)$, cannot be more than $Q(t)$, since inventories do not exist. But it could be less. If prices are low relative to wage rates, less acreage will be harvested; conversely, if prices are high relative to wage rates, more will be harvested. Thus, $X^s(t)$ can take the following form

$$X^s = g \frac{P(t)}{W(t)} + hQ(t) + k \quad \text{or} \quad X^s = Q(t)$$

and where

$W(t)$ represents wage rate

K is the random element of this equation

g and h are constants whose value remains to be determined.

Lastly, an equation has to be stated to represent demand for the product. We can assume that consumer disposable income, market price, the size of population, and the price of competing products will affect the demand function as follows:

$$P(t) = \alpha \frac{Y(t)}{N(t)} + \beta \frac{x^d}{N(t)} + \gamma Z(t) + \delta$$

where

$Y(t)$ is the consumer disposable income in the marketing year

$N(t)$ is the population

$Z(t)$ is the composite price of all competing products

α, β, γ are constants and δ is a random element

In this demand function, income and quantity purchased are expressed in "per capita" form. On the market an average price will be arrived at for which

$$X^s = X^d.$$

Here, we have two equations in three unknowns. The unknowns are Q, X, and P. Disposable income, population, wages and prices of competing products are considered as data to be collected for independently forecasted figures.

The next step in the analysis is to determine the values of the constants and of the random factors. In this study, the estimation would use the least square method, and historical data which are available for all variables. Thus, we will end up with equations that contain numerical values for the parameters. We can perform analytical work with these equations to gain information on the order of magnitude of price changes as a function of the changes in the other variables.

The parameter values of some econometric relations can be estimated from data on consumer behavior. Such approach is called "cross section analysis" as compared to time series analysis. The latter is applicable in the above case. Consumption as a function of income could also be determined from data on a sample of households; thus cross section analysis also could have been applied in the example.

Marketing research collects voluminous data on consumer behavior through test marketing, panels, interviews, and give-away programs. Econometric analysis of the data can provide a useful method for data reduction and interpretation; indeed, it could even orient marketing research to the collection of really pertinent information.

APPORTIONING AN ANNUAL SALES FORECAST

To serve the purposes of budgeting and control, a simple mathematical procedure can be used. This can be programmed for electronic computers, and applied routinely to prepare and revise monthly sales forecasts and other reports for several products. The procedure consists of the following basic steps:

(1) Preparation of an annual sales forecast for the product
(2) Apportioning of the annual forecast over the months of the year
(3) Computation of an upper and lower error limit on the monthly forecast
(4) Revision of the annual forecast and repetition of (2) and (3) whenever the control limit is exceeded

The sales forecast is prepared by any method. It may be done simply by the least square estimate of the annual sales data of the product, or by setting desired (and reasonable) annual sales quotas in view of the planned marketing effort for the year. It might be derived from econometric analysis. The annual sales forecast is an input, an exogenous variable to the forecasting procedure, but its preparation might also be performed by routine calculations and can conceivably be programmed for an electronic computer. In view of item (4), the revision of the forecast, this may be very useful since the apportioning and controlling of the forecast can also be performed by computer.

Historical data on monthly sales by year form the basis of estimating what percent of the expected annual sale should accumulate as each month passes. Two of the many methods by which this can be done are as follows:

(1) Averaging the data on cumulative monthly sales over the same months of several years
(2) Computing a trend line of the monthly percentage sales from the historical data

In either case, a measure of variability can be computed (the standard deviation of a month's sales or the standard error about the trend line) and a control limit established at, for example, the level of two standard deviations about the average or the trend line.[1]

In operation, the actual cumulative sales data are computed monthly as percent of the forecast and are compared with the forecasted cumulative sales up to that month. If in, say, two consecutive months the actual sales figure is beyond the same tolerance limit, then the annual forecast, its apportionment by months, and the tolerance limit are computed again.

---

[1] Other rules also can be used to determine when to prepare a new forecast. The procedure is very flexible. Before implementation, it might be advisable to test several different rules for the preparation and revision of the annual forecast. Prior to the testing, a suitable measure of success should be selected and applied rigidly to the result of each variant.

This approach, similar to the quality control chart approach, is widely referred to in textbooks and handbooks.[2] Reportedly, major industrial firms have adopted it with success.

EXPONENTIAL SMOOTHING—A SYSTEM TO PREPARE
WEEKLY OPERATIONAL FORECASTS

Day-to-day warehouse replenishment can use a relatively simple formula, called exponential smoothing, for the forecast of sales from the warehouse by products. In conjunction with the use of an electronic computer, the formula has an advantage over comparable approaches in that its use normally requires less memory space.

The forecast for the period i, $\bar{x}_i$, of the volume of sale x_i of a product is prepared with the use of the following formula:

$$\bar{X}_i + 1 = \alpha x_i + (1 - \alpha)\bar{x}_i$$

Thus the new forecast is the weighted sum of the last value of the variable and its forecast. If $\alpha = .3$, the sales next week are expected to be 30% of this week's sales figure plus 70% of the forecast for next week. Experimentation with the formula indicates that under certain circumstances the prediction will be biased. If the bias is due to a systematic trend in the time series, the forecasting will lag behind the trend. The formula can be adjusted for the trend factor as follows:

$$\bar{X} + 1 = \alpha x_i + (1 - \alpha)(2\bar{x}_i - \bar{x}_i - 1)$$

The last term contains the weighted difference between the last two forecasts as the adjustment for trend. If $\alpha = .2$, then the value of the forecast of next week's sales equals the sum of 20% of the current sales and 80% of the latest forecast and change in the two latest forecasts. Other similar adjustments of the smoothing formula can be developed to improve the forecast over seasonal and cyclical fluctuations.

The value of the smoothing constant affects the rapidity with which the forecasted time series adjusts to changes in the direction of the actual sales data. For some values of α, the forecast is very sensitive to changes of the data; for others it is insensitive. There are no quick ways to determine the best value of α for the best forecast of sales of a product. This problem becomes magnified when the use of historical data introduces another smoothing factor into the formula for which a best value also has to be determined. Simulation of the forecast over several years' sales history and a comparison of each simulated forecast with the actual data will indicate the consequence of different values of α on the forecast.

Which value of α (or values of several smoothing constants) should

---

[2] See for instance Gordon B. Carson, ed., *Production Handbook*, 2nd Ed. (New York: The Ronald Press Company, 1959), pp. 214, 215.

then be adopted? The answer depends on the measure of effectiveness used for the evaluation of the forecast. Such measures can be

The standard error of the forecast
The cumulative error over a fixed number of forecast periods
The average length of a biased sequence of forecasts
The maximum length of biased sequences.

Experimentation with several possible values of the smoothing constants over the sales history of numerous products will require the handling of a large volume of data and computations. Computer codes to perform these calculations can easily be written and even moderate size computers can perform the required calculations relatively rapidly. The computer codes developed for the experimentation remain useful parts of an operating system, even after the values of the smoothing constants have been determined. The measure of effectiveness of the forecasts of each product can continuously be updated and the simulation code can be used to recompute the values of the smoothing constants whenever the measure reaches certain predetermined limiting values.

OTHER MATHEMATICAL AND COMPUTER APPROACHES TO FORECASTING

One interesting use of the moving average approach was developed by the National Bureau for Economic Research. The approach consists of the analysis of economic time series to identify the following components:

Trend
Business Cycles
Seasonal Fluctuations
Random Movements

Historical data (for five or ten years) are entered into a computer routine of various moving averages and other relatively simple mathematical calculations, and the separate time series of the above factors are printed out. This information can be very useful as a basis of, say, the exponential smoothing approach. The cyclical trend and seasonal factors can be used as "base series" about which the actual sales data fluctuate.

A computer code was recently developed for the Radio Corporation of America to forecast the outcome of the latest presidential election. Reportedly, the mathematics that was the basis of the code represented a complex model of voting behavior. It covered the voting patterns by involved statistical techniques. It apparently was a large scale econometric type model and analysis. In operation, a network of data transmission lines brought last minute information on voting tabulations to a central computer which computed the latest forecast and the odds. It was a large real time system in forecasting and, apparently one that gave the most accurate forecast.

In forecasting, to have a real time system means to be ahead of time hour by hour, or whenever the forecast triggers a new decision. The RCA forecasting method, and for that matter the forecasting methods of the other television networks, foreshadow large scale real time systems. These tabulate sales of products practically by the day in each sales district of a company and prepare reports immediately to initiate actions by the marketing, production and shipping departments. Such systems are not feasible as yet; it would be difficult to justify their economy. But they are within the realm of possibility.

THE LOGISTIC SUPPORT OF MARKETING

It is commonplace to say that marketing management requires the products to be at the point of sale in the required quantities when needed. It is a matter for *good* management to have the right quantities on hand and yet not in excessive amounts. Further, since the production may take place at several geographic locations, the products have to be brought to the point of sale at the least total production and transportation cost. Finally, orders from the points of sale should be scheduled for production at the plants in such a way that the fluctuations of production (over time) should not be excessive.

A properly working administrative system continuously resolves these problems. Mathematical techniques and their routine computer applications have been assisting the movement of the supply to the point of sale.

The three basic logistic problems mentioned above can be restated as follows:

Management of point of sale inventory
Allocation of customer warehouses to supplying plants
Allocation of production over time.

Some mathematical solutions to these problems will be described briefly.

MANAGEMENT OF POINT OF SALE INVENTORY

We can consider point of sale inventory either from the standpoint of the retailer or from that of the manufacturer-wholesaler. The retailer's inventory consists of the items on display, a small-back-room inventory, and the warehouse stock from which the retailing units are supplied.

The size of display inventory depends on the total useful floor space (or shelf space) available. A department's inventory is the result of the floor space allocated to the department and the use of the space within the department for the display of different merchandise. Economic analysis teaches us a simple rule for space allocation and one that is grounded on mathematical principles of differential calculus: Allocate as much space to each line (or department) so that the net return on the last unit of each should be equal. In addition, of course, the total space allocated cannot exceed the space available. If a unit of space, say a foot width on a display gondola were as valuable as any other unit of space, and if net return on the merchandise were easy to calculate, the implementation of this rule would be very simple. Empirical studies of consumer behavior in self-service stores, however, indicate that a complex interaction exists between location, shelf width, depth, jointness of purchase of certain products, and other factors. Once a more complete model of a store is developed, the display rules become more complex. A detailed model and continuous evaluation and readjustment of allocated space is conceivable with the use of a computer, but the practical value of such an approach over the present continuous experimentation remains to be proven.

Back room inventory normally is a back-up for shelf replenishment. Problems with the handling and moving of such inventory usually override the importance of quantitative considerations. For this reason, these inventories will be neglected in the discussion here. Retail warehouse inventory replenishment will not be discussed separately. It is similar in principle to wholesale warehouse replenishment.

Warehouse inventory management (either wholesale or retail) requires the continuous forecasting of sales and the determination of reorder quantities and safety stocks. Good inventory management normally uses some mathematical formula for determining the least cost reorder quantities and a satellite formula for determining the minimum necessary safety stock levels.

A large number of different formulae exist for the computation of reorder and safety stock quantities. These formulae were designed to satisfy the needs of many different warehousing and reordering conditions. A formula that best applies in the case of a single warehouse may not perform as well for a chain of regional and customer warehouses. Economies can be achieved by applying the correct formula or, in some cases, a simple one that approximates the quantities that could be computed with the use of the correct but complex formula.

In some instances, correct formulae cannot be established at all, or only after extensive mathematical research. This is true in the case of reordering for each member of a chain of warehouses which can replenish each other and also draw from several production centers according to some complicated management rules. In order to find the best formula or formulae, computers are used with codes that simulate the requirement pattern of each warehouse in the chain. Various safety stock and replenishment formulae are then tried out on simulated operating data. The formulae which result in the "best operating pattern" will then be implemented in practice. The criterion for "best operating pattern" may be the least total inventory cost for the system, an upper limit for the frequency of back orders, or some other more specific condition. Often the computer has to be instructed to select the best set of reorder and safety stock rules from several that were programmed into the simulation runs because the volume of data generated in the simulation may be too great for manual review and analysis.

The following example illustrates the use of an inventory reorder formula and indicates its application. This formula is particularly useful in a system which replenishes warehouse inventories from a central warehouse or plant. Orders placed by the warehouses normally are processed on a weekly or semi-weekly basis and require a few weeks' replenishment lead time. The lead time is usually fairly constant (in terms of number of weeks elapsed) and is the sum of data processing time, loading, transit and unloading time. Sales forecasts are prepared weekly either for the week during which the items ordered will be available in the warehouse, or for all weeks over and immediately beyond the order lead period. Table I illustrates the forecasting and reordering procedure. Orders are

Table 1

FORECASTING AND REORDERING PROCEDURE FOR A WAREHOUSE
Lead Period : Five Weeks

Calendar week	23	24	25	26	27	28*	29	30	31
	23	24	25	26	27	28			
	24	25	26	27	28	29			
Forecast revised	25	26	27	28	29	30			
for week	26	27	28	29	30	31			
	27	28	29	30	31	32			
New forecast and order									
for week	28	29	30	31	32	33			
Sales data available									
for week	27	28	29	30	31	32			

* Current week.

placed on the basis of the new forecast of warehouse sales and the latest revised forecast of sales over the lead period. The error of the sales forecast is known up to the previous week.

Let us denote the most recently prepared forecast for j week as x_j and the order placed for that week as y_j; the difference

$$x_j - y_j$$

is the expected amount of addition to or subtraction from the week's expected opening inventory as we see it now. If the week's opening inventory is zero, the above difference is either the week's ending inventory or the amount to be back ordered.

Errors of the forecast can be tabulated and a frequency distribution can be obtained. The variability of the error will be measured by σ, the standard deviation of the frequency distribution. We shall assume that the error has a normal probability distribution, but the argument and the reorder and safety stock formulae do not depend on this assumption.

If I_0 designates the opening inventory when the order is placed n weeks hence, the quantity to order, y_n, can be obtained from the following formula

$$y_n = x_0 - y_0 + x_i - y_1 + \ldots + x_{n-1} - y_{n-1} - I_0$$
$$+ x_n + k\sqrt{n+1}\,\sigma$$

The top line of the formula is a computation of the expected back order for, or expected inventory of, the product during the lead period. The second line contains the latest requirement forecast for the delivery week, and the desired safety stock level.

The safety stock factor, $k\sqrt{n+1}\,\sigma$ requires further explanation. It depends on the relative magnitude of

the unit cost of holding unsold inventory and
the unit cost of a back order.

This ratio is embedded in the value of the quantity k. Tabulated values of k are shown in Table 2 for various ratios of the two costs. In this table, c_1

Table 2

VALUES OF SAFETY STOCK FACTOR k

$\dfrac{c_1}{c_1 + c_2}$	k
.01	2.33
.05	1.65
.10	1.28
.25	.67
.50	0.00

designates the unit holding cost and c_2 the unit back order cost. The left hand column expresses the unit holding cost as a percentage of the total unit cost.

The following example illustrates the use of the formula in conjunction with the use of some forecasting method, say exponential smoothing. Let us assume that the lead period between placing an order and the arrival of the order is five weeks, or $n = 5$. Warehouse inventory of each item is reviewed and orders are placed weekly. Furthermore, in order to avoid the placement of a very small order, a minimum order quantity is established. At each review, the reorder quantity is computed. If this is less than the minimum quantity, nothing is ordered; if it is more than the minimum quantity, the computed number of units are ordered. (NOTE that according to the formula for y_n, the "reorder" can be a negative quantity. This will happen whenever the opening stock plus the orders already placed exceed the latest forecasted requirements and desired safety stock level.)

Table 3 presents the illustration. The "report" above the horizontal line is the output of a weekly computer run for one product. It contains

Table 3

SAMPLE COMPUTATION OF REORDER QUANTITY

PRODUCT		207RT90		COST RATIO	10%
OPENING INVENTORY		50		SIGMA	10
SAFETY STOCK		30			
MINIMUM ORDER		20			
Week	28	29	30	31	32	33
Forecast	100	110	130	131	120	90
Order	110	125	140	150	100	45*
Difference	-10	-15	-10	-20	-20	

1. Safety stock is computed by the computer and remains unchanged until either COST RATIO or SIGMA changes.

   Compute k $\sqrt{n+1}\,\sigma = 1.28 \times 2.45 \times 10$ 31.36.   Round to 30.
2. Compute cumulative difference (top row of y_n): -35

3. Compute

	Opening inventory	-50
	Safety stock	30
	Forecast for week 33	90
	Cum. difference	-35
	Order	45

1. The forecast of sales for each of the weeks in the lead period and for the delivery week
2. The orders placed earlier with the central warehouse for each week in the lead period
3. Opening inventory
4. The cost ratio $c_1/c_1 + c_2$
5. The error of the weekly forecast, σ
6. Minimum order quantity
7. Safety stock

Other information could also be in the report, such as the value of the smoothing constant (or constants) if exponential smoothing is used; the value of the measure of forecasting efficiency and its limiting value; data on sales quotas over the period or percent accomplishment; last year's sales figures and quotas in the same period; accumulated sales figures up to the period within the span of the forecast. Below the line is the computation. The resulting order quantity (if larger than the minimum) is centered in the "Order placed" row and is starred.

In order to prepare the report, the computer performs the following tasks weekly:

1. Reads the latest sales data (last line on Table 1)
2. Computes the new forecast (column 28 on Table 1)
3. Computes order quantity
4. Prints out report (Top of Table 3) on-line or off-line
5. Prepares any other required information

Additional work is performed either weekly or less frequently:

1. Check of forecast error
2. Recomputation of the alpha factors, or new estimation of the annual forecast, its monthly apportioning, and the new error limits
3. Preparation of monthly summary data

In practice, the procedure is not as simple as it is presented here, but the report, which is the focus of attention from the marketing standpoint, will be similar.

DISTRIBUTION PROBLEMS

Shipments to and from warehouses may be organized by the transportation department of a company. Often, however, the organization and determination of least cost shipment patterns are the responsibility of the marketing department. The contribution of linear programming to the determination of the least cost shipping pattern has been recognized for some time. In the past, however, it was found that the order of magnitude of problems associated with the computation of shipping schedules often defied the capability of even the largest computers.

A company that produces numerous different products in several plants and ships them to tens or hundreds of warehouses and ultimately to a large number of customers has a very large computational problem. To date, the best computer codes can handle only up to about 500 constraints on the shipping pattern simultaneously. Tremendous as this code is, it may be insufficient for many purposes. Various ways are available to resolve the problem of size.

1. Aggregation of variables and reduction of the number of constraints
2. Division of the problem into subproblems of manageable size

3. Development of larger computers
4. New computational codes

The first two items contain pitfalls. Specifically, they either do not lead to an optimum solution or they do not provide the information necessary for a real time system. The third item is subject to future developments in computer technology. It should be noted that the larger a computer, the more expensive it is per hour of operation, but the cost of computing solu-

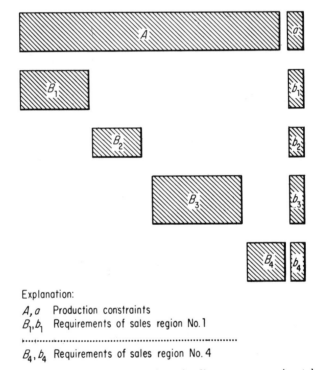

Explanation:

A, a Production constraints
B_1, b_1 Requirements of sales region No. 1

B_4, b_4 Requirements of sales region No. 4

Fig. 1. Schematic representation of a linear programming tableau with special structure.

tions to a problem is reduced with the increase in computer size. For example, the computation of a solution to a linear program of modest size (70 equations, 120 variables) required approximately three to four hours on the first generation of commercially available computers eight to ten years ago. The same problem was recently computed on a new large scientific computer with four different optimizers in a few minutes.

New developments can be reported on the fourth item. A revolution in linear programming has occurred within the last two years that may result in entirely new ways of computing solutions, particularly to problems of special nature. Distribution problems, joined with the allocation of the production capacity of several plants among products, usually fall into this category. To the reader who is familiar with linear programming, Figure 1 illustrates such problems.[1] It is a schematic tableau of the arrangement of the coefficients of a linear programming matrix. The shaded areas contain the location of the parameters; the blank area contains zeros only.

A new computational procedure known as the "decomposition algorithm" can take advantage of the special configuration of the numbers in the linear programming tableau. This procedure can be interpreted as the logical means for subdividing a large problem into manageable sections. There is, however, a very important difference between this approach and those which fall under item 2 in the previous listing. The decomposition approach does separate the smaller linear programming problems, identified with the letters B and b and referred to as Sales Region Requirements, and solves each problem separately. In addition, however, it introduces the individual solutions into a "master program" which checks the feasibility of the individual solutions against the quantities of resources to be used in production (the A, a part of the tableau); provides an interim evaluation of the solution to the subproblems, and allocates bonuses to and penalties upon the use by the subproblems of certain resources used in production. The subproblems are solved once again with reference to the penalties and bonuses, and the process is repeated until an optimum solution is attained. All this, of course, takes place inside the computer.

Since the use of the decomposition approach subdivides a large problem into smaller problems which can be solved on existing computers, it is reasonable to anticipate an expanded use of linear programming in the area of marketing distribution planning and the development of real time administrative systems built around the central computer code. In view of the discussion of real time systems presented in the preceding section on warehouse inventory management, systems built around programming techniques could become very effective.

ALLOCATION OF AN ADVERTISING BUDGET

Research effort is currently being expanded to find the right structure of the problems associated with the allocation of the advertising budget and to develop sufficient experience with the use of the results. A real time marketing data system, however, is conceptually feasible and should become a reality in the foreseeable future. A brief review will be presented of

---

[1] To the reader not familiar with the representation of linear programming problems the review of any of the numerous textbooks and popular articles in technical and business periodicals is recommended. The space allocated here does not permit a detailed discussion of this well treated topic.

some elements of such a system. The focus of attention is the marketing of consumer oriented differentiated products which are subject to promotional effort and which are sold on a competitive market.

The example of floor space allocation can be paraphrased to apply for the allocation of a fixed budget (= floor space) to the use of various media (= product lines or departments). The mathematical model of marginal analysis or differential calculus can be introduced here also for the solution of elementary models. In reality, the appropriate functions which describe consumer response to advertising are not easy to obtain. Two approaches to this empirical procedure will be noted.

One approach establishes a single mathematical function for the consumer response to the advertising of each individual product by advertising medium. Such functions indicate that when a product is promoted, sales increase at a rapid rate until a plateau is reached. From then on the marginal return on the advertising dollar falls. The parameters of such functions can be estimated from empirical observation and the rule for allocation of the advertising budget on the margin to each product and advertising medium can be applied. We can tag this as the "deterministic" approach to the problem.

A more elaborate approach, which we may term "stochastic," studies the probabilities that the buyer of a brand name product will switch from the preferred brand to a competing brand. With the knowledge of these probabilities, called "transition probabilities," the expected results of an advertising campaign or a test marketing experiment can be projected. The transition probabilities are used to compute the percent of those who, after all brand switching took place, will buy the promoted (or researched) product.

The advertising expenditure in this example is very similar in its effect to the budgetary deficit which "primes the pump" of the economy, and the transition probabilities resemble the income multiplier.

The continued application of the stochastic approach (or its more elaborate versions) requires the use of data on consumer behavior. Such data are collected and, indeed, their interpretation might benefit from theoretical models of this sort. The use of large displays (matrices) of transition probabilities also requires the use of electronic computers. Once reliable models and reliable data are brought together in a computer for continuous analysis, the step to a real time system in conjunction with continued returns of data on consumer behavior will not be difficult to make.

Business management generally cannot choose competitive strategies that will enable the firm to earn maximum net profits—because the necessary "marketing intelligence" is simply lacking. Because much of the needed information is now not generally available to management, the choice of what seems to be the best competitive strategy results in much lower than maximum net profits.

THE DIFFERENTIATED PRODUCT

When the marketing expenditures of any single differentiated product are being increased, two separate but related phenomena are typically encountered: (see Figure 1).

1. Market share soon tends to increase at a decreasing rate—flattening out and approaching (but never reaching) 100 percent as its upper limit.

MEASURING THE PRODUCTIVITY OF

MARKETING EXPENDITURES

2. Net profits reach a maximum, then decrease, then even become negative.

Together, these two relationships pose an obvious dilemma for management in choosing competitive strategies, i.e., in planning what market share to reach for in order to attain maximal net profits rather than mere survival:

1. A competitive strategy aimed at getting a high and stable market share for a differentiated product may require such a high level of marketing effort that net profits are much lower than maximum.

2. A competitive strategy striving for maximal net profits may require such a low level of marketing effort that the differentiated product has a low and unstable market share and is exceedingly vulnerable to competitive pressures.

In reality, strategic planning proceeds in a manner different from both these over-simplified alternatives, not only because the actual market situations are much more complex, but also because *none* of the seemingly rudimentary information involved in the two functional relationships illustrated in Figure 1 is, in fact, generally available to management. Neither the market share nor the net profit productivity of the firm's marketing efforts for any single differentiated product are generally

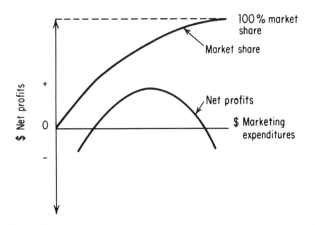

Fig. 1. Product A market share and net profit as functions of marketing expenditures.

known. The complexity of the competitive situation and of the required strategic planning, and the lack of the necessary marketing intelligence interact in their cumulative effects. Management is more or less in the dark in difficult and complex competitive situations and almost inescapably engages in strategic planning that results in profits less than the maximum.

THE TYPICAL FIRM

"The Differentiated Product" was discussed up to now. But most firms are multi-product firms; the typical business manufactures and/or markets a fairly large number (sometimes several thousands) of separate and distinct differentiated products, each one of which shares a different market with competing products of other firms. For example, this is obviously so for Procter and Gamble, General Foods, General Electric, Eli Lilly, Scott Paper Company, etc. In fact, it is hard to think of a firm which manufactures and/or markets only *one* differentiated product.

But in the multi-product firm, that part of the total marketing outlay which is currently spent on each separate and distinct differentiated product is not generally known to management. In the typical multi-product firm, alleged single product marketing cost figures now available to management are patently inaccurate and grossly misleading for strategic planning. It is actually very difficult, expensive, and sometimes even impossible to obtain accurate marketing costs for each separate and distinct differentiated (branded and advertised) product in the typical multiproduct firm—even on a one-time basis, let alone recurrently.

Some important variable marketing costs, not true "joint" costs, are incurred in common for several products, e.g., selling costs when the salesman sells the entire line, advertising and sales promotion which benefits many products, etc. Many of these marketing costs which are incurred in common are not allocated to individual products at all. More frequently, on the other hand, many marketing costs which are incurred in common are arbitrarily and illogically allocated to individual products by some rule of thumb, as for example, on the basis of dollar sales volume. Correct and useful allocations to individual products of variable marketing costs require some sophisticated analytical techniques not used by the typical multi-product firm.

Even an accurate total of the marketing and physical distribution costs for the multi-product business as a whole may not be known to management. Some of the firm's important marketing costs are buried in manufacturing cost figures or in general and administrative cost data, (e.g., storage of finished goods inventories, shipping costs, order-processing costs, transportation costs, etc.). Such hidden marketing costs are not, of course, allocated to individual products.

Individual product dollar gross profit figures either are not regularly available or cannot even be used to make marketing decisions. Where the same product is manufactured in several different plants with varying unit manufacturing costs in each plant, a unilateral production planning decision can change a company's cost of goods sold, and therefore its gross profits, substantially, even though no change in marketing or in selling price has occurred.

Consequently, net profit contribution figures for individual differentiated products in a multi-product firm either are not available at all, or are substantially inaccurate and misleading because of the deficiencies in marketing cost and gross profit figures.

Moreover, accurate market share figures for each separate differentiated product sold by a multi-product firm are usually not available because of the high cost of the necessary marketing intelligence activities. At best, market share figures are approximate estimates of the demand for groups of the firm's products. Thus, for example, it appears that National Dairy Products does not know accurately its brand's share of the fluid milk market in any given city.

We see that whatever strategic planning may be done by the marketing management of the typical firm with the objective of maximizing net profits is certainly performed in a marketing intelligence void. But, even if the typical multi-product firm did have accurate current marketing costs, net profit and market share information for each differentiated product, management would still be operating largely in the dark in planning for its profit maximizing competitive strategy. This point can best be demonstrated by an actual case study below of one corporation which did acquire such information.

THE LEADING FIRM

One year and considerable research dollars later, a large and progressive corporation was in a position substantially to improve what had originally been a much better than average marketing intelligence system. The newly available information for one of the corporation's sales divisions showed management how wide of the profit maximization mark were the results of the divisional sales management's past competitive strategies. Some of the results of the new marketing intelligence system for this one sales division are summarized in Table 1.

It was a surprise to top marketing management to learn that products K, L, and M were unprofitable, being responsible for a negative marketing profit amounting to 25.9 percent of the Sales Division's total marketing profit contribution.

Management was also unpleasantly surprised when comparisons were made between the distribution of marketing profits, (column 1), market shares (column 2), and the allocations of selling, advertising and sales promotion costs by products (columns 3 and 4). Products A and B brought in 76 percent of the marketing profits, and yet only 27 percent of the advertising and sales promotion outlays and 23 percent of the selling expenses were devoted to these products. Products K, L, and M were responsible for a marketing loss which amounted to almost 26 percent of the Division's total profits, and yet about 35 percent of the advertising and sales promotion effort and 28 percent of the total selling efforts were devoted to those unprofitable products.

There is no apparent logic in the relationships between the market share figures and either profit contributions or marketing expenditures. Products with the highest market shares (B, F, and J) absorb very low shares of total marketing expenditures (3.8 percent at the highest) and are fairly profitable. Products with the lowest market shares, I, E, and C, also generally absorb low proportions of marketing costs, though C is the third most profitable product. The market shares for the three unprofitable products K, L, and M, do not appear to be unduly high, as a possible explanation for their negative profit contribution.

Discovery of the existence of three unprofitable products and the apparently gross mal-distribution of marketing expenditures among products focussed the attention of management on the following specific questions:

Table 1

MARKET SHARE, MARKETING PROFITS AND MARKETING COSTS
FOR PRODUCTS IN ONE SALES DIVISION

Products	% of Total $ Marketing Profit Contribution* 1	Market Share 2	% of Total $ Expenditures on Selected Mkt. Expenses	
			Advertising and Sales Promotion 3	Selling 4
Totals, Sales Div.....	100.0	—	100.0	100.0
A................	59.2	22.6	26.2	19.6
B................	16.8	85.0	1.0	3.8
C................	15.8	7.1	15.3	13.7
D................	11.8	27.0	3.8	5.2
E................	7.8	4.9	1.2	4.6
F................	4.8	88.0	0.3	3.0
G................	4.5	45.3	15.0	15.7
H................	3.3	60.0	0.7	3.5
I................	1.4	2.7	1.6	2.5
J................	0.5	46.0	0.2	0.4
Subtotal........	125.9	—	65.3	72.0
K................	−5.7	24.1	7.1	8.8
L................	−8.8	15.2	6.9	4.0
M................	−11.4	12.6	20.7	15.2
Subtotal........	−25.9	—	34.7	28.0

* Marketing profit contribution = $ gross profits − $ allocated marketing costs.

1. By how much (if any) would the profit contribution of the most profitable products A, B, or C be increased if there were a given dollar increase in their marketing expenditures?
2. How would such an increase in marketing effort affect the strategy of competitors—would it result in a viable and stable market share?
3. By how much (if any) would the net losses of unprofitable products K, L, and M be reduced if there were a given dollar decrease in their marketing expenditure?
4. How would such a reduction in marketing effort affect competitive reaction—would it result in a viable and stable market share?
5. By how much (if any) would the marketing profit contributions of profitable products A, B, and C be affected by a change in the mar-

keting expenditures on unprofitable products K, L, M, etc.—and vice versa, i.e., it is necessary to compete with a full line?

MARGINAL PRODUCTIVITY

To answer these questions, management needs to know the marginal or incremental marketing profit contributions and the marginal changes in market shares that are associated with changes in the amount of the marketing effort for each differentiated product. In other words, management needs to have information of the kind illustrated in Figure 1 for *each* differentiated product A through M.

Added effort spent on product A may not bring in the same increment of profit contribution or market share as the same amount of additional effort expended on product B. Conversely, reduced expenditure on product K may not affect its profit contribution or market share to the same extent as a similar reduction on product L. Changes in the level of the marketing expenditure on different products will result in increasing or decreasing incremental returns but at different rates for different products.

But another source of complexity is that each differentiated product's marketing expenditures comprise a mix of different kinds of marketing effort; e.g., personal selling, various types of advertising, sales promotion, point-of-purchase display materials, technical sales engineering, and many other kinds. To know the incremental productivity of any single differentiated product's total marketing effort it is necessary to know the separate marginal productivity of every single (important) element of that product's marketing mix. What is the marginal productivity of advertising expenditures on product A? of personal selling effort? of point-of-purchase materials?

To answer the above questions, it was necessary to add new dimensions to the company's marketing intelligence system. To estimate the separate influence on profits of each element of, let us say, product A's marketing mix—while "holding constant" the effects of all other variables—the use of a computer and fairly sophisticated multivariate correlation analysis techniques was required. Although attention is focussed on the statistical techniques and experiments employed, the entire undertaking would not have been practical without the availability and use for data processing of a medium size computer.

STATISTICAL ANALYSIS

Something beyond a relatively simple linear regression analysis was necessary because:

1. The Company, like most other companies, had in the past allocated

many important elements of its marketing budget, such as national advertising, to individual products in some fairly fixed ratio to sales. This meant that while sales were a function of marketing total expense, at the same time some marketing expenses were a function of sales.

2. It was hypothesized that with increasing marketing expenditures there is a diminishing return (see Figure 1). Accordingly it appeared necessary either to rely on an unusual interpretation of linear regression results, or to use some type of more complex non-linear model (by introducing quadratic elements into the models).

Working with data for product *A* first on an experimental basis, 15 different multiple regression equations or models were tried out in 15 separate computer runs—each model comprised of as many as 20 variables. These variables represented each element of the product's marketing mix such as advertising of various types, promotion, and personal selling; various demographic factors, or consumer characteristics; and finally, measures of competitive marketing efforts. For each of these 20 or so variables, readings were taken in approximately 100 sales territories, in order to take advantage of the "uncontrolled experiments" resulting from the "random" mix of many types of marketing effort by geographical area.

There were discrepancies and contradictions in the results of these different models, but the most productive of these 15 different models turned out to be "difference" equations, i.e., all the variables were redefined and recalculated from the original data to represent the *change* from one year to the next. It was, therefore, hypothesized that the *change* in a marketing expense variable within a territory from one year to the next is responsible for a systematic change in sales and profits within that same area. The results for some of these marketing expense variables are shown in Table 2.

Table 2

MEASUREMENTS OF THE INCREMENTAL PROFIT PRODUCTIVITY OF
SEVERAL TYPES OF MARKETING EXPENDITURE FOR PRODUCT A

Marketing Expenditure, Variable Number	Time Period 1 (Year 2 − Year 1)		Time Period 2 (Year 3 − Year 2)	
	Regression Coefficient	"t" Value*	Regression Coefficient	"t" Value*
#12	$ 54.87	2.42	$ 102.73	2.01
15	−171.63	−2.34	−59.95	−2.89
11	38.66	2.60	−328.29	−1.99
13	−74.71	−2.03	283.54	2.87
14	313.82	2.05	−750.48	−2.12

* A "t" value of 2 or more is considered statistically significant; t = the regression coefficient divided by the standard error.

INCREMENTAL PROFIT RESULTS

The "regression coefficients" in Table 2 may be interpreted as representing the additional or incremental dollars of profit that would result from an addition of "X" dollars on any one type of marketing expenditure or effort for product A—everything else affecting product A profits remaining the same. In any one time period, the different elements of the marketing mix had markedly different effects on product A profits. Thus, in the first period, an additional expenditure of "X" dollars on variable No. 14 had a positive effect on profits of $313.82, while the same additional expenditure on variable 15 would reduce profits by $171.63.

Two of the expense variables, 12 and 15, seem to affect product A profits in the same direction in both of these time periods; 12 had a positive effect on profits and 15 had a negative effect. The three other marketing effort variables, 11, 13 and 14, show seemingly changed effects on profits as between the two time periods; showing a positive effect in one period and a negative effect in the other (or vice versa).

There were, of course, numerous possible hypotheses that appeared reasonable in seeking an explanation for the change in the behavior of certain marketing effort variables in the different models and time periods. Two of these hypotheses that seemed more reasonable to management are outlined below:

A. In responding to evolving changes in the consumer and to changes in competitive efforts, management consciously changes product A marketing mix from one time period to the next. Changes in product A marketing mix relative to changes in competitive marketing mix may result in some of the product A marketing cost variables shifting from increasing returns in one time period to decreasing returns in another (or vice versa). There may also be a dynamic effect from significant changes in marketing effort or in marketing mix per se; as in fashion, new product design, etc., a change in product A marketing mix or in the level of one of the marketing efforts may increase its marginal productivity simply because it is new.

B. A second hypothesis is that the relationship between some of the "independent" marketing cost variables and product A profits (or market share) is curvilinear rather than linear—such as the net profit curve in Figure 1—and the data for the different time periods estimate or "cover" different portions of these curves. For example, consider variable 11. It appears plausible to hypothesize that time period 1 estimated the rising portion of such a curve while time period 2 estimated the falling portion of the relationship illustrated by the lower curve in Figure 1 (although it is not intended to conclude that the average change from period 1 to period 2 represents a uniform change in that variable for all market areas).

Assuming that both of these hypotheses were applicable to the statistical estimates of the productivity of the various forms of product A marketing effort (shown in Table 2), the following recommendations were made to management:

1. Increase expenditures on marketing efforts 12, 13.
2. Decrease expenditures on marketing efforts, 15, 11, 14.

Even with the above positive and specific recommendations, however (and similar recommendations for other products), management still did not have sufficient quantitative marketing intelligence to plan a competitive strategy likely to result in maximal profits:

1. The statistical analysis indicated the directions of change in the allocation of product A's marketing budget but not the magnitudes. Rapidly diminishing returns might be encountered.

2. The statistical estimate (i.e., the regression equation) probably holds only within, say, a 10 to 20 percent change of the variables and represents only static conditions.

3. It is possible that some effort variables showed increasing returns because competition had not been sufficiently aware of the territorial differences in the company's marketing efforts (on which the statistical analysis was based) to take retaliatory action.

CONTROLLED MARKET EXPERIMENTS

It appeared that controlled local market experiments could provide the most conclusive answers to these and similar problems, short of a sustained major change in the national marketing program. Thus by market experiments it is possible to avoid or reduce the degree of extrapolation otherwise necessary with respect to time, range of expenditure and competitive responses.

Different experimental designs were used for the different types of marketing expenditures or combinations of marketing expenditures. One of the experimental designs is shown in Table 3. With this design, it was possible to conduct the two experiments for variables 12 and 13 simultaneously in the same territories and cities, and to determine the linear effects and the quadratic, or diminishing return effects, separately for each variable. Moreover, the design made it possible to determine the interactions between the linear and quadratic effects of the two variables.

In other words, the experiment yielded (1) direct measures of the "main" effects, i.e., of the extent to which marketing efforts 12 and 13 can be deemed to be operating independently on profits, (2) measures of the extent to which they are complementing or reinforcing one another in producing profits, and (3) specific measures of diminishing returns.*

Some of the marketing variables were advertising expenditures where the difficulty of matching treatments (expenditures) with results (sales and profits) usually precludes controlled market experiments. Where predominantly non-local media, i.e., "national" media, are used, the sales territory or city cannot be the experimental unit for most media employed as in the case of the experiment described above. In this case, there was a single exception where one type of local media was involved, and this class of media was used as a basis for an experimental program.

ADVERTISING EXPERIMENTS

Contrary to the experimental design covering the other types of expenditures shown in Table 3, which was a one time period experiment, the advertising experiments involved the application of several treatments in sequence over time.

The time periods used in the advertising experiments were chosen on

Table 3

EXPERIMENTAL DESIGN FOR VARIABLES 12 AND 13

Territory	City 1 Variable #12	#13	City 2 Variable #12	#13	City 3 Variable #12	#13
1................	Base	Base	Base	Med.	Base	High
2................	Med.	Base	Med.	Med.	Med.	High
3................	High	Base	High	Med.	High	High
4................	Base	Base	Base	Med.	Base	High
5................	Med.	Base	Med.	Med.	Med.	High
6................	High	Base	High	Med.	High	High
7................	Base	Base	Base	Med.	Base	High
8................	Med.	Base	Med.	Med.	Med.	High
9................	High	Base	High	Med.	High	High

Base or zero level corresponding to present national average
Medium a moderate increase above the base level
High an increase above medium level equal to difference between moderate
    increase level and the base level

---

* Information on interactions were not obtainable from the correlation procedure but only from an experimental design such as the one used. Statistical tests of significance were used to determine the reliability of each of the measured effects.

the basis of the following criteria; long enough for the designated treatments to take effect, long enough to minimize the problems of lags in response, and long enough to minimize the residual or carry over effects from treatments applied in a previous period. However, one of the main advantages of the experimental design used was the possibility of estimating fairly readily the residual or carry over effects. That is, it was possible to estimate separately the effect of a given level of advertising after excluding the carry over effect of the level of advertising used during the previous period.

The results of the advertising experiments satisfactorily answered the question as to whether there were very small diminishing returns or sharply diminishing returns. Additionally, the advertising experiments, together with the results of the statistical correlation analysis, also provided other insights into the productivity of advertising expenditures.

The same correlation analysis for product A—some of the results were shown in Table 2—also yielded regression coefficients for *competitive* advertising of +23.65 in time period 1 and −70.65 in time period 2. The advertising experiments also showed similar puzzling changes in productivity for product *A* advertising versus competitive advertising.

A reasonable explanation appeared to be the assumption that each product *A* or competitive advertisement performed two functions: it advertised brand and product type. Thus, for relatively small decreases in competitive advertising, product *A* sales increased (everything else being equal); and, conversely, when competitive advertising increases slightly, product *A* sales will decrease. But for *large* decreases in competitive advertising, the effect of this decrease on product type purchases becomes noticeable; consumers buy less of both product *A* and its principal competitors and presumably shift to substitute products (and every group of competitive differentiated products has a more or less closely substitutable group of other products).

The advertising experiments utilizing non-national media also indicated significantly more sharply diminishing returns from any one "issue" of an advertising medium containing a large number of advertising "messages" (e.g., number of pages of advertising in a newspaper or Sunday supplement) than in another issue of the same medium containing a relatively smaller number of advertising messages. It appears that all advertisers of all products may encounter diminishing returns as the total volume of advertising messages in any one issue of an advertising medium increases substantially.

CUSTOMERS AND TERRITORIES

A marketing intelligence system that develops information with regard to products even as deeply as has been described above still really treats with only one of the parameters of the complex of problems with which marketing management has to deal; two other principal parameters may be defined as customers and territories.

Consequently, there is a need for planning competitive strategy with the objective of maximizing profits in terms of interrelated products, customers and territories. The further consequence is that a really adequate marketing intelligence system needs to provide interrelated information with regard to products, customers and territories.

REAL TIME AND MAXIMAL NET PROFITS

Obviously, a complete marketing intelligence system which takes into account all relevant parameters in sufficient depth requires large resources devoted to research; but much time necessarily elapses between the initiation of research and the completion of information in a form useful for management decision making. Of these two limitations, real time is the more important factor, and here electronic data processing and similar developments are of great assistance. While it is at present not yet possible for a truly adequate marketing intelligence system to keep current with fast moving strategic developments in the market, still such marketing intelligence does help management to plan competitive strategies that result in more nearly maximal net profits.

PROFIT FUNCTIONS

Upon completion of the marketing experiments and of the statistical analyses of the significance of the results, the marketing intelligence operation moved from the experimental model to the national or company-wide projection; and to the generation of a profit framework. Expressed most succinctly, this final overall analytical step required the development of an equation which expressed profit as a function of the market effort variables that were explicitly treated in the correlation analysis and in the market experiments.

This last analytical step enabled management to arrive at reasonably specific answers to questions such as the following: (1) what is the optimum size and (2) what is the optimum mix of product A's marketing budget? These two questions were answered by application of the following principle: Expand whatever type of effort is yielding the greatest additional returns until diminishing returns sets in to an extent where it pays to begin concentrating on some other form of effort. The answers had a large pay-off in terms of more nearly maximal net profits.

chapter five | *Borge M. Christensen and J. R. Greene*

Continued survival of a firm in an increasingly competitive market environment requires a sound program of new product offerings. Those companies which have been able to maintain a steady stream of improved products, in timely anticipation of customer needs, not only have survived but also normally have prospered.

Recognizing this fact, during recent times more and more dollars have been invested in research and development efforts in the laboratories to insure that business enterprises will be well stocked with promising new ideas. However, hard experience has shown that the mere generation of product ideas is not sufficient to guarantee commercial success. There also must be a well integrated approach to the planning, scheduling, and controlling of new product programs.

Although the elements which are part of any new product program are

PLANNING, SCHEDULING, AND CONTROLLING THE LAUNCHING OF A NEW PRODUCT VIA CPM

discussed extensively in the literature,* little has been provided in the way of a systematic methodology which will assist marketing managers in answering such questions as:

What is the detailed schedule of activities to complete the launching from beginning to end at minimum cost and time? If a delay occurs at

* See, for example: American Management Association, *Developing a Product Strategy,* Management Report Series Number 39, New York, 1959.

Conrad Jones and Samuel C. Johnson, "How to Organize for New Products," *Harvard Business Review,* Vol. 35, No. 3, May-June 1957, pp. 49-62.

Philip Marvin, *Planning New Products* (Cleveland: Penton Publishing Company, 1958).

C. Wilson Randle, "Weighing the Success of New Product Ideas," *Industrial Marketing,* July 1957, pp. 37-40.

a specific point, how much additional effort, time, or cost must be expended to counteract the delay, and where?

What and how much labor in various skills is required at a particular time?

What is the status of the project in relation to the scheduled completion date?

Conceptually, the problems and questions associated with the launching of a new product are analogous to those encountered in a variety of other programs. For example, the construction of an office building requires integration among, and the successful completion of, a great number of interrelated activities within time and cost restraints. Similar situations are found in the development of large-scale military weapon systems or the maintenance shut-down of a refinery.

In recent years competition on one front or another has led to the development of several mathematically oriented techniques which, in conjunction with computers, provide factual project management data.[2] The result has been faster and more accurate answers to questions related to the planning and scheduling of projects, and tighter and more effective control during their implementation.

In the following sections of this article, we shall show how the first of these techniques to incorporate both time and cost information, namely the Critical Path Method, developed by Mauchly Associates Inc., can be applied to the important marketing problem of launching a new product.

FUNDAMENTALS OF THE CRITICAL PATH METHOD

The initial step in applying the Critical Path Method (CPM) involves definition of each activity which must be performed in a project and its relationship to all other activities. This is facilitated by the use of a graphic technique—the arrow diagram. In the diagram, arrows indicate each activity in the project. The presence of an arrow depicts the existence of an activity. Time flows from the arrow's tail to its head. The length of

---

[2] A. Astrachan, "Better Plans Come from Study of Anatomy of an Engineering Job." *Business Week,* March 21, 1959, pp. 60-66.

Børge M. Christensen, "How to Take the Guesswork Out of Project Planning," *The Iron Age,* August 3, 1961, pp. 67-69.

Børge M. Christensen, "The Critical Path Method, an Optimizing Time-Cost Planning and Scheduling Method," General Electric Company Publication CPB 184, July 1961.

D. G. Malcolm, J. H. Roseboom, G. E. Clark and W. Fazar, "Application of a Technique for Research and Development Program Evaluation," *Operations Research,* Vol. 7, 1959, pp. 646-669.

an arrow carries no significance; only relative position of arrows is of interest.

An example of a very simple arrow diagram is shown in Figure 1. A

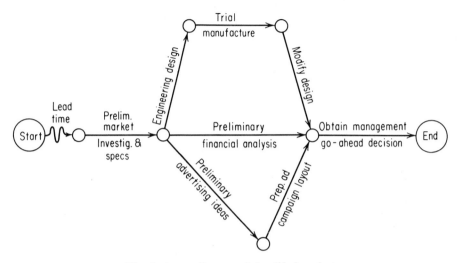

Fig. 1. Arrow diagram of simplified project.

few of the precedence relationships among the activities in this hypothetical project are as follows:

1. "Preliminary Market Investigations and Specifications" can be started following any lead time between the time of planning and the time the project is to be started.
2. "Engineering Design" must be fully completed before "Trial Manufacture" can be started.
3. A "Management Go-Ahead Decision" cannot be made until the financial analysis, the final design, and the layout of the advertising campaign are all fully completed and their results available.

With respect to the number of arrows in the network, it is often found that considerable detail is beneficial and that a gross treatment tends to obscure significant relationships and lessens the advantages of the technique. In practice, therefore, one would expect that each of the arrows in Figure 1 would be replaced by several arrows in series or parallel and with additional head-tail connections. The comprehensiveness of the diagram will depend in large measure on the purposes for which it is drawn.

Construction of the network is facilitated by determining three precedence relationships for each arrow: (1) activities that must immediately precede, (2) activities that immediately follow, and (3) activities that can be performed concurrent with the one under consideration. Proceeding in this manner, one builds the diagram arrow-by-arrow.

Considerable benefit can be derived from the arrow diagramming phase of project planning alone. The concept of the arrow diagram provides an orderly procedure for planning and results in an easily interpreted visual representation of the project scope. Consequently, it is an excellent vehicle for communicating both the macroscopic and microscopic aspects of the program to all project personnel.

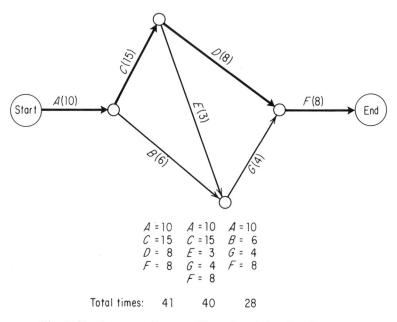

Total times: 41   40   28

Fig. 2. Simple arrow diagram. Normal activity durations are shown on the arrows. The critical path is shown with heavy line arows.

Although the logic of the plan as established in the diagram may be agreeable to all concerned, it does not necessarily represent a feasible or desirable way of implementing the project. Only when time and costs are associated with each of the planned activities will it be possible to evaluate the over-all plan.

For each activity there exists a range of possible completion times. In general, as time is compressed direct costs increase. The shortest time in which an activity can be completed is termed the *crash time;* the minimum direct investment required to complete the activity in the crash time is defined as the *crash cost.* The lowest direct cost to complete the activity is known as the *normal cost;* the corresponding minimum duration constitutes *normal time.* Investments in excess of the crash cost do not contribute to expediting the activity; extensions beyond the normal time only result in additional costs.

The over-all project investment and completion time will vary with the combination of duration times selected for the individual activities. The sum of selected durations along one or more directed sequences of arrows —or paths—will be higher than the sum along all remaining paths. The largest sum indicates the required duration for the entire project, and the activities represented by the arrows along the corresponding path are

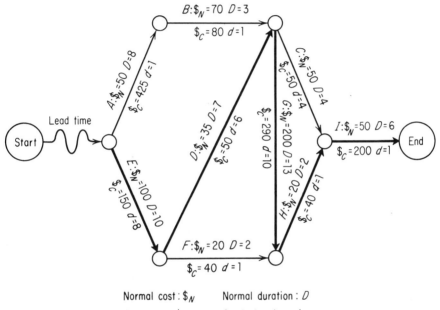

Fig. 3. Simple arrow diagram. Normal and crash time and cost information is given along each arrow. Normal project duration is 38 days at a cost of $595. Fully crashed, the project can be done in 26 days at a minimum direct cost of $920.

critical activities. This is the *critical path*. Thus, in Figure 2 the critical path is comprised of activities A, C, D, and F, since the numerical values associated with these letters represent the longest path through the network.

Since the activity durations along a critical path always add up to the project duration, the non-critical activities will have some leeway for their performance, i.e., the available time is longer than the required time. As critical activities are compressed in order to obtain alternative project durations, the leeway may be absorbed and new critical paths may develop. Conversely, if any critical activity is delayed during implementation of the project, the over-all project duration will be extended by an equal time

As an illustration, a simple arrow diagram is shown in Figure 3. The activities are identified by letters, and normal and crash cost and duration information is given directly on each arrow. Considering only normal

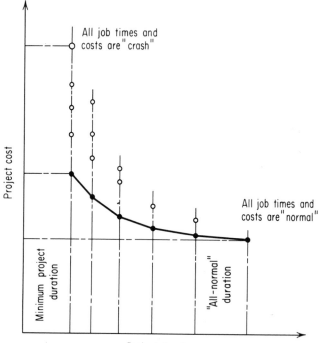

Fig. 4. Typical Direct Project Cost Curve. Between the "all-normal" and minimum project durations exist (in this case) four partly expedited possible project durations. In any real project hundreds of possibilities exist for project duration and cost combinations. The mathematical procedure of CPM determines the lowest direct cost and the associated activity characteristics for each possible project duration. In the figure, the lowest direct costs are connected to form a piecewise linear curve.

times and normal cost, the activities shown with heavy arrows form a critical path with an over-all project duration of 38 days and result in a minimum planned project cost of $595.

If it were desired to complete this project in less time, say 37 days, it could be accomplished only by planning to expedite one of the critical activities E, D, G, H, or I. Expediting non-critical activities (A, B, C, or

F) would not affect the project duration but would only serve to increase project costs.

The least expensive way of expediting this project is accomplished by planning completion of activity D in one day less than the normal time. This is true because the cost to expedite D by one day is $15, which is less than that for any other activity on the critical path.

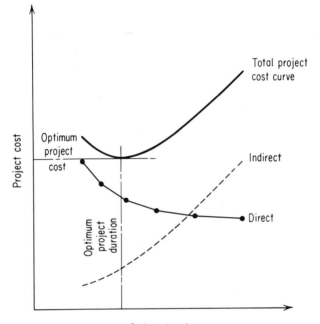

Fig. 5. Typical Total Project Cost Curve. The Total Project Cost Curve is the sum of the Direct Project Cost Curve determined my CPM and the Indirect Project Cost Curve decided upon by the user. The optimum schedule is indicated by the minimum on the Total Project Cost Curve. The associated activity characteristics are found directly from the information produced by the GE CPM program.

To obtain the shortest possible time for the project, it is necessary to compress all of the *critical* activities to their crash points. Doing this, the project duration becomes 26 days and the corresponding cost $920.

Successive compression of project duration and the associated minimum project costs can be shown graphically as a curve with the general shape indicated in Figure 4. The points above the curve indicate alternative, but more expensive, combinations of activity durations to obtain similar over-all project lengths. In most practical projects there will be an astronomical number of project-duration, project-cost combinations.

The least cost curve in Figure 4 is called the Direct Project Cost Curve because only direct costs were considered when the activity time-cost relationships were established.

Computational procedures have been established not only for development of the Direct Project Cost Curve but also for simultaneous calculation of activity characteristics corresponding to each project duration, such as earliest possible start time for an activity, latest allowable finish time, criticality status and amount of leeway, and scheduled cost. Using electronic computers programmed for CPM, one can in a matter of minutes obtain all of this information in a clearly tabulated form. (See Figure 8.)

There are great advantages in selecting from all existing project-duration, project-cost combinations those schedules for which direct cost is the lowest possible amount. In addition, the Direct Project Cost Curve shows the range of *possible* project durations and, therefore, immediately informs the planner of the possibility of meeting a pre-set project deadline.

Although the analyses based on the direct project cost data are useful in themselves, additional benefits can be derived by considering the *indirect* project costs so that the total anticipated cost of implementing the project under alternative schedules can be determined. The sum of direct and indirect costs results in a "U" shaped Total Project Cost Curve. An idealized case is shown in Figure 5.

The Total Project Cost Curve finds many uses. Its primary function is in the selection of that schedule which will require a minimum total investment for its implementation. The project duration corresponding to this minimum is indicated at the bottom point of the "U" shaped curve.

With this brief introduction to the Critical Path Method in terms of its fundamental building blocks, let us consider a hypothetical but realistic application of the method.

IMPLEMENTING THE CRITICAL PATH METHOD: A CASE STUDY

The Victoria Company's Appliance Division has been charged with the responsibility of expanding the company's consumer product line by placing a small appliance on the market. A decision has been made to take advantage of the seasonal demand which occurs for this kind of appliance prior to each Christmas period. It is known that many small appliances are purchased as gift items and that most gift sales occur between the middle of November and the 24th of December. After Christmas day, gift sales fall off sharply. Consequently, it has been decided that sales should start on or about November 15. A project manager has been named and has decided to use the Critical Path Method. A properly programmed computer is available. Five steps are involved.

STEP 1: PREPARING THE ARROW DIAGRAM

The project manager's first job is to arrange for the construction of an arrow diagram. While consulting with the many functional groups that will be involved in the project, a diagram is prepared which depicts the logical precedence between each major activity in the contemplated project. The resulting diagram is shown in Figure 6.

The level of detail in Figure 6 is sufficient for over-all project management. At a later time, functional managers may draw additional arrow diagrams which will assist them in planning, scheduling, and controlling the identified project tasks that are under their individual jurisdictions.

In Figure 6 some of the work elements are subdivided into several phases. This indicates that the start of some activity is dependent upon the partial, but not final, completion of the subdivided activity. For example, the engineering work must be brought to some state of completion before patent search can be started.

Four additional comments should be made about the diagram. First, it will be noted that the junctions where arrow heads and arrow tails meet have been numbered. This is done to provide a unique reference for each activity which can in turn be communicated readily to the computer. For example, the activity "Motivation Research" from Junction 1 to Junction 3 is identified as (1, 3). The junctions are called *events* since they signify the event of starting or completing one or more activities.

Second, several activity arrows are shown as broken lines and are known as *dummies*. These arrows do not indicate actual work elements, but rather are restraints used to maintain a proper precedence relationship in the diagram. They are treated by the computer as ordinary activities but do not require the expenditure of resources—either time or money. For instance, the restraint (27, 29) indicates that "Review and Revise Design" together with "Refining Advertising Campaign Ideas" must both precede the "Preliminary Media Selection." However, only "Review and Revise Design" must precede "Consolidate Trial Manufacturing Specifications."

Third, the wavy line (0, 1) is known as *Lead Time*. Event 0 is the current instant of time and Event 1 is when the project is scheduled to start. These two events, of course, could be concurrent. Arrows have been drawn from Event 0 to Events 17 and 36 to show that top management must be available at the latter two points if the project is to proceed. If management can only be available at earlier times, it may be possible to shorten the lead time to conform to their schedule restraint. If in this situation the

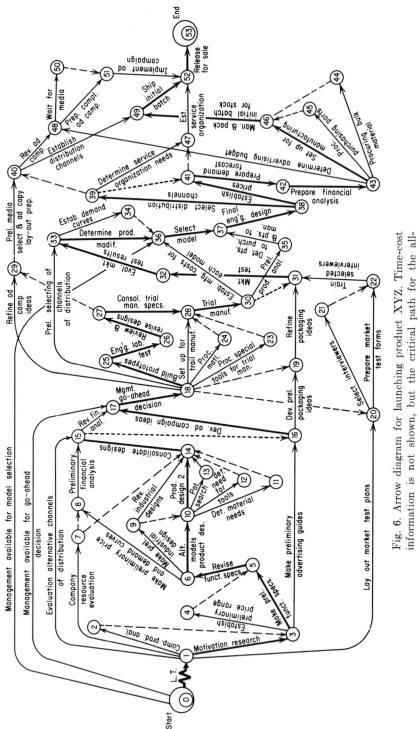

Fig. 6. Arrow diagram for launching product XYZ. Time-cost information is not shown, but the critical path for the all-normal case is indicated with heavy lines.

188

amount of lead time is less than the required compression, some activities may be forced into otherwise unnecessary crashing. The resulting increased costs can be related directly to management's unavailability. At times, the elimination of all lead time and a complete crashing of the project will not provide sufficient time compression and project completion will be unavoidably delayed. Again, responsibility can be placed where it belongs. In case management can only be available after Events 17 and 36 should start, lead time may be extended with a possible corresponding delay in project duration.

The fourth and final comment is that the diagram has been drawn so that both project START and project END are identified by single events, Events 0 and 53, respectively.

STEP 2: COMPLETING THE INPUT DATA
FOR COMPUTER CALCULATIONS

In addition to the numbered diagram the project manager must arrange to provide time-cost information about each activity. In the great majority of cases it can with sufficient accuracy be assumed that cost rises linearly as attempts are made to expedite an activity. It is therefore only necessary to establish normal costs, normal durations, and crash costs and crash durations. In cases where the linearity assumption does not hold, a piecewise linear approximation can be made. The linearity assumption eases the burden of data collection considerably. There also exists the possibility that only normal *or* crash duration can be implemented. Such discontinuity must be specified.

The successive expediting of the project duration is based on the relative slopes of the activity time-cost relationships. By specifying artificially large time-cost slopes for selected activities, the project manager can exert his influence on the sequence in which these activities are considered for expediting.

The computer program used for the processing of this example—the GE 225/CPM program—offers the user an opportunity to bias the allocation of leeway or float time. To this end, a priority weight—a number from one through nine—is given to each activity. The priority weighting scheme allocates any available float to activities in proportion to the established weights. In cases where uncertainty on duration estimates is abnormally high, one would use a high priority weight and consequently would expect a proportionally high amount of float to be scheduled for that activity. For practical reasons, the float allocation by priority weights is augmented in the GE 225 program by a built-in bias which conserves float for activities located late in a project.

Step 2 is completed when all of the required information is collected and listed on input code sheets. Figure 7 shows page 3 of the code sheets

GENERAL ELECTRIC — GE 225 Critical Path Method Input Code Sheet

I	J	D	d	NORMAL COST	CRASH COST	SLOPE (Option-W al)	C/W	CODE	ACTIVITY DESCRIPTION
6	9	4	2	400	700			4 N 3 0 2	INDUSTRIAL DESIGNS PHASE 1
6	10	2	18	4000	4200			9 C 3 0 1	MAKE ALTERNATIVE MØDELS PRØDUCT DESIGN PHASE 1
7	8	0	0	0	0			1 C 0 0 0	DUMMY
7	14	0	0	0	0			1 C 0 0 0	DUMMY
8	15	2	2	300	300			5 C 4 0 2	PRELIMINARY FINANCIAL ANALYSIS
9	10	0	0	0	0			1 C 0 0 0	DUMMY
9	14	8	5	800	150			4 N 3 0 2	REVISED INDUSTRIAL DESIGNS PHASE 2
10	11	3	3	120	120			6 C 3 0 3	DETERMINE MATERIAL NEEDS
10	11	3	3	120	120			6 C 3 0 3	DETERMINE NEED FØR SPECIAL TØØLS
10	13	4	20	1000	1500			8 C 4 0 1	PATENT SEARCH

Column numbers for ACTIVITY DESCRIPTION: 28 29 30 31 32 33 34 35 36 37 38 39 40 41 42 43 44 45 46 47 48 49 50 51 52 53 54 55 56 57 58 59 60 61 62 63 64 65 66 67 68 69 70 71 72 73 74 75 76 77 78 79 80

LEGEND

I - THE EVENT NUMBER AT THE TAIL OF THE ACTIVITY ARROW.

J - THE EVENT NUMBER AT THE HEAD OF THE ACTIVITY ARROW.

D - THE NORMAL DURATION FOR THIS ACTIVITY.

d - THE CRASH DURATION FOR THIS ACTIVITY.

W - A DIGIT FROM 1 TO 9 - THE WEIGHT OF THIS ACTIVITY IN RELATION TO OTHER ACTIVITIES (FOR PURPOSES OF FLOAT ASSIGNMENT).

C/W - A CONTINUOUS OR NON-CONTINUOUS COST CURVE (SPECIFY).

Prepared By JRG - BMC   Date 10/1/61

Fig. 7. Page 3 of the GE 225 CPM input code sheet for the new product launching project shown in Figure 6.

prepared for this example. Each line on the page corresponds to one activity and can contain up to 80 columns of information. Columns 1 through 28 contain precedence, time, cost, slope, weight, and continuity information. The dummies are entered with zero time, zero cost requirements, and minimum weights. Activities that cannot be expedited, such as "Determine Material Needs" (10, 11) have normal time equal to crash time and normal cost equal to crash cost.

The remaining columns, 29 through 80, are reserved for an alphanumeric activity description. A code can be included in this description to facilitate identification of, for instance, areas of responsibility. Similarly, job account numbers or any other desired code may be included.

Activity responsibility resting with Executive Management has been coded in this example in the 500-series, Finance and Legal responsibility is coded in the 400-series, Engineering in the 300, Manufacturing in the 200, and Marketing responsibility in the 100-series.

STEP 3: COMPUTING SCHEDULES

A deck of input cards is next keypunched on the basis of the input code sheet, one card for each activity. The cards will contain all the project information necessary to communicate with the computer. If processed with a CPM program package which contains the proper step-by-step interpretation of the mathematical CPM formulation, the result will be a computer output consisting of a series of tabulated, alternative schedules. Each schedule will constitute a complete, detailed timetable for a given project duration. Besides repeating the pertinent portion of the input information, the output table will list:

Criticality status of each activity.

Time and cost required for each activity in order to implement the particular schedule.

Change in activity times and costs as compared to the preceding schedule.

Scheduled finish of each activity in view of specified priority weights.

Scheduled float for each activity as determined by priority weights and the activity's proximity to the last event in the project.

Earliest possible and latest allowable start and finish of each activity.

Total and free float for each activity.

Total float and *free float* have different significance. If total float is zero, the corresponding activity is critical. Free float is the amount of leeway available after implementation of an activity if all other activities in the project were started as early as possible. Should an activity last

Fig. 8. Launching product XYZ—The Victoria Company, New Product Division. Example of CPM prepared on the GE 225

i	j	Description	Crit. Status	Time	Chng.	Cost	Sched. Fnsh	Sched. Float	Earliest Start	Earliest Fnsh	Latest Start	Latest Fnsh	Total Float	Free Float	Pri. Wt.
000	001	Lead Time	Crit	0					0		0				1
000	017	Management Available for Go-Ahead Decision		0				102	0		102	102	102	102	2
000	036	Management Available for Model Selection		0				205	0		205	205	205	205	2
001	002	Competitive Product Analysis	Crit	20		675	20		0	20	0	20			5
001	003	Motivation Research	Crit	20		15000	20		0	20	0	20			5
001	007	Company Resource Evaluation		8		480	8	1	0	8	87	95	87		2
001	015	Evaluate Alternative Channels of Dist.		10		500	10	90	0	10	90	100	90	90	2
001	020	Lay Out Market Test Plane		5		300	5	99	0	5	131	136	131	99	2
002	003	Dummy	Crit	0			20		20	20	20	20			1
003	004	Estimate Preliminary Price Range		2		130	22		20	22	33	35	13		2
003	005	Make Preliminary Functional Specifs.	Crit	15		1200	35		20	35	20	35			4
003	016	Make Preliminary Advertising Guides		10		1500	30	70	20	30	90	100	70	70	2
004	005	Dummy	Crit	0			22	13	22	22	35	35	13	13	1
005	006	Revise Functional Specifications	Crit	2		250	37		35	37	35	37			2
006	008	Make Preliminary Price & Demand Curves		3		175	40		37	40	95	98	58		4
006	009	Preliminary Indust. Designs Phase 1		4		400	41		37	41	51	55	14		9
006	010	Alter. Models Product Design Phase 1	Crit	18		4200	55		37	55	37	55			1
007	008	Dummy		0			9	31	8	8	98	98	90	32	1
007	014	Dummy		0			9	86	8	8	95	95	87	87	5
008	015	Preliminary Financial Analysis		2		300	42	58	40	42	98	100	58	58	1
009	010	Dummy		0			41	14	41	41	55	55	14		4
009	014	Rev. Industrial Designs Phase 2		8		800	49	46	41	49	87	95	46	46	6
010	011	Determine Material Needs		3		120	58	1	55	58	92	95	37	37	6
010	012	Determine Need for Special Tools		3		120	58	1	55	58	92	95	37	37	8
010	013	Patent Search	Crit	40		1000	95		55	95	55	95			8
010	014	Alter. Models Product Design Phase 2	Crit	40		11000	95		55	95	55	95			9
011	014	Dummy		0			59	36	58	58	95	95	37		1
012	014	Dummy		0			59	36	58	58	95	95	37		1
013	014	Dummy		0			95		95	95	95	95			1
014	015	Consol. Designs & Select Three Models	Crit	5		1300	100		95	100	95	100			8
015	016	Dummy	Crit	0			100		100	100	100	100			1
015	017	Revise Financial Analysis		1		60	101	1	100	101	101	102	1	1	1
016	017	Develop Advtg. Campaign Ideas	Crit	2		1000	102		100	102	100	102			6

192

i	j		Activity Description	Crit Status	Time	Chng.	Cost	Scheduled Fnsh	Scheduled Float	Earliest Start	Earliest Fnsh	Latest Start	Latest Fnsh	Total Float	Free Float	Pri. Wt
016	019	101	Develop Preliminary Packaging Ideas		2		300	102	5	100	102	143	145	43	2	6
017	018	500	Management Go-Ahead Decision	Crit	2		2500	104		102	104	102	104			9
018	019	000	Dummy		0			104	3	104	104	145	145	41		1
018	020	000	Dummy		0			104		104	104	136	136	32		1
018	023	202	Procure Special Tools for Trial Mfg.		10		500	114	1	104	114	118	128	14		8
018	024	202	Procure Materials for Trial Mfg.		20		20	124		104	124	108	128	4		7
018	025	302	Build Prototypes	Crit	10		1800	114		104	114	104	114			3
018	028	203	Set Up for Trial Manufacture	Crit	24		8400	128		104	128	104	128			4
018	029	101	Refine Advertising Campaign Ideas		1	–	200	105	27	104	105	200	201	96	20	2
018	033	100	Preliminary Selection of Dist. Channels		2		250	106	95	104	106	199	201	95	95	2
019	031	101	Refine Packaging Ideas		3		450	110	38	104	107	145	148	41	41	2
020	021	102	Select Interviewers		10		200	114		104	114	136	146	32		2
020	022	102	Prepare Market Test Forms		3		120	107	7	104	107	143	146	39	7	1
021	022	000	Dummy		0			114		114	114	146	146	32		5
022	031	102	Train Selected Interviewing Personnel		2		600	116	32	114	116	146	148	32	32	1
023	028	000	Dummy		0			115	13	114	114	128	128	14	14	1
024	028	000	Dummy		0			124	4	124	124	128	128	4	4	9
025	026	302	Engineering Lab Tests	Crit	8		1100	122		114	122	114	122			9
026	027	302	Review and Revise Product Design	Crit	3		650	125		122	125	122	125			7
027	028	203	Consolidate Trial Mfg. Specifications	Crit	3	–	650	128		125	128	125	128			1
027	029	000	Dummy		0			125	7	125	125	201	201	76		7
028	030	201	Trial Manufacture	Crit	20		9000	148		128	148	128	148			2
029	040	101	Prel. Media Select & Ad Cpy, Lay-Out Prep.		15		3000	147	69	125	140	201	216	76	76	1
030	031	000	Dummy	Crit	0			148		148	148	148	148			2
030	035	303	Preliminary Product Analysis		4		400	152	2	148	152	200	204	52		3
030	036	201	Establish Mfg. Costs for Each Model		3		400	151	54	148	151	202	205	54	54	8
031	032	102	Market Test	Crit	50		10000	198		148	198	148	198			3
032	033	102	Evaluate Market Test Results	Crit	3		1500	201		198	201	198	201			3
033	034	102	Establish Demand Curves		3		300	204		201	204	202	205	1		3
033	036	303	Determine Product Modifications	Crit	4		800	205		201	205	201	205			9
034	036	000	Dummy		0			204	1	204	204	205	205	1	1	1
035	037	203	Determine Parts to Purchase & to Mfg.		3		300	157	50	152	155	204	207	52	52	2
036	037	500	Select Model	Crit	2		1000	207		205	207	205	207			5
037	038	303	Make Final Engineering Design	Crit	8		1200	215		207	215	207	215			9
038	039	100	Select Distribution Channels	Crit	1		400	216		215	216	215	216			2
038	041	100	Establish Prices	Crit	2		200	217		215	217	215	217			2

Fig. 8 (con't.)

i	j	Activity	Description	Crit. Status	Time	Chng.	Cost	Scheduled Fnsh	Scheduled Float	Earliest Start	Earliest Fnsh	Latest Start	Latest Fnsh	Total Float	Free Float	Pri. Wt.
039	040	000	Dummy	Crit	0			216		216	216	216	216			1
039	041	000	Dummy		0			216	1	216	216	217	217	1	1	1
039	047	103	Determine Service Organization Needs	Crit	5		500	221	14	216	228	249	254	33		4
039	048	101	Revise Advertising Campaign		12		2500	228	21	216	256	216	228	21	21	8
040	048	104	Establish Distribution Channels	Crit	40		4000	256		216	219	237	277	21		2
040	049	102	Prepare Demand Forecast		2		200	219	18	217	217	217	219	37	4	2
041	042	000	Dummy	Crit	0			217		217	222	254	254			1
041	047	402	Prepare Financial Analysis		3		600	222	7	219	247	219	222	20		2
042	043	202	Procure Bulk Material		25		50	247	5	222	252	242	267	15	5	8
042	044	202	Procure Purchased Parts		30		200	252		222	267	237	267	15		9
043	044	201	Set Up For Manufacture	Crit	45		22500	267	5	222	223	222	228	5	5	2
043	045	100	Determine Advertising Budget		1		300	223	13	222	247	227	267	20	20	2
043	046	000	Dummy		0			254	10	222	252	267	267	15	15	1
043	048	000	Dummy	Crit	0			257		247	277	267	277			1
044	046	201	Manufacture & Pkg Initial Batch for Stock	Crit	10		20000	277	19	267	258	254	291	33	33	9
045	046	103	Establish Service Organization	Crit	37		3700	272		221	288	228	288			3
046	049	101	Media Availability Lead Time		60			288	38	228	250	266	288	38	38	2
047	052	101	Prepare Complete Advertising Campaign	Crit	22		5200	250		228	291	277	291			5
048	050	204	Ship Initial Product Batch to Distrib'rs.	Crit	14		1334	291		277	288	288	288			2
048	051	000	Dummy	Crit	0			288		288	291	288	291			1
051	052	101	Implement Advertising Campaign	Crit	3		350	291		288	288	288	288			2
052	053	100	Release Product for Sale	Crit	2			293		291	293	291	293			1

Project Duration in Days   293
Direct Project Cost   148,184

Fig. 8. (con't.) 19th expedited schedule for the new product launching project. The table includes information identical to that prepared by the computer for each schedule.

194

longer than planned but not long enough to absorb more than its free float, the delay will not interfere with the timely completion of any other portion of the project.

Figure 8 shows one of the expedited schedules, taken from the computer print-out. It includes all of the detailed activity characteristics for that schedule.

The least direct project costs corresponding to various project durations as prepared by the computer are summarized in Figure 9.

Schedule	Project Duration in Days	Least Direct Project Cost in Dollars
All-normal schedule	399	129,940
1st expedited schedule	395	130,080
2nd expedited schedule	390	130,280
3rd expedited schedule	389	130,330
4th expedited schedule	388	130,380
5th expedited schedule	383	130,680
6th expedited schedule	380	130,860
7th expedited schedule	378	131,060
8th expedited schedule	348	134,060
9th expedited schedule	346	134,260
10th expedited schedule	344	134,460
11th expedited schedule	343	134,560
12th expedited schedule	342	134,760
13th expedited schedule	302	143,760
14th expedited schedule	301	144,060
15th expedited schedule	300	144,460
16th expedited schedule	299	144,894
17th expedited schedule	297	146,284
18th expedited schedule	295	147,234
19th expedited schedule	293	148,184
20th expedited schedule	283	153,184
21st expedited schedule	278	157,350
22nd expedited schedule	272	162,350
23rd expedited schedule	267	167,350
24th expedited schedule	252	182,350
Minimum-duration schedule	247	188,850

Fig. 9. Summary of computed alternative schedules.

The range of project durations span from an all-normal duration of 399 days to a minimum duration of 247 days beyond which the project cannot be expedited. Had *all* jobs been expedited, the project duration would still have been 247 days, however, the cost would have skyrocketed to $219,000. This represents an unnecessary outlay of approximately $30,000, or 16 percent of the necessary direct project cost for the minimum duration.

The computation time required for each alternative least cost schedule for this example averaged four seconds.[1] In general, required processing time depends on the size and complexity of the arrow diagram. In addition to computation time, read-in of the activity cards and print-out of

---

[1] Four seconds processing time on the General Electric GE 225 Information Processing System corresponds to a processing cost of approximately 17 cents.

the tabulated schedules each require approximately two-tenths of a second per activity.

The range of project durations and the associated costs in Figure 9 are shown graphically in Figure 10 as the Direct Project Cost Curve. To

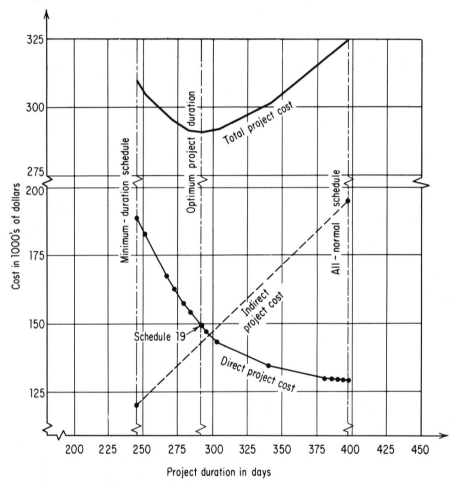

Fig. 10. Direct, Indirect, and Total Project Cost Curves for new product launching example.

show the total project cost picture, indirect expenses must be estimated and added. In most cases, indirect cost is considered to be a fixed percentage of some base cost. In the Victoria Company, a constant indirect cost rate of 150 percent of total normal duration cost is used. Therefore, the indirect cost of implementing the all-normal schedule is 150 percent of $129,940, or $194,910, corresponding to an indirect cost rate of $488 per day. The indirect cost for the minimum duration schedule is a total of $488 times 247 days, or $120,536. The constant indirect rate is shown as the straight, broken line in Figure 10.

STEP 4: ESTABLISHING THE PLAN OF IMPLEMENTATION

The final step of the planning and scheduling procedure is to select a specific plan of implementation, then translate relative times to a calendar-based schedule and allocate resources in accordance with the selected schedule.

The project manager can observe the variation of total project cost associated with alternative project schedules by adding the Direct and the Indirect Project Cost Curves in Figure 10. The resulting Total Project Cost Curve—the "U" shaped curve in the figure—clearly indicates that the least expensive project duration can be obtained if the implementation is executed in accordance with Schedule 19 wherein the project time is 293 working days.

It is known that a high percentage of the total year's volume will occur between the middle of November and the 24th of December. Therefore, to maximize seasonal sales and minimize implementation cost, the most desirable schedule would be the one for which the 293rd working day corresponds to the calendar day of November 15.

The selected schedule, Number 19, is converted into a calendar-based schedule by properly accounting for Saturdays and/or Sundays, holidays, vacation shutdowns, and other non-working days, and then setting an appropriate lead time. If the time period from the current date to November 15 is greater than the calendar time required by Schedule 19, then of course that schedule—with its minimum total project cost benefit—can be used. If, however, the actual calendar time available is less than that required by Schedule 19, then a further expedited—and therefore more costly—schedule must be used in order to achieve a November 15 completion date.

Total company profit can be maximized *only* if the total project cost (from Figure 10) and the cost of lost sales volume resulting from delays beyond November 15 are considered simultaneously. Summing these costs results in a Composite Cost Curve. The minimum point on the Composite Cost Curve determines the over-all optimum schedule.

The composite cost situation for the Victoria Company is portrayed in Figure 11. In this case it is found to be the schedule corresponding to a project duration of 270 working days (i.e., Schedule 23). Thus, even though Schedule 19 would result in the lowest project implementation cost, the Christmas trade would be missed if that schedule were used and the composite cost would be $30,000 higher than that resulting from Schedule 23.

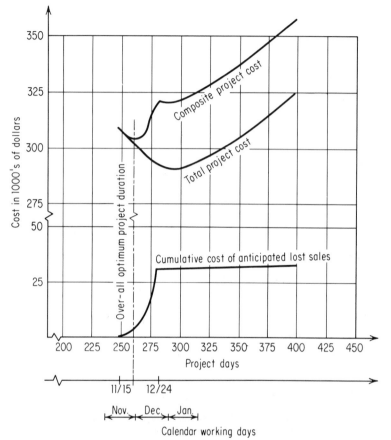

Fig. 11. Composite cost variation with calendar time and project duration for product XYZ. The composite project cost is the sum of the total project cost and the cumulative cost of anticipated lost sales. "Project Day O" must be specified before the calendar scale can be established.

Placing the selected schedule on a calendar is accomplished by the computer with a simple calendar dating routine. The established timetable is then communicated to the various organizational components under whose jurisdiction responsibility for completion of individual activities belongs. Once in the hands of functional management, duration and cost information as tabulated in the computer output (cf., Figure 8) is used for allocation of manpower, equipment, and other resources.

STEP 5: CONTROLLING THE PROJECT

Although originally developed as a project planning and scheduling tool, the Critical Path Method lends itself very well to the *controlling* of programs such as the one considered in this example. The project manager should receive periodic reports from functional managers, with frequency depending on project durations and personal preferences. Reports should include information regarding time and cost required for completion of activities under their respective jurisdictions. Based on these reports, new input cards are prepared for those activities for which time-cost requirements deviate from previous data. Using the computer the project plan can be rapidly updated. In addition to the regular reports, the project manager must be informed immediately when critical activities are delayed or non-critical activities extend beyond the available free float.

Analysis of the revised information may indicate that a new schedule is required for the remainder of the program if the original project duration is to be realized. If slippages have occurred, normally it is possible to eliminate their effect by developing a new schedule which specifies that subsequent critical activities be executed on a more expedited basis than was originally planned. When all remaining critical activities have already been scheduled to be fully crashed, management must resort to alternative approaches. Redefinition of critical activities yet to be implemented, and revisions in the arrow diagram, constitute two alternatives which can be taken.

Both of these possibilities usually require managerial risk decisions. CPM aids management by specifying the only activities for which such decisions will have the desired influence.

For example, redefinition of critical activities in the product launching project described above could occur if management decides that time does not permit the construction of more than two prototypes if the project completion date is to be met. The development of two prototypes, rather than many, increases the risk of not finding a suitable product. Management then must use its judgment as to whether it is willing to accept this risk.

Alternatively, the arrow diagram could be revised by a decision to eliminate all or portions of one or more activities. For example, in Figure 6 "Trial Manufacture"—and consequently "Consolidate Trial Manufacturing Specifications"—may be eliminated, causing the junction points labeled 27, 28, and 30 to coincide in the revised diagram. Since both activities were on the critical path, additional time is made available for subsequent activities.

If all activities along the critical path have not been fully crashed, trade-offs can be considered between the cost of further crashing and the risk of changing the nature and quality of planned activities. By studying alternative computer runs before the actual method of expediting to be applied is decided upon, management decisions can be based on a wider range of factual data than is possible without CPM and the high-speed computer.

CONCLUDING REMARKS

In the foregoing portion of this article the Critical Path Method was discussed in some detail. Emphasis was placed on the application of the method to an important class of marketing management problems. It was demonstrated that CPM represents a basic tool available to all levels of management and that the technique included elements of timeliness, selection, and evaluation. CPM provides for true management by exception. The mathematical structure and the computational details of the method were omitted.

As presented here, the method considers only one project at a time, and allocation of *total* company resources is not necessarily optimum. Computer programs can, however, also be applied to inter-project scheduling and can be used to take into account the allocation of scarce resources among competing projects. In addition, methods exist which will incorporate the uncertainty of time estimates more directly than does the priority weighting scheme. The result is a statistical evaluation of the *probability* of completing a project within established time and cost limits.

Discussion of these and other extensions of the fundamental principles of the method would lengthen this presentation unduly. Although the article has been limited to a consideration of the basic features of the Critical Path Method, the discussion has been sufficient to demonstrate that CPM is an extremely powerful tool which—in conjunction with the electronic computer—stands ready to help the business manager minimize the guesswork in decision-making.

It must surely be a sign of mental weakness to agree to write a paper with so broad a title, one which almost constitutes an invitation to provide a summary of the remainder of this book. Yet I do believe that this chapter can serve some useful functions. First of all, it offers the reader an overall view of the entire analytic process whereby computers are brought to assist in the solution of managerial problems. More important, it can help management to see the process as a whole from the point of view of the analyst, to understand his problems more clearly and to recognize the value as well as the limitations of the product which he has to offer.

FROM PROBLEM TO MODEL . . .

GENERAL DESCRIPTION

Selection of a specific problem is obviously the first stage in the use of computers as an aid to managerial decision making. The firm has either

FROM PROBLEM TO MODEL

TO COMPUTER TO SOLUTION*

recognized that it has decision problems for which these tools can be help-ful or the computer application specialist is consulted to explore whether such problems exist. In any event, no quick and easy answers can be ex-pected of him and it will generally be a long time—very likely a matter of three to six months—before he is ready to employ the computer.

First of all, the analyst must acquaint himself with the details of the operations of the firm and the workings of the problem. This is particu-larly important if he is a consultant brought in from outside the company. For every company and almost every problem is an individual which differs in at least some details from others which the investigator has previously encountered.

Next comes the difficult task of model building—the selection of the most pertinent features of the problem on which the analysis must be

* I would like to acknowledge my gratitude to the Ford Foundation whose grant to Princeton's Department of Economics helped in the completion of this paper.

based, and the translation of the problem into analytically tractable terms. This requires ingenuity, experience and above all, time. Unfortunately it is difficult to illustrate this point tellingly, for like the solutions to so many problems, most analytic models seem to be perfectly obvious to hindsight—that is, after the laborious task of their construction has been completed.

SIMPLIFICATION IN MODEL BUILDING

A basic characteristic of any real problem is the complexity introduced by the profusion of heterogeneous details which are usually involved. These details are often of secondary relevance. For example, in evaluating plans for an advertising campaign it is not only relevant to know what audience it will reach and how their purchase plans will be affected by it both in the near and the more distant future. It may also be important to investigate whether the advertisements will be seen by the company's salesmen and to what extent they will bolster sales force morale. Information on the availability of the product is also sometimes pertinent —if an item is not displayed on the shelves of the supermarkets of the southwestern region it may be wasteful to advertise in publications which have a relatively large circulation in that area. It may also be relevant in planning the campaign to take into account the aesthetic opinions of management, the company image which it is trying to create in the mind of the public, and indeed, even its prestige aspirations. The reader will surely find it easy to add to this list many other complications which play some role or potential role in advertising planning. It is quite obvious, however, that not all of these considerations will be of very great importance, though appearances in this respect are, unfortunately, often quite deceiving.

These details constitute a major nuisance from the point of view of the analyst. They clutter up the problem, obscure its structure, adding to the task of requisite fact gathering and complicate the mathematical techniques which must be employed in its investigation. In fact, it is usually impossible to take all or even most of these details into account in the analysis. In order to put the problem into a form where it is sufficiently tractable for machine calculation, a considerable amount of simplification and pruning away of unimportant elements must first be undertaken.

However, it should be recognized that this process of simplification is not a peculiarity of the use of computers. It is part and parcel of any piece of analysis. After all, the use of *controlled* experiments in laboratory work is at least partly motivated by the same considerations. If temperature changes represent a complicating factor in the study of some physical phenomenon, then in the laboratory an artificial situation is created in which temperature is not permitted to vary while the behavior of the elements of immediate interest is scrutinized. In this way, the tidy, well-ordered world of the experimenter is substituted for the relatively chaotic features of reality.

Indeed, this association between analysis and simplification is a characteristic feature of everyday thinking, whether in ordinary discourse or in the most hard-headed business decision making process. Statements that begin "the recession was caused by . . ." or "the new package size isn't selling well because . . ." surely are virtually certain to encompass only part of the picture, though they may well focus on what, for the purposes at hand, are the most important elements.

The management which uses computers as a decision making aid should therefore not be surprised to find that the problem as it is actually brought to the computer is only a skeletal version of the circumstances with which it has to wrestle. Almost all problems must be simplified to some extent in order to analyze them successfully. In its own thinking management undoubtedly tries to go right to the heart of the matter and to disregard minor and only mildly relevant considerations. However, it is quite different when this is done in the privacy of one's mind and when the results of the process of abstraction are put down on paper, stark naked, for all to see. The latter is always likely to produce some degree of shock.

There is nothing wrong, then, with the fact that computer analysis of decision problems must involve the use of *models*, the name given to the simplified versions of reality that are examined in place of the facts themselves. However, the process of construction of these models does involve very serious dangers. If one ignores a consideration which is actually an essential feature of the problem at hand, the result will be a serious misrepresentation of the facts and any recommendations which are obtained with the aid of such a model are apt to be unacceptable.

This means that the businessman must play a very important role in the process of model building. No one is as well acquainted with the circumstances relating to his problems. The computer technician, the programmer, the operations researcher or the mathematician are unlikely to have the requisite business know-how.

The businessman must therefore be prepared to examine the model in detail, to point out important omissions, and, indeed, to suggest other elements in the model whose role is likely to be secondary in practice and which are therefore likely candidates for deletion. In sum, model building requires two types of expertise, that of the technician who is well acquainted with the nature of modern analytic techniques and the capabilities and requirements of computers, and that possessed by the people who live with the facts and therefore know them most intimately—the members of the managerial group.

ILLUSTRATION: PRODUCT LINE EXPANSION DECISIONS

Throughout this chapter, I shall refer back to one specific problem for purposes of illustration. In this way a degree of continuity will perhaps be imparted to what must be a rather disjointed discussion.

The illustrative problem involves a firm considering the expansion of its product line as the magnitude of its operations and the resources at its command grow with the passage of time. That is, as the firm grows it will frequently wish to increase the number of products which it handles and not simply add to the outputs of its current manufactures. There are many reasons why it should want to do so—it may have begun to saturate the markets for portions of its existing line, or it may wish to reduce risk by increasing the number of baskets in which its eggs are deposited, etc.

Now, after some thought it may be recognized that there exists a standard mathematical model which would appear to be helpful here. This is the classical linear programming production model. For that model is designed to determine the company's optimal product line (as well as the optimal combination of production processes to be used in its manufacture). If, then, it is possible to determine the best product line for the firm with any given set of resources, one would expect that the same calculation, or a simple extension thereof will enable us to determine how and where that product line should be expanded as company resources grow.

The basic procedure involves the selection of a set of, say, 2000 products which the firm considers potential candidates for its product line. Corresponding to each such product we define a variable Q which represents the *quantity* of that item which should be produced. We thus have the 2000 variables $Q_1, Q_2, \ldots, Q_{2000}$, and the answer to the linear programming computation will be of the form

$$Q_1 = 0; \quad Q_2 = 57{,}300; \quad Q_3 = 0; \quad Q_4 = 0; \quad Q_5 = 737{,}450, \text{ etc.}$$

This means that products 1, 3, and 4 should simply not be included in the company product line, while items 2 and 5 (say refrigerators and food mixers) should, indeed, be produced, and in the quantities indicated.

The model itself contains two basic parts. The first, the so-called *objective function,* indicates how the goals of the firm will be served by the various alternative output combinations. For example, to adopt the standard assumption, suppose our firm's aim in life is (at least approximately) to maximize profits. Then our objective function will be a mathematical expression designed to indicate how the output level decisions affect profits. Thus, if item number 1 yields a profit of \$20 per unit and there are Q_1 units of this item produced, total profit from this source will be

$20Q_1$ dollars. Similarly, item number 2 might yield, say, $17Q_2$ dollars, etc., so that, considering all of our candidate products in the same way, we obtain a profit function of the form

$$\text{Profit} = 20Q_1 + 17Q_2 + 32Q_3 + \ldots + 12Q_{2000}.$$

It may appear at first glance that item 3 is a better bet than item 1 or 2 since the former yields a unit profit of 32 dollars—an amount considerably higher than the unit return to the other two. However, this disregards the firm's capacity and resource limitations. For example, if the firm's cash resources are being used fully, and it takes twice as large an investment to produce a unit of item 3 (say $200) as it does to produce a unit of item 2 ($100), then item 2 will very likely prove the better investment. For that commodity yields $17 per $100 of investment whereas the other good which returns $32 per $200 of investment only yields $16 per hundred. Thus, the extent to which these items make use of company resources becomes an important consideration in the problem. This is taken into account in the second part of the statement of the programming problem, *the constraints*. For example, our firm will have a cash availability constraint. If each unit of item 2 ties up 100 in cash, the total cash use involved in producing Q_2 units of this item will of course be $100Q_2$. Similarly, item 3 will tie up $200Q_3$ units of money. In total, the cash needs of the company will then be given by an expression such as

$$164Q_1 + 100Q_2 + 200Q_3 + \ldots + 79Q_{2000}.$$

If the company has 12 million dollars to invest, the total cash used by all of its products cannot exceed this quantity. In other words, we must have

$$164Q_1 + 100Q_2 + 200Q_3 + \ldots + 79Q_{2000} \leq 12 \text{ million.}$$

This is our first constraint. There are likely to be a number of other constraints representing the limits of physical plant capacity, limitations of managerial time availability, capacities of various specific pieces of equipment which represent potential bottlenecks, etc.

Thus the model which we are proposing to use to analyze the product line expansion problem is of the following form:

Find the magnitudes of the outputs of each of the 2000 possible products, $Q_1, Q_2, \ldots, Q_{2000}$ which maximize company profits

$$20Q_1 + 17Q_2 + 32Q_3 + \ldots + 12Q_{2000}$$

given the limitations imposed by the constraints

$$164Q_1 + 100Q_2 + 200Q_3 + \ldots + 79Q_{2000} \leq C_1 \text{ (cash constraint)}$$
$$2.1Q_1 + 1.4Q_2 + 9.6Q_3 + \ldots + 8.3Q_{2000} \leq C_2 \text{ (capacity of stamping machine)}$$

etc.[1]

---

[1] There will very likely be a substantial number of these constraints. Problems in-

That is all there is to the statement of the model.[2] The symbols C_1, C_2, etc. have been substituted for the specific capacity figures (such as the 12 million $= C_1$ money capital availability datum) to indicate that these are to be treated as (independent) variables. That is, the firm's expansion will be represented by the increases in the quantities of resources C_1, C_2, ... which are available to it. By solving the programming problem for larger and larger values of the C's we can see what happens to the composition of the company's optimal product line. Presently we shall see that, as it stands, the use of our model for this purpose involves some difficulties, but for the moment they can be ignored.

Now the reader should observe how simplified are the bare bones of our model as they have been described in comparison with the rich and complex texture of a real product line expansion problem. Actual decisions are heavily dependent on the fortuitous experiences of management which make it more qualified to produce some item A than some other item B. It will reflect the availability of raw material suppliers and their relationships with the company. It will be influenced by the past history of the company and a variety of tangible and intangible considerations of varying importance.

Actually, more of these matters are or can be taken into account in the model than may at first appear to be the case. For example, the list of 2000 items which are initially selected for consideration will presumably already have excluded commodities for whose production management is entirely unfitted by the nature of its past experience.

Nevertheless, it must be clear that the model represents a very considerable simplification of the facts of the matter. This is precisely the point which the illustration is designed to bring out at this stage—that models *necessarily* represent a simplification of reality. It is hoped that this example will help to reduce the reader's uneasiness when he sees how drastic are the simplifications introduced in the models which he encounters in the future. We shall return to our product line expansion model presently.

---

volving more than 100 constraints are not rare. In the present problem every element in the firm's operations which constitutes a potential bottleneck will correspond to a constraint.

[2] There is a third portion of every linear programming problem, the non-negativity requirements $Q_1 \geq 0$, $Q_2 \geq 0$, ... , $Q_{2000} \geq 0$. These fairly unimportant sounding constraints state merely that the smallest amount of any product which can be turned out is zero—it is impossible to manufacture a negative number of refrigerators! Despite their slightly ridiculous appearance these restrictions are really highly important. However, they play no significant role in our present discussion.

. . . TO COMPUTER . . .

GENERAL DESCRIPTION

Having discussed the examination of the marketing problem and the construction of the model we turn now to the next stage of the procedure— the translation of the model into computer language and the collection of the materials required to process it on the computer.

This stage of the analysis consists of three major types of operation: data gathering, programming, and processing on the computer. Although the data-gathering phase is the most familiar of the three, it is likely to be the most time consuming and perhaps one of the most demanding of the analyst's sophistication and ingenuity. More will be said on this point subsequently.

Before programming can begin, it is necessary to make a choice of computer. It should be recognized that the biggest most powerful computer is not always the most efficient in handling the particular problem at hand, nor is it always wise to employ a computer which is currently owned or rented by the company for other purposes.

Once the choice of computer has been made, the programming can begin. Programming is the term used to denote the compilation of instructions for the computer and the translation of these instructions into a language which can be followed by the machine. Sometimes programming is an extremely difficult process calling for great exercise of care and patience. For electronic computers have no native common sense and are usually not built to learn from experience. As a result, every little step must be specified precisely and there is no instruction so obvious that it can be omitted or even abbreviated. In adding the numbers 17 and 32 it is never necessary to tell anyone "pick up a pencil, write down the first of the two numbers specified in this sentence on the piece of paper in front of you; now write down the second number immediately underneath the first; now add the two numbers; finally, write the answer down immediately below the other two numbers." Rather, we just say "add 17 and 32 and write down the answer." However, the programmer must always be just as specific as the first long-winded set of instructions. For example, the computer must always be reminded specifically to record an answer, and it must be told exactly where to record it. Since we are thoroughly versed in short cuts, ellipsis and reliance on our colleagues' common sense, it is extremely difficult to bring ourselves down to the low mental level required for communication with computers. This is one of the most taxing problems involved in programming, and a great many mistakes can be traced to the omission of apparently trivial details.

However, the difficulties of the programming phase of the analysis need not always be formidable. For one thing, there exist great and growing libraries of "canned programs"—programs which have been developed and tested in the past and which are now available for use. But here a warning is in order. The pedigree of a canned program should, wherever possible, be examined before it is used. Electronic computers are, after all, a very new invention—for all practical purposes they can be considered about a dozen years old. As a result, it is not surprising that it has been impossible to test all canned programs adequately and sometimes one turns up which is rather an amateur effort, and which is fairly inefficient or even not fully "debugged." But then, no library can be held responsible for the quality of every opus it contains.

Programming is also not always as difficult as it may appear to the untrained observer. One must not be misled by the apparently obscure and esoteric language in which the programmer usually works—one which may seem like an advanced form of the secret codes of our childhood. It is true that some very difficult programming tasks require extreme skill and intelligence. But there is also a great deal of relatively routine work in programming and the training for this sort of work can be acquired in a matter of weeks or, at most, months. Much programming also consists, in effect, of cutting and pasting, with several existing (canned) routines being put together to produce a new more powerful program.

A simple example of this is provided by our product line expansion model. Here it will be noted that, at least so far, the calculation has been described as a matter of linear programming in which we examine what happens as the capacities (the firm's resources) expand. What is called for here is, therefore, a number of repeated linear programming calculations with only the capacity data undergoing change. For this purpose it is likely to be expedient to employ one of the standard linear programming routines with a few additional instructions to the computer telling it to change the data as required at the end of each calculation and then to begin the computation over again. (This task could, of course, be done by hand changing the data and starting the machine working again at the end of each round of linear programming calculation. Such a procedure, however, is likely to be slow and inefficient, and it will be particularly costly if it wastes a great deal of time on a large and expensive machine.)

Once the data have been gathered and the program completed, there remains only the feeding of the required information into the machine and the calculation of the results. This stage is strictly routine and need not concern us unless we are interested in the workings of the electronic computer itself. Instructions and data are passed on to the machine by the use of punched cards or punched or magnetic tape and the machine returns the answers by similar means, from which they can be printed out in fairly readable form by automatic typewriters or high speed printers. If desired, they can even be obtained in the form of graphs by connecting the digital computer up to an analogue unit which can make the translation.

PROBLEMS OF DATA GATHERING

It was stated in the previous section that data gathering can be one of the most demanding tasks in the preparation of the model for computer analysis. It is often second after the model building stage in terms of time required for completion. Although every company keeps masses of data and there are many standard services offering still more statistics to management, this information is rarely available in the form required by the analyst. The basic difficulty is that a managerial decision requires information of a very special and hard to obtain variety. It is necessary to determine what difference it will make to the welfare of the company if one rather than another of the possible decisions being considered is selected. If it has been decided to introduce electric can openers into the product line, before deciding whether to produce 10,000 or 20,000 per month it is necessary to know how much it will cost to turn out these numbers and also how much it will cost to market them. In other words, we must know not just the costs and demands for current outputs, but also the corresponding figures for the alternative outputs which are being considered. But most statistics which are available to the firm only report the current situation and leave it up to the analyst to infer the other *marginal* data he requires for his optimality calculation.

Even the production cost information provided by the cost accountant normally offers only a first clue to the required data. It takes considerable analytical skill and probing of the construction of the accountant's figures which give the cost of the current 5000 units per week output to infer how much it would cost to produce 10,000 or 20,000 units per week. To guess simply that the total cost of supplying 10,000 units is twice as large as that of 5000 units is to ignore the possibility of either economies of large scale production or of diminishing returns. Such an assumption essentially ducks the basic issue.

Obviously, similar and often far more difficult problems are involved in the collection of the required marketing data.

In our product line expansion problem the data gathering stage involves:

a. The determination of the list of products to be considered for inclusion in the company product line;

b. the determination of the *marginal* input requirements for every such item and for every potential bottleneck input, e.g., it must be determined how much *additional* cash would be tied up by each additional automatic can opener produced;

c. the *marginal* profitability of each such output must be determined, i.e., how much each additional can opener turned out will contribute to profit and overhead after deduction of variable production and marketing costs.

These figures or some reasonable approximations must be obtained not only for items which the company has manufactured in the past, but also for every product which it is considering adding to its product line and on which it may have available no direct experience or records of past costs and market performance. The difficulties involved in gathering such information should be sufficiently obvious.

WHY COMPUTERS?

Before turning to a few remarks on the selection of the computer model to be used in the analysis, it is well to recognize that not all marketing problems can profitably employ computers as an aid to their solution. This may even be true of problems where mathematical models can be helpful, for sometimes the main purpose of the model is to serve as a device to get management to examine aspects of the problem which are ordinarily overlooked. That is, the model may be designed to reorient management's thinking or just provide a very helpful check list for its deliberations. Even if a model is to be used for calculation purposes, the computation may be so simple that pencil and paper or a desk calculator will suffice. In such cases the use of an electronic computer can only represent either swank or folly.

However, many marketing problems are inherently intractable without the help of powerful calculators. This will be so, where, as is often the case, a vast number of interrelationships and interactions exist. Many problems also involve vast numbers of combinations for examination— numbers which are well beyond the capacity of unaided human intelligence. Indeed, these problems are characteristically of such a magnitude that they would be well beyond the capability of the most powerful computers were it not for the short cuts provided by the mathematician.

WHICH COMPUTER?

It is obviously not feasible in advance to lay down a set of fixed rules for the selection of the right computer to deal with every conceivable marketing problem. All that will really be done here is to make one relevant observation. The specialized computers which have been developed for accounting, record keeping, and billing tasks (the so-called business data processing machines) are often highly specialized calculators designed to attend to their bookkeeping tasks very effectively. For that very reason they are sometimes not very adaptable to the needs of the analyst of managerial problems. Costs of programming and computing a non-bookkeeping problem on such a machine may be substantially higher than it would be on a "scientific machine." Consequently, in such a computation a firm may well find it appropriate to rent time on someone else's computer rather than using its own, or it may find it more satisfactory to employ one of its medium sized computers (e.g., the adaptable IBM 650) rather than a large machine (such as the IBM 705) which it also has available.

. . . TO SOLUTION

GENERAL DESCRIPTION

There is really very little to describe in this stage of the analysis. The computer has reported the results of its calculations and the analyst, in turn, transmits them to management. However, for reasons which will presently be discussed, it will rarely if ever be appropriate to employ the answers produced by the machine without modification and further analysis. The unfortunate fact is that the computer will at best provide approximations to the best answers to marketing problems, and often the answer obtained from the electronic calculator will only serve as an effective starting point for further consideration of the problem.

As a result, the analyst must give a great deal of thought to the results and must often process them further before he presents them to management. Management, in turn, must reconsider the findings of the analyst very carefully and modify them to take into account the detailed business considerations which it knows better than anyone else. Only then, out of the cooperative efforts of the computer, the analyst and the businessman is it possible to produce results which can be employed with confidence and which will be of maximum effectiveness.

DATA IMPERFECTIONS AND THE COMPUTER SOLUTION

Since a few of the difficulties involved in obtaining the required data have been discussed, the probable inaccuracies in the information employed in the analysis should be clear enough.

Sometimes random inaccuracies in the input figures offset one another and so produce only relatively small distortions in the answers which are put out by the computer. But we cannot usually be confident in advance that we will encounter this happy circumstance. In addition, in the multitude of arithmetic operations performed by the computer, small errors in the data can sometimes compound and end up producing serious errors in the answers.

One obvious way of dealing with this difficulty is to exercise more care in the collection of input figures. But there are clearly limits to this approach. There are other alternative ways of coping with the matter. One powerful approach, well suited to the computer, is a *sensitivity analysis*. Here one assumes a range of likely error in the data and instead of using only one set of figures one makes several alternative calculations employing different numbers within the reasonable error range. For example, if the marginal cost of some item may not plausibly be expected to be less than $10 or more than $15 then we may make three successive calculations using, in turn, 10, 12.5 and 15 dollars as our cost figure. The purpose of this exercise is to see whether these data changes produce substantial effects on the solution. If the solution turns out to be relatively insensitive to data changes this will increase the analyst's confidence in his results. It means that errors in the data used in this particular calculation are not likely to make much difference to the validity of the recommendations. Fortunately, such error insensitive conclusions are not as rare as pessimism might lead us to expect.

Even if the calculation is revealed as somewhat sensitive to data errors, a sensitivity analysis may give the investigator a far better idea of the consequences of these errors and it can help him to correct for them. For example, suppose it turns out from the sensitivity analysis that a difference of $2.50 in the marginal cost figure produces a $4.00 change in recommended price. Then, if the analyst can, from his discussions with the accountants and management, infer the direction and amount by which his cost data are likely to be biased, he is in a good position to estimate by how much and in what direction the calculated price may be expected to differ from the true optimum.

OMISSIONS FROM THE MODEL

At the beginning of this chapter, the necessary process of simplification involved in model construction was discussed at some length. Clearly, the details which were ignored in the construction of the model can sometimes affect the conclusions drawn with its aid. For example, our product line expansion analysis may now recommend the introduction of dishwasher soap into the company's product line. But this calculation may ignore the fact that the company is already a major manufacturer of the chemicals employed in producing soap and that by going into soap production itself the company will endanger its far more valuable sale of chemicals to other soap manufacturers. If this consideration has not explicitly been introduced into the model there is no way in which the electronic computer can take it into account. Consequently, the computer's recommendations will normally require at least some degree of revision because of the oversimplifications of the model construction.

DANGERS IN APPROXIMATIVE CALCULATIONS

Often, because of limitations of data availability or research budget restrictions, the analyst will find it expedient or even necessary to employ approximative computations. But this, too, can have its serious dangers and may produce very badly distorted results unless the technique is used with very great caution and unless answers are carefully corrected for the resulting biases.

To illustrate this point it should be recognized that one of the most

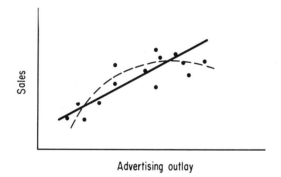

Advertising outlay

Fig. 1.

popular types of approximation is the use of linear relationships where the facts of the matter involve some slight degree of nonlinearity. For example, in fitting a statistical curve to the data represented by the dots in the following diagram, the statistician is likely to employ a straight line, even though the dots exhibit some degree of curvature.

A linearity assumption has a very simple economic interpretation. It means that results increase in strict proportion with any increase in effort. If a $100,000 increase in advertising expenditure will add $600,000 to sales, then a million dollar increase in advertising will augment sales by $6 million. Linearity amounts to the absence of either diminishing returns or economies of large scale operation.

Now, diminishing returns mean that it will pay the company to conduct a relatively wide variety of operations, for over-specialization in any one of its activities will soon become unprofitable because that activity runs into diminishing returns. Similarly, increasing returns to scale in any of its operations mean that it is likely to pay the company to become highly specialized in its activities—to sacrifice diversification in order to obtain the economies of large scale associated with concentration on a few specialty lines.

We see, then, that a *linear* programming calculation is likely to produce mistakes in its recommendations. It is apt to recommend overspecialization to the company whose marketing effort is subject to significant diminishing returns. Similarly, it is apt to call for overdiversification of the operations in which economies of large scale are important. Fortunately, the analyst is usually aware of these biases and can correct for them in the recommendations he presents to management.

The dangers of the linearity approach to approximation occur in an extreme form in our product line diversification model. The reader may already have concluded correctly that we should really have employed a *nonlinear* programming analysis in the first place, and that the standard linear programming analysis, described above, will probably not call for a sufficient degree of diversification as the company expands.

In fact, here the situation is even worse than it appears at first. It can be shown that in a *linear* programming situation, no matter how much company resources expand, it will *never* be profitable to add new items to its product line! The explanation is simple. In the absence of diminishing returns, if management has found a few good products to turn out, it should stick to them—it should simply turn out larger quantities of the same items. Of course, in practice more output usually means increased marketing costs, but this is precisely the main diminishing returns phenomenon omitted from a linear programming model.

CONCLUSION: TECHNOLOGICAL UNEMPLOYMENT FOR MANAGEMENT?

There has been some loose talk to the effect that the use of electronic computers as an aid to managerial decision making is likely to result in some members of management working themselves out of a job. The discussion of the preceding sections should provide management with strong reassurance on this point. Business firms are not about to be taken over by science fiction monsters constructed of circuits, tubes and transistors. Particularly in the marketing area, computers cannot be helpful in dealing with every problem, and where they are useful they can serve only as a tool for better decision making. Except in a few highly restricted areas, they cannot now and probably will never be able to produce recommendations which can be accepted without extensive review and emendation by management.

But, at the same time, one must not underestimate the really revolutionary contributions which computers can make to the decision making procedure, and the number of important problems which were formerly intractable but can now be handled on a systematic basis with the aid of these machines. The potential savings and other advantages which computers offer are truly enormous. In dealing with computers, then, management must beware equally the Scylla of overenthusiasm and uncritical acceptance, and the Charybdis of naive skepticism and unwillingness to accept the assistance of the vastly improved management tools of tomorrow.

PART III

THE COMPUTER AND PLANNING

It makes obvious sense to talk about using computers to design and test electric motors or inventory control systems because we performed similar design and testing functions before computers became available. But if by "design" we mean a rational process of planning and specifying something to meet certain constraints and goals, if by "test" we mean a systematic process of collecting and evaluating performance data, it is more difficult to talk about using computers to design and to test organizational structures. For although we put organizations together and tear them apart, we usually do so in ways that really do not merit the labels "designing" or "testing." We are guided more by fad and fancy than by facts.

We ignore basic questions and focus on trivia. We hide real issues about relationships between authority, expertise, and seniority in organizations behind sterile debates about "line" and "staff" functions. We try to tackle the severe barriers that inhibit creativity in organizations by

USING COMPUTERS TO DESIGN AND TO TEST ORGANIZATIONAL STRUCTURES

making a few changes in the rules by which group discussions are conducted. New packages like "brainstorming" or "decentralization" divert us from the hard labor of defining the real problems that face us and of developing solutions of a fundamental nature.

When we plan changes in an organization, we often do it casually and carelessly. A colleague of mine spent six months in a large corporation observing managers as they explored their needs for a large electronic data processing system and as they planned ways in which the system could be used. When the time came to prepare recommendations about the sort of organization that would grow up around the computer, the managers drafted these hurriedly in one afternoon. In another case, a team of men from a university research group worked with a company to develop rules for scheduling operations in a chemical plant. The rules are widely recognized as a major contribution to our knowledge of production planning and control; but within the plant, their implementation was almost frustrated because no one asked how best to put them into effect.

We cast our thoughts about organizational processes into rigidly over-simplified categories and propositions that do not reflect the dynamics of the manager's situation. Who knows of two men who agree enough on the meaning of "line" and "staff" that they could agree on how to classify the personnel in someone else's organization? If an organization says that it has "centralized" its operations, what does this really tell us about the changes that have taken place? How often do we make exceptions in our actions to the maxims that we should preserve "unity of command"; that no manager should have more than five, or seven, or ten direct subordinates; that all our decisions should be made in a way that will maximize profits for the firm?

We seldom make experiments; and when we do experiment, we are likely to finesse an evaluation of the outcomes. Sometimes we are too busy, sometimes we do not know how to make sense out of the results, and sometimes we do not care because we have "known" from the start that the experiment was a good one.

Too much of the time in business (and in universities, too) we give organizational matters short shrift. Why? There are many reasons—good and bad. Let me summarize the most legitimate ones that I have heard:

We do not have good measures of organizational effectiveness. It is hard for us to know, even in a small and tightly controlled "laboratory" organization, when changes in structure are called for, or if changes are made, whether they are successful. The arguments about measures of organizational performance may be less strident than the disputes about television rating services, but the confusion is as great. How do we recognize a "well organized" or a "poorly organized" distributor? Their sales, profit, or cost record may reflect characteristics of the region or the customers that they serve more than the way they are set up to provide the service. Concepts of profit or cost are seldom as precise as they seem on accounting statements; and the impression they give in the short-run may be quite different than the one they would provide over a longer period. Other important indicators of performance—like employee morale, skills in developing new managers, or flexibility to meet emergencies —are intangibles that are hard to assess.

We are not very imaginative about new strategies for organizing. The structures we use reflect centuries of tradition about how we proceed. In the case of machinery for a plant, we usually have a cadre of engineers and scientists who draw on research results to produce new proposals. They are in a fair position to support their proposals with preliminary performance measures or to get approval for a "test" or "experiment." In the case of organizational suggestions, though, we do not have the same systematic accumulation of knowledge to generate new ideas. New proposals that are made must withstand skepticism and reluctance to change under conditions where predictions or "tests" of effectiveness are difficult to make.

We are seldom willing or able to experiment with real people and real organizations. It is only in the last few decades that we have begun to do serious experimental studies of group and organizational behavior. We are hindered by the slow development of useful theories of behavior and of sensible ideas for collecting and analyzing data from our experiments. We are hindered by the sheer cost and complexity of these studies. Time, money, and talented observers and analysts must be present in abundance. We are hindered finally by fears, well or ill-founded to varying degrees, about the things that may happen if an experiment fails. The effects of a poorly chosen piece of equipment may disappear as soon as it is replaced by something else, but the effects of a poorly designed organizational structure may linger long after it is abandoned. Once an experiment has been started there is no way to restore the conditions which existed beforehand.

For many of the challenges of developing better organizations and of getting better measures of when organizations need to be changed, computers are irrelevant. But in other ways, computers can make impressive contributions to the processes of design and evaluation. They are already helping by creating conditions under which managers must pay more attention to the structures and systems which they establish and endorse. And in the next few years, they will provide new ways for managers to evaluate how well they are doing on organizational matters, to search for new ideas, and to try them out without disrupting the normal functioning of their firms.

Do computers really force us to pay more attention to organizational problems? Although the evidence is mainly anecdotal, the answer definitely seems to be "yes." Their mere existence helps. Together with the broader information processing and control systems in which they are imbedded, computers are one of a number of pressures for innovation and change in management today. They share the stage with other advances in technology; with new media for the promotion and distribution of goods; with significant changes in the relationships between business and all levels of government; with political, economic, and social changes that are taking place in other countries; and with radical improvements in the educational background that we can provide to men preparing for managerial careers. To realize even the applications of computers to marketing that have been suggested in this volume, we will have to face many issues and questions about the structure and staffing of the marketing departments and about the relationship of such departments to other units in the organization.

The disruptive force of computers is accentuated because it is focused largely on white collar and managerial segments of organizations. Managers may have been casual during the first Industrial Revolution about the effects of new technology on hourly workers, but it is not likely that they will be as casual about a new technology that may eliminate or drastically modify some of their own jobs.

Many possibilities for change and improvement often seem to be suggested simply in the process of deciding how a computer can be used and of writing programs for it. Some users, in fact, have argued that they saved more by rethinking procedures and policies before they got their computers than they did by automated data processing after the machines were installed. Other possibilities are suggested by the discovery that supposedly "stupid" machines, programmed by men who often do not have much real business experience, often make decisions about things like inventory, factory scheduling, and product distribution better than men who have specialized for years in making these decisions. When this occurs, a company is likely to ask how much slack there is in other phases of its operations.

Over the longer run, computers are also going to have a more subtle but no less important impact on our approaches to organizational design and evaluation through their impact on the training of the next generation of managers. Young men will be exposed increasingly to teaching machines, management games, simulation techniques, and other facets of information processing technology. For the last five years, for example, every man in Carnegie Tech's graduate program in industrial administration gets basic training in the use of computers as part of his core training in management. Every effort is made to equip him so that he can use them as easily as he would a slide rule, a reference library, or a staff assistant to tackle problems in marketing or other fields that he may choose. Similar though less intensive experience is also given in the School's program for executives. To the extent that the computer is embedded in the environment in which men learn about management, it is going to be an important influence on their approach to all kinds of managerial problems.

I might suggest other ways in which computers are helping to make us more attentive to questions of how to build and how to assess organizational structures, but these seem to me to be the most important ones. Computers help by disrupting and discrediting old patterns and structures, by forcing us to seek alternatives to our traditional ways of operation, and by assuming an increasingly important role in the preparation of new candidates for management.

Computers ought to be able to do more, though, than raise questions and create new problems for us. They should be able to help find solutions. Returning to the problems that I stressed in the beginning of this paper, computers can help overcome:

—Our lack of adequate information about how good existing organizational systems are and about where our attention ought to be focussed.

—The difficulties of finding good ideas about new directions in which we might move, new kinds of organizational arrangements we might try.

—The difficulties of assessing in a systematic way what the effects of a change are likely to be.

—The need for ways to experiment with new ideas and arrangements without damaging or destroying an existing organization.

It will be easier to illustrate these points if we look at a sample problem of organizational design with which marketing executives may sometimes be concerned. In any organization where salesmen or sales offices are dispersed geographically and where one or more intermediate levels of supervision can be found between the field salesman and the top marketing executive, there are problems of how to organize communication procedures and how to assign "authority" to insure effective organizational performance.

Our first problem in such a situation would be to collect data that will let us estimate the effects of rules for communication and assignments of authority on the performance variables we are interested in. Suppose that we know what data will help us. These data are hard to collect without a computer. In the first place, they must be available quickly. If they are delivered four to six weeks late, as much hand calculated information is, they come too late for us to initiate useful supplementary investigations about the problems they reveal. Computers do not always deliver data promptly, but they can be many times faster than most clerical operations.

With a computer, we can collect more sophisticated measures. To compare two subunits of an organization which are organized differently, we should have more than each unit's *average* performance. We should have some measure of variability of performance within each unit so that we can estimate whether the differences we observe between units are meaningful differences or simply random variations that are not likely to persist. If you have tried, you know that it is harder to teach a human clerk to compute a standard deviation or perform a test of significance than it is to teach him to compute a percentage or an average. Given one of the modern algebraic programming languages with adequate pre-packaged subroutines, it is as easy to get a computer to do many kinds of complex analysis as it is to get it to do simple calculations.

In preparing many kinds of data, computers are also more accurate. Many errors occur in hand calculations, more than most data users realize. If data for a computer are once correctly recorded and punched and if the program, or set of instructions, for the machine has been carefully designed and "debugged," the work that the computer does should be substantially error-free. In cases where there is a risk of error or a risk that the computing instructions may be wrong, computers are much more cheerful and more patient than many clerks about checking their work.

Faster, fancier, and more accurate data will be a great help if we know what data we need. If we do not know what data we need, our first task is to find out what information is worth collecting and how we can use this information to develop possible solutions for the problems that we discover. Knowing what questions to ask and what avenues to explore is a major mark of distinction between the effective and the ineffective manager. How can computers assist us in our search?

At first glance, they do not play a very important role in our search for relevant ideas, facts, and experience. If we want to know more about the relationships of communication procedures and authority structure to performance today, we are likely to begin by talking to other executives or consultants whom we know about their experiences. We or one of our assistants may call or visit other companies or attend a seminar on the subject. More and more, we are likely to refer to books or periodicals that offer advice or that summarize, in the form of case studies or reports on experimental studies, the relationships that have been found among these variables in other situations.

Computers will eventually be a key element in this search process, however. They are becoming important, first of all, in accumulating useful facts and theories about the kinds of communication and authority structures that work well. Until recently, most of our "wisdom" about these questions has been anecdotal in nature. Where we have tried to do systematic research, we have had to choose between the extremes of closely designed and controlled, but highly unrealistic laboratory experiments on one hand and of realistic, but loosely formulated case studies and surveys on the other. Computers greatly expand the possibilities for getting reliable and useful conclusions from organizational research.

More specifically, we can already point to three ways in which computers are aiding research on problems of designing communication and authority structures.

1. Computers make larger and more comprehensive surveys possible. The studies that the Survey Research Center at Ann Arbor has undertaken on the effects of various supervisory patterns on morale and productivity (8) and the efforts of men at Ohio State to identify the "factors" of effective leadership performance involve quantities of data and levels of complexity in calculations that would be difficult to carry through without computers.

2. Computers provide a means of trying to generalize the results of small-group laboratory studies to large-scale organizations. There is a large collection of experimental literature about the effects of

different kinds of communication restrictions on the performance of four- and five-man teams. To do similar experiments with larger teams, such as we would have to organize in real-life is a slow and expensive process. Efforts are now underway at Carnegie, via a computer simulation model, to predict how larger networks might behave, and thereby, to identify the aspects of large-group performance that are most worth exploring with human subjects.

3. Computer programming languages provide an important alternative to ordinary English or to the languages of mathematics, geometry, and statistics for the statement of theories about human behavior and for the generation of predictions which we can test through various kinds of research. A computer program, for example, which enables a machine to simulate the flows of information or the responses to authoritative actions in a real organization is, in effect, a "theory" about the communication or authority structure of that organization. Computer program theories are more precise, and thus easier to test and evaluate, than most verbal theories; and they can describe many kinds of behaviors more flexibly than the highly formal techniques of mathematics and statistics.

As computers help us to generate more useful facts and theories about organizational behavior, we are going to need their help in finding the information that will really help us answer the specific questions with which we are immediately concerned. As we are already doing in law, medicine, and the physical sciences, we are likely to establish one or more central libraries that will store on media like magnetic tapes that computers can read, theoretical writings, research data, and case experience about organizational processes. If these materials can be indexed appropriately and if ways can be found (as they have been in other fields) to put our problems and questions directly to the computer, we should be able to get:

—A report on whether there is any theory, research, or case experience relevant to the questions in which we are interested.

—Copies of the relevant documents, summaries and abstracts of the parts that are of most interest to us, or information about where the documents can be obtained.

—Comments and data that may help us evaluate the applicability of the theories, research results, and experience that are reported to us.

Much of the computer technology for such a library is now available. Working with overviews of organizational questions such as the one that March, Simon, and Guetzkow (10) have proposed, we need to develop better systems for classifying and indexing the information that we have and will accumulate. We must make a substantial initial investment in finding, sorting, and preparing materials for the library and in setting up procedures that will keep it up to date.

Once we have defined the problems that face us and put together some alternative proposals for their solution, we usually want some estimates of their probable consequences before we decide which one to put into effect. We can derive these estimates from the experience of others, but often this is not appropriate because of differences between their organizations and ours. We can also generate estimates by selecting an alternative and trying it out in some part of the organization. If we are interested in long-term results, though, it may take months or years before we can assess whether to extend the experiment to the rest of the organization. Sometimes, as in setting up an air defense organization, we may be most concerned with the ability of a plan for organization to meet emergency conditions which may occur only rarely in real life. Or we may be faced with circumstances where even the tentative installation of one plan for organization will set off employee reactions that limit our freedom to experiment with others.

To get faster feedback, to explore a system's ability to deal with rare but critical emergencies, and to avoid being forced into premature commitments about plans for organizational structure, firms can often use simulation techniques to help estimate the consequences of various organizational proposals. That is, they can set up models or replicas of the main features of the organizational or organizational-environmental system that they are dealing with, and then check proposed new policies with the model or the replica rather than with the real organization. Simulation techniques are for the organizational planner what the wind tunnel is for the aeronautical engineer.

Depending on the kinds of effects we want to explore, we may try to simulate the reactions of an individual executive or worker, the reactions of a work group or subunit in the organization, the total organization, or a larger system which embodies both the organization and large segments of its environment. Effective simulations may not be terribly complicated; and they may not involve any use of computers. We are simulating, crudely but perhaps adequately, in situations where we simply sit down and ask: "If we promote John Jones to be supervisor of the other district salesmen he has been working with, how will the other salesmen react?" By using what we know about John Jones and the other salesmen, we may be able to predict fairly accurately that Dick Smith will quit, that Harvey Hendricks will not care, and so on. We are simulating in many training sessions when we expose trainees to role playing situations in which the roles of people they are dealing with are played as they might be in real life.

But when the effects we want to trace involve larger organizational units or very complicated sequences of interactions, we often need the facilities of a computer to aid in the simulation.

In the RAND Corporation's simulation of the nation's air defense system, for example, computers were used to generate the environment in which radar crews, central plotting and tracking groups, and interceptor squadrons operated. Computers simulated the flight paths of friendly and enemy aircraft and missiles in a much larger variety of combinations than the crews had experienced in real life and translated these paths into "blips" on the radar screens which the air defense units were watching. It was then possible to put Air Force personnel into this synthetic environment, and by observing the kinds of communication and authority patterns that they developed, to derive policies both for organizing an air defense system and for training personnel to perform effectively within it (2). In another study at RAND, computer models were used to generate interactions among crews at a large number of "simulated" air bases which were trying to maintain inventories of spare engine parts sufficient to keep enough planes in operation at reasonable cost-levels under a variety of peace-time and war-time conditions (5).

In other cases, computers have been used to simulate both the organization and its environment so that effects of a variety of organizational conditions and managerial policies can be tested. The Systems Development Corporation has constructed an analytic model of a total business system that simulates information flows, decision rules, and physical production processes within an organization. With this model, they have been able to explore some general effects of using alternate channels for making decisions, of installing different kinds of control systems, and of setting different objectives within the organization (9). In another study, Bonini (1) has set up a general computer model of a business firm and tested some of the long-run effects of factors like the stability of the external environment, characteristics of the internal communication systems, and the amount and "contagion" of top management pressure on such dimensions of the firm's performance as profits, cost control, pricing policy, and sales. Even in their general form, these models lead to some interesting and provocative predictions about factors that determine how well an organization will perform.

Computer models may also be used to generate predictions of how individuals will react. We have already had a great deal of success in building models that will simulate and predict the behavior of people making fairly complex managerial decisions. There now exists something called "the rote marketer"—a computer program which simulates the behavior of real teams making sales forecasts and marketing decisions in the highly complex Carnegie Tech Management Game (6,7). For real-world decisions, there are simulations of the behavior of a department store buyer making many of the decisions that his position requires (4) and of an investment officer in a bank deciding what stocks and bonds should be bought for various trust funds (3). We cannot yet point to good computer simulations of emotionally-loaded behavior, such as of how an individual will react to a new policy that threatens his status or security as an employee. But given further growth in our understanding of the psychological processes involved and in our ability to design and use computers, we are not many years away from these kinds of simulations.

Some firms are looking forward to quite specific simulations of their own organizations and of the environments in which they operate. Whenever they have a question about the implications or effects of a broad class of problems and policies, they question the computer in the same way that we now question staff experts or outside consultants. It is not likely that the computer will render either the staff expert or the consultant obsolete; but in many areas that we now handle by crude kinds of crystal-ball gazing, a good computer simulation will serve us as well or better. More and more we may expect our staff men and consultants to become less useful for their ability to answer questions directly and more important for their ability to design simulation models to which they can put questions.

Progress in developing simulations that are relevant to the design and evaluation of organizational structures has been substantial, but it is not as great—or as prominent—as our progress in simulating various production processes or the aggregate characteristics of consumer demand or interfirm competition. To simulate a system effectively, one must be able to make fairly precise specifications about how it will behave. We are not as precise in our knowledge of organizational processes as we are in our knowledge of many other kinds of systems. We have concentrated, in computer design, on the development of machines and programming languages that are very efficient at manipulating numbers but less efficient in manipulating the kinds of qualitative language in which most of our knowledge of organizations is couched. We will benefit from the continued expansion of research on organization processes, whether or not it involves computers; and we may expect to see an increase in machines and programming languages that are designed especially to analyze qualitative relationships and to work efficiently with words as well as with numbers.

For many of the processes we are interested in studying, our simulations are likely to be combination man-machine simulations. In these, we will use computers most effectively to generate the environment and the gross workings of the organization. We will use human subjects, though, to work within these organizational and environmental constraints because for many purposes we cannot yet specify their behavior completely enough to replicate it with a computer. Because, for example, of differences in our understanding of the kinds of behavior involved, we are likely to see earlier progress in the development of computer simulations of communication processes than of authority relationships within organizations.

We are now near the end of the chain. Once we have used simulation techniques to predict what alternative proposals for organizational design might lead to, we—or perhaps in the not-too-distant future, our computers —make a choice. This is implemented; and we begin the cycle again, using computers to help us collect the data which helps us to evaluate how well the innovations are working and helps us, more generally, to keep track of other parts of the organization and to recognize new problems which need attention.

The eventual importance of computers in designing and testing organizational structures is clear; the speed with which their various potentialities can be developed is less so. At the moment, computers are creating many problems for us to work on. They are helping in many cases to give us better information and ideas to work with. But when we talk about their ability to undertake the search for data and experience that are applicable to our problems or to help choose solutions and simulate their effects before we commit ourselves to them, we are talking about developments that for the most part lie ahead of us.

To help bring these developments about, three problems need to be dealt with. The first is the one with which I introduced this paper:

We need to become much more sensitive to the importance of organizational design in achieving good performance and much more analytical and critical about the ideas which we accept in this area. The second has to do with cost: Adequate libraries of organizational research and experience cannot be established by single companies or single universities acting on their own. Pilot research on effective ways to simulate organizational behavior on a large scale is going to cost millions of dollars. Arrangements for cooperative support of these undertakings can greatly speed their realization. The third problem has to do with effective monitoring of what we achieve: The prospect is that within another decade we shall have the power to plan and control the performance of organizations—and of the men within them—to much closer tolerances than we can now. This power implies a responsibility to use it in ways that make organizations more satisfying to the men who work within them and to the people whom they serve than they often are today.

REFERENCES

1. Bonini, C., "Simulation of Information and Decision Systems in the Firm," Graduate School of Industrial Administration, Carnegie Institute of Technology; ONR Memorandum #77, 1961 (dittoed).

2. Chapman, R. L., et al., "The Systems Research Laboratory's Air Defense Experiments," Management Science, 5 (April 1959), pp. 250-269.

3. Clarkson, G., "The Meno Anew: A Simulation of Trust Investment." Unpublished Ph.D. thesis, Carnegie Institute of Technology, 1961.

4. Cyert, R., and J. G. March, "A Specific Price and Output Model," Graduate School of Industrial Administration, Carnegie Institute of Technology; Behavioral Theory of the Firm Working Paper #30, 1961 (dittoed).

5. Enke, S., "On the Economic Management of Large Organizations: A Laboratory Study," *Journal of Business,* **31** (October 1958), pp. 280-292.

6. Haines, G., F. Heider, and D. Remington, "The Computer as Small Group Member," *Administrative Science Quarterly* (forthcoming).

7. ———, "The Rote Marketer," *Behavioral Science* (forthcoming).

8. Likert, R., "Measuring Organizational Performance," *Harvard Business Review,* **36** (March-April 1958), pp. 41-50.

9. Malcolm, D. G., and A. J. Rowe, "Computer-Based Control Systems," *California Management Review,* **3** (Spring 1961), pp. 4-15.

10. March, J. G., H. A. Simon, with H. Guetzkow, *Organizations* (New York: John Wiley & Sons, Inc., 1959).

chapter two | *Alfred A. Kuehn and Ralph L. Day*

Computer models based on business operations are now being used in many ways. The educational use of computer models in business games has tended to overshadow their application to the analysis of actual business operations. However, an increasing amount of interest is being shown in the development of simulation models and operational games. This article discusses the nature of these promising new tools and illustrates their use in a marketing context.

The distinctions among the various approaches to the analysis of business operations which make use of computer models are frequently not recognized. Most of these techniques are still in an early stage of development, and terminology has not yet crystallized to the point where one can apply a single term to a specific model without the risk of being misunderstood. As a result, in some quarters all computer models of business situations are called "simulations" unless they are applications of a single well-known algorithmic technique such as linear programming or

SIMULATION AND

OPERATIONAL GAMING

a standard statistical approach such as regression analysis. There is also a tendency to invent new names with which to identify one's own particular work, even though it may be virtually indistinguishable from the approach used by others in the field.

It is not the purpose of this article to establish either precise definitions for such new terms as "industrial dynamics" [1] and "heuristic programming" [2] or to coin additional terminology. Nevertheless, it does seem necessary to clarify the sense in which the terms "simulation" and "operational gaming" are used.

---

[1] Jay W. Forrester, *Industrial Dynamics* (New York: John Wiley and Sons, 1961).

[2] Herbert A. Simon and Allen Newell, "Heuristic Problem Solving: The Next Advance in Operations Research," *Operations Research,* Vol. **6** (January-February, 1958), pp. 1-10.

COMPUTER SIMULATION

The term "simulation" is frequently used in a much broader sense than will be adopted for the purposes of this article. A dictionary definition of "simulate" is "the act of assuming the appearance of, without the reality; to feign." This definition could include a wide range of things and activities from the use of Link trainers to "role playing" sessions, not to mention economic theories and operations research models. In this article the term "simulation" will be restricted to computer models of some phase of business activity, which possess all of the following characteristics:

1. The structure of the model seeks to represent the operational characteristics of some segment of the actual business world, be it a part of a firm, an entire firm, an industry, or even the whole economy.

2. The model containing the essential features of the simulated business operation is an abstract, computational system of mathematical and logical expressions designed to accept inputs depicting actual or hypothesized changes in the real situation and to provide outputs approximating the operating results of its real world counterpart.

3. The model is a self-contained system with a structure (consisting of functional relationships and parameter values) that remains stable over time. The structure is not altered by changes in the environment.

Thus, a simulation model is a theory of the dynamic mechanisms of the business system being modeled. Environmental conditions influence the predictions of behavior generated in the simulation study only insofar as they represent variable inputs to the model. The output describes the changes in behavior of the elements (e.g., firms) in the system over time as determined by the structure, functional relationships, parameter values, environmental inputs, and starting conditions incorporated in the model.

A computer model is then a simulation, in the specific sense considered here, only if it is a self-contained model based on an actual business operation, and remains structurally stable over time while generating predictions of outcomes in the business system. The structural stability requirement does not limit the flexibility of the model but rather emphasizes that a simulation model is a theory which, in some sense, must be tested. If the output of the model is not consistent with the observed behavior of the system being modeled, the theory reflected in the model should be modified, extended, or perhaps even rejected completely. Revisions of theory require adjustments in the structure of the simulation model.

The three characteristics of a business simulation outlined above contain no restrictions with regard to structural details. A simulation can be either stochastic (that is, contain probabilistic elements) or "exact." Its structure can consist primarily of mathematical expressions or it might consist entirely of logical operations such as "conditional transfer" or "branching"; usually it contains important elements of both. The role of the computer is in one sense very limited. It merely performs the calculations specified by the model, calculations which an individual could do with a desk-top calculator. Yet, the computer is essential to the development and testing of simulations of even moderately complex situations. The computational speed of the computer is necessary if a solution of a complex mathematical structure is to be obtained within a reasonable period of time and expenditure of effort. Also, the flexibility of computer programming imposes few restrictions on the structural formulation of models and provides procedures for obtaining solutions to problems which cannot be solved with existing formal mathematics.

The intent of the foregoing discussion has been to provide a more precise definition of simulation in the context of computerized business models. To the extent that this has been accomplished, related techniques employing computer models can be more precisely identified by appropriate terminology.

PEDAGOGICAL MODELS

Business games, for example, are often referred to as simulations, even when they are based on purely hypothetical business situations. Such contrived games are clearly simulations only in the very broad sense of the word since they often have none of the essential features of a business simulation outlined above. In developing business games, there is frequently no attempt to represent faithfully the operating characteristics of a real situation or to provide a predictive theory. The game model is often an incomplete representation of even the hypothetical situation on which it is based. Game administrators often portray parts of the business world and modify parameters of the game while play is underway.

The form and objectives of the business game distinguish it from simulation in a more fundamental way than does its lack of "realism." It is quite possible for portions of a business game to be based on a simulation model but the game must allow for the participation of players. The game model would not be a simulation of the industry unless the players were to simulate the behavior of their specific counterparts in the business firms. Therefore, the prime purpose of game models is not to predict the behavior of an actual industry but rather to provide an educational tool.

The educational purposes suggested for such games have included the teaching of concepts and principles in a dynamic environment, the conveying of truths which scholars have not yet formulated verbally ("teaching the unteachable"), acquainting the student with organizational problems, and providing practice in the application of various skills in the face of an uncertain future. The business setting of the games is generally thought to increase the student's motivation and to provide an orientation to managerial subject matter.[1]

Most of the broad educational benefits outlined above can be obtained by using games which are not based on realistic simulations of an industry or market situation. This is indeed fortunate since constructing a realistic simulation of business and consumer behavior which reflects the influence of marketing variables is no simple task. The outward trappings of a marketing situation can be incorporated into a game quite easily whereas a realistic simulation requires a deeper understanding of the operation of the underlying behavioral and influence mechanisms.

For purposes of general business education, the student can be admonished to play the game and not the world. The emphasis can be upon the player learning about his game environment just as he might in another setting be required to learn about the mechanisms operating in a specific business situation. This does not, of course, answer such questions as what should be taught and what should be the characteristics of games so as to facilitate initial learning and subsequent transfer of acquired knowledge to practical application. Although there is disagreement among business educators on this point, it seems clear that realistic games, once they are available, will be more effective in providing "synthetic experience." [2]

To say that business games are not simulations in the sense reserved for the predictive model of a real operation is in no way derogatory to business gaming. It is merely a recognition that business gaming for teaching purposes is a fundamentally different use of a computerized business model, both in terms of structure and objectives. Since "business game" and "management game" are well established and generally recognized terms for such pedagogical models, it seems desirable to use these terms, rather than simulation, to refer to such models.

OPERATIONAL GAMING

Of all the terms applied to computer models of business operations, perhaps the most amorphous is "operational gaming." One of the early statements of the nature of operational gaming was "the use of war gaming

---

[1] William R. Dill, James R. Jackson, and James W. Sweeney, eds., *Proceedings of the Conference on Business Games as Teaching Devices* (New Orleans: Tulane University, 1961).

[2] Alfred A. Kuehn, "Realism in Business Games," *op. cit.,* pp. 56-60.

in a context broader than that of military situations alone."[1] Defined in this way, operational gaming would include business games and the simulation of competitive situations, since both of these techniques are descendants of the war game. The issue is further clouded by the fact that early references to operational gaming emphasized its potential as an educational device.[2] However, it should be noted that these references preceded the adaptation of the war game to business situations as a management training device.

The terms "business game" and "management game" now adequately cover the educational applications of the war gaming approach. Therefore, it seems desirable that "operational gaming" be used in a more restrictive sense. Even before the development of the business game, some operations researchers were using the term to refer to the use of the gaming situation as an aid to problem solving and as an approach to strategy formulation for participants in actual situations involving conflict.[3]

As more realistic business games are being developed, there are increasing opportunities to use the game model for operational purposes as well as for training purposes. When a game model reflects the major operating characteristics of an actual situation in a reasonably realistic way, it can be used to study the implications of alternative strategies. Knowledgeable executives can play the game as if it were the real situation in competition with other experienced businessmen representing competing firms, or against computer models programmed to react in the way it is believed that competitors would react.[4] The objective is not training in the broad sense but the testing of actual operating procedures and policies in the synthetic environment of the game.

"Operational gaming" will be used here to mean the use of a game structure based on a realistic simulation of a business environment in conjunction with one or more players (or teams of players) for the purpose of problem solving or policy evaluation. An operational gaming model will then have striking similarities to a business game model in those cases in which the former permits players to compete with each other in the context of the game. It differs from business gaming in that the ob-

---

[1] Walter E. Cushen, "Operational Gaming in Industry," in Joseph F. McCloskey and John M. Coppinger, eds., *Operations Research for Management* (Baltimore: The Johns Hopkins Press, 1956), Vol. 11, p. 358.

[2] *Op. cit.*, p. 361.

[3] Clayton J. Thomas and Walter L. Deemer, Jr., "The Role of Operational Gaming in Operations Research," *Operations Research,* Vol. 5 (February, 1957), pp. 1-27.

[4] George H. Haines, Jr., "The Rote Marketer," *Behavioral Science,* Vol. 4 (October, 1961), pp. 357-365.

jectives are different and much more stringent requirements of realism are placed on the model.

An operational game is like a simulation in that it is intended to reflect realistically the major operating characteristics of an actual business situation and to provide operating results which can be considered as predictions of what would be the outcomes in the real situation, given the actions of the participating units. The operational gaming model differs with respect to the simulation model in that it is not self-contained, humans being assigned to play important roles in interaction with the model and thereby influencing its output.

SIMULATION AND GAMING IN MARKETING

The applications of simulation and gaming to marketing situations are still relatively limited in number. A few simulation studies of an exploratory nature have been made in recent years. Among these are the simulation of a local lumber market by Balderston and Hoggatt,[1] and a simulation of the major appliances department of a large department store by Cyert, March, and Moore.[2] Other simulation studies which have long-run implications for marketing have been made by Orcutt, et al.,[3] and by Simulmatics, Inc.[4]

The early business games were generally of the "top management" type and did not depict marketing activities in detail. They used purely hypothetical models in which business firms were depicted at a very abstract level. The marketing segments of these games were little more than hypothesized schedules of demand with each period's potential being allocated among firms according to "reasonable" assumptions about price and promotional elasticities.

More recent "total firm" games, particularly the Carnegie Tech Management Game,[5] have had more complex marketing functions but still

---

[1] F. E. Balderston and A. C. Hoggatt, "The Simulation of Market Processes," Management Science Research Group, University of California, Berkeley, October, 1960.

[2] R. M. Cyert, J. G. March, and C. G. Moore, "A Model of Retail Ordering and Pricing in a Department Store," in R. E. Frank, A. A. Kuehn, and W. F. Massy, eds., *Quantitative Techniques in Marketing Analysis* (Homewood: Richard D. Irwin, Inc., 1962).

[3] Guy H. Orcutt, Martin Greenberger, John Korbel, and Alice M. Rivlin, *Microanalysis of Socioeconomic Systems: A Simulation Study* (New York: Harper and Brothers, 1961).

[4] Ithiel de Sola Pool and Robert Abelson, "The Simulmatics Project," *The Public Opinion Quarterly*, Vol. 25 (Summer, 1961), pp. 167-183.

[5] K. J. Cohen, et al, "The Carnegie Tech Management Game," *The Journal of Business of the University of Chicago*, Vol. 4 (October, 1960), pp. 303-321.

have not attempted to achieve a high degree of realism. A still more recent development is the complex computerized "marketing game" which
eliminates or simplifies other aspects of the business firm and concentrates
on marketing variables. One such game, the MIT Marketing Game, is
discussed elsewhere in this book. The CIT Marketing Game, perhaps the
most recent game of this type, will be discussed below.[1]

THE DEVELOPMENT OF AN INDUSTRY SIMULATION

Most of the remainder of this paper will be devoted to a discussion of the
research, extending over a period of several years, which contributed to
the development of a simulation model of the detergent industry and the
CIT Marketing Game. This now offers promise of a game structure suitable for operational gaming applications in industry. It will be shown
how this work progressed from the analysis of empirical data to the construction of analytic models, thence to more complex simulation models
and finally to the development of the game model.

THE INITIAL RESEARCH—AN ADVERTISING MODEL

The research which eventually led to the CIT Marketing Game was not
originally intended to result in either a simulation of an industry or a
marketing game. The initial goal was to develop an analytical model of
market influences and consumer behavior which could be used to develop
decision rules for use by management in the budgeting of advertising.[2]

An analytical model was constructed treating consumer brand shifting as a first order purchase-to-purchase Markov Process. The implications of this model were then examined under the assumption that the
managements of the competing firms would independently seek to maximize their operating profits. In addition, some of the consumer behavioral
assumptions underlying the model were tested with the purchase records
of a consumer panel. Finally, an analysis was made of the consistency of
the sales and profit results generated by the model with comparable data
available for competing brands of a variety of grocery and proprietary
drug products. These first tests led to additional research in the development of an improved model of consumer brand shifting and to the incorporation in this model of the influence of price, product characteristics

---

[1] Alfred A. Kuehn and Doyle L. Weiss, "CIT Marketing Game," Research in
Marketing Project, Working Paper No. 4, Carnegie Institute of Technology, Pitts-
burgh, Pennsylvania.

[2] Alfred A. Kuehn, "A Model for Budgeting Advertising," in Frank M. Bass,
et al., eds. Mathematical Models and Methods in Marketing (Homewood: Richard
D. Irwin, Inc., 1961).

and retail availability upon consumer purchasing behavior, due regard being paid to the interaction of these factors with advertising and related forms of sales promotion.[1]

The empirical evidence examined in the course of the above research appeared to suggest that the general lack of progress of researchers in developing a sound model for the budgeting of advertising might have been due to the way in which the field of marketing had been partitioned for purposes of research. Traditionally, such individual influences as price and advertising have been regarded as essentially independent of one another. Since the total consumer influence structure appeared too complex to be studied at one time, the problem was partitioned and most researchers concentrated either upon advertising or the effects of price and gave little explicit consideration to possible interrelationships. When success appeared elusive, marketing practitioners and theorists began to look upon marketing as a complex maze of influence mechanisms in which little could really be done in the way of scientific analysis. Consumers came to be regarded as erratic, unpredictable, inconsistent and irrational. This seemed to be considered by marketing men as evidence that marketing would not be amenable to the types of mathematical analysis and model building which brought order into the physical sciences.

THE DEVELOPMENT OF MORE REALISTIC MODELS—SIMULATION

A more realistic model of consumer behavior was developed next, consumer brand choice being treated as a probabilistic process. The probability that a consumer would buy a specific brand was influenced by competitive merchandising activity. Similarly, the past buying patterns of the consumer (reflecting his consumption habits and, to a degree, his satisfaction or dissatisfaction with the items purchased) were recognized as being closely related to the probability that the consumer would buy specific brands in the near future. The model appeared to describe consumer brand shifting behavior quite well. It specifically recognized that there may be some element of chance in a consumer's choice of a brand and treated consumer brand shifting as an adaptive or learning process.

Similarly, the influences of price, advertising, product characteristics and retail availability were recognized as not being independent. These components of the marketing mix were incorporated as interaction effects in an expanded form of the original model (which had previously contained only advertising).

A continual process involving the building of models, the testing of assumptions, the evaluation of implications, and comparison of the results

---

[1] Alfred A. Kuehn, "How Advertising Performance Depends on Other Marketing Factors," *Journal of Advertising Research*, Vol. 2 (March, 1962), pp. 2-10.

with empirical data on consumer buying behavior and the merchandising activities of competitors, led to successive refinements of the model. It then appeared to describe the underlying market and behavioral systems quite well. Seldom did the model produce implications not considered reasonable or at least plausible by marketing managers and it frequently provided unforeseen results regarded as intriguing and worthy of test market experimentation.

On the other hand, several gaps were evident in the above analytic formulation of the model and the "optimum" advertising and pricing decision rules which were derived from it. For example, retail availability was treated as an independently determined variable, whereas in fact there is some evidence to support the feedback influence of market share and the interacting effects of advertising, sales calls, and retail promotions upon the "per cent distribution" obtained by brands. Similarly, segmentation of the market according to differences in consumer preferences for product attributes introduced problems too complex to permit the development of analytic solutions. To facilitate the exploration of these problems, the analytic models studied and tested above were incorporated into a computer program simulating the consumer, wholesale and retail levels of the detergent industry. In the process of preparing this simulation model, several additional assumptions were made. Patterns of behavior were assumed for wholesalers and retailers with respect to their decisions to stock or not stock a brand, recognizing the influences of customer demand for the product, its market share, and the merchandising activities in its behalf relative to that of competition. These assumptions, however, were based upon a substantial amount of preliminary research and the analysis of statistical evidence. Improvements in this aspect of the simulation model (perhaps in the form of the model, certainly in the setting of the parameter values) can be expected in the course of continued research with the model.

CURRENT AND FUTURE RESEARCH

The model on which the CIT Marketing Game is based might be considered a simulation of the market for packaged detergents. By the definitions outlined earlier in this paper, the game could be developed into an operational game as the mechanisms are further tested, modified, and perhaps extended to better simulate behavior in that industry.

The research now underway to evaluate the structure of the simulation so as to provide directions for future improvements is proceeding along lines similar to those outlined earlier with respect to the testing of the analytical model of consumer behavior and market influences. First, the implications of the simulation are being examined with respect to its equilibrium characteristics, that is, the levels of expenditures which competing manufacturers would be required to make for advertising and sales personnel and the prices that they would have to charge to maximize independently their profits. This type of analysis is being done for identical products and for products that are differentiated in terms of physical characteristics. The sensitivity of these results to various parameters in the model (e.g., industry and inter-brand price elasticities, probability of consumer being influenced by advertising, degree of habitual purchasing behavior by consumers, etc.) are also being examined. A variety of other types of related studies with the simulation model are also planned for the near future. For example, what is the optimal way within the framework of the model to introduce a new product? What kind of investment is justified in establishing a market position for a new brand? How does the answer to this question depend upon future product developments within the industry and the ability of the firm to incorporate such developments into the brand in question?

The above questions can be studied within the simulation model and the results obtained from the model can then be examined with respect to past market data. It may also be possible to test directly individual assumptions within the model. Also desirable would be the testing of results of the model in practice. This can be done in those cases where marketing managers see the results of the model as reasonably consistent with their experiences and find opportunities for new strategies in the implications of the model. Such comparison and test results can be expected to provide information with which to improve the simulation model, suggest areas for future research, and open areas for application. It should be noted that perfection in a simulation model is not needed for application. All that is required is a model which can help management make better decisions. Whether the simulation model described in this paper will prove to be of operational value is yet to be demonstrated. It seems certain, however, that much will be learned in the course of this research, and these findings should help lead to a better understanding and improved models of the market under study. In any event, some of the analytical models which have been incorporated into the simulation have already been found useful in various areas of application.

What is the role of the simulation technique in the research outlined above? Clearly, much emphasis has been placed on using tests of internal consistency and the findings of empirical research to evaluate assumptions and the implications of the analytical models at each stage of their development. These models were combined into a computer simulation model only after the various parts were understood and tested in some detail. If the simulation model combining these analytical models also included the behavior of the individual firms, it would generate the time path of results predicted by the entire system, a system much too complicated to evaluate analytically. As yet, however, no attempt has been made to simulate the behavior of competitors. Only the reaction of the channels of distribution and of consumers to the merchandising activities and product offerings of competitors have been considered. This type of simulation would therefore be limited to predicting market results, given independent estimates of the behavior of competition. When assumptions are made about the behavior of competitors, the simulation should indicate (to the extent that it correctly depicts the real situation) the results which would occur in practice, within random error limits for probabilistic models.

The computer model logically followed from the development of more conventional analytic models which serve as its basic components. The availability of computers enabled the construction of a larger, more complex model than would previously have been amenable to analysis. Ironically, it appears that the availability of computers is not an unmixed blessing. The use of computers in simulation may actually prove, for a time, to delay progress in the development of sound theory. The computational ability of the machine has led researchers to expand greatly the number of variables included in models and to increase the complexity of feedback loops. The ease with which this can be done gives the researcher a feeling of great power. Unfortunately, means of equivalent simplicity are not yet available for evaluating the individual and interaction effects of large numbers of variables in complex dynamic systems. It seems likely that more progress in the development of theory will be forthcoming once researchers learn to concentrate on a relatively few variables in the early stages of the construction of a model. Additional variables can then be incorporated as more is learned about the mechanisms operating in the system being simulated, or, as was done in the example outlined above, a series of models can be developed and tested before being combined as a rather complex simulation model.

THE CIT MARKETING GAME

Once the simulation model was developed and improved to the point that it seemed to reflect adequately most of the major operating characteristics (other than individual firm behavior) of the industry on which it was based, it provided the foundation for a comparatively realistic marketing game in which the teams of players represent the individual firms.

The game has provision for three firms operating in four geographical regions. The marketing aspects of the game are quite detailed while the production, financial and accounting operations are highly simplified so that the players' interests are focused upon marketing variables. This also serves to keep the time demands of the game upon the players and the administrator at a level which permits its use as a supplementary part of a marketing course. Each firm may market from one to three brands of detergent in each region and has the opportunity to revise or alter its prices, advertising budgets, size of salesforce and retail promotional allowances once each game month. Other decisions made by the players include the quantities ordered from the production department and the shipping schedules to and between regional warehouses. If the firm does not take positive action to change these policy decisions, they are treated as constant from month to month. Thus, the players need take action only when they wish to redirect the firm's efforts and resources.

In addition to the above merchandising and distribution decisions, a firm may buy information about the market and its sales position relative to competitors. It may purchase market survey reports containing estimates of total industry retail sales and market shares, retail distribution and stockouts by brand, retail shelf prices, competitive advertising expenditures, wholesale and retail inventory levels, and the size of competitors' salesforces. The firm can also undertake to develop new and better products by allocating funds to product research. The firm can direct such research toward several ends: basic research; research aimed at developing products with specific characteristics; the synthesis of a competitor's product; and the alteration of the characteristics of one of the firm's own products. (The product research function is believed to be similar to the mechanisms operating in industry but is not claimed to be realistic and is not a part of the underlying simulation model.) Products developed by the research department are made available to the players, accompanied by a laboratory report outlining its product characteristics (washing power, gentleness, and a measure of sudsing) and estimated manufacturing costs. The players must make the decision as to whether any given product should be marketed on the basis of the laboratory-determined characteristics and consumer "blind" product preference tests. One of the four regions in which the firm may market its products could also be used as a large test market if this appeared to be desirable.

The teams are given similar starting conditions in terms of their market positions and resources. Thus, the "firms" in the game do not attempt to portray actual firms and the game is not a simulation of the U.S. detergent industry. On the other hand, the reasonably realistic environment (representing wholesalers, retailers and consumers) in which the teams operate does provide an opportunity for participants in the game to learn something about the behavioral characteristics of the market and the operating problems faced by marketing managers in industry.

In addition to its value to the players, the game provides a useful laboratory setting for the researcher since he can study the response of the simulated environment to patterns of behavior exhibited by the teams of players. It also provides the opportunity to observe the effectiveness of analytical techniques and decision rules used in playing the game. Thus the "controlled environment" of the game offers an inexpensive means of testing hypothesized strategies and techniques of business analysis which would be very costly to test in actual practice.

The game structure is designed to be self-contained. That is, subjective judgments by game administrators are not required during play of the game. While this precludes the consideration of such essentially qualitative factors as package design, it has the advantage that players know that the basic structure is stable throughout the game and not influenced by subjective judgments of administrators. This encourages their efforts to try to understand the workings of the game structure and the relationships embodied in it.

The next stage in the long term program which has produced the simulation model and the game structure described above is the play of the game by business executives in the industry being modeled. (The game can be modified to represent any of a number of consumer grocery and drug product industries with a much smaller amount of additional work than was required in establishing the initial model. The changes required would primarily concern the physical characteristics of products and the related consumer preference structures.) When the game is played by marketing executives of the industry to which it related, suggestions for improvements and data helpful in simulating the firm's behavior should be forthcoming. This should contribute to both an improved simulation model of the industry and a useful operational game structure.

SUMMARY

This article has attempted to provide useful guidelines for increasing the preciseness of terminology for computer models of business situations, particularly simulation and operational gaming. Some of the interrelationships among different kinds of computer models have been illustrated by reference to the development of a simulation model of the packaged detergent industry and a marketing game based upon it. Some directions have been suggested for future work which should lead to improved simulations and better operational games for use in marketing.

Simulation and operational gaming have so far played only a limited role in business research and an even smaller role as a practical aid to managerial decision making in marketing. However, a start has been made and the results are promising.

INTRODUCTION

One must first set forth the properties of an analog computer before considering the use of such computers in the simulation of marketing systems. Let me take the three words analog, marketing and marketing systems and say a little about each of them. The dictionary definition of the term "analog" (spelled analogue), of which analog is a variation, is as follows:

1) That which is analogous to some other thing,
2) Biological: an organ similar in function to an organ of another animal or plant but different in structure and origin—

It is similar *effects* or *results* that we are looking for without concern for differing structures or even origins. The term "analog computer" is perhaps a better one to examine. Again referring to Webster, we find the following definition:

ANALOG COMPUTERS IN

THE SIMULATION OF

MARKETING SYSTEMS

"A type of calculating machine that operates with numbers represented by directly measurable quantities as voltages, resistances, rotations, etc."

This "combined term" has come to imply a means of handling continuous variables and thus an ensuing sense of continuity—a continuing process or system, a closed loop system which does indeed have continuity within itself. There are by nature two kinds of analogs: the direct analogy type and the mathematical analogy type. The simplest example of the direct type is a slide rule, a device with which we are all familiar, at least by sight. It consists of two sticks on which the distances are analogs of the logarithm to be multiplied or divided. Thus, some of the distances on the stick are analogous to the sum of the logs or products of the numbers being handled. Since the sticks are calibrated in analogs, the result is a direct reading multiplier or divider. It is interesting to note here that the inputs and outputs are in digital form. This in no way destroys the analogous nature of the operation of the solution.

More complicated direct type analog computers exist, of course, and a good example is the AC network analyzer. In this type, the component parts of large electrical systems, e.g., generators, loads, transformers, transmission lines, etc., are simulated by use of resistance and reactors. Here there is usually an identifiable element in the computer which is analogous to each of the physically recognizable functional units of the system. This type of computer, although easier to understand, is of course less flexible than the second type, the mathematical analog computer. The operation of the mathematical analog, on the other hand, basically involves the use of equations or systems of equations in which identifiable operations in the solution of these equations, such as addition, multiplication, and integration, are simulated by devices or a combination of devices which are components of the mathematical computer.

SIMULATION

Now after this first discussion of analog computers, I would like to say a little about simulation. There are two ways to look at it: one as far as teaching is concerned, and the other as far as practical application is concerned. However, I can't see much difference between a simulation to teach students the effects of a marketing system on production or one designed to demonstrate the effects to management of following a fixed cost plus policy. We can manipulate this and that and see what is going to happen in our system. Thus, in industry we use simulation to teach ourselves. However, one cannot say much about such simulation until we talk about systems because the systems concept has great relevance to marketing operations. Therein lies the real value of the analog to the simulation of marketing systems. There has been a great surge of interest in systems analysis, such as the complex problems in communication networks. It is not surprising to see marketing people begin to realize that they can do something with this approach.

SYSTEMS AND ANALOGS

It might as well be stated now that with systems analysis "Via Analog Computers" you cannot get four decimal places. But if you deal with approximate data, as we usually do in marketing, and are interested in the sensitivity of the system (about which we shall say more later) this is the computer made for your problem. There are, indeed, close enough analogies between systems such as the previously mentioned communication networks and some of our marketing systems to warrant a further look.

At the Operations Research Society meetings in June of 1961, the chairman of one session was talking about simulation and computers. He made a great point to the effect that the person using the computer (digital) did not need to know anything about the system being simulated. I think this is a very unhealthy approach to the simulation of marketing systems. If you want to simulate and do not know anything about the system, don't play with the analog because it does demand that you do in fact know something about the system which you wish to simulate.

Moreover the very nature and construction of the analog wherein identifiable components simulate physical functions in our system implies (and in fact demands) that the problem solver know the nature of the flow in his system.

As I have previously said, we are finding in marketing more and more that we have things in common with other systems. I think much better use of these structural similarities can be made with the analogs than with the digital computer because the problem solver can inject himself into the system and experiment with it. For example, Dr. Lysle Peterson, of the School of Medicine of the University of Pennsylvania, has been using analog computers for some time to introduce artificial surges into the cycles of blood flows. This, I believe, has its counterpart in our economic systems. Slowly, we in the social sciences (of which marketing is a part) are beginning to see in operating analogies patterns for possible simulation. One can, I believe, profitably exploit developments in the techniques of systems simulation originally designed for the use of analogs in many other fields.

I recognize that some of the components of the flow systems seem to be most elusive. But I do not believe that these problems exist to any significant degree in the solution of marketing problems. The analog solution will give you information on which you can base a decision as a marketing manager. The systems analysis technique, again, may give us insight into the *type* of decision that might be made, *or* tell us whether a decision is needed at all. The latter is a frequently overlooked point. Many times the simulation of the marketing system (along inventory lines, for example) does not give us what we think we want but it tells us that we do not need that degree of sensitivity at all. That is, we discover there is no real need for the degree of accuracy in inventory levels previously considered essential for reasonable decision making. This has been found to be true in the work of Richard Maffei, at the Massachusetts Institute of Technology. In the main, these techniques (such as sensitivity analysis) are really tools and are of greatest assistance in providing an insight into the problem. But again, if you choose to use these techniques, you have to look first at an elementary system.

ELEMENTARY SYSTEMS

The systems with which we are most familiar are production control systems. Marketing and production, of course, are linked together, and the systems concept may bring us to a point ten years from now when we will no longer remember the functional areas of marketing and production as being separate.

We ought first to look at an extremely basic concept of a system. The simplest kind would involve production, sales, interest charges, etc. And you would have, dropping out at the bottom of the system, some sort of a profit concept. This, then, would represent a human, mechanical complex. This system should be a *closed loop* operation, but many examples of open loop operations, such as embezzlement (to be figurative), can be found. Essentially, then, one would have a very simple control system regulating a rate of production which has to be geared to marketing if a sensible distribution or marketing system is to exist.

Further, the elements and values in this system must be known if we are to be responsible for its manipulation to best assure total consumer satisfaction, which might be liberally interpreted as the best well-being for all. I do not choose to (nor can I) comment on the subject of the ethics involved here. It is for far greater minds to argue this. However, the marketing institution must strive toward the goal of adaptability, guided by those bench marks which it can find with respect to total consumer satisfaction. Market adaptability is the gearing of our productive and distributive system to the changing character of the market. This is the essence of any sensible marketing system, and although it does not seem to bear directly on the subject at hand, it is inextricably involved, for again we are talking about systems and their adaptability in marketing and the ease with which analogs simulate this adaptation process.

The balancing of market demands and productive capacity would be an extremely simple task if our marketing costs and economic costs systems were infinitely variable. That is, if it would cost us nothing in effort, dollars, etc., to change the system, make mistakes, etc. Knowing this is not possible, we seek an optimum between adaptability to satisfy the market and facility to produce and distribute most efficiently. It is in this latter area that the analog seems to me to be extremely helpful. It always seeks a stable solution.

AN ELEMENTARY COMPANY SYSTEM

Consider more about the nature of simple systems. Figure 1 is a highly simplified block diagram of a company's operations. However, even in this simplified form, certain fundamental characteristics can be noted. The block diagram shows clearly the behavioral or human possibilities that exist and have been observed in analogous systems. For example, owing to the closed loop or *feedback* character of the system, possibilities for instability in all or parts of the system exist and will manifest themselves as oscillations. In particular, an inventory oscillation will result from a poor choice of policy decisions or parameters. It can then be seen that the decision operator which determines, on the basis of information as to the current deficit or excessive inventories, at what rate manufacturing should be carried on is a very critical parameter. Should this alarm one? No, because "borrowing" from the theory of servo-control systems we know that to base changes in production rate solely on the size of inventory will produce violent fluctuations in the system. It is also known that to keep the inventory within narrow bounds, the rate of production should be increased or decreased by an amount proportional to the deficiency or excess of inventory, plus an amount proportional to the rate at which the inventory is decreasing. In other words, what we call derivative control is essential to the stability of the system.

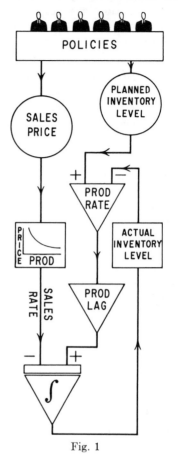

Fig. 1

The purpose of the system or an analysis of the system is to evolve some optimal policy decision which will, on the one hand, allow us to adjust the production rate and minimize inventory while taking into account long-run fluctuations in sales; and, on the other hand, stabilize production and also allow inventories to fluctuate as orders fluctuate. As was mentioned earlier, the two types of analog computers previously described are very useful in determining just how sensitive the relationship is between these fluctuations.[1]

Let us now examine the system to see whether it can be simulated on

---

[1] Unpublished manuscript, Dr. W. H. Boghosian, University of Pennsylvania, 1956.

an analog computer. In the system, we need to add, subtract, multiply, integrate, and to generate what is mathematically called a function. These operations are all fairly self evident. In actual practice, such a very simple system would require two *policy inputs:* sales price and planned inventory level. The relationship between price and the number of units offered for sales which is labeled "production" in the chart, would be a mathematical function which would be generated as the problem went along. This simple system would seek to stabilize itself at a production rate which would satisfy the requirements of the policy inputs. This is the very essence of analog simulation.

In our example of this business system, the mathematical model is quite easily obtained by using readily available computer components which would be inter-connected in exactly the same way as the system block diagram (Figure 1). On paper, the system diagram and the corresponding or analogous computer model diagram would be interchangeable, including the use of human operators in conjunction with models. It is worth pointing out here again that such computer models frequently prove useful in evaluating the advantages, if any, of incorporating computers as operational entities in some part or parts of an actual business system. At this point, some words of caution are required.

An optimum business system does not necessarily follow from the use of an optimized model. And, in general, it will only be a matter of chance if the actual system works better than the model. Also, models are no better than the data available for use with the model. This latter fact still remains as a crucial problem, but model evaluation will tell the systems designer what type and how much data are important or relevant. Here, again, of course I am referring to the concept of sensitivity.

I do not wish to belabor the point, but the concept and theory of the analog computer is such that it facilitates making a sensitivity judgment in the analysis of a marketing system. Now that we have a simple system on paper, let us see what we really want to do as far as simulation is concerned. We have a proposed system and a desire to construct a model of how this system will work. After experimenting with the model and manipulating it price-wise to achieve some sort of an evaluation, we then design our system for actual operation and put it into effect. It is a comforting thought and something which I always like to think of, that we are talking about pennies, as it were, in simulation and dollars in actual operation. So much, then, for the words that I thought must be said about simulation in general.

SPECIAL AND GENERAL PURPOSE ANALOGS

Now let us consider the two types of computers in use—special purpose and general purpose analogs. As its name implies, the special purpose analog is designed to solve a special or particular type of problem. To be more correct, it is designed to do one specific kind of mathematical operation which will, in turn, solve one particular type or class of problem. One of the simplest special purpose computers ever designed by man is shown here in Figure 2.[1] It was a crude, electrical analog designed to

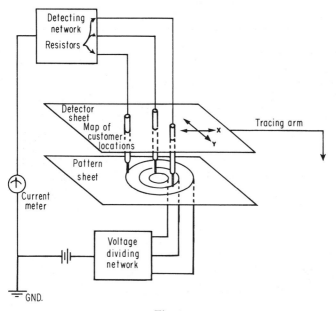

Fig. 2

calculate the dissemination pattern of minute, solid particles released in the atmosphere from one or two sources—for example, the dispersion pattern of air pollution from a factory chimney. You may very well ask what this has to do with marketing, and the answer is nothing. However, this same physical system can be reversed. Assume now that "marketing demands" (and I mean demands such as consumers') arise from a series of points or clusters (customer locations) in a plane. Further assume that these points or clusters are situated about some unknown theoretical point which would be the best location point to satisfy these various demands at a minimum transport cost.

A trivial approach and solution to this problem of analogy is shown in Figure 3. The map represents the various buildings of the University of Pennsylvania which house faculty members. The problem is to locate a faculty club (or retail outlet) in such a way, or such a place that the total

---

[1] For a description of this analog see "An Analogue Solution of the Generalized Transportation Problem with Specific Application to Marketing Location," Proceedings of the First International Conference on Operational Research, Operations Research Society of America, Baltimore, Maryland, 1958.

faculty (or customer) miles walked is at a minimum. This is purely and simply a location problem which is met again and again in marketing. Figure 3 shows the solution. The faculty club, or we might say a retail store, would be ideally located at the innermost *Maltese* cross, and it will minimize the total faculty miles walked. Furthermore, the plotted contours give a general solution to the problem; any position on contour num-

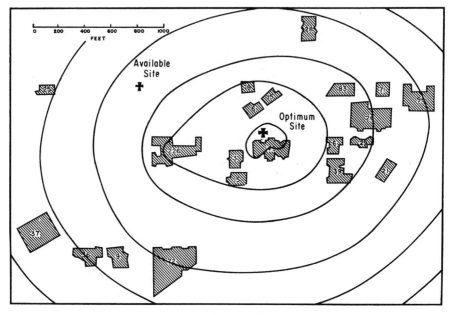

Fig. 3

ber will be equally less acceptable than the ideal solution. Thus any location beyond (toward the perimeter) the outermost cross which was an available site would be less acceptable. This may all seem very impractical and so it is, except that it solved the problem immediately at hand.

A far more complicated and practical special purpose analog is the ALPAC, or Analog Linear Programming Algebraic Computer, designed and built by the Scott Paper Company. The problem which gave rise to the need for this computer was primarily a distribution problem or, again, a transportation problem. As in the previous illustration, the attempt is to minimize transportation costs. The problem involves ten paper manufacturing plants with the ability to convert and manufacture sixty major products which will then be distributed to 140 sales districts. The demand for the sixty products varies week by week for each of the 140 districts. The problem in the simplest form is to instruct each mill at the beginning of the week as to which and how much of each of the sixty products it shall produce, and which and how much of each product it shall ship to each sales district's wholesale point. Immediately, of course, the problem is to arrange the production and designate the destination in such a way that the total amount of shipping costs will be at a minimum for the company. On the ALPAC, the problem is solved quite easily. We must define the cost of producing *each* product at *each* plant and the cost of transporting *each* product from *each* plant to *each* sales district. The cost factor,

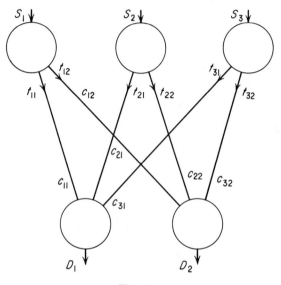

Fig. 4

for purposes of solution, includes both the differential costs of transfer and the differential costs of producing.

The ALPAC is also an electrical analog. In Figure 4 we have a simplified example of this problem. S_1, S_2, and S_3 represent three plants in supply points and D_1 and D_2 two wholesale centers in demand points. Each possible path for the flow of goods has a corresponding cost (i.e., C_{11}, $C_{21} \dots C_{32}$). At the same time, t_{11}, $t_{12} \dots t_{32}$ represent the quantity of goods transferred. Desired are those t values which when multiplied by corresponding costs will yield a minimum total transportation cost for the system. The voltages are set equal to costs and, at the same time, other voltages are set which correspond to the demand for the various products at the wholesale center. Thus, we have an electrical representation of supply and demand in the form of current. The analog is now solved for the production and distribution schedule which will minimize transportation costs to the company. This is true because the problem is simulated by a physical system, namely, an electrical network, and a solution is obtained from a general network theorem which states, loosely speaking, that the distribution of currents in the network which contains sources of voltages and resistances will so arrange themselves as to minimize the total power in the network. In this case, the total power in the network is analogous to the total cost of transportation.

Given demands and supplies which are known and costs which can be calculated and assigned, production and distribution can be arranged in such a way that the total shipping costs are at a minimum for these condi-

Fig. 5. Desk-type Analog Computer.

tions. It should be noted that this system displays the same basic characteristics as the simple one which was previously described. It is a closed system with feedback characteristics. Policy decisions such as fixed production rates at various plants can be set in the system (computer), and the system is capable of instabilities. Finally, the system controls itself to give the desired solution.

Now that a special purpose analog has been examined let us turn to its companion, the general purpose analog. The question inevitably arises: why two kinds? The simple answer lies in the nature of the problem to be solved by the users. The special purpose will usually have far greater capacity and do the special problems assigned more efficiently and less expensively than the general purpose. We might make a comparison in the realm of mathematics. If you want to get the value of a logarithm of a given number, it is very efficient and inexpensive to look it up in a table rather than go through the mathematics of calculating the logarithm each time for each number. And thus we might have book after book of results of such mathematical calculations, ranging from a simple table of squares and roots to the values of complex functions. But is this a good substitute for a knowledge of mathematics to solve new and different problems when they arise? The ability to reason mathematically is more valuable than any given set of specialized tables when we are dealing with a variety of problems. And so it is with the general purpose analogs. They range in complexity (as the special analogs do) from the simple table model shown in Figure 5 which is manufactured by Electronic Associates, to very large installations which are usually combinations of/or compilations of smaller units and which occupy the size of a very large room.

MARKETING USES OF ANALOG COMPUTERS

Finally then what can be said in summation about analogs in marketing systems?

Professor Baumol in his book *Economic Theory & Operations Analysis* has suggested several types of marketing problems that are capable of treatment by operations research. These include:

1. Pricing Problems
2. Optimum Use of Selling Effort
3. Choice of Distribution Arrangement
4. Queuing Analysis
5. Monte Carlo Techniques
6. Pricing Decision Models
7. Transportation Storage Model
8. Warehouse Location Model

In my opinion, and this is shared by others more familiar with analogs, all of these problems except possibly Monte Carlo Techniques (5) and Queuing Analysis (4) lend themselves to simulation by analogs. I have, of course, not touched upon the relative advantages of digital and analog computers. It was not my intention to make a formal comparison.[1] As I have said, there are many types of marketing problems which lend themselves to analog simulation. Analog computers not only are suitable for such purposes but, as I have tried to indicate, they also involve the user and give that feeling of man-machine relationship which I hold very high in the simulation of marketing problems.

---

[1] For a brief comparison see *Marketing, a Maturing Discipline,* p. 105-110. American Marketing Association, Chicago, Illinois, 1961.

chapter four | *Helmut Weymar*

Marketing policies are adopted in the context of dynamic systems. These systems consist of relationships between pools and flows of information, money, goods, equipment, and men. Effective marketing policies must be based on an understanding of the structures of the relevant systems and how these structures determine system behavior through time.

These notions present the basic message of industrial dynamics to marketing men. Before saying more about the nature of the industrial dynamics approach, I want to drive home the above ideas in the context of an example.

ADVERTISING AND STABLE OPERATIONS[1]

Demand fluctuations are found in many industries, often leading to excess capacity for long periods coupled with costly shortages during de-

---

[1] The research underlying this article was made possible by grants from the Sloan Foundation and the Ford Foundation. The necessary computer time was made available by M.I.T.'s Computation Center.

INDUSTRIAL DYNAMICS:

INTERACTION BETWEEN THE

FIRM AND ITS MARKET

mand peaks. Such fluctuations are generally attributed to factors beyond the control of the industries involved, or at least beyond the control of the member firms. I will suggest in the following discussion of a typical consumer durables industry how such fluctuations may be caused by industry marketing policies.

Figure 1 shows a schematic diagram of a typical consumer durables industry. The relationships indicated in the diagram and explained below comprise a *model* of the industry. The product in question is well established, so that for the industry as a whole, long-term growth is due only to population expansion. Since it will not affect our conclusions, we shall ignore population growth in our model.

The consumers of the product are divided into two pools. The first consists of those persons who have recently bought and are not currently in the market. The second is made up of old consumers considering the purchase of a new unit. As consumers buy the product, they flow from the pool of prospective customers to the pool of users not in the market. After a certain average delay, these users begin to consider replacing their units, and thereby flow back into the pool of prospective customers. The process of deciding to buy a new product also involves a delay.

These two time delays—the purchasing decision delay and the satisfied product usage delay—are both variables depending on the advertising pressure applied to the market by the industry. Figure 2 indicates the

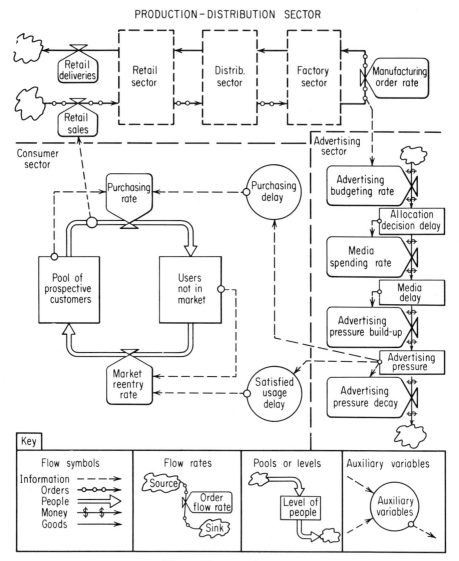

Fig. 1. Diagram of system.

form of these relationships in the model. At very low advertising pressures relative to normal, here implying a timeless style with no industry efforts toward inducing artificial obsolescence or speeding the purchasing decision, the usage and purchasing decision delays are quite long. Conversely, with saturation advertising, implying rapid superficial style change, the two delays are reduced considerably below their normal operating values. As these delays increase, the consumer purchase rate (i.e., retail sales) falls, while if they decrease, consumer purchases rise.

The relationship between advertising pressure and the purchasing decision delay shown in Figure 2b would be valid at each point in time in the absence of various random influences in the market. Weather, holidays,

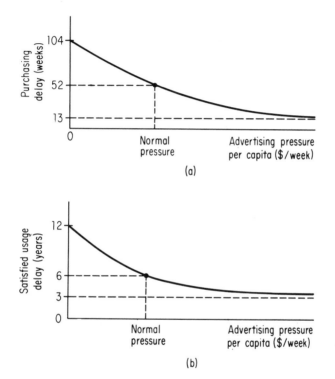

Fig. 2. (a) Purchasing decision delay vs. advertising pressure. (b) Satisfied usage delay (consumers not on market) vs. advertising pressure.

national and international events, and other occurrences which may be considered random with respect to our system all tend to make the actual purchasing decision delay vary in a noisy fashion about the value indicated by the existing level of advertising pressure. We shall include such random fluctuations in studying the dynamic behavior of our system.

Consumer purchases are made from the retail sector of the industry's production-distribution system. An increase in retail sales causes retailers to increase their ordering rate from distributors, not only to replace the extra units sold, but also to build up inventories on hand and on order to a level commensurate with the new higher consumer purchase rate. Moreover, should the increased retail order rate begin to curtail product availability at the distributor level, then this rate will be even further increased as retailers begin to order further ahead of their anticipated needs. A similar relationship exists between the distributor and factory sectors, with the result that a small increase in retail sales is in the short run amplified into a considerably larger increase in factory shipments and production. Conversely, a small drop in average consumer purchases temporarily leads to a much larger drop in factory production, as retailers and distributors act to reduce their inventory positions.

The industry system is completed by the advertising budgeting policy, and the series of delays which take place between this decision and its eventual effect on advertising pressure. It is conventional in many industries to base advertising spending on recent sales. Consequently, advertising increases when sales climb, and decreases when sales fall. We will initially incorporate this policy into our system in such a way that the size of the advertising budget is directly proportional to a recent average of manufacturing orders received at the various factories. After the budgeting decision is made, there ensues first a delay for deciding how to spend the allocated funds, and then a delay for transmitting the message through the advertising media. Finally, the media advertising rate does not have its full effect instantaneously, but rather entails a delay for building up advertising pressure on consumers, or allowing this pressure to decay.

This completes the description of our system. Figure 3 shows the behavior of the major system variables over a fifteen-year period in response to a sudden independent increase in the level of prospective customers. I have, for the moment, omitted the random fluctuations in the purchasing decision delay. If we can understand the way in which the system responds to this simple though artificial input, we will be in a good position to understand system behavior when the purchasing delay varies randomly.

The major fluctuations in Figure 3 with an average period of approximately five years are caused by the interaction of our advertising policy with the remainder of the system. The increase in the number of prospective customers causes retail sales to increase. After a delay, manufacturing orders increase by a larger amount due to the amplification in the production-distribution system. Advertising spending increases proportionally, eventually leading to a further increase in retail sales. Without this further increase in retail sales, manufacturing orders would begin to fall, reflecting the fact that retailers and distributors have placed most of the extra orders needed to increase their inventory positions. With the decline in inventory orders offsetting the further increase in retail sales due to advertising, manufacturing orders eventually level off, as does

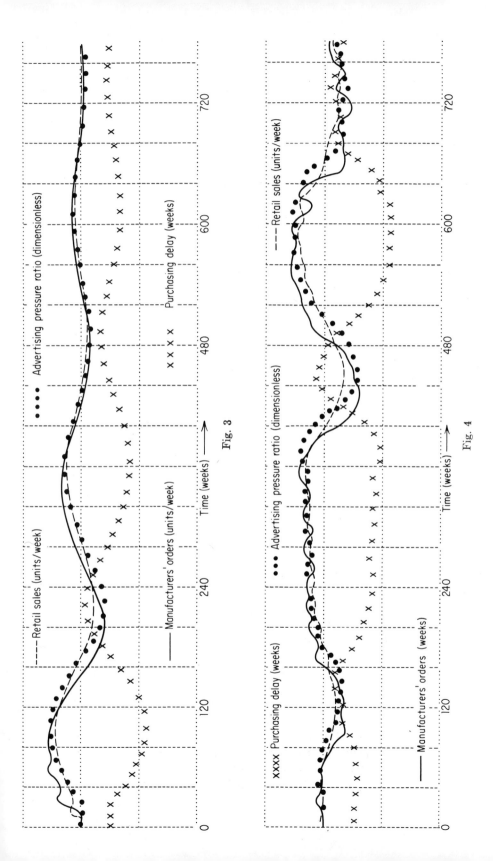

Fig. 3

Fig. 4

advertising spending and the purchasing decision delay. This whole process from the initial increase in prospective customers until the eventual peak in manufacturers' orders represents a quarter cycle and takes some 70 weeks.

As the purchasing delay approaches its trough, retail sales begin to level off and manufacturing orders fall reflecting a further decline in inventory orders. Advertising spending, therefore, declines, eventually causing the purchasing delay to increase and retail sales to decrease. This process continues until inventories are cut to a level low enough such that manufacturing orders and advertising spending reach their troughs, and the purchasing delay reaches its peak. Forces corresponding to those which caused the purchasing delay to climb from its trough now cause it to fall from its peak as the cycle continues.

The pronounced five-year cycle shown in Figure 3 indicates that our system is particularly sensitive to any external fluctuations having a period of roughly five years. The fact that the system will amplify these fluctuations much more than it will amplify disturbances with periods much greater than or less than five years is characteristic of naturally oscillatory feedback systems. It can be shown that random disturbances are effectively made up of a continuous spectrum of fluctuations ranging from very short periods (i.e., less than one week) to very long periods (i.e., more than fifteen years). Therefore if we allow the purchasing decision delay to vary randomly around the value indicated by advertising pressure, we should expect that our system will "pick out" the fluctuations at or near its natural period such that these fluctuations will be predominant in the system's output.

Figure 4, showing system behavior when the only external input consists of random variations in the purchasing delay, confirms this notion. Superimposed on top of the five-year fluctuations are variations with a period of some forty weeks. If we look carefully at the early part of the response shown in Figure 3, we again see these forty-week fluctuations. These are manifestations of the fact that the production-distribution system taken alone (i.e., without the advertising and consumer sectors) tends to generate forty-week cycles. The forty-week cycles are heavily damped, so that when the system is subjected to a single sudden external input, they diminish rather rapidly, as in Figure 3. They persist, on the other hand, when the system is subjected to a continuously varying input, as in Figure 4.

Based on the above discussion of how the structure of our system has determined its behavior, the imaginative reader perhaps will have already concluded that sales fluctuate mainly as a result of the policy causing advertising spending to be proportional to manufacturing orders. Given this conclusion, a policy leading to a decrease in advertising spending when manufacturing orders climb and an increase when they fall would seem

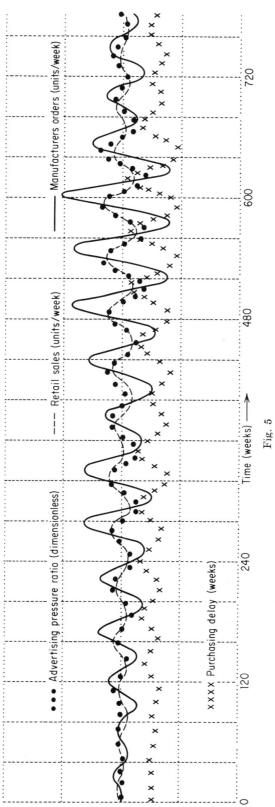

Fig. 5

more appropriate. Certain corporations have claimed to be pursuing such "countercyclical" policies in recent years.

Incorporating a countercyclical advertising budgeting policy in our system is a simple matter. Under such a policy, advertising spending would vary around a "normal" value which would be proportional to a long-term average (covering, say, three years) of manufacturing orders. If a recent average of manufacturing orders was above the long-term average, then advertising spending would be dropped below its normal value; and conversely if orders were below their long-term rate then advertising would be increased above normal. Figure 5 shows system behavior in response to random variations in the purchasing delay when the original advertising budgeting policy is replaced by such a countercyclical policy.

The amplitude of the fluctuations is still large, though the average period is now only 50 weeks. We can again explain this behavior in terms of the structure of the system. Just as before, an initial increase in retail sales causes a still larger increase in manufacturing orders. The latter increase now causes a *decrease* in advertising spending, which soon leads to an increase in the purchasing delay and a decrease in retail sales. Thus, the trough in the purchasing delay need not wait for inventory orders to die down as before, but rather is brought about as soon as the delays in the production-distribution system and the advertising chain have been traversed. This accounts for the shorter period. The high amplitude arises largely from the fact that the inventory control policies in the production-distribution sector cause it to amplify the 50-week fluctuations in retail sales.

The moral to this example is not that countercyclical policies don't work. It is, to repeat, that marketing policies operate in the context of dynamic systems, and that such policies cannot be effective unless they take into account the structures of the relevant systems. If, for example, the consumer usage and purchasing delays in our system were subject to fluctuating influence from factors outside of the industry, then well-conceived policies could largely eliminate the effect of such fluctuations. Such policies would be based on an understanding of the interaction between the amplification of the production-distribution system, the nature of the delays in the advertising process, and the structure of the consumer sector.

INDUSTRIAL DYNAMICS

These notions linking system behavior to system structure form the core of the industrial dynamics approach. Let us move on now to a discussion of this approach: its background, its major aspects, its objectives, and its relation to marketing.

BACKGROUND

Industrial Dynamics finds its origin in four related developments, each largely a product of this country's military effort during and after World War II. These are: (1) the development since the middle 1930's of analytical techniques for studying the dynamic behavior of complex engineering systems, (2) the invention and refinement of digital computers starting a decade later, (3) the translation of tactical military policies into mathematical form during the middle 1950's, and (4) the use of simulation techniques during the same period for studying and improving complex nonlinear military systems largely made up of these formalized policies.

Research in the area of industrial dynamics has now been under way at M.I.T.'s School of Industrial Management for six years under the leadership of Professor Jay W. Forrester.[1] The Industrial Dynamics Research Group now includes some ten members working on various externally and internally sponsored projects. These include, among others, a study of the dynamic interrelationships between order-filling, production, and labor force control within a company manufacturing electronic components, an investigation of the process of research and development for military products, analysis of the dynamic implications of various procurement and marketing policies in a firm processing agricultural products, and an investigation of the corporate growth process within the context of a young electronics company. In addition, work essentially similar to industrial dynamics is getting under way in other companies and universities.

MAJOR ASPECTS

The major aspects of industrial dynamics are fourfold: (1) the systems viewpoint, (2) the emphasis on the information feedback characteristics of business systems, (3) the description of business policies and environment in precise mathematical form, and (4) the use of digital computer simulation techniques.

---

[1] For a more detailed discussion of industrial dynamics, see:

Jay W. Forrester, "Industrial Dynamics—A Major Breakthrough for Decision Makers," *Harvard Business Review*, July-August, 1958.

For a fully comprehensive treatment, see:

Jay W. Forrester, *Industrial Dynamics*, John Wiley and Sons, Inc. and the M.I.T. Press, 1961.

In addition, an intensive two-week summer session in industrial dynamics is taught each year at M.I.T. for interested persons in industry and universities.

THE SYSTEMS APPROACH

The business systems approach has as its fundamental axiom the notion that corporate performance is largely determined by a *structure* or system of relationship between variables. We have already seen such a system in our advertising example.

Within a system, the dynamic behavior of each corporate variable of interest—such as profit rate, market share, or growth rate—is determined by all of its relationships with other variables, whether direct or indirect, and can only be understood by taking into account all such relationships. In most corporate problems of interest, the relations between variables which must be taken into account are many and complex, generally crossing the traditional functional lines within a company and often crossing the bounds between the company and the external economy as well.

EMPHASIS ON FEEDBACK

As a corollary of the systems viewpoint comes the notion that dynamic corporate behavior of interest is largely determined by the array of information feedback loops within the relevant system. A feedback loop exists whenever an action is taken which affects an environment, and the environment in turn affects the action. In our earlier discussion of countercyclical advertising policies, we saw that an increase in manufacturing orders led to a decrease in advertising spending, which after a delay led to a decrease in advertising pressure and in retail sales, causing in turn a decrease in manufacturing orders and an increase in advertising spending. This is an example of a feedback relationship causing fluctuations. As an alternate example, an increase in profits often causes an increase in earnings retained for investment in new equipment or research and development, leading to new products and increased productive capacity and in turn to higher profits. Here we have an example of a feedback relationship underlying growth.

Even a seemingly weak relationship between two variables (i.e., so weak as to be rejected by most tests of statistical significance) can, if it is included in a feedback loop, be a major factor determining system behavior. When this fact is ignored, the effectiveness of both formal and intuitive reasoning processes aimed at explaining or improving industrial performance is often curtailed.

Processes involving fluctuations, growth or decline are often recognized as being *regenerative* in nature. The use of this vocabulary implies the existence of feedback loops within the structures underlying such processes. Within the set of problems which have traditionally bothered management, there are many which may be primarily characterized as involving growth, decline, or fluctuations. It is, therefore, particularly important that we place emphasis on the feedback characteristics of business systems.

PRECISE DESCRIPTION OF POLICIES AND ENVIRONMENT

By the late 1940's there were many people with experience in dealing with engineering systems who recognized the analogy between the dynamic behavior and structure of these systems and the dynamic behavior and structure of business and economic systems. For those among this group who wished to push further, the next step—presented here as the third fundamental aspect of the industrial dynamics approach—was clear. In order to use the systems notions to their full advantage, the relationships of interest would have to be stated in a form *precise* enough to be treated explicitly. This is the only way systems of scope large enough to be of managerial interest might be treated without the ambiguity characteristic of discussions of over-all business problems.

In an industrial dynamics study, each variable of interest is defined as a mathematical function of other variables of interest. The entire set of such relations comprises the industrial dynamics *model* of the system under investigation. The primary criterion employed in formulating these relationships is their *plausibility* to the model builder as representations of the corresponding relations in the actual business system.

SIMULATION

The final major aspect of the industrial dynamics approach is digital computer simulation, the need for which we anticipated in the previous section. The business problems for which the systems approach is particularly useful are generally large in scope, with the result that the related models generally involve many variables. Moreover, if the relationships between these variables are to be plausible, they must include saturation and threshold effects, mentioned here as just two examples of the broad class of relationships labeled "nonlinear." Analytical (equation-solving) techniques have been developed which obtain general solutions describing the behavior of certain engineering systems under all circumstances, but these are only easily applicable to simple systems involving relatively few variables. They have not yet been well developed for dealing with general nonlinear systems of any magnitude. While these techniques are therefore not useful as the primary vehicle for investigation of business systems, familiarity with the fundamental concepts involved is valuable as background to such investigation, and direct application of the techniques as a secondary mode of research has proven useful in certain cases.[1]

In the absence of techniques capable of yielding general solutions for the behavior of complex nonlinear systems, industrial dynamics utilizes simulation. As applied in industrial dynamics studies, simulation is a technique for observing the dynamic behavior of a model given a specified set of environmental or "input" conditions. If the model and its environment are plausible representations of an actual business system and its environment, then the dynamic behavior of the model "simulates" the behavior of the actual system. Figures 3, 4, and 5 showed results of simulations using the model diagrammed in Figure 1.

The mathematical relations between the variables comprising an industrial dynamics model can be directly transcribed onto punched cards. The simulation process can then be carried out on a digital computer, with data concerning the behavior of any variables of interest returned to the analyst in printed and/or plotted form.[2]

OBJECTIVE

We have discussed the four major aspects of the industrial dynamics approach, but taken alone these cannot ensure—or even make it likely—that the adoption of this approach will be useful. It is important that its objective be clearly understood. The objective of industrial dynamics is to provide the manager with additional insight into the dynamic behavior of his firm so that he can more effectively design the policies which control that behavior. Its aim is to *improve* the manager's intuition rather than *replace* it.

It is our experience that as the manager studies the dynamic behavior generated by a system simulation, his understanding of the way in which the structure of his firm determines its performance is inevitably improved. On the basis of such improved understanding, he can call upon his creative abilities to devise new policies to improve performance. It is an important aspect of industrial dynamics that such policies can first be tested within the context of the model, before being tried in the actual business system. Industrial dynamics works to broaden the spectrum of

---

[1] For an example of the direct application of systems analysis techniques in an industrial dynamics investigation, see:

Willard R. Fey, *The Stability and Transient Response of Industrial Organizations,* Electrical Engineering S. M. Thesis, M.I.T., 1961.

[2] More specifically, the equations are written in difference equation form, and the simulation is run by means of the DYNAMO compiler, currently written for the IBM 704, 709, and 7090 computers. For a fuller discussion of DYNAMO, see:

Alexander L. Pugh, III, *DYNAMO User's Manual,* M.I.T. Press, 1961.

alternatives which the manager is able to consider, and to guide him in choosing among these alternatives.

MARKETING AND INDUSTRIAL DYNAMICS

The marketing concept properly refers to a viewpoint rather than a functional area of the firm. To adopt the marketing viewpoint is to emphasize the firm's efforts to meet the needs of its market. This viewpoint must take into account areas of the corporate structure outside of that which would traditionally be called marketing. I say this in the face of the fact that corporations of nearly all sizes in almost every industry have officers whose responsibilities are narrowly confined within the marketing area.

The implied contradiction here is real and explainable. There exists a vast body of institutional knowledge concerning marketing activities. Moreover, these activities are directly related in various ways to the nonmarketing operations of a company. In the absence of a general framework within which to consider the over-all activities of his firm, it is enough to expect the marketing executive to develop an effective working knowledge of these institutional facts and direct structural relations. To ask more would in many cases be to ask for superficiality. *Under these circumstances*—i.e., in the absence of an effective way in which the executive can view his firm as a dynamic system without being overwhelmed by its complexity—perhaps it is best that marketing be viewed as a function rather than a viewpoint. Then, at least, the company has one or more officers well versed in the purely marketing aspects of its activities, even if these officers lack the perspective of an overall system point of view.

It should be clear, however, that industrial dynamics potentially offers the missing framework. Through this approach management's understanding of the separate dynamic characteristics of the marketing, production, financial, and other activities of its firm may be integrated. Management can then be free to accept marketing as a viewpoint, an emphasis upon the firm's efforts to meet the needs of its market, rather than as a separate functional area. Issues of interfunctional concern can be decided on the basis of integrated understanding rather than equivocal committee compromise.

There is still the oft-raised objection that the business of meeting the needs of a market is fraught with intangibles, that many of the variables of interest are difficult to quantify conceptually let alone measure empirically, or in short, that these variables cannot be meaningfully included in a mathematical model. This difficulty is likely to add to rather than detract from the usefulness of the industrial dynamics approach.

When dealing with tangible variables such as out inventory, a labor force, or a flow of orders, an experienced manager can probably keep track of the dynamic interactions between five or perhaps ten variables. As the variables of interest become less tangible or less conceptually quantifiable, his ability to keep track of the relationships between more than two or three variables in a consistent manner declines sharply. The result is that many of today's marketing decisions are made on the premise that similar decisions were made in the past with apparently successful, or at least not disastrous, results. Rarely are the full implications of these decisions in terms of the performance of the over-all firm taken into account. Under these circumstances policies are formulated on the basis of the past performance or "output" of the related business system, rather than on an understanding of the structure which generated that performance.

The potential improvement which industrial dynamics offers over such an approach lies in the clarification of relationships between variables and in the increased scope afforded by a formal system model. To be included in a mathematical model, variables such as consumer awareness, market penetration, or product image must be clearly and precisely defined. At least within the context of discussions concerning the model, the confusion which arises when such concepts mean different things to different people is effectively eliminated. Moreover, the only limit on the number of such relationships which may be usefully included in a model is that set by the manager's ability to understand their dynamic interactions even when the relationships and variables are clearly defined. Our experience at M.I.T. has been that at present this limit lies somewhere between 100 and 500 variables.

In precisely defining relationships between intangible variables, the model builder will either examine and retain such assumptions as he has already had in mind, or he will adjust these in the direction of increased plausibility. His initial efforts may yield models which of themselves offer no direct benefit by way of improved policies, but which are likely to be extremely helpful in two indirect ways. First, his concept of the structure of the system with which he is dealing will almost inevitably be sharpened, with the result that his intuition concerning the behavior of the system is likely to be improved. Second, even early models tend to indicate which relationships are critical to model behavior and which are relatively unimportant. On the basis of such indications, the manager may redirect his data gathering effort in order to improve his empirical foundation in the critical areas. Coupled together, these notions argue that one of the major benefits of industrial dynamics in an area of intangibles is that it offers a flexible but precise framework within which to carry on the continuous managerial learning process.

OTHER MARKETING APPLICATIONS

I have already discussed one marketing situation in which the industrial dynamics approach proved enlightening. Let me now mention a few other marketing problems which might usefully be dealt with via this approach:

(a) *Product Growth*—During the early stages of product growth, the timing of the expansion of sales effort relative to production effort is critical. Too early a sales effort leads to orders without production capacity and attracts competition sooner than might otherwise be the case. Too late a sales effort leads to expensive overcapacity. The requirements of a coordinated set of policies in the sales, production, and other activities involved in product growth are more readily understood against the background of a system study.

(b) *Research and Development*—In defense industries, a company's marketing effort often consists largely of writing proposals aimed at gaining military research and development contracts. Overallocation of engineering manpower to these activities can lead to expensive crash programs in the face of understaffed engineering departments, and eventually to failure in meeting contract terms. The dynamics involved in managing the marketing and other aspects of military research and development are manifestations of fairly general system structures common to many companies, and can only be fully grasped in terms of these structures.

(c) *Product Differentiation*—For any given basic product line, one can conceptualize a curve relating product quality to the size of the market willing to pay for that quality. Normally, a large portion of the total market is concentrated in one region of this curve, around what might be termed the "average desired quality." During the early phase of a product's life cycle, companies typically tend to crowd together in this central region, each vying for a larger share of the consumers desiring "average quality." Meanwhile the sector of the total market willing to pay for higher quality goes unsatisfied. The frustration of such a sector not only represents a potential profit for one or more of the industry's members, but also provides a lure for the development by other industries of higher quality substitutes for the product in question, and thus tends to shorten the total life cycle of this product. The consistency and plausibility of the judgments which must go into any decision as to when and how to broaden a product line in order to segment, maintain, or extend a market can be effectively analyzed in the context of a dynamic model.

(d) *Commodity Price Dynamics*—The commodity portion of the costs of certain manufactured products is large. In these cases, price and market share in the market for the finished product are heavily dependent upon price and market share (i.e., procurement share) in the commodity market. The policies coupling a firm's activities in the two markets largely determine the firm's profit rate. A system study provides an ideal framework within which to test alternative coupling policies in this situation.

These are but a few examples of situations in which the industrial dynamics approach can be useful. It is important to note that while in each case the emphasis was on what would normally be classified as a marketing problem, the implications of the problem regarding other traditional functional areas were taken into account as well. This is consistent with my earlier remarks concerning the nature and importance of the systems point of view as it is applied to management.

CONCLUSIONS

I said earlier that the marketing concept should refer to a viewpoint rather than a functional area of management, and that a management ought *not* to have officers whose designated responsibilities are limited to the marketing aspects of its activities. Needless to say, if a company is to be successful, its sales, advertising, distribution, and other marketing efforts must receive individual attention from talented personnel experienced in these areas. This implies a sector on the company organization chart which might meaningfully be labeled "marketing." My objection is not aimed at the existence of such a sector. I object instead to the prevailing notion that the marketing executive's responsibilities are effectively *limited* to the marketing activities of the firm.

Marketing managers are just as responsible for high production costs resulting from destabilizing advertising policies as they are for low sales resulting from ineffective sales management. Similarly, production managers should be held accountable for any of their decisions which have an adverse albeit indirect effect on the firm's marketing efforts.

Each of the problems which I mentioned in the previous section was a matter of specific concern to marketing managers. Yet each was also a matter of over-all corporate concern involving nonmarketing areas. The role of the marketing manager in dealing with such problems will continue. But he should—and now he *can*—view these problems as resulting from a specific system structure, and should base his design of new policies on an understanding of that structure.

INTRODUCTION

While much has been written on the use of electronic computers in the day-to-day tasks of keeping track of where the business is and producing data summaries on where the business has been, the purpose of this paper is to explore the use of computers in answering questions about where the business might be heading. This latter area of interest has been relatively neglected in the reported studies concerning computer applications in industrial firms.

Perhaps the need for the computer in business planning may be suggested by considering the following little vignette, caricatured to be sure.

The Time—About the year 2 B.C. (before computers), or could this time be even the present?

The Place—The executive presentation room of the Old Mud Coffee Pot Company.

THE COMPUTER'S PLACE IN

BUSINESS PLANNING:

A BAYESIAN APPROACH

The Characters—Three executives, unceremoniously labeled **1**, **2**, and **3**; one slightly harassed market research man and his two assistants (chart flipper and Vu-graph operator, respectively).

The Scene—The chart flipper has just placed an impressive three-color graph on the easel. This chart purports to show estimated unit sales of Old Mud Coffee Pots over the next ten years. The chart flipper then strikes an unobtrusive pose as the market research man affixes pointer to said chart.

Market Research Man: "Gentlemen, as you can see from the trend line on this chart, we expect **1970** sales of Old Mud Coffee Pots to reach 7.4 million units, a virtual doubling of current sales. Our **1970** estimate was based on a careful study of anticipated changes in personal income, age distribution of the population, and the rate of new household formations, just to name a few of the broad economic factors. We also considered various competitive trends affecting total industry sales of coffee pots (e.g., the swing to instant coffee, the outlook for future tea consumption) as well as the intra-industry activities of rival coffee pot producers."

Executive 1 (singularly unimpressed by the tri-colored chart) : "What rate of growth did you use for changes in personal income?"

Market Research Man: "Approximately 3.4% annually, on a compounded basis, of course."

Executive 1: "I wonder what effect it would have on our sales if personal income increased faster than that, say maybe 5% a year?"

Market Research Man (somewhat flustered) : "Well, off hand I couldn't say. We could work it out for you, however."

Executive 2: "I was thinking of a somewhat different line of interest. You say that you have considered the trend toward consumption of instant coffee insofar as it adversely affects brewed coffee sales and hence the demand for coffee pots. What assumption did you use in your analysis and what chance do you think exists that this assumption will be borne out?"

Market Research Man (a bit haltingly) : "As I recall, we assumed that the trend toward instant coffee consumption would level out in the 1964-65 period. However, I don't believe we ascribed any particular odds to this trend actually occurring . . . I suppose *some* chance exists that the trend could continue perhaps through 1967, although I don't think that this would be very probable."

Executive 3 (obviously thinking about another matter) : "Frankly, I don't see how your estimate on that chart up there relates to the *plans* we are considering. As you know, our research people are working on a new model coffee pot with a separate replacement bottom. I'd like to know whether bringing this model out is a better financial bet than sticking with the old model. We don't want the Cafe Klatch Co. to get the jump on us, you know."

Market Research Man (hapless and perplexed, as the executives start moving toward the door) : "I think that given a little time, we can evaluate these alternatives. I say, given some more time we can. . . ." (Fade-out as chart flipper starts dismantling easel and Vu-graph operator starts unplugging machine, tripping over the extension cord in the process.)

While the above description is, of course, only fictional insofar as *our* companies are concerned, a consideration of the moral of this little fable— to be offered in subsequent sections of this paper—might serve to show the role which the computer can play in extending the operational aspects of business planning. At this point, however, some comment should be made on what is meant by the activity of business planning.

Concomitant with trends in the growing complexity of business enterprise, faster obsolescence of products and processes and increasing expenditures on research and development, the function of business planning has found a definite niche in the activities of many business firms.

Despite its own newness, however, the formal concept of business planning has managed to spawn a host of progeny. For example, choosing the time dimension as a modifier leads to the categories, long range and short range planning. If we care to introduce the concept of purpose, we have strategic planning and tactical planning. Expressed in terms of financial measures, the basic phrase leads to profit planning or sales planning. An application of the functional dimension leads to market planning, product planning, development planning, etc. This list can be expanded almost endlessly depending upon our combinatorial ability to produce hybrids like long range, strategic, product planning.

In an effort to avoid a quicksand of adjectives, we will restrict ourselves to the more generic term: business planning. As a beginning approximation, we can define business planning to cover those activities associated with making high level, high risk decisions which must consider the relationship of the firm to its environment and which involve the deployment of significant amounts of the firm's resources in order to reach desired "end states" in a future time period. Our conception of business planning is thus decision and problem oriented rather than just a consideration of forecasting some general future setting for the firm, devoid of explicit consideration of the alternative courses of action available to the firm.

Even a cursory reading of the literature on business planning, however, would reveal that little unanimity exists on what this concept means. No attempt will be made here to summarize exhaustively the various definitions which have been proposed. However, the perceptive statements of Peter Drucker[1] on this subject would seem to bear repeating. Drucker, in an effort to dispel some "misunderstandings" about the meaning of planning, has proceeded to describe some things which planning is *not:*

(a) "(Long range planning) is not forecasting . . . Any attempt to do so is foolish. Human beings can neither predict nor control the future . . .

---

[1] P. F. Drucker, "Long Range Planning, Challenge to Management Science," *Management Science,* April, 1959, pp. 238-40. Drucker then goes on to define (long range) planning as "risk taking decision making" (p. 248).

(b) ". . . it does not deal with future decisions. It deals with the
futurity of present decisions. . . .

(c) ". . . (it) is not an attempt to eliminate risk. It is not even an
attempt to minimize risk. Indeed any such attempt can only lead
to irrational and unlimited risk and to certain disaster."

While it is well to keep Drucker's thoughts in mind, business planning
activity does embody some *expectations* about the future as related to
present alternative courses of action (including, naturally, the case of
maintaining the firm's current course) which are available for choice.
The question of the length of this future time period is moot. While many
firms consider five years and longer as constituting the "long range," this
selection is, of course, arbitrary. The length of the planning horizon will
vary with the problem under study.

Just where the computer fits into this activity is a question which will
be approached in the following way:

First, planning decisions obviously arise out of planning problems.
Accordingly, the first portion of this paper will be concerned with describing the components of a problem generally and then showing within
this frame of reference how planning problems may be, at least crudely,
distinguished from other classes of problems.

Next, some of the descriptive aspects of traditional planning procedures used by business firms will be discussed. It will be shown that conventional techniques contain certain inadequacies, some of which may be
overcome through application of the tools of *applied decision theory.*

The place of the computer will be introduced in the next section of
this paper as discussion proceeds to a consideration of the "spirit" of
modern decision theory (more specifically, Bayesian decision theory) and
the role it can play in dealing with problems in planning. It will be shown
that the computer can supply *implementation* to the concepts of decision
theory and thereby increase the scope of the planning problems which
can be handled.

Finally, the writer will discuss briefly the results of using the decision
theory-computer approach in actual planning situations and what has
been learned from these applications.

THE CHARACTERISTICS OF BUSINESS PLANNING PROBLEMS

The line between business planning vs. non-planning problems is hardly
clear and sharp. Most differences are differences in degree. However, one
means to distinguish the characteristics of this former group from the latter group is to list the components of a problem and to contrast the characteristics of planning problems (in the context used in this paper) with
the characteristics of what might be called "better-structured" problems,

i.e., those problems which appear to be more tractable to the traditional techniques of operations research and related disciplines.

As is generally known, the types of problems which have yielded so successfully to the "classical" operations research tools of linear programming, queuing theory, inventory analysis, etc. have for the most part arisen in the lower levels of management. Although in many cases the solution of these problems has been very tedious, computationally, this problem class can be nonetheless characterized by the presence of certain desirable attributes, e.g., reasonably good problem definition and input data, few judgmental variables, relatively high control over the outcomes resulting from pursuing the courses of action under evaluation, reasonably simple payoff functions, and a relatively short time horizon over which the effects of the decision extend.

In contrast, the particular characteristics of business planning situations leave much to be desired in terms of overall problem structure. This may be shown by commenting upon these characteristics within the following frame of reference which lists the general components of a problem, involving the aspect of uncertainty.

a. *Decision Maker*—person or group having the authority to choose the course of action which will be initiated.

b. *States of Nature*—environmental setting of the problem which may affect the outcome of each specific action being considered. From the planner's standpoint, uncertainty exists regarding the occurrence of alternative states, i.e., he is not certain which state of nature, of these conceptualized, is the true state.

c. *Courses of Action*—choices under evaluation for achieving desired ends.

d. *Outcome-Payoff Relationship*—the conjunction of a given course of action with a given state of nature and the "value" (utility or financial measure) which the decision maker assigns to this outcome.

e. *Probabilities*—the chances that alternative states of nature (which affect the relative efficiency of various courses of action) will prevail.

The particular characteristics of business planning problems may be described within the preceding format.

The *decision maker* in most business planning problems tends to be located at a high level in the organizational hierarchy and is responsible for dealing with problems for which clear-cut decision rules are not usually available. This is obviously not to say that the decision maker might not enlist the aid of lower level management people. In practice, he usually does rely on subordinates for either supplying data inputs or for study design and computational assistance. But whether the decision maker consists of an individual or group (e.g., planning committee) the final responsibility is usually placed high in the organizational structure.

The *states of nature* of business planning problems can be typified as emphasizing the relationship of the firm to its external environment. In this setting, the outcomes of decisions may be only partially under the executive's control. Decision areas thus include the category of adaptation as well as control, and typically relate to the interaction of the firm with its environment (competitors, customers, government, etc.).

The characteristics of the alternative *courses of action* associated with business planning problems also differ from those typically associated with lower level problems in terms of diversity, lack of structure, and general emphasis on the longer run future. As a consequence, emphasis must be placed on the consideration of flows of revenues and costs and the time pattern of these flows. But emphasis on the futurity of present courses of action tends to lead to a wide range of feasible alternatives available for reaching longer term goals. The process of searching for feasible alternatives and then screening these courses of action in order to reach a manageable number of alternatives comprises an important aspect of business planning problems.

The *outcome-payoff relationships* found in business planning problems are also characterized by complexity, both in terms of considering the interaction of courses of action with states of nature in the determination of outcomes and in the "value" assignment to these outcomes. This latter problem reflects, of course, the firm's business goals. In business planning problems, these goals are frequently diverse and qualitative in nature, if commensurable at all. Quite frequently, in order to simplify the problem, the planner is forced to use some portmanteau variable, e.g., long term profits, in an attempt to reduce possibly conflicting goals to some manageable criterion.

In business planning problems, the probabilities associated with the occurrence of alternative states of nature are almost always of the subjective type. That is to say, the business planner must usually resort to expressing degrees of belief (these probabilities usually being obtained from the experienced judgment of the decision maker) that demand for a new product, for example, will be "high" vs. "low." Inasmuch as the planner is usually working with unique events, the relative frequency concept of classical probability is rarely applicable to this class of problems. These subjective probabilities can also be noted by their fluid and evolutionary nature. For example, in the early stages of evaluating a new product for possible future commercialization, little is known (or assumed known) about alternative levels of consumer demand. However, through employment of sample product testing at the consumer level, trade evaluations, etc., expectations about the product's potential for success are gradually formed. (Also, to a large extent, decision makers attempt to protect themselves from the repercussions of uncertain (and possibly adverse) future events by following the practice of committing resources sequentially in the pervasive desire to maintain flexibility for future positive action, or "stop loss.")

In summary, the foregoing problem characteristics suggest some plausible reasons for the relative lack of success which the quantitative techniques of operations research and allied disciplines have had in dealing with business planning problems. As a next step, we can examine the characteristics of methods traditionally used for dealing with planning problems in order to see how adequately these procedures are able to cope with the preceding problem characteristics.

TRADITIONAL PLANNING TECHNIQUES

The activity of business planning is, of course, hardly new. What has come about in recent years, however, is the emphasis which has been placed on (a) extension of the planning horizon (the impetus for which has been described earlier in this paper) and (b) increased formalization of the planning activity in the sense that this function has achieved departmental status in many companies and full-time people are being used to carry on this activity. Despite increased awareness of the need for planning, it is relevant to note that some of the *techniques* of planning have tended to lag the gains which have been made in need recognition. From a perusal of the planning studies which have appeared in the literature and the writer's own experience, certain characteristics of traditional planning techniques stand out. The main characteristics of these procedures can be listed as follows:

(a) Conventional planning procedures tend to emphasize end-of-planning-period (i.e., "snap-shot") views of payoffs rather than flows of sales and costs through time which are related to the courses of action under evaluation. In some planning studies no attempt is even made to provide a simple accumulation of profit experience throughout the period required to reach the firm's expected position in the terminal year of the planning period.

(b) Associated with the preceding point is the fact that little formal use is made of discounting longer term revenues and costs to present value in order to reduce different patterns of cost and revenue flows to a common denominator basis.

(c) The complexity of real business problems tends to force the use of polling procedures of one sort or another where persons knowledgeable of particular facets of the firm's activity (e.g., experts on end use markets or competitive activity) are asked to supply data estimates for their particular sphere of expertise, subject to a set of over-all ground rules. Planning activity (at least in large corporations) thus tends to involve the activities of many personnel in the organization even though coordination may be restricted to a relatively small study group.

(d) Estimates obtained by this polling procedure, however, are usually stated in "certainty equivalent" terms. That is, rather than being asked to state their estimates in terms of a range of possibilities or to attach numerical probabilities to the occurrence of alternative future events, data contributors are usually asked to supply simply a single, e.g., "most probable" estimate, for those subject areas which fall within their purview.

(e) The selection of alternative courses of action for evaluation tends to be narrow. Emphasis is placed on reducing some feasible set to a "representative" sub-set of courses of action. Emphasis is also placed on the search for dominant courses of action, i.e., those acts which are expected to yield at least as large a payoff as some other act under all states of nature (environmental factors) being considered.[1]

(f) Little or no attempt is made to consider even low order interactions of the courses of action being evaluated.

(g) The probleim of formally considering the corporate multiple goal structure is frequently avoided at the outset of the study, i.e., in the screening process used for obtaining candidate courses of action. Some type of formal check list may be used in this screening process. A portmanteau variable like total profits or return on investment is then usually selected as the payoff criterion to be applied to those candidate courses of action which have survived the screening test. Risk attitudes are not explicitly introduced by means of utility functions or similar conceptual devices.

(h) Little or no attempt is made to test the sensitivity of the outcomes of the study to departures in the basic assumptions.

(i) Few formal devices are used to incorporate feedback data from the field (e.g., market surveys, early sales results, etc.). Insofar as the use of informal means (e.g., salesmen's reports) is concerned, the typically unreliable aspects of early feedback data tend to be neglected in the sense that highly generalized inferences may be made on the basis of a very small sample, particularly if there exists some "spectacular event" in this sample (e.g., Company ABC definitely does not think that the new product has sales potential!).

In line with comments in the preceding section of this paper which dealt with the characteristics of business planning problems, it is relevant

---

[1] And, yield a *larger* payoff under at least one state of nature.

to note that traditional planning procedures have surmounted few if any of the difficulties encountered in trying to apply classical operations research techniques to this class of problems. If anything, traditional techniques appear less adequate.

For example, although the element of uncertainty abounds in business planning problems, few attempts have been made to incorporate a probabilistic framework in the analysis of these problems. Although the futurity aspects of courses of action constitute an important characteristic of business planning problems, little use is made of the tools of capital budgeting, e.g., discounting. Other examples could, of course, be derived from the preceding description of traditional planning procedures.

It would appear that the deficiencies of traditional planning techniques stem from two sources (a) lack of a suitable conceptual framework within which the characteristics of planning problems can be viewed and (b) lack of a means to implement this conceptual framework from a computational standpoint. In the next section of this paper we will try to show that the use of a decision theory-computer approach may overcome some of the inadequacies of conventional techniques for dealing with the characteristics of business planning problems.

APPLIED DECISION THEORY-COMPUTER APPROACH TO BUSINESS PLANNING

It is hardly surprising that relatively little use (at least by business planners) has been made of the procedures developed under the general heading of applied decision theory. First, these techniques are, for the most part, of recent origin. Furthermore, with few exceptions,[1] contributions in this area have had rather specialized distribution (largely limited to technical journals) and have been associated with substantive areas of interest (e.g., the foundations of statistics) that are largely outside the purview of business planning personnel.

While several decision models have been proposed (e.g., maximin, minimax regret, the Laplace criterion, the Bayesian approach, the Hurwicz criterion) this paper will focus on what appears to the writer to represent the most fruitful of these procedures, viz., the Bayesian approach to decision making under uncertainty.

In this section of the paper the following topics will be covered:

---

[1] A non-technical discussion of decision theory and its applications may be found in: R. Schlaifer, *Probability and Statistics for Business Decisions,* New York: McGraw-Hill Book Co., Inc., 1959.

C. J. Grayson, Jr., *Decisions Under Uncertainty,* Harvard Business School, 1960. D. W. Miller and M. K. Starr, *Executive Decisions and Operations Research,* Englewood Cliffs: Prentice-Hall, Inc., 1960.

(a) A brief description of the Bayesian approach in terms of an illustrative and hypothetical problem situation will first be presented.[1]

(b) Some of the limitations which this procedure shares with other formal or prescriptive models will next be pointed out.

(c) A brief description of the role which various ancillary techniques (e.g., sensitivity and indifference probability analysis, simulation, capital budgeting) can play in overcoming some of the limitations of the basic Bayesian approach will then be discussed. This section of the paper concludes with a description of the role which the computer can play in implementing the above procedures.

THE BAYESIAN APPROACH

The Bayesian approach to decision making under uncertainty can perhaps be most easily described within an illustrative problem situation.

This illustration will be drawn from the textile fibers industry. Data are hypothetical and the problem is necessarily simplified.

Let us assume that a decision maker in a firm producing synthetic fibers faces the problem of whether or not to expand the production capacity of a fiber called Texcel (a pseudonym) by adding a modification of the basic fiber to the existing product line. His decision is to be predicated upon whether or not the modified version of Texcel will appeal to prospective consumers. It is also assumed that a relevant experiment (survey) can be made so as to determine the modified fiber's appeal, or lack thereof, among the respondents in the survey.

The decision maker has two courses of action, A_1—expand and A_2—do not expand capacity. In this simplified illustration, it is assumed that the effectiveness of these two alternatives depends on which of two mutually exclusive, collectively exhaustive "states of nature" actually obtains. The case of "unfavorable" demand (as measured by the probability, $p_1 = .03$ of a potential customer's purchase of q or more units in time, t_i of the modified Texcel), will be labeled S_1. The case of "favorable" demand (as measured by the probability $p_2 = .20$ of potential customer purchase of q or more units of Texcel fiber in time, t_i) will be labeled S_2. We will further assume in this illustrative case that the decision maker can attach numerical utilities[2] to the conjunction of each of the two

---

[1] No attempt will be made within the scope of this paper to compare the strengths and weaknesses of the various decision models mentioned earlier. For a discussion of detailed aspects of these models, see: D. W. Miller and M. K. Starr, op. cit.

[2] The utilities described here are defined in the von Neumann-Morgenstern sense. See appendix for a description of how these utilities are derived.

courses of action with each of the two states of nature. The following payoff table (in which cell entries are in terms of utilities) summarizes these hypothetical data.

Table 1

UTILITY PAYOFF MATRIX

	S_1 ($p_1 = .03$)	S_2 ($p_2 = .20$)
A_1 (Expansion)	-12	15
A_2 (No Expansion)	0	-4

As the above table indicates, were the state of nature S_2 to obtain, the decision maker is assumed to attach a high positive utility, viz. 15, to taking action A_1, i.e., expanding capacity, inasmuch as he would then incur favorable sales and profits under this alternative. If he did not expand capacity, however, i.e., took action A_2, profits which could have been made would be foregone. Suppose he assigns a negative utility of -4 to this cell. Should the decision maker take A_1 when S_1 actually would prevail, then costs of idle capacity, etc., would be involved. Assume that he assigns a large negative utility of -12 to this outcome. Finally, the decision maker assigns a utility of 0 to the conjunction of S_1 with A_2. In this case, neither costs of idle capacity nor costs of foregone profits would be incurred.

However, the decision maker does have some beliefs about the likelihood of S_1 vs. S_2 obtaining. It is assumed, in his present state of knowledge regarding future demand, that he attaches a subjective probability of 0.4 to the event S_1 obtaining and a probability of 0.6 that S_2 will take place. Using the Bayesian approach we can then proceed to calculate the expected utility for this hypothetical decision maker under each act.

Table 2

APPLICATION OF PRIOR PROBABILITIES

	Pr ($S_1 : p_1 = .03$) $= 0.4$[1]		Pr ($S_2 : p_2 = .20$) $= 0.6$		EU
A_1 (Expansion)	0.4 (-12)	$+$	0.6 (15)	$=$	4.2
A_2 (No Expansion)	0.4 (0)	$+$	0.6 (-4)	$=$	-2.4

[1] The expression, Pr ($S_1 : p_1 = .03$) $= 0.4$ means "the subjective probability that state of nature S_1 (such that purchase probability is equal to .03) would obtain is equal to 0.4."

The preceding table shows the calculation of EU, expected utility, as a result of applying the decision maker's subjective probabilities regarding the likelihood of S_1 vs. S_2 occurring, to the utility entries. Under the Bayesian approach, he would then select the act which led to the highest expected utility of all acts being considered. In this illustration, the decision maker would select act A_1, viz., plant expansion.

However, it is next assumed that the decision maker can perform some relevant experiment, in order to secure additional (sample) evidence about the likelihood of S_1 vs. S_2 actually occurring.

For purposes of illustration,[1] it is assumed that the decision maker can conduct and is desirous of conducting a survey on whether or not potential consumers would purchase the modified product, Texcel fiber, were it commercialized. A decision is then made to select a random sample of $N = 50$ potential consumers, the survey is then conducted and $R = 4$ potential consumers out of the 50 indicate a willingness to purchase (q or more units in time period, t_i) if the product were marketed.

The introduction of additional sample evidence now leads to the use of Bayes' theorem[2] in order to calculate revised or posterior probabilities for the occurrence of S_1 vs. S_2.

The use of the sample evidence is shown:

Table 3

DETERMINATION OF POSTERIOR PROBABILITIES

Variable, p_i	Prior Prob.	Conditional Prob.* $Pr\ (R = 4/S_g = p_i)$	Joint Prob.	Posterior Prob.
$S_1 : p_1 = .03$	0.4	.0460	.01840	.71
$S_2 : p_2 = .20$	0.6	.0128	.00768	.29
	1.0		.02608	1.00

* The entries in this column were obtained by applying the binomial distribution; using p_i equal to .03 and .20, respectively, and the number of "successes" equal to 4.

As can be noted from the above table, the employment of the sample evidence has revised the probabilities for the occurrence of S_1 vs. S_2 rather

---

[1] In this brief, introductory section a discussion of additional aspects of the Bayesian approach, e.g., decision to sample vs. taking terminal action will be omitted, since the purpose is only to compare this simple illustration with actual problem situations. For more extensive exposition, see: R. Schlaifer, op. cit.

[2] Bayes' theorem can be described as follows: Let $S_1, S_2, \ldots S_g, \ldots S_n$ be n mutually exclusive and exhaustive events and let R be an event for which the conditional probabilities, $Pr(R/S_g)$, and the prior probabilities, $Pr(S_g)$, can be stated. To find the conditional probability, $Pr(S_g/R)$ for any S_g, given R, the following formula (Bayes' theorem) is used:

$$Pr\ (S_g/R) = \frac{Pr\ (R/S_g) \cdot Pr\ (S_g)}{\sum_{j=1}^{n} Pr\ (R/S_j) \cdot Pr\ (S_j)}$$

markedly, e.g., the probability associated with the event S_1 has changed from 0.4 to 0.71.

The decision maker, following the Bayesian approach, would then proceed to recompute the expected utilities for each act, A_1 vs. A_2, using the posterior probabilities just derived.

Table 4
APPLICATION OF POSTERIOR PROBABILITIES

	$Pr\,(S_1 : p_1 = .03) = .71$		$Pr\,(S_2 : p_2 = .20) = .29$	EU
A_1 (Expansion)	.71 (−12)	+	.29 (15)	= −4.17
A_2 (No Expansion)	.71 (0)	+	.29 (−4)	= −1.16

As the resultant expected utilities indicate, according to the Bayesian approach, the decision maker would now select A_2, i.e., not expand, since this act leads to a higher (less negative) utility. The incorporation of additional information has served to reverse the decision. The implications of this hypothetical illustration can next be examined.

LIMITATIONS OF THE BAYESIAN MODEL

The preceding hypothetical and simplified illustration of the Bayesian approach has nevertheless made several assumptions about the state of knowledge possessed by business planners and/or business executives:

(a) The decision maker is presumed capable of being able to list all relevant states of nature and courses of action. In practice, of course, a great deal of time is spent in the actual search and screening of these variables. Ultimately, however, incomplete optimization must, perforce, be the rule if only because of the exigencies imposed on planning activity in a going business organization.

(b) The outcome-payoff relationships in the hypothetical illustration were assumed to be given. Moreover, the problem appeared in a timeless framework. But in practice a great deal of calculation may be required to yield the relevant payoff measures and many sub-assumptions usually have to be made when dealing with courses of action whose effect may extend so far into the future.

(c) The model also expressed payoffs in terms of utilities (in the von Neumann-Morgenstern sense). In practice this concept is for the most part not even known to business men, let alone used in actual planning studies. Proximate payoff measures like discounted cash flow must be employed at this stage in technique dissemination. Furthermore, the theoretical power of the utility framework for dealing with the multiple and sometimes incommensurable goals of higher level management still leaves much room for improvement.

(d) The model also assumes that the decision maker and/or supplier of data inputs can state explicit, albeit subjective, probabilities about the occurrence of alternative states of nature bearing on the courses of action under evaluation. However, in actual business planning problems, the decision maker may hold only rather vague notions about the likelihood of various states of nature prevailing. It would thus appear that some means would be welcomed for indicating how sensitive his choice might be to variations in these probabilities.

(e) Finally, the opportunity to conduct meaningful surveys for the purpose of revising prior probabilities on the basis of sample information is not always practical in real planning problems. Some studies, e.g., long range price strategy, may preclude the opportunity for developing market data on the grounds that future actions would be disclosed in the data gathering process. In other studies (e.g., capacity expansion) the long lead time from decision point to implementation of the decision may make it virtually impossible to secure relevant consumer data before the fact. In planning studies, it would thus appear that the collection of meaningful information as a basis for revising prior probabilities assumes a much more subtle (and perhaps limited) role.

However, the Bayesian procedure is, after all, an abstraction or model. While the preceding limitations should be recognized, the relevant question is whether the model, on balance, is a *useful* one.

With regard to this more important question, the writer hopes to show that the Bayesian framework is decidedly useful. First, however, we might explore the role which various ancillary techniques (including the use of the computer) can play in overcoming some of the limitations of the basic Bayesian model.

ANCILLARY TECHNIQUES AND THE ROLE OF THE COMPUTER IN PLANNING

Quite independently of the development of the Bayesian decision model, other techniques have emerged from the management sciences which are relevant to increasing the effectiveness of the Bayesian approach.

For example, the tool of sensitivity analysis, wherein departures from original assumptions are made so as to test the sensitivity of outcomes to changes in these original assumptions, represents an important procedure for incorporation into the Bayesian framework. As mentioned earlier, in business planning problems at least, decision makers may hold rather vague notions about prior probabilities. Through use of sensitivity analysis, tests can be made of the sensitivity of final choice (i.e., the course of action leading to the highest expected payoff) to changes in the study's original assumptions. "Indifference probabilities" (those probabilities assigned to states of nature which would make the expected payoff associated with some "inferior" course of action equal to the expected payoff associated with the preferred course) can be calculated to measure this sensitivity.

Moreover, in many problem situations, more or less "objective" information (on, say, total market size and associated growth rates) is available. Various analytical frameworks can be constructed which combine this more or less "known" information with the decision maker's subjective probabilities regarding less documentable variables (e.g., anticipated market share for the firm).

Finally, the technique of simulation provides a powerful yet straightforward means for determining the flows of revenues and costs which are associated with course of action-state of nature combinations over the length of the planning period. The application of the discounting technique (e.g., discounted cash flow) may be easily built into the model.

Where can the computer fit into these procedures? It would seem that the computer can play a very important role toward implementing these (and other) techniques:

(a) The computer can be used in screening possible courses of action. In diversification planning, for example, the usual procedure is to set up a list of criteria, against which candidate products and/or companies are matched. In large scale programs of this sort, the computer can provide a ready means to perform this screening function.

(b) The computer can also be used to explore relevant states of nature via various types of forecasting models. Not only may the usual techniques of regression analysis and related statistical procedures be employed, but also forecasting models incorporating various dynamic features can be devised and tested retrospectively on the computer.

(c) After various courses of action or states of nature are screened, the computer also provides a way to implement the Bayesian model and the various ancillary techniques noted earlier:

   (i) The computer provides the capacity for expeditiously evaluating a greater number of courses of action, if relevant.

   (ii) The computer may be used to establish the initial payoff functions—a difficult calculational task when a long planning period is involved.

(iii) The computer provides a means to perform the desired sensitivity calculations after initial outcomes have been determined. In the case of multi-stage problems, the computer may also facilitate the use of a combination Bayesian-dynamic programming approach.

(d) Last, but hardly least, the computer can be used to provide a flexible model in which field data can be entered for the calculation of revised probabilities via the Bayesian approach. In other words, this model (i.e., computer program) can be established and maintained on a reasonably current basis, for incorporating *new* estimates as needed and then determining the implications stemming from these revisions of original data.

In summary, the Bayesian approach constitutes a decision framework which appears well suited to the characteristics of business planning problems. Ancillary techniques, like sensitivity analysis and simulation can be used to augment the workability of the Bayesian model as used in actual practice. Finally, the computer provides a helpful tool for implementing all of these techniques, should the extent of the calculational burden warrant its use.

Discussion can now be directed to what has been learned in the application of these procedures to actual problem situations.

REFLECTIONS ON THE USE OF THESE TECHNIQUES IN ACTUAL PLANNING PROBLEMS

From the writer's use of the decision theory-computer approach in actual planning problems in the Du Pont Company, it may be of interest to make some more or less general observations on our experience to date.

In this company, the decision theory approach has been used experimentally in a variety of applications ranging from capacity expansion problems to questions concerning the introduction of new products and long range price and promotional strategy. In cases where the problem detail warranted it, a digital computer was used in the simulation. In smaller scale problems, desk calculator procedures sufficed.

In terms of the mechanics of using the decision theory approach, it is hardly surprising that the determination of data inputs, particularly subjective probabilities, still represents an important educational problem. In our studies, however, we have found that managerial people—although generally unfamiliar with the technical aspects of probability theory—

can usually grasp the salient points of what is involved if the questions are framed in a step-by-step manner.

Typically, we attempt to derive their subjective probabilities concerning the variables of interest (e.g., consumer demand for a new product) through a sequential approach. The respondent may first be asked to estimate a "most probable" value for consumer demand. He is then asked to state a maximum and minimum value within which he would feel virtually certain (say, 95 per cent "confident") that the variable would fall. Intermediate values are then placed between the most probable value and the end points of the range and he is asked to state the probability that demand would fall within these intervals. Probability mass functions are then constructed and the graphs are shown to the respondent for possible alteration. In practice we have found that a five or six point mass function is about as detailed as one can go in constructing subjective frequency functions. Discrete (probability mass) functions are thus typically used to approximate density functions, even though the variable may be continuous. While the approach obviously lacks mathematical elegance, the fact remains that it is operational.

In planning problems concerning existing products (in which an appreciable amount of past experience is available) we have found that respondents can express their subjective probabilities on a reasonably detailed basis. Moreover, in this class of problems, respondents are frequently able to express probabilities covering cases where even low order interactions of the variables are involved. In other situations where less experience prevails, e.g., the introduction of a new product, a more gross structuring of the problem is obviously required.

In instances where problem detail suggests the need for computer simulation, we have found it expedient to use an automatic coding system (e.g., IBM's FORTRAN) inasmuch as programming time is a more scarce resource than computer run time in problems of this type.

In terms of the reception of this approach by the sponsors of various studies, a few observations of general interest can be made. First, it would seem that a large part of the value of the approach lies in the need for the decision maker to think about the problem in a somewhat different (and hopefully more fruitful) way. The relatively rigorous structure of the approach forces him to consider the implications of each of his assumptions on other assumptions and to quantify, if crudely, some variables which he would not ordinarily consider for quantification. Emphasis is thus placed on achieving internal consistency among the assumptions. It is not surprising that a good part of the value of the approach is derived in the formative stages of structuring the problem well before the outcomes are finally cranked out of the computer.

Secondly, the use of sensitivity analysis appears to have made a worthwhile contribution to these studies by showing that many factors which had apparently been thought to influence the outcomes markedly, often turn out to be relatively insignificant in terms of their effect on final choice.

Use of a computer model also provides an efficient means for conducting tests on the effects of several other assumptions not included in the original set of variables in order to permit a range of questions to be answered in the presentation of the study results. In our experience, however, a general caveat on this point is in order. The computer, of course, can generate an almost inexhaustible set of outcomes, depending upon one's imaginative ability to vary assumptions. This feature may prompt the temptation to include in the final verbal presentation (and written report) a whole series of possible (but rather implausible) outcomes, thereby confusing the listener and/or reader and detracting from the main findings of the investigation. The results of these auxiliary computer runs (while pertinent at times) are usually better placed in the appendix of the report.

Moreover, the many advantages of the decision theory-computer approach over traditional planning techniques should obviously not be construed as indicating that these procedures offer any foolproof predictive device for making optimal planning decisions. Further research of at least two types is needed: (a) improving the usefulness of the decision model itself and (b) improving our ability to predict outcomes related to states of nature affecting the courses of action under review.

With respect to the first area, it is well to point out that, in our experience, managerial choice has not always agreed with the choice implied by application of the model. Nor can full documentation be made of the extent to which the implications of the model have influenced management's choice. Research has been and is being conducted on such areas as the applicability of the utility framework in describing risk attitudes and the possible use of payoff measures other than strictly monetary measures (like discounted cash flow) for incorporation into the model.

But good decision rules are one thing and good *predictive* tools for ascertaining outcomes associated with taking alternative courses of action are another. And in this latter area much research remains to be conducted. As a starter, work has been done on (a) measuring product life cycle characteristics regarding the sales and profit experience of older products and on (b) examining opportunities for using field or survey data to revise prior probabilities held regarding the occurrence of external events relevant to the problem. However, these are only illustrative of the many possibilities for further research on the predictive aspects of planning theory.

In summary, however, it would seem that the decision theory-computer approach can offer a useful aid to the business planner by both providing a conceptual framework for decision making and supplying implementation for this framework. While the hapless market research man of our introductory fable cannot be guaranteed immunity from the "slings and arrows of outraged executives" by merely adopting this approach, it is felt that these procedures will find increasing application on the part of business planners in the future. At worst, this approach provides a useful "if . . . then" model for answering questions like "what would happen if such and such were to occur?" At best, applied decision theory, aided by the computer, may provide not only an internally consistent, flexible device for marshaling the best executive estimates regarding the future but also a going means to incorporate field information and revision of prior probabilities in effectively dealing with the more realistic world of dynamic and sequential decision making.

APPENDIX

THE VON NEUMANN-MORGENSTERN CONCEPT OF UTILITY

In the body of this paper, reference was made to the von Neumann-Morgenstern utility framework. The purpose of this addendum is to present a brief and non-technical description of this concept.

"Utility" in the sense used here is a very different concept from that typically associated with micro-economic theory. The latter concept, i.e., utility in the neoclassical economics sense, goes back at least to W. Stanley Jevons.[1] As used in value theory, the concept of utility was psychologically oriented and referred to the "subjective satisfaction" derived by an individual from possession of given numbers of units of some commodity. The so-called cardinalist school of economists constructed a theoretical apparatus which postulated the existence of degrees of psychic benefit attributed to the possession of varying quantities of some good or service. However, the inherent difficulties in measuring this subjective concept later gave rise to the ordinalist school of J. R. Hicks et al. which developed the indifference map approach.

Although the same term is used, utility in the von Neumann-Morgenstern sense[2] (the sense used here) is a very different concept than used by the neoclassical economists.[2] Based on a particular set of postulates

---

[1] For a discussion of some of the history of this concept, see: N. Georgescu-Roegen's "Choice, Expectations and Measurability," *Quarterly Journal of Economics,* Vol. **68**, 1954.

[2] A lucid discussion of this concept may be found in W. J. Baumol's *Economic Theory and Operations Analysis,* Englewood Cliffs, N.J.: Prentice-Hall, Inc., 1961, pp. 331-346. J. von Neumann and O. Morgenstern's original development may be found in *Theory of Games and Economic Behavior,* Princeton, N.J.: Princeton University Press, 1944, pp. 15-29.

about an individual's preference for certain "prizes," i.e., outcomes, the
von Neumann-Morgenstern framework can be used to assign an index
number for the purpose of predicting which "gamble" (having the prizes
as payoffs) the individual would choose if the attainment of the prizes
were subject to risk.

For example, suppose an individual were asked to rank three prizes
in order of preference, viz., $A = \$500$, $B = \$200$, and $C = \$10$. The indi-
vidual states that he prefers A to B to C. The von Neumann-Morgenstern
concept postulates that for some (conceptual) lottery containing A and
C as prizes, where the probability of obtaining A equals $Pr\ (A)$ and the
probability of obtaining C equals $1 - Pr\ (A)$, the individual would be
indifferent to choosing either B for certain or the lottery which contained
A and C as prizes.

Suppose that the individual states that he would be indifferent to receiving B for certain and participating in a gamble in which he would
receive A with a probability of 0.6 and C with a probability of 0.4. (For
all gambles where $Pr\ (A)$ exceeds 0.6, it is assumed that the individual
would choose the gamble and for all gambles where $Pr\ (A)$ is less than
0.6, it is assumed that the individual would prefer receiving B for certain.)

Within the von Neumann-Morgenstern apparatus, one could arbitrarily assign some utility number to A and C, e.g., 1 and 0. The utility
of prize B would then be computed from the following equation:

$$U\ (B) = Pr\ (A) \cdot U\ (A) + \{1 - Pr\ (A)\} \cdot U\ (C)$$

$$U\ (B) = 0.6\ (1) + 0.4\ (0)$$

$$U\ (B) = 0.6$$

Suppose further that the individual, when confronted with prize $D = \$400$, states that he would be indifferent to receiving D for certain and
participating in a gamble in which he would receive A with a probability
of 0.7 and C with a probability of 0.3. The utility of D could be found
similarly.

$$U\ (D) = Pr\ (A) \cdot U(A) + \{1 - Pr\ (A)\} \cdot U\ (C)$$

$$U\ (D) = 0.7\ (1) + 0.3\ (0)$$

$$U\ (D) = 0.7$$

If the individual were then asked to choose between two gambles involving, say, as prizes A and B and A and D, respectively, one could
predict (if the individual's behavior were consistent with the von Neumann-Morgenstern framework), the gamble which would be selected. As
Table 1 shows the individual (were he complying with the postulates
of the von Neumann-Morgenstern concept of utility) would select gamble
1 inasmuch as the expected utility (EU) of this gamble (at .84) exceeds
the expected utility associated with gamble 2 (at .82). In contrast, if the

Table 1

HYPOTHETICAL GAMBLES

Prizes	Probability (Gamble 1)	Probability (Gamble 2)	Utility	Expected Utility (Gamble 1)	Expected Utility (Gamble 2)
A ($500)	.60	.40	1.0	0.60	0.40
B ($200)	.40	—	0.6	0.24	—
D ($400)	—	.60	0.7	—	0.42
				0.84	0.82

individual were guided solely by expected monetary value, his choice would have been the opposite, viz. ($500 × 0.6) + ($200 × 0.4) = $380 for gamble 1 vs. ($500 × 0.4) + ($400 × 0.6) = $440 for gamble 2.

As could be inferred, business planning problems, which are noted for the uncertainty surrounding the outcomes of alternative courses of action might be expected to involve considerations which could be placed within the von Neumann-Morgenstern utility framework.

However, attempts to measure empirically individual utility functions (and to use these functions to predict behavior under real or simulated conditions) have been only sporadic. These attempts can be classified under two bases, controlled experiment vs. measurement under field conditions.

The work of F. Mosteller and P. Nogee represented a pioneering attempt to construct utility functions under more or less controlled conditions.[1] D. Davidson, P. Suppes, and S. Siegel's study represents another attempt (using a somewhat different procedure) to derive empirical utility functions within a laboratory setting.[2] W. Edwards has conducted several experiments on the determination of individuals' subjective evaluations of probabilities.[3]

Even less work has been done to date with respect to deriving utility functions under field conditions. H. Grayson, Jr.'s, work stands out as the major, if not sole, investigation within this category.[4] His study con-

---

[1] See: F. Mosteller and P. Nogee's "An Experimental Measurement of Utility," *The Journal of Political Economy*, October, 1951, pp. 371-404.

[2] D. Davidson, P. Suppes, and S. Siegel, *Decision Making: An Experimental Approach*, California: Stanford University Press, 1957.

[3] W. Edwards, "Probability-Preference Among Bets with Differing Expected Values," *Psychological Bulletin*, Vol. **51**, No. 4, 1951.

[4] C. J. Grayson, Jr., op. cit. The writer's own work in deriving utility functions for a sample of middle management personnel has been summarized in the paper: *The Derivation of Utility Functions in a Large Industrial Firm*, presented at the First Joint National Meeting of TIMS and ORSA, November, 1961, San Francisco, California.

cerned the derivation of utility functions for a group of people employed in oil and gas drilling operations. His purpose was largely educational in the sense that he was primarily interested in determining whether the functions could be readily derived (i.e., the consistency with which his respondents could state risk preferences) and his respondents' reactions to the practicality of the concept. No attempt was made to determine whether or not the empirically derived functions could predict respondents' actual behavior.

While the utility concept offers some provocative possibilities regarding possible use in actual business planning situations, it is fair to say that applications to actual business problems are virtually non-existent as of this writing.

To the casual reader, the title of this chapter might seem confusing. What possible connection can there be between marketing problems and military planning? It is the purpose of this paper to indicate that there is, in fact, a strong relationship between the two fields. We hope to demonstrate to the designer of market planning systems that the advanced military planning techniques are a source of conceptual ideas, experience, and design criteria. The intent, however, is not to detail the appropriate military techniques but to outline them, indicating how they can be applied.

The largest single organization in the world, in terms of number of computer installations, is the United States Department of Defense. More than 500 commercially available digital computers, as well as a large number of special "military systems" are in use in that agency. In this discussion, it is important to recognize that an "installation" represents both hardware (the machine itself) and software (the programs, routines, and models which the machine manipulates). Unlike most industrial users

MARKETING APPLICATIONS OF ADVANCED MILITARY PLANNING TECHNIQUES

of computers, the government and particularly the Department of Defense, invests heavily in software as well as hardware. A good deal of this "software" investment is for advanced techniques for planning, control and intelligence, or information processing. It is to these techniques that we wish to direct our attention.

Since such techniques and systems are now being employed as an aid in the determination of military expenditures, which make up a large part of the Gross National Product, all marketing men should be aware of their general effect. But the size and shape of the total U.S. market is only of passing interest in this discussion; the real concern is with the marketing function, and how computers can be used to assist in market planning.

At the same time, it is the task of the "marketeer" upon which the attention is to be focussed. The computer is, at best, a servant, not a replacement for the *man* in marketing. In our concern for developing aids for the marketing man, we must be careful to define his role and mission in the firm rather than to generalize. The marketing function can run the full gamut; from the hot dog salesman at a baseball game to the executive level technical marketeer of large scale defense systems such as the Polaris weapons system or the Sage defense system. Each type of salesman has specialized needs and interests. The computer system which might serve one type of marketing function well might be very ineffective in a different environment.

This paper deals with applications for the marketing man at the far end of the spectrum; the salesman in a large defense or industrial systems organization. This type of individual is definitely not an "order-taker." He sells a small number of very large, complex, and expensive products to a limited number of customers. Competition is intense in this "game," and the tactics and timing of each product innovation and sale are extremely important. In this type of marketing environment, some of the newly developed military planning techniques can be directly applied. We envision an integrated data processing system that will aid the marketeer-manager in both the long and short run. Such a system would serve to support the long run market planning and control function as well as the short run programming and market research (intelligence) function.

In pin-pointing military techniques which can serve as the basis for this integrated market planning system design, we demonstrate their existence and usefulness as feasible tools. In listing marketing applications which can follow from these techniques, we show that such tools have interesting and vital carry-over for industrial systems. Finally, it should be recognized that a significant percentage of the concepts and applications detailed in the other chapters of this book also resulted from Government expenditures to solve comparable military systems problems. It is a well known fact in the computer industry that military developments and applicators in the Electronic Data Processing field precede industrial applications by two to three years.

EXAMPLES OF MILITARY PLANNING TECHNIQUES

Military planning and control techniques utilizing electronic computers can be classified and examined under three topical areas:

1. Strategic models for planning[1]
2. Tactical models for planning
3. Intelligence system techniques.

---

[1] Strategic models can be defined as those which consider the short as well as long term effects of competitive engagement, with emphasis on the competitive aspect. Tactical models are generally short term in nature, with only minor considerations on the competitive aspect.

In each case, we will select an example and describe it briefly with appropriate references for those desiring more information. It should be noted that details of some of these techniques are still classified. However, enough information in each area has been released to make the broad concepts available to potential users.

STRATEGIC MODELS FOR PLANNING

Strategic models for planning are normally a type of operational game. A well known example of such a model currently used by the U.S. Air Force for planning analysis is the Air Battle Model [1] (ABM). The ABM, with its supporting computer program, is "a device for simulating a large-scale two-sided global war. The model incorporates interrelations between most of the offensive and defensive air and ground support operations of both sides that are believed to affect air operational capabilities significantly in the first day or two of a general war." The model is a logical dynamic statement of the interacting effects of a complex *operation*. It is a *game* in the sense that two (or more) players are involved. It is an *operational game* in the sense that, once pre-planned inputs are introduced into the system, play will proceed automatically, providing a chronological history of the game (war) as output.

It is this latter result which makes such a tool important to the strategic planner. With an operational game available, the planner can develop several alternative plans which appear feasible. These "pre-plans" are then tested on the model, allowing a high speed computer to assess the effects of one alternative versus another. The plan selected is the optimal one among the several alternatives, based on the test results. [2]

The Air Battle Model is quite complex. Work on the model started in 1955 at the Rand Corporation, Santa Monica, California. After feasibility testing of the model, the Air Battle Analysis Division, under the War Plans Division, Headquarters U.S. Air Force, was established as a focal point for USAF war gaming requirements, and given the responsibility for the development and application of the Rand model. The Operation Model Evaluation Group, Air Force (OMEGA), was established in Washington, D.C. [3] to help apply the model to Air Force problems.

---

[1] Developed under Contract AF 33 (600)-35190 with the United States Air Force. A good description of this model is to be found in "Simulation of Air Operations with the Air Battle Model" by R. Adams & J. Jenkins in *"Operations Research,"* Vol. 8, No. 5 (1960).

[2] The results, of course, must be reviewed critically, as should be the output of any machine system. However, it is the alternative "pre-plans," plan testing, optimal plan selection sequence which is important. By utilizing a strategic, all encompassing test model to evaluate alternatives, the strategic planning process is improved.

[3] Under a contract with Technical Operations, Inc.

The Air Battle Model system which resulted, consists of three parts:

1. *Plan Converter*—provides mechanized conversion of Air Force Operational Plans into proper form for model input.
2. *The Air Battle Model*—the operational game simulation itself. The ABM consists of a master control program and seven major operational programs.
3. *The Output Programs*—which sort, compile and tabulate the detailed histories of all parameters and operations in each game or run.

This "software" system is run on an IBM 7090 computer. The entire program has cost approximately $3.5 million so far. Approximately $2.0 million was for the programming of the ABM proper. This game, probably the world's largest and most detailed operational war game played on a high speed digital computer, takes about 11 months for a complete evaluation of a set of plans. This involves 4-6 months of pre-planning, one month of running time (e.g., manipulation of the ABM proper), and 4 months of data reduction. Present development work on this system is designed to materially reduce the overall time to a more desirable figure.

The important aspect of this technique, however, is not its cost or complexity, but in its ability to support the strategic planning function in a working situation. By providing a simulated environment or model in which a vast operation involving a two-sided engagement can be logically evaluated,[1] the technique serves an important purpose. The capability to assess logically and mechanically the strategic effects of a broad plan can materially improve the over-all planning process.

TACTICAL MODELS FOR PLANNING

In the strategic model, the important factor was the ability to simulate an "extensive" environment which considers the competitive interaction of two players on a broad front, involving a series of separate engagements. In the tactical models, the orientation is to planning in a limited or short run sense, in which nature is the only competitor. The problem is usually one of program planning,—with limited resources, and in limited time, how to schedule and assign tasks to the appropriate capabilities or

---

[1] A description of the Air Battle Model can be most easily seen by an illustrative mission, as played by the model. A group of planes take off from their base, refueling at designated points, and penetrating enemy territory. En route, they are subject to defensive action such as detection by radar, attack by fighters and surface to air missiles, etc. The invading planes may defend themselves while moving to the target area where specific targets are bombed. The flight then returns to base. This entire mission is simulated by a 25,000 instruction program on a digital computer. The outcome of such a mission, included losses, targets hit, etc., can be determined by the model.

resources in order to complete a specific mission or project. A good example of a tactical planning model or system of this kind is PERT (Program Evaluation Review Technique[1]). PERT, a statistical technique developed and applied by the Special Projects Office of the United States Navy Department in 1958, was initially used to coordinate and evaluate the prog-

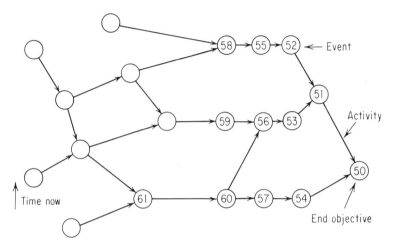

Fig. 1. Typical PERT project network.

ress of the FBM (POLARIS) Weapons System project. Essentially using time as a variable, the PERT system provides:

.A measure of current status against approved plans and schedules
.A forecast of future progress and problem areas with the probabilities of meeting schedules for planned efforts
.The effects of proposed changes in plans on established schedules for meeting program goals

The PERT-System is composed of three separate sections:

---

[1] PERT publications available from the Superintendent of Documents, U.S. Government Printing Office, include:

> *PERT Summary Report, Phases I and II, Polaris Management, Proceedings of the PERT Coordination Task Group Meeting, Instruction Manual and Systems and Procedures for the Program Evaluation System.*

See also "Application of a Technique for Research and Development Program Evaluation," by Malcom, Roseboom, Clark, and Frazer in *OPERATIONS RESEARCH*, Vol. **7**, 1959, pp. 646-669, as well as "Critical-Path Planning and Scheduling," by J. Kelley, Jr., and M. Walker, in the 1959 Proceedings of the Eastern Joint Computer Conference. This latter paper discusses a parallel industrial application in construction planning.

1. *Data Input*—A project structure or diagram (network) is defined which describes the interdependencies, time relationships, and sequence of a set of events. The events, depicted in Figure 1, as circles, are defined as recognizable points in time at which specific tasks or activities start or end. The arrows between two events represent activity or work required to proceed from one event to the next, implying a fixed amount of resources operating on a specific task. A set of elapsed time estimates are obtained for all such activity by collecting data from each individual responsible for performing them. This time-estimate data,[1] as well as the project sequencing diagram represent the input.

2. *PERT Simulation and Computation*—The above data is fed to the PERT model which is programmed on a large scale data processor. A probability density function is fitted to the time estimates for each activity, and mean time to completion as well as the variance from the mean are computed. The expected earliest and latest event times (time when event will occur) and the probability of completing each event are then determined, utilizing the computed data and the sequencing information. In this manner, the critical events in the project can be defined, and the over-all estimated project completion date and probability of completion (at that date) can be derived. If this over-all target date is not satisfactory, alternative courses of action can be simulated and evaluated, using the same procedures.[2]

3. *Data-Output*—Standard print-outs from the computer provide a variety of information to management. If one compares the PERT estimates with the original or desired plans, potential schedule slippages and other critical events can be determined. Utilization of the simulation capabilities of PERT allows alternatives to be evaluated and tested before actual implementation.

The PERT system was originally programmed on the NORC digital computer at the Computation Laboratory of the Naval Weapons Laboratory, Dahlgren, Va., at an estimated cost of approximately $21,000. The system has been subsequently programmed for several different computers in a wide number of locations, and is now being used by several major weapons systems contractors including General Electric, Lockheed, and Sperry Rand. Although there are some elements of the PERT system to which exceptions might be taken, its over-all effectiveness as a planning technique at the tactical (program planning) level cannot be questioned.

---

[1] Several projects are now under way to include cost of the activity in the data analysis. In these more advanced techniques, each activity would be specified in terms of both elapsed time and estimated costs.

[2] Such alternatives could include: changes in project sequencing, changes in the allocation of resources to activities which would increase or decrease elapsed time estimates, adding new activities, or changing the task assignments on existing ones.

It has been shown to be an extremely valuable tool in the management of the Polaris-FBM project, and is now being expanded for use in the National Aeronautics and Space Administration (NASA) and other areas of the Department of Defense.

INTELLIGENCE SYSTEM TECHNIQUES

In military intelligence system techniques, as in the other techniques discussed above, there is an implicit element of competition. Nature acts as a somewhat antagonistic agency, attempting to hide or conceal important facts and information from our view. In many cases, intelligence systems are engaged in acquiring data and information concerning a competitive organization which would prefer not to have this information revealed. The purpose of advanced intelligence techniques utilizing computers is to improve the efficiency and decrease the time involved in obtaining necessary information in the face of this uncooperativeness.

There are many military and governmental intelligence systems and techniques now available or under development.[1] One example of the general intelligence system techniques now available is the WALNUT system developed for the United States Central Intelligence Agency (CIA) by IBM Corp. The WALNUT system[2] is a large capacity, random access, document retrieval system which utilizes the storage of highly reduced photographic images providing a rapid, selective output. The system consists of a *random access document index*, a *document image converter*, and a *random access image file*.

Documents, containing written or graphic information are microfilmed. This microfilm copy and associated data describing the contents of the copy are then forwarded to the WALNUT system. The data description is filed in the *document index*, and the microfilm copy is transferred to a specially prepared film strip, utilizing the *document image converter*. The image converter automatically assigns the film strip to a particular location in the image file, recording this location on a punch card. The film strip is then physically stored in its assigned location in the *random access image file*.

---

[1] A good survey of unclassified techniques may be found in *"Documentation, Indexing and Retrieval of Scientific Information,"* prepared by the Committee on Government Operations of the U.S. Senate, 1960. Another good source is *"Current Research and Development in Scientific Documentation,"* prepared semi-annually by the Office of Science Information Service of the National Science Foundation. Both documents can be obtained from the U.S. Government Printing Office.

[2] The WALNUT system has been described in "Photo-Image Storage—Its Role in Modern Business," by John Veyette, Jr., in BUSINESS AUTOMATION, Oct. 1961. Detailed information can also be obtained directly from the IBM Corporation.

Documents are retrieved by filling out a search form which describes as specifically as possible the type and nature of the information desired. Using this search request, the document index is automatically scanned for all documents which meet the criteria of the request. A list of all such documents is prepared for the requester along with a special address card for each document in the list. The requester reviews the prepared list and asks for copies of individual documents by returning the appropriate address cards. The requester then receives copies of the microfilmed documents in the form of specially prepared photo-aperture cards which can be viewed directly or used to make full sized reproductions. At no time do the original document copies leave the file, and the system provides the capability to search hundreds of millions of pages rapidly and efficiently.

Essentially, the WALNUT system, as in any intelligence technique, consists of three basic functions:

1. *Data Input*—Acquisition and initial processing of raw data or information, usually in some qualitative format.

2. *Information Processing and Storage*—The raw data is evaluated with respect to other information known or already stored. New trends or facts are analyzed utilizing models or structural representations of the real world. Significant data is then forwarded for dissemination, and the newly acquired and evaluated (e.g., processed and analyzed raw data) information is stored for future use.

3. *Information Dissemination and Retrieval Output*—Significant data is forwarded to the appropriate user. The user can also request and retrieve desired information from the storage files by describing the characteristics or criteria of search. Utilizing this search routine, the system retrieves and forwards copies of the appropriate information to the requester.

Intelligence systems can be appropriately classified as planning techniques in that they assist planners in recognizing actual or potential changes in the operating environment which require re-planning. Advanced mechanized techniques can provide the planner with the capability to recognize changes and competitive activities quickly and accurately. The information retrieval capability provides an efficient means of calling up the information needed to assist in the planning process.

TRANSITION FROM MILITARY TO MARKETING PROBLEMS

Summarizing, the three military techniques outlined above consist of:

.An operational game used in the evaluation and analysis of strategic level plans—*The Air Battle Model*

.A set of computer programs used to evaluate the status and plans of a tactical level project or program—*PERT*

.A mechanized intelligence system for information storage and retrieval—*WALNUT*.

All of these techniques have certain elements in common which differentiate them from normal run-of-the-mill accounting and financial applications of computers:

1. Each of these techniques performs a function which is fairly complex. That is, they are not simply a mechanization of clerical or tabulating procedures which previously existed. This function simply would not be performed if it could not be mechanized. Thus, the first aspect of these techniques is that they were primarily developed to increase the decision-making capabilities rather than to decrease clerical costs.

2. Each of the techniques relies heavily on the human as part of the input and output process. They are essentially *man-machine* systems.

3. There is an element of competition implicit in the design and operation of each technique.

4. The techniques operate on qualitative data in which there is some judgment or evaluation required. The systems, therefore, are not completely rigorous, e.g., they work efficiently most, but not all, of the time.

It is interesting to note that these characteristics might also be the criteria which one would adhere to if he were designing a market planning system utilizing computers. The marketing system would certainly be for a new functional area, designed primarily to assist in the market decision-making process. Because marketing is primarily a human art, any realistic system must be designed with the human as an integral part of the process. The system must be geared to the marketplace and its inherent element of competition. Finally, the computer system must be designed to operate on qualitative data to the extent that the system is effective at least most of the time.[1]

If, as we assert, there are some very close relationships between the characteristics of certain military planning techniques, and the design requirements of analogous industrial market planning systems, then it would be appropriate to try to apply these military tools. The next section outlines the characteristics of such marketing applications with some recommendations for further development. In this discussion, as in the preceding one, our purpose is to pinpoint some realistic examples rather than to describe them in detail.

---

[1] It is this qualitative aspect of the marketing man's information spectrum which most laymen point to in developing a list of reasons why computers cannot be useful in the marketing function. Yet, we have demonstrated that there now exist useful techniques in military applications which operate on this kind of qualitative data.

MARKETING APPLICATIONS OF MILITARY PLANNING TECHNIQUES

Our discussion of marketing applications follows the same framework as in the examination of military techniques. Three types of applications can be described:

.An industrial strategic level model applied to the planning of a large industrial and defense systems manufacturer

.A market-product programming application for the same type of organization

.An intelligence system supporting the market research function in the same type of organization.

In each case, we have successfully applied the broad concepts and techniques presently utilized in military applications to solve complex market planning problems. Although these applications have not all been reduced to computer programs at this time, they have been "hand played," e.g., programmed using desk calculators. The problem of computer selection and programming, although a difficult task in itself, is primarily a technical one, once the models and techniques have been developed. Since we are primarily concerned with the *transition* from military to marketing applications rather than the details of the applications themselves, this lack of complete mechanization is not too important. It is sufficient to state that such applications can be programmed and run on a computer if required.

The strategic planning application is depicted in Figure 2, Strategic Planning for the Federal Market. As noted in the introductory comments, emphasis is on the broad market planning problems of a large systems corporation in the defense market. The initial step was to obtain data on the structure, economics, requirements, and state of the art in the federal market. From this information, an operational model of the environment was developed. Information concerning the past sales, profits and operations of the corporation as well as its present capabilities, plans, and R and D programs were analyzed. This was done to determine a set of possible or feasible alternative plans which broadly met the criteria of initial objectives developed by the study team on the basis of long range corporate goals. At this point, an initial strategic plan (e.g., a set of alternative plans, any one of which appeared to meet our initial objectives), and an operational model had been developed.

A market research team provided data on the key competitors in the market place, evaluating each one to define its probable course of action. Using this competitive capabilities information and the operational model previously developed, we proceeded to "game" the initial strategic plans.

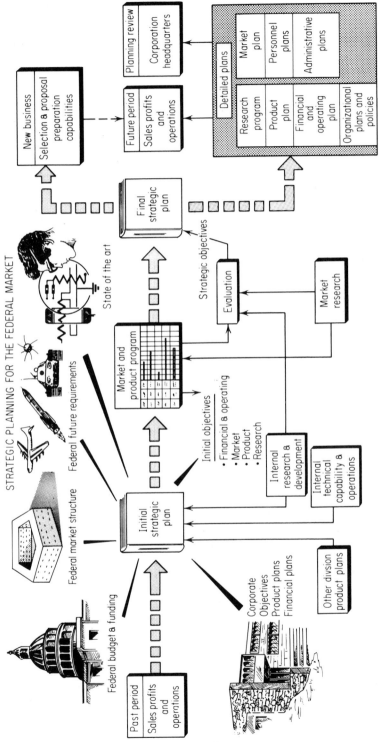

STRATEGIC PLANNING FOR THE FEDERAL MARKET

Fig. 2.

313

The implementation of each plan was simulated and the results were determined in the form of probable market sales and product programs over a five to ten year period. During the course of the simulated games, initial objectives were modified and reviewed, and a final set of strategic objectives were drawn up. The market-product results for each plan were then evaluated with respect to the final objectives in order to select the most desirable among the several alternatives. In performing this selection, we relied on both the quantitative results of the games as well as qualitative market research and R and D "breakthrough" estimates. The result of this complex planning process is a final strategic plan, the actual long and short range programs of action expressed in the form of detailed operating, market and product plans.

This strategic planning technique, drawn in concept directly from the analogous military system, produces an over-all marketing and operating strategy, and gives a structured guide to the market place. It provides a set of integrated plans in which timing and interplay between different activities have been considered rigorously. An additional feature of such an approach is that the consideration of competitive dynamics can materially aid the new business selection and proposal preparation capabilities of the company, an important aspect of short term market decision making in this type of firm.

It is true that this planning process is quite cumbersome unless it is mechanized; one study of this type involved three men working for approximately one year. However, the bulk of this effort is usually for initial data gathering and structuring of the operational model. Once this has been completed, new planning evaluations can proceed relatively quickly.

The second application, the use of a tactical program planning technique is also quite similar to the military version. In the industrial and defense systems firm, product timing decisions are extremely critical. The product research and development program must be closely geared to the development of supporting services. A technical and sales force must be trained, drawing upon key personnel who have usually already been committed to several different programs, and a coordinated market program and publicity campaign must be initiated. The actual scheduling and timing must be programmed such that the new products are announced at a time when market requirements for such products are increasing, competitive products have not yet gained general acceptance, and other company product line sales can not be drastically affected. A relatively simple form of the tactical program scheduling and planning technique can materially alleviate the often harassed marketing manager from detailed planning and control of complex programs. Elapsed time estimates are made by those responsible for executing discrete activities. This data is fed into the mechanized system, and the probable product announcement date can be determined. The marketing manager can, by manipulating his resources, or rescheduling activities, program the announcement and marketing operations for the optimum point in time.

Finally, we can pinpoint an application of intelligence techniques to market planning. Several proposals have already been advanced for just such systems, and some now do exist.[1] However, the existence and nature of industrial intelligence systems, as in the case of military systems, is a closely guarded topic. It is fairly easy to see that in our industrial and defense systems firms, an intelligence system supporting the market research function would be a practical and valuable tool. Information and data on competitive equipment, bids, new personnel acquisitions, managerial changes, contract awards, etc., is placed on punch cards or in a tape memory. Graphic or extensive textual material is stored on microfilms, whose contents and location are also indexed. A complex file indexing, analysis, and retrieval program is then written which allows the mechanical systems to automatically scan the amassed data for required information, and to assemble new trends. By keying the operational model data requirements of the strategic planning programs to the indexing programs of the intelligence system, it might be possible to eventually allow the mechanical system to perform a large portion of the market research task internally. This latter proposal is still in the planning stage but is certainly a feasible technique. In any case, we have developed some simple, yet effective market intelligence systems utilizing punch card equipment which effectively aid in the market research-market planning function. These applications are also conceptually quite similar to military intelligence techniques.

SUMMARY AND CONCLUSIONS

In summary, we have reviewed a wide variety of military computer techniques for planning and control which have been developed at government expense. The concepts, designs and development of these techniques represent, within limits, a large storehouse of ideas and operating experience upon which the marketing oriented systems designer can draw. Although one must be both careful and critical in directly applying military techniques, the close similarity (in terms of the computer system design) between the marketing and military planning functions deserves some attention. We have demonstrated that, at least in certain kinds of market

---

[1] See "Commercial Intelligence Services" by Dr. Roy Soukop, in the Chemical Business Handbook, edited by John H. Perry, and "A Business Intelligence System," by H. P. Luhn in the IBM Journal of Research and Development, October 1958.

planning situations, the military computer techniques are quite easily applied. It is hoped that the focus on strategic planning and intelligence techniques has brought to light some new ways of looking at how computers can be useful and has served as a platform, a jumping off point, in developing new and advanced computer systems for market planning.

PART IV

CASE STUDIES

chapter one | *Edwin M. McPherson*

EXAMPLE 1 — CONSUMER PRODUCTS — DEVELOPMENT OF AN IM-
PROVED ANNUAL FORECAST

A manufacturing firm using manually prepared short-range forecasts derived from sales statistics suffered a disastrous year. Inventories were out of control, cash-flow was hampered, field returns were increasing, dealer-distributors were complaining of stock overloads and the structure of management decision making was undetermined. A crash project was undertaken to improve the accuracy and effectiveness of intermediate and long-range forecasting.

Sales statistics for the total period of available records were reduced to punched paper tape. These records included as much detailed data in respect to customer description as possible. The punched paper tape was read into an RCA computer, stored on magnetic tape, and subjected to a series of editing and grouping runs. Similar buying patterns

CASE STUDIES OF THE

COMPUTER AND FORECASTING

were related. As a result of this editing, two distinct markets were isolated for further analysis.

During the time period in which the sales statistics were being reduced to computer language and being analyzed, a separate team prepared for computer use data for comparable periods which were descriptive of the United States economy. Records of the activity of the Gross National Product, Installment Loans Outstanding, Unemployment, etc., were placed on tape.

It was not known which, if any, of the indices of economic activity were descriptive of the sales activity to be forecast. A computer program was written which compared the variation between measured time periods of the index with the historical variation of sales during the same period.

Indices which had the same or similar variations were isolated. The analysis continued by shifting the index activity to a preceding time period and comparing this shift with sales statistics. Indices which showed similar patterns of activity, but which preceded sales shifts of activity were isolated.

As is usual in analysis of this sort, no single index pattern exactly matched the pattern of sales activity. Several seemed close, but deviated enough so that if used as a basis of guiding inventory buildup or cutback, the deviation could be costly to management. This meant that an index of activity, peculiar to each of the two discovered markets, would have to be constructed from those indices which seemed related to each market.

A computer program was written which matched (correlated) multiple indices with the sales data. This was done by a simple correlation of each index with the sales data, calculating how close the fit of this data might be, then repeating this calculation for each index tested. When the calculations were completed, each index was ranked as to the importance of its contribution, and all indices were averaged together to form a total match to the sales statistics.

If the combined indices produced an exact match of prior sales history, the job would be completed. If not, then indices would be substituted and the analysis made again. A set of standards was effective or ineffective. Ineffective indices were eliminated after each comparison.

This approach, which relies upon commonly accepted economic indicators for predictive purposes, finally developed a set of indices which could be used by the manufacturer to guide his production and inventory policy. Under the first year of testing and operation, it predicted within a half of a percent the sales activity for the consumer item being produced. Since that time the technique has been further refined and is reported producing still more accurate results.

The effect of this marketing forecasting technique on the flow of goods for this specific firm has been to bring productive activity more closely in line with consumer demand. This improves service to customers by reducing costs of the product which are attributable to error and waste.

EXAMPLE 2 — CONSUMER PRODUCTS — SEASONAL FORECAST OF STYLE, SIZE, AND COLOR REQUIREMENTS

A manufacturer using tabulated equipment to prepare intermediate range forecasts of sales activity found the forecasts, while reasonably accurate, required more time to prepare than could be tolerated, if the forecast was to be of value to the firm. The basic cause for this shift in timing was due to the changing character of the market. More calculations were required to fix sales trends.

These calculations arose from two sources, first the industry as a whole was offering wider selections of merchandise to dealers and distributors;

and second, the life of each offering as a part of the product line was decreasing due to the variety offered.

In a seasonal business, where decisions have to be made for the short run and erroneous decisions can only lead to unrecoupable losses, the importance of analyzing trends early and correctly cannot be overemphasized. Items in the product line, once placed into production, are useless for any other purpose; but withheld from production, they could be disposed of with minimum loss. The product line consisted of three thousand items offered in thirty-two sizes and several alternate styles for a total set of variables in excess of 540,000 possible decision errors.

Analysis of the sales statistics established relationships between sizes, styles, patterns and colors. Size shifts existed but were quite slow in taking effect. Style shifts occurred more frequently but still were predictable within reasonable tolerance. Cross-link relationships existed between colors and patterns which were reducible to percentage factors. Seasonal patterns existed which formed another set of cross-link percentage relationships.

The existing system required from six to ten days to compile, to calculate, and to project early sales into orders for raw materials. In an industry with limited sources of reliable supply and a high degree of free competition, delay in reordering increased raw material supply or of cancelling optioned materials could mean a sales season lost to competition. Such a loss could lead to financial instability in this close margin business.

Historical data on a reasonable sales period were developed. Known and suspected mathematical relationships were established. Limits of sample reliability were determined. These limits were established on the basis of total customers ordering to date, size of customers ordering, number of units ordered by major buyers as well as number of units ordered by smaller buyers. In order to establish a definite trend, both "quantity ordered" and "number of customers ordering" standards had to be met. Limits were established both for an item and for the total line offering.

The basic formula for projection, based primarily upon prior history percentage relationship, was placed in the computer, together with the inventory of raw materials. As orders were received they were prepared for the computer, entered, calculation was made of raw material requirement and orders applied against inventories on hand, on order or reserved.

As each order was applied against raw materials, the number of customers ordering that item was entered by size, and the number of units ordered was entered in the proper size group. These numbers were automatically checked against reliability limits and if, for the time span involved, a projection of sales could be made of that item, the projection was prepared, placed on tape and read out of the computer at the end of the run as a management report. Twice weekly, all items were reviewed and a complete forecast made. Items below normal sales frequency criteria were separated from those above. A prepare-to-cancel and prepare-to-reorder report was made. The total anticipated demand in each instance was calculated, both by weekly time periods during the sales season and for the entire season.

The effect of this forecast was to reduce inventory in anticipation of reduced sales or to reorient the sales force toward greater effort where such reductions could not be freely accomplished. The effort of salesmen to alter the sales pattern was readily measurable. Where demand was increasing beyond normal expectancy, management was in the position of being able to place emergency orders early in the season before competition tied up suppliers' reserves.

EXAMPLE 3 — CONSUMER PRODUCTS — SHORT-RANGE FORECAST OF INVENTORY REQUIREMENTS

A manufacturer of non-perishable, non-style consumer items found that it could predict total demand for the products it manufactured but not its own share of these markets. The firm established a system of full inventory at consumer level since point of sale coverage had been proven of greater importance than advertising or other sales approaches to the market. In order to establish nationwide coverage in retail, wholesale and distributor outlets, substantial inventory was required. The product line consisting of from eight to twelve basic sizes in from fifteen to twenty styles and merchandised in units of one through one dozen represented approximately one thousand line items normally stocked.

The manufacturer established distribution points at his plants and major shipping centers. He stocked on consignment inventories at distributor, wholesaler and dealer levels. In short, the manufacturer assumed complete horizontal inventory responsibility. Lack of a size or an item at the consumer level meant diversion of a sale to a competitor. Excess inventory meant losses in breakage, damage to stock, and increased servicing costs. Population shifts resulted in increased or decreased consumption. Consumption of the product was related to use and use from point to point was not predictable. Prior history of consumption within geographic areas was useful in establishing the quantities necessary to the replenishment of stocking points.

Analysis of the prediction problem and of the inventory control problem indicated the need for a "levels of control" system. Inventory records were established centrally for stock at major distribution points, at regional warehouse points, and at the factories. These points were tied together through use of leased lines and teletype. Inventories at each level were placed on a central inventory control computer.

Prior sales history was compiled for each item in each area where stock control was centralized. Shipping time between alternate distribution points and between regional or factory warehouses was calculated on an emergency and a routine basis. Average daily consumption as influenced by seasonal cycles for all points, major and minor, were computed. The average manufacturing cycle for each item was established.

From the foregoing, tables were placed in the computer which contained regional, branch (wholesale), and central shipping and consumption data. Upper and lower limits for each item in each stocking point were derived from this data. A formula which modified upper and lower limits based on changes in frequency of demand was generated.

As orders were received to replenish dealer stocks, these were processed against wholesale stocks. If a deviation from prior historical norms— either more or less than usual consumption within a given time period— was observed, an exception report calling this condition to the attention of wholesale management was prepared. The same type of analysis was conducted at the regional and factory levels together with appropriate reports to management.

The system detected early significant changes in demand which permitted shifting of inventories between sales, warehouse, and factory points to maintain full service to customers. It reduced total inventories while improving specific service to customers. The calculations and timing of the system are such that it cannot be accomplished without a wire network and without a computer to maintain current records. Total sales increased for this firm, presumably at the expense of its competitors.

CONCLUSIONS

As the volume and complexity of business increases, the need for accurate current data on sales activity also increases. The computer offers the opportunity to satisfy volume data processing needs. It also presents the opportunity for creating specific methods of measurement to extend current sales activity into the immediate, near immediate, and long-range future. The cost of developing and installing proper programs is substantial. However, the rewards are being proven more substantial each day.

Linear programming is an economical way for the multi-product, multi-plant corporation to determine the location at which orders received from widely scattered points should be filled. Some computer users have prepared standard programs which can be adapted to the scheduling needs of such firms. A corporation wishing to use such a program provides information as to its demand requirements, its supply capacities, and its cost structure. More specifically, it forecasts the demand over time for each of its products as well as the purchasing pattern of each of its large customers or distributors. The supply information provided includes the location and productive capacity of each of the various plants, unit costs for each product at various levels of output, and transportation charges from the possible production sites to each of the major customers. Once such information is obtained, the prepared computer program will indicate the allocation of resources which would minimize the total costs of production, transportation, and warehousing.

The popularity of standardized programs is due to a combination of

THE TRANSPORTATION PROBLEM

AS APPLIED TO A MAJOR

CHEMICAL MANUFACTURER

economic and technological factors. The wide range of possible applications and the promotional advantages provided have enabled computer manufacturers to absorb the high developmental costs of such programs. Potential users, in contrast, find that the expense of designing a more specialized scheduling program usually exceeds the possible gains. This follows from the fact that once the adjustments necessary for computer application have been made, the production and distribution problems faced by all large, decentralized manufacturers are structurally similar. Because of these twin limitations of cost and computer capacity, most corporations prepare a simplified model of their operations which will enable them to use a generalized computer program. Important problems still remain, however, when this procedure is employed. The necessary information must first be obtained and then put in a form acceptable for use in the prepared program. The following paragraphs indicate the possible complexities of such an undertaking.

Computer Applications, Inc., was retained by a large chemical manufacturer desirous of employing "MITRI"—a transportation program prepared for the IBM 7090. The division in question manufactured its four products at ten plants with each plant working two shifts. There are marked monthly fluctuations in the demand for the four products and the division's customers consist of 450 widely scattered distributors. The dimensions of this system were beyond the capacity of the prepared program which could not allow for the 450 customer classes. It was thus necessary to assign each of the 450 customers to 100 aggregated customer classes. The available cost data, however, were based on the shipment of products from the plants to the original 450 customers. Consequently, a weighting system had to be employed to determine the cost of shipping from each of the ten plants to each of the 100 aggregated customers. Further complication was introduced since some products were shipped from plants to warehouses and then from warehouses to customers. Production costs at various levels of operation and warehousing expenses were also considered. At all times, the computer consultant restricted himself to applying the data provided by the client company.

The model did not contain opening or closing inventories because of the significant computational and programming effort that would have been required. In addition, no allowance was made for the fact that the costs of transportation would depend upon the mode of shipment—truck or rail. Instead, a weighting device was employed whenever alternate methods of transportation were available. Within the limitations of the model, resources were allocated in a manner which would minimize costs.

The value of any solution obtained by the method described above depends in large part upon the quality of the inputs. Such a computer program would be of little assistance if the initial estimates of cost and demand are greatly in error or grossly inappropriate methods of aggregating and weighting are employed. In most cases, however, satisfactory methods of averaging and aggregating can be developed. Also, estimates of cost functions and demand fluctuations are necessary whatever the method used to schedule production.

Aside from sheer computational ease, there are two other advantages to the use of computers in scheduling. First, the data requirements of the program may lead to a more scientific approach to forecasting. Conversely, the effect on scheduling of changes in one's assumptions concerning cost and the structure of demand are revealed. The course of action most appropriate, given the existing range of uncertainty, can then be determined. The ability to vary inputs can also be helpful in such tasks as assessing the impact of technological innovations or freight rate changes and determining the relative merits of proposed factory or warehouse locations. When properly employed, MITRI and programs similar to it can indicate the effects of many major corporate policies before irrevocable actions are taken.

chapter three | *John R. Parks and Dr. L. H. Krone*

Reproduced below is the text of a report prepared by the Research and Engineering Division of the Monsanto Chemical Company. The material is in the exact form in which it was presented to corporate officials and the marketing directors of each of the company's divisions. The report was submitted in November 1961 with the expectation that it would influence future company policies. Although limited mention is made of the fact, the problem could not have been solved without the use of a computer.

INTRODUCTION

The problem of optimally locating sales offices relative to customers has been mathematically analyzed and the analysis used to

MINIMUM COST LOCATIONS

FOR SALES OFFICES

1) select the sales office locations that will serve the customers at minimum total cost, or
2) make better assignments of customers to present locations.

As an example of the use of these programs, it has been shown that the total cost of operating sales offices at the present locations of the offices of the Organic, Plastics, and Inorganic Divisions is 13.6 percent higher than the cost of operating fifteen offices consolidating the sales functions of the divisional offices.

This problem originated in Marketing Services. The Operations Research Group collaborated with Marketing Services in analyzing the problem to determine the important data and a method of processing these data to answer questions on sales office locations.

The results of this study are being used by Marketing Services to make recommendations to the marketing directors on problems of divisional and corporate marketing.

SUMMARY

APPROACH TO THE PROBLEM

The approach to this problem was to develop a mathematical model that described, as closely as presently possible, the total cost (occupancy, personnel, telephoning customers, telecommunications) of operating a sales office as related to the volume of orders to be processed. Customers were grouped by counties in which they are located. Limitations on the number of customers assigned to a sales office were affected by requiring that the cost per order handled should be either a minimum or less than some preselected maximum. In order to study the model, several 704 programs were developed.

One program involved free choice of sales office locations guided by a criterion of "best" location. "Best" location was used in the sense of that county with the maximum volume of unassigned orders. After a location has been selected, counties are assigned until the total cost per order at that location passes through a minimum or exceeds a preassigned maximum. This process is repeated until the county list is exhausted.

The preassigned maximum cost per order has a more important function than being a limit on the cost per order as counties are assigned to a location. A low value of the preassigned maximum forced the program to choose a larger number of sales office locations and a high value forced the program to choose fewer office locations.

The program computed the total operating cost for a chosen set of offices for a given value of the preassigned maximum. Over a range of values of the preassigned maximum cost per order, the total cost passed through a minimum representing a balance between the cost of long distance calling of customers from a few sales office locations and the leased line costs and fixed costs for a large number of sales office locations. This was the optimizing feature of this program.

A second program operates with preassigned locations of sales offices and assigns customers on the basis of the nearest location. This process is repeated to exhaustion of the county list.

The third program analyzes the corporate sales data at each office and tabulates the orders by division. This makes possible the statement of the relative strength of each division at each office. The first and second programs can be used on divisional as well as corporate sales data. The third program is used only after corporate sales data have been processed by one or both of the other two programs.

LIMITATIONS AND ASSUMPTIONS

The basic limitations and assumptions of these programs are 3 in number:

1. The sales offices are assumed to be independent of each other. This assumption is not true in regards to telecommunications between a sales office and the General Offices and plants. More efficient use of telecommunications capacity is obtained by having groups of sales offices share lines. The assumption of independence increases the cost of telecommunications. The increased cost can be removed by having the selected sales offices organized into a proper network by the Communications Department.

2. There was no control (in an accounting sense) over the input data. The input data were the county locations, the order and sales dollar volumes associated with each county. These data have not, previous to this work, been available since there has been no accounting records of the geographical location of the origin of Monsanto business. The listings of the 1959 business of each division originating from each district office were sent to the home office so that clerks could enter the state and county of origin of each order on the list. This information was summarized to obtain the geographic distribution of orders for each division separately. The division summaries were combined to obtain the corporate summary. Even though no attempt was made to reconcile the results with accounting totals, it was found that the total order and sales dollar volumes were within 95 percent of the total. It should be noted that the cost to push the precision of the data from 95 to 99 percent is not warranted since the past histories of the divisional sales offices are not sufficiently well known to be accounted for this closely by the mathematical model.

3. It was assumed that occupancy and personnel costs are independent of geographic location. While not strictly true, the variations were not significant enough to affect the final result.

CONCLUSIONS

1. The programs can not check the detailed performance of the sales offices as they presently operate.

2. The programs *can approximate* the performance of the sales offices as they are now located.

3. The programs *can show* whether or not such locations yield least cost operations.

4. The programs *can choose* a set of locations of consolidated sales

offices and associated county assignments so that Monsanto may present a corporate front to all its present and potential customers at minimum cost.

5. The programs *can be used* to estimate the cost of operating any configuration of sales offices and will determine the divisional structure of each consolidated office.

RECOMMENDATIONS

The mathematical solution of this problem is more general than it appears. The objective of the present solution is to minimize the cost of passing information from customers to the General Offices and the plants. The objective could just as well be minimization of the cost of passing finished goods to the customers. From a larger point of view, these processes of passing information and finished goods form a loop which could be approached with the present model.

It is recommended that the activities of the various departments that center around transfer of information and/or goods be viewed in the light of the solution of the sales office location problem.

DETAILS OF CALCULATION

The cost function describing the operating cost of a sales office as related to the order volume contained the following factors:

1. Occupancy cost per clerical person
2. Salary cost per clerical person
3. Number of clerical people to handle the orders
4. Local telephone charges (including equipment) per clerical person
5. Long distance charges based on an average 9 minute call to customers
6. Frequency of calls to customers
7. Leased line cost to General Offices
8. Message frequency to General Offices
9. Service people per clerical person.

The value of these factors plus additional data required in the solution are given in the Appendix. The long distance telephone charge tables and the leased line cost formula based on air line miles were obtained from the Communications Department. Estimates of the other factors were obtained from Marketing Services.

As counties were assigned to a sales office, the above factors were used to compute the total cost of handling the accumulated order volume. A running cost per order could then be calculated. Initially, the cost per order would decrease. Sometimes, the cost per order would pass through a minimum at which time the assignment of counties would be terminated. Sometimes the accumulated total cost would increase sufficiently fast that the cost per order would increase until it reached a preselected maximum at which the county assignment was terminated.

Among the cases studied with these programs was a comparison of the total operating costs of the Organic, Inorganic, and Plastics Divisions' sales offices as they are presently located and the cost of operating fifteen corporate sales offices in best locations and combining the functions of the divisional offices. The following table summarizes the results:

Table 1

COMPARISON OF TOTAL OPERATING COSTS
OF DIVISIONAL OFFICES AS PRESENTLY
LOCATED AND 15 CORPORATE OFFICES

Division		Cost ($1000)
Organic		592
Inorganic		370
Plastics		663
	Total	1625
Corporate		1405
	Difference	220 = 13.6 percent.

A by-product of this work was a program which presents the divisional and corporate sales data in a statistical form. The program was written to present the data in three ways:

1. Distribution of orders by county order volume
2. Distribution of sales dollars by county dollar volume
3. Distribution of dollars per order by size of this ratio. The distribution of orders has been tabulated and presented to Marketing Services. Data such as this can be useful in inquiring about Monsanto's depth of penetration of the Nation's business.

chapter four | *Hans B. Thorelli*

The simulation of organization structure and behavior is certainly one of the most exciting areas of computer application in marketing-oriented business planning. This applies with equal force to the organization of entire marketing systems comprising producers, channels, and consumers and to intra-firm organization for marketing decision making. In the latter area applications so far have largely centered on various aspects of physical distribution and inventory control. Much less has been done with regard to marketing's principal role as a data processing and circulating medium and a link in entrepreneurial decision making on such matters as the areas in which the firm should be active.

The International Business Operations Game (INTOP), the case-type model to be discussed, was explicitly designed for use in tackling some of these aspects of business planning. This game was developed at the Graduate School of Business of the University of Chicago.[1] While the

---

[1] INTOP is eminently a product of teamwork. The author served as a coordinator of a group which also included Professor Robert L. Graves, Associate Director of the Operations Analysis Laboratory of the School and Lloyd T. Howells, M.E., M.B.A., Research Assistant. Much advice and assistance was obtained from other faculty members at Chicago.

GAME SIMULATION OF

ADMINISTRATIVE SYSTEMS

area of application of the case is related most immediately to Dean Dill's essay on design and testing of organizational structure it has points of contact with several other papers, notably Michael Halbert's on information requirements in decision making and Dr. David Hertz's on the coordination of business functions.

The word *simulation* is used somewhat extravagantly in the title of the case. It should be thought of in the same relativistic sense as a link trainer in the context of flight simulation, or small group study as a highly simplified tool of simulating large organizations. We are dealing here with gross approximations of the "simulated" reality rather than with accurate or perhaps even well-balanced projections thereof. It should also be emphasized that while our intentions are honorable the use of INTOP for organization simulation is in its infancy.[1]

Perhaps the most crucial problem facing the organization planner is to design a system of structure and behavior conducive to satisfactory attainment of the overall goals of an organization while keeping intraorganizational conflict and suboptimization among departments within

---

[1] The game was "checked out" only in May 1961.

reasonable bounds.[1] This problem becomes the more troublesome, the more complex the organization. It comes to a head in the international operations of diversified companies, a prime reason for focusing INTOP in this area. However, the game by analogy—or by simple change of parameters, if desired—is equally applicable to the internal coordination problems of any dispersed and diversified concern operating exclusively in domestic markets.

More specifically, we shall discuss the use of INTOP as an instrument of organization planning in the following areas:

1. Structuring approaches (organization by area, product, function, etc.)
2. Centralization—decentralization (delegation)
3. Communications

Before going on to that discussion, however, the reader is entitled to a brief description of the game.

CAPSULE DESCRIPTION OF INTOP [2]

INTOP provides for the play of 3-25 teams representing as many companies. The game has been played with 4-7 executives on each company. When the game is used for organization planning and simulation (rather than as hitherto, largely for educational purposes) a greater number of members on each team is likely to be desired. Certainly the game models are complex enough to provide realistic decision-making tasks and processes for up to a dozen members per team—especially if the company teams are subjected to such non-computerized shock-type environmental developments as strikes, currency devaluations, etc., in which real life also abounds. The fact that INTOP permits a great number of teams is especially valuable in that it allows testing of different organizational arrangements under similar environmental conditions, i.e., the special circumstances which develop in any sequence of play. (As in bridge and other complex games the chances of any one sequence being repeated in the lifetime of the players is slim.)

The companies may operate in one, two or all of three areas, i.e., Brazil, the European Economic Community (EEC), and the United States. "Operate" is a broad concept and covers any one, or any combina-

---

[1] Cf. H. B. Thorelli, "The Tantalizing Concept of Productivity," *American Behavioral Scientist* (November, 1960), 6-11.

[2] A complete Player's Manual is obtainable from the author at the Graduate School of Business, University of Chicago, Chicago 37, Illinois. An Administrator's Manual is also being prepared.

tion, of the functions of manufacturing, marketing of one's own product, serving as distributor, and licensing. It is even possible for a company to restrict itself to the role of financier. All corporations are assumed to have their home office in Liechtenstein, well-known international tax haven.

As in real life, each area will have its peculiar characteristics in terms of size, demand and production functions, as well as economic climate and governmental policies with regard to corporate taxation and international trade. Countries in balance-of-payments difficulties may, for example, place restrictions on the remittance of profits abroad.

Each *decision period* represents three months in real life.

Each company may manufacture and/or market either or both of *two different products*. As an assist to the imagination, it may be instructive to think of these as two medium-priced electrical appliances. As the purpose of the exercise is to tackle general business problems, however, and to emphasize the necessity of learning about an industry by experience and research, we have deliberately avoided any attempt to "reproduce" any one specific real-life market in detail. Product line planning is further emphasized by the fact that research and development may be prevailed upon to secure patented improvements. Each of the two products may have up to four improvements (or "grades") in the course of the game. Patents may be licensed, globally or nationally, selectively or exclusively, and with provision as to the maintenance of minimum prices, etc. (In the event that markets get too highly organized, the U.S. Department of Justice may bring an antitrust suit resulting in a court decree for compulsory licensing or dedication to the public of any patent controlled by violating concerns manufacturing or marketing in the United States.)

To avoid unrealistic and exasperating complication it is only possible to manufacture two grades of each of the two basic products in any given area during any given quarter. Furthermore, a company may only *market* two grades of each of the two products in any given area in any given quarter (whether it manufactured these goods, bought them from another company, or did both). For convenience reasons these two grades are called the standard and the deluxe versions.

In the field of *production* management, optimum plant size and fixed-variable cost relationships vary by area and product. Depreciation is linear and by percentages which are uniformly and automatically applied to all companies. Manufacturing costs increase as plants grow obsolete. However, plant efficiency may be increased by spending money on methods improvements. Plants which are obsolete or represent over-capacity may be disposed of, and new plants may be constructed at any time.

Due to the plurality of products, grades and geographical markets with different demand characteristics *marketing* decisions are of cardinal importance. Price elasticity varies with all three of these categories, while advertising extends to both grades of a given product which a company may market in an area at any given time. In addition to selling to the "computerized" consumer market, the company may also want to engage in industrial selling, i.e., use another company as distributor. This may be done nationally as well as internationally, and the company may also transfer its own goods from one area to another (intra-company transactions). Inventory charges (for warehousing, etc.) as well as Commercial and Administrative expense are automatically applied. Both of these functions are exponential, placing a premium on low inventory but high sales volume.

Financial management is important in this exercise as in real life. Companies are provided with an initial starting capital. Working capital may be increased by ploughing back profits, by short-term borrowing for current needs in the different areas of operation, and by long-term borrowing (within sound banking limits) by the Home Office, presumably for long-range expansion or general consolidation of a shaky company. In cases of outright distress, materials suppliers may be counted on to extend credit, but only on stiff terms. In addition, companies are free to arrange loans between themselves at any time.

Surplus liquidity may be absorbed in the areas by the purchase of short-term, low-interest bonds, and at the Home Office by investing in higher-yielding securities.

Negotiation between companies is ordinarily a prominent feature of the game in view of the provision for inter-firm trading, licensing, and financial transactions, and the urge of several companies to specialize in certain areas, products or functions. This feature—as yet quite rare in management games—may be retained or excluded in organization simulation exercises depending on their purpose.

Timing problems are also forced to the surface in INTOP. There are time lags of one or several quarters in plant construction, international transfers, use of patents, maturing of accounts receivable and payable, the international spread of business cycle effects, etc. These dynamic features, added to the impact of competitive interaction, place a premium on planning and effective managerial organization.

The procurement, processing, and communication of *data* for decision-making is of crucial import in all organizations and especially in competitive business. The information furnished each company on a routine basis is quite rich, and some of it is detailed enough to make selective screening and use imperative at both headquarters and operating levels. In addition, companies may or may not choose to incur extra expenditure for some or all of a score of market research items which the computer will provide on special request.

Sample copies of the two most important data output sheets furnished each company on a quarterly basis are reproduced here. They represent a Balance Sheet and an Income Statement of a somewhat more sophisticated

COMPANY 07

INTOP - UNIVERSITY OF CHICAGO

BALANCE SHEET

PERIOD

	AREA 1	AREA 2	AREA 3	HOME OFFICE	CONSOLIDATED 08
ASSETS					
CASH	3,493	713,639	0	37,650	754,783
A/R FIRST QUARTER	1,020,000	478,447	0		1,498,447
A/R SECOND QUARTER	0	482,955	0		482,955
INVENTORY STANDARD X	174,914				
DELUXE X	0	96,000	0		
STANDARD Y	622,376	0	0		
DELUXE Y	609,090	573,812	0		
TOTAL		0	0		
SECURITIES	1,406,382	669,812	0	2,150,000	2,076,194
	0	0	0		2,150,000
TOTAL CURRENT ASSETS	2,429,876	2,344,855	0	2,187,650	6,962,381
NET PLANT AND EQUIP.	5,250,000	900,000	0	0	6,150,000
INVESTMENT INTERCOMP.				6,616,000	0
SUBSIDIARY CONTROL					
TOTAL ASSETS	7,679,876	3,244,855	0	8,803,650	13,112,381
LIABILITIES					
A/P FIRST QUARTER	1,128,267	504,095	0		1,632,363
A/P SECOND QUARTER	0	170,529	0		170,529
SUPPLIER CREDIT	0	0	0	0	0
BANK LOANS	0	0	0	0	0
TOTAL CURRENT LIABILITY	1,128,267	674,625	0	0	1,802,893
LOANS PAYABLE				0	0
TOTAL LIABILITIES	1,128,267	674,625	0		1,802,893
STOCKHOLDER EQUITY					
COMMON STOCK AT PAR				10,000,000	10,000,000
PAID IN CAPITAL			0-	0	0
RETAINED EARNINGS	1,125,806	1,380,230		1,196,350	1,309,488
HOME OFFICE CONTROL	5,426,000	1,190,000			0
TOTAL EQUITY	6,551,608	2,570,230	0	8,803,650	11,309,488
TOTAL LIAB. AND EQUITY	7,679,876	3,244,855	0	8,803,650	13,112,381

Table 1.

COMPANY 07

INTOP - UNIVERSITY OF CHICAGO

INCOME STATEMENT	AREA 1 PRODUCT X	AREA 1 PRODUCT Y	AREA 2 PRODUCT X	AREA 2 PRODUCT Y	AREA 3 PRODUCT X	AREA 3 PRODUCT Y	HOME OFFICE	CONSOLIDATED
STANDARD SALES								
CONSUMER	174,000	1,430,000	210,000	1,399,852	0	0		3,213,852
INTRA-COMPANY	96,000	0	0	0	0	0		96,000
INDUSTRIAL	0	0	0	0	0	0		0
LESS: COST OF GOODS	173,532	674,471	150,000	532,526	0	0		1,530,530
GROSS MARGIN	96,467	755,528	60,000	867,326	0	0		1,779,322
DELUXE SALES								
CONSUMER	0	0	0	0	0	0		0
INTRA-COMPANY	0	0	0	0	0	0		0
INDUSTRIAL	0	0	0	0	0	0		0
LESS: COST OF GOODS	0	0	0	0	0	0		0
GROSS MARGIN	96,467	755,528	60,000	867,326	0	0		1,779,322
TOTAL GROSS MARGIN								155,771
OPERATING EXPENSES								
COMER. AND ADMIN.	19,000	59,999	18,571	58,200	0	0		155,771
METHODS IMPROVEMENT	0	5,000	0	5,000	0	0		10,000
ADVERTISING	15,000	20,000	10,000	17,000	0	0		62,000
SHIPPING	36,000	0	0	0	0	0		36,000
INVENTORY	0	0	0	8,470	0	0		8,470
SALES EXPEDITING	0	0	0	0	0	0		0
DEPRECIATION	60,000	90,000	0	60,000	0	0		210,000
NET OPERATING EXPENSE	130,000	174,999	28,571	148,670	0	0		482,242
NET EARNINGS FROM OPER.	33,532	580,528	31,428	718,655	0	0		1,297,080
TOTAL NET OPER. EARNINGS		546,996		750,084		0		1,297,080
NON-OPERATING INCOME								
INTEREST INTERCO. LOANS							0	0
LICENSES							0	0
MISC. INTEREST		0		0		0	36,550	36,550
TOTAL NON-OPER. INCOME		0		0		0	36,550	36,550
NON-OPERATING EXPENSE								
MARKET RESEARCH							0	0
LICENSES							0	0
R & D NEW PRODUCT X							60,000	60,000
R & D NEW PRODUCT Y							100,000	100,000
TOTAL INTEREST		0		0		0-	0	0
TOTAL NON-OPER. EXPENSE		0		0		0-	160,000	160,000
GROSS EARNINGS		546,996		750,084		0-	123,450	1,173,630
LESS: TAXES		284,438		337,537		0-	0	621,976
LESS: CAPITAL TRANS. TAX								
NET EARNINGS		262,558		412,546		0-	123,450	551,654
LESS: DIVIDENDS							200,000	200,000
TO RETAINED EARNINGS		262,558		412,546		0-	323,450	351,654

Table 2.

340

COMPANY 15
BALANCE SHEET

PERIOD 11

	AREA 1	AREA 2	AREA 3	HOME OFFICE	CONSOLIDATED
ASSETS					
CASH	2,191,884	1,583,638	261,057	217,110	4,253,690
A/R FIRST QUARTER	3,339,600	696,426	200,000		4,236,026
A/R SECOND QUARTER	0	714,000	160,000		874,000
INVENTORY STANDARD X	164,720	68,054			
DELUXE X	0	0			
STANDARD Y	577,699	181,514			
DELUXE Y	683,688	0			
TOTAL	1,426,108	761,624	249,569		2,437,301
SECURITIES	0	0	0	3,000,000	3,000,000
TOTAL CURRENT ASSETS	6,957,592	3,755,688	870,626	3,217,110	14,801,018
NET PLANT AND EQUIP.	6,960,000	2,640,000	2,770,000		12,370,000
INVESTMENT INTERCOMP.				0	0
SUBSIDIARY CONTROL				16,600,000	
TOTAL ASSETS	13,917,592	6,395,688	3,640,626	19,817,110	27,171,018
LIABILITIES					
A/P FIRST QUARTER	1,959,701	651,622	141,350		2,752,674
A/P SECOND QUARTER	0	228,487	99,827		328,315
SUPPLIER CREDIT	0	0	0		0
BANK LOANS	0	0	0		0
TOTAL CURRENT LIABILITY	1,959,701	880,109	241,178		3,080,989
LOANS PAYABLE				9,950,000	9,950,000
TOTAL LIABILITIES	1,959,701	880,109	241,178	9,950,000	13,030,989
STOCKHOLDER EQUITY					
COMMON STOCK AT PAR				10,000,000	10,000,000
PAID IN CAPITAL	3,157,891	1,015,578		239,813	239,813
RETAINED EARNINGS	8,800,000	4,500,000	99,448-	372,703	3,900,215
HOME OFFICE CONTROL			3,300,000		
TOTAL EQUITY	11,957,891	5,515,578	3,399,448	9,867,110	14,140,029
TOTAL LIAB. AND EQUITY	13,917,592	6,395,688	3,640,626	19,817,110	27,171,018

Table 3.

COMPANY 15   PERIOD   11

INCOME STATEMENT	AREA 1 PRODUCT X	AREA 1 PRODUCT Y	AREA 2 PRODUCT X	AREA 2 PRODUCT Y	AREA 3 PRODUCT X	AREA 3 PRODUCT Y	PERIOD HOME OFFICE	CONSOLIDATED
STANDARD SALES								
CONSUMER	0	0	0	1,280,000	0	0	0	1,280,000
INTRA-COMPANY	0	0	0	0	0	0	0	0
INDUSTRIAL	860,000	2,528,000	0	0	120,000	280,000	0	3,788,000
LESS: COST OF GOODS	298,889	1,303,530	0	453,760	70,089	183,112	0	2,309,383
GROSS MARGIN	561,110	1,224,469	0	826,239	49,910	96,887	0	2,758,616
DELUXE SALES								
CONSUMER	0	2,178,000	0	0	0	0	0	2,178,000
INTRA-COMPANY	0	0	0	0	0	0	0	0
INDUSTRIAL	0	0	0	1,100,000	0	0	0	1,100,000
LESS: COST OF GOODS	0	678,299	0	669,813	0	0	0	1,348,112
GROSS MARGIN	0	1,499,700	0	430,186	0	0	0	1,929,887
TOTAL GROSS MARGIN	561,110	2,724,169	0	1,256,425	49,910	96,887	0	4,688,503
OPERATING EXPENSES								
COMMER. AND ADMIN.	0	73,333	0	59,999	0	0	0	133,333
METHODS IMPROVEMENT	0	50,000	0	30,000	10,000	10,000	0	100,000
ADVERTISING	0	0	0	0	0	0	0	0
SHIPPING	144,000	100,000	0	44,000	9,000	15,000	0	312,000
INVENTORY	0	0	0	0	0	0	0	0
SALES EXPEDITING	100,000	394,800	0	70,800	0	0	0	565,600
DEPRECIATION	120,000	180,000	0	120,000	20,000	30,000	0	470,000
NET OPERATING EXPENSE	364,000	798,133	0	324,799	39,000	55,000	0	1,580,933
NET EARNINGS FROM OPER.	197,110	1,926,036	0	931,625	10,910	41,887	0	3,107,570
TOTAL NET OPER. EARNINGS		2,123,146		931,625		52,797	0	3,107,570
NON-OPERATING INCOME								
INTEREST INTERCO. LOANS		0		0		0	0	0
LICENSES		0		0		0	0	0
MISC. INTEREST							51,000	51,000
TOTAL NON-OPER. INCOME							51,000	51,000
NON-OPERATING EXPENSE								
MARKET RESEARCH							0	0
LICENSES							0	0
R & D NEW PRODUCT X							100,000	0
R & D NEW PRODUCT Y							0	100,000
TOTAL INTEREST							0	0
TOTAL NON-OPER. EXPENSE							100,000	100,000
GROSS EARNINGS		2,123,146		931,625		52,797	49,000-	3,058,570
LESS: TAXES		1,104,036		419,231		15,839	0	1,539,107
LESS: CAPITAL TRANS. TAX								
NET EARNINGS		1,019,110		512,394		36,958	49,000-	1,519,462
LESS: DIVIDENDS							200,000	200,000
TO RETAINED EARNINGS		1,019,110		512,394		36,958	249,000-	1,319,462

Table 4.

and informative nature than is usually supplied for public consumption by diversified and/or divisionalized concerns. Less detailed than internal accounting records, they are nevertheless explicitly designed with organization simulation in mind, allowing separate breakdowns by product, area and/or function. (Each company is further supplied with an internal staff report analyzing sales, production and inventory in units of various products and grades by area as well as their cost. There are also two optional output sheets of market research data.)

While this is a highly condensed description of the International Business Operations Game, it should bring out two points of importance. First, that although specifically focused on international concerns INTOP is indeed a well-balanced *general* top management game, giving broad representation to such classical business functions as production, marketing, finance, and accounting in addition to overall corporate planning. Secondly, the game has sufficient complexity to make a fairly elaborate division of labor (i.e., organization) most desirable, and the data furnished the teams are presented in such a form as to make possible deliberate experimentation with different types of organization patterns and decision-making processes. By virtue of the modular design, the degree of complexity may be varied to reflect any given real-life situation with sufficient faithfulness to permit efficient testing of different organizational designs.

At this stage someone may object that the game is not specifically enough directed towards *marketing* problems to suit the interests of readers of this work. We will readily admit that it is not devoted to marketing subfunctional problems such as sales management, salesmen training and compensation, media and channel selection, etc. But it does have the core of marketing functional decisions of price and advertising. More importantly, the game is squarely focused on the *entrepreneurial aspects of marketing,* dealing with such crucial problems as to the businesses and areas in which the company should be active in the first place, whether products should be sold by a captive outlet or through intermediaries, the procurement and processing of market data, and, not least, the integration of marketing with other parts of the business (both horizontally and vertically in the organization). It is in these areas we claim that INTOP would be quite useful as a simulation device in marketing organization planning.

USE IN ORGANIZATION PLANNING AND SIMULATION

The most powerful reason for using simulation in organization planning is that it frequently may be a great deal cheaper both in direct costs and indirectly in human relations and lost time costs than experimental tinkering with the real organization itself. Where this is the case, simulation is likely to become increasingly used, provided there is any reason to believe that tenable conclusions can be reached. It would seem that on the latter point we may be moderately optimistic. Organized behavior systems seem to be governed largely by three major sets of interacting variables:

    a. The personalities involved
    b. The goals and structure of the organization
    c. The environment in which the organization operates

As to personality types the military for many years have been using games to study the behavior of more or less risk-minded commanders in varying organizational and environmental circumstances. It should be equally feasible to use other criteria, such as production-centered vs. employee-oriented leaders. As at the present time, we have little knowledge of how the game experience itself will affect the behavior of the players. It would seem advisable for the time being not to use the people who will themselves be affected by the organization planning effort in the simulation, at least not in the positions they may expect to take up in real life.[1] Other personalities with somewhat similar characteristics to the real-life personnel available may be used. It is, of course, also possible to hold the personality variable "constant" in some degree by a randomized composition of teams.

The goals of the organization would presumably be stated by management in advance of the simulation exercise, and thus be a parameter rather than a variable in the exercise. As organization structure is likely to comprise the set of variables of prime import in game simulation of decision-making systems, we shall discuss this area separately in the last few pages of the paper.

Whether the environment in which the organization operates should be a given or a variable in organization simulation would again be dependent on the purpose in mind. If the environment is known in salient respects and the intention is to try out alternate types of organization, the thing to do is to set the parameters of the game model in such a way as to reflect principal features of the environment. If the organization is more or less given, at least initially, and the intention is to examine ways in which it might most effectively cope with environmental change, a great degree of variability in the market variables in the course of the simulation exercise is clearly desirable. Again, it may be stated with considerable confidence that INTOP offers great possibilities in the area of environmental change—from many to few competitors, from homogeneous to

---

[1] It is another matter that management games may be used educationally to "break in" personnel into an organizational scheme which already has the official stamp of approval by top management.

highly differentiated markets, from relative stability to violent change, etc. Its modular design also facilitates its use in trying to simulate a *particular* real-life market with some effectiveness, although this would involve more work. Generally speaking, the author feels that the simulation of particular environments with appreciable degrees of faithfulness and detail usually will require models of such complexity and specificity that one might prefer to abstain from the game feature as such.

Proceeding, then, to the core area of organization simulation, we shall discuss the aspects mentioned initially in this paper, namely problems of structure, centralization vs. decentralization, and communications.

SIMULATION OF STRUCTURING APPROACHES

A crucial problem in marketing-oriented diversified companies is whether to structure primarily by customer groups, products, geographical areas, or management functions at the various levels of organization. Assuming that field-level organization is oriented toward customer categories, balanced performance usually requires emphasis on one of the other structuring approaches at the level or levels immediately below the executive officer. INTOP was explicitly designed with this type of organizational problem in mind. Areas, products, and management functions are all labels on sets of variables in the game vital and complex enough to stimulate experimentation with different types of structure. As indicated by the operating statements reproduced earlier, data outputs (as well as decision inputs) are arranged in such a way that far-reaching divisionalization based on profit responsibility by area or products is possible. As many successful businesses have a functional top management organization, such a structure must have other, compensating advantages. These may be most clearly apparent in a fairly centralized operation based on division of labor according to professional specialties of the management group.

At this point, it may be worthwhile to recount briefly an informal experiment in the structure area undertaken with a cohort of some seventy Chicago area middle managers during the Spring of 1961.[1] The men were randomly distributed over 14 different INTOP company teams. Believing the game was played for educational purposes exclusively, they were unaware of participating in an experiment. It was merely pointed out to them that the complexity of the game, and the relatively brief decision periods, was apt to require an efficient division of labor within each team. Their attention was drawn to a passage in the Player's Manual empha-

---

[1] These men were going through the final semester of the two-year Executive Program run by the Graduate School of Business at the University of Chicago.

sizing that game data would be continuously presented in a manner making divisionalization based on profit responsibility by area or product possible, and that functional organization has other, compensating advantages. The executives were encouraged to take up positions in the company teams other than those corresponding to their own real-life jobs, and most of them did.

Focusing the discussion on the level of line executives reporting directly to the President, we find that although a majority of companies (8 of 14) were in both the product X and the product Y businesses none of them went in for a product-oriented top management structure. Five companies started out with area managers, while the other nine adopted a functional setup. At mid-game, all companies were required to rotate managerial positions in order to broaden the experience of participants. They were also asked to reconsider in this connection their division of labor. All five area-oriented companies retained their structure. Interestingly, however, no less than six of the nine functionally organized groups switched to area management. Four of these expanded into one or two new areas around the time of management reorganization.[1] Three firms had functional administration throughout. Of these, two were engaged in only one product business each, and all three at the beginning of the game were active only in one area (in the latter part all three conducted multi-area operations). Not a single company changed from area to functional organization.

It should be emphasized that most area organizations included some type of functional officer on the first line level, or in a parallel staff position, most commonly a controller. Where personnel resources permitted, companies were prone to add a level of product or functional managers below the area manager in the most important area, rather than to add staff specialists at the corporate level. This example is suggestive of organizational change to meet changing environmental conditions, or of a re-interpretation of existing conditions.

One of the chief merits of organization simulation by gaming is that it rapidly and tangibly will make the planner aware of many of the problems likely to arise under different administrative schemes. A good example is the introduction of corporate "services," i.e., functional specialists with staff authority only in relation to principal line managers but with varying degrees of line authority over corresponding line or func-

---

[1] In a written review of operations at the end of the game the President of one of these companies stated that "the original company organization was structured functionally and therefore had a President, Chief Financial Officer and Production, Marketing and R & D Specialists. It was soon found that the peculiarities of each market were such that we could better operate with area decentralization. We now have a President, Chief Financial Officer and three Area Managers, each completely responsible for all operations in his area."

tional specialists below these managers. INTOP would seem well qualified to simulate such situations.

SIMULATION OF CENTRALIZATION VS. DECENTRALIZATION (DELEGATION)

Strongly suggestive evidence concerning the efficacy of varying degrees of centralization and decentralization (the term used in the sense of delegation of authority *per se* rather than geographical or other divisionalization of operations) in a given type of environment should be obtained by game simulation. Given sufficient time and resources for the experiment, a game of the INTOP type could also be used to get at least preliminary answers to such vexing problems as whether centralization or decentralization of authority should be emphasized in a highly competitive or rapidly changing market.

One aspect of authority delegation of particular interest in the simulation of marketing organization concerns the effects of given policy constraints in various areas of decision making. Management may wish to know how far authority to set prices (or deviate from posted prices) should (or can) be delegated; where in the organization authority to negotiate contracts with the outside for sales, licensing, purchasing, loans, etc., should be vested; whether there should be provisions for pre- or post-audit in such instances, etc. In many real-life situations, a given manager at a subordinate level may have general authority in his sphere of activity but still be subject to a number of specific exceptions of withheld authority in matters such as those just illustrated.

A group of policy constraint and authority allocation problems for whose simulation INTOP is especially well suited are in the area of intra-corporate marketing. In shipments from the U.S. to the EEC (or from one product division to another), what rules should govern transfer pricing? If division manager B feels division manager A is charging him too much or otherwise is uncooperative, should B be allowed to buy from sources outside the company, or even go into the making of A's product himself? If B develops new patents, must he give his inside customer A an exclusive right to use them for a certain time, or can he decide to license the innovations to outsiders at once? If area managers are measured on profit performance and the Brazilian manager finds he can export to the U.S. market profitably, shall he be allowed to do so over the protests of the U.S. area manager? By what decision-making machinery should these various types of questions be resolved? These are the types of problems INTOP teams are often grappling with, and they have a suitably realistic background.

COMMUNICATIONS

One would expect that organization planning would consider problems of communication mostly in connection with problems of structure and/or authority allocation. The operational question for the simulation exercise then becomes, What are the information needs at various points in the organization, and by what communications processes shall they be met? Players in INTOP soon observe, just like real-life decision makers, that over-communication may be as much of a problem as under-communication and scarcity of data; the processing and routing of vital data should indeed be part of organization planning. Communications systems may be tried out by simulation both for general efficiency and to examine the need for special committees or management meetings for cross-communication.

The realism of simulation efforts in organization planning generally and with regard to communications in particular, may be enhanced appreciably by limiting the amount of face-to-face communications within company management groups to somewhat realistic proportions. This may involve locating the members of a team in different rooms, and placing a limit—or cost—on the amount, type, or duration of direct communication within the group. In some cases it might even be realistic to place the members of a team ostensibly located, say, in the EEC in a room with the EEC managers from all other companies. In this manner the fact that managers tend to generate a dual loyalty to their own local operating environment in addition to their loyalty to the company itself may be built into the simulation.

The Shrank Company is a dynamic growth concern with strong, active management control. A great amount of information had been received as to the many forms of electronic computers available and the benefits associated with the use of such equipment. The executives of the firm wished to determine the feasibility of electronic data processing. The estimated value of information not presently attainable, the costs of changing to a new information processing system, and many other factors had to be considered.

In their evaluation of E. D. P., company executives found it necessary to examine their entire operation. This review revealed a number of conditions that made a computer installation desirable: a 500% increase in paper work, sharp rises in sales volume and the cost of inventory, a wide range of new fabrics, industry sales dependent on the Mother's Day and Christmas trade, and a sales division desirous of information for planning rather than statistics of historical interest.

THE SHRANK COMPANY: USE OF THE COMPUTER IN DATA PROCESSING, SALES FORECASTING, AND MANAGEMENT CONTROL

Shrank and the computer firm from which it was to purchase the equipment made a detailed examination of all the procedures used in accounting, inventory control, production management, and many other areas. Upon completion of this study, a complete program showing how the computer should be employed by the Shrank Company was prepared by the computer manufacturer. This program specified the functions to be performed by the computer, the type of information to be fed into its memory units, and the procedures to be followed in operating the machine. The prepared program was designed primarily to coordinate the flow of information from scattered manufacturing plants, sales and executive offices located throughout the country, and the more than 5,000 customers of the company. The objective was to provide data on raw materials inventory, costs and profits by product line, as well as style and sales trends early enough in the season so that appropriate adjustments could be made.

APPLICATION OF THE IBM. RAMAC 305 TO THE SHRANK COMPANY

Shrank does 15 to 20 million dollars a year gross business in the manufacture and sale of women's sleep wear. This firm has several plants
scattered throughout the country, six regional sales offices, sales headquarters in New York City, and executive and accounting offices as well
as major manufacturing facilities in southern New Jersey. Shrank wished
to coordinate all plant activity, inventories, sales, and accounting records
on its new equipment. This task is carried out in the manner described
below.

The storage or memory unit of the computer contains (1) the firm's
complete list of over 6,000 accounts; (2) a breakdown of the sales force
by region, and by salesmen; a coding of all the many styles of clothing
manufactured and sold; the firm's complete payroll; and additional information. Incoming orders are processed on a series of punched cards.
All that need be recorded on the card is the department and style numbers, the quantities purchased, the customer code and whatever special
information is desired. All other necessary data is stored in the RAMAC
305's memory unit. After punch cards have been prepared for each of the
day's orders, the information is fed into the equipment and a number of
operations take place.

The printer attached to the machine prints on the firm's record forms
the complete order with all prices and discounts, the customer's address,
and the date of expected shipment. Realistic delivery dates can be assigned as estimates are made by the machine with full realization of the
nature and number of prior orders. The record forms are in quadruplicate
and the process provides an accurate invoice ready for mailing at the
time of shipment.

Simultaneously, the equipment updates existing information as to the
customer's pattern of sales, and his purchases on a monthly, a seasonal,
and a year-to-date basis. Similarly, the machine adjusts the salesman's
performance record so as to indicate his sales by month and by year-to-
date, the discounts he offered, and the company's profit or loss on his
activity. The RAMAC 305 also compiles a perpetual inventory record
which reports on availability by size and style, and facilitates the accurate estimation of delivery dates. Inventory figures are immediately adjusted to reflect the filling of orders or the manufacture of finished stock
by the production department. Data is also available on the cost of inventory, the amount of work-in-progress, and the volume of raw material
arrivals.

The day's orders are completely processed in a manner of hours. At
the close of the day, a report is compiled which shows the complete sales

by style, salesman and region; the price of the items sold; and the cost of the items.

DATA PROCESSING AS AN AID TO MANAGEMENT CONTROL

Many executives in the textile industry believe that the improvements in record keeping and delivery date estimating made possible by electronic data processing justify its use. The equipment, however, also provides a number of reports that facilitate the exercise of management control. The following information is made available to Shrank executives.

Stock Status Report: Complete sale, authorizations of stock, stock in process, availability and coverage of styles.

Sales to Production Analysis: A report which includes percentages of sales by style groups and seasons.

Salesman's Booking Report: His quota, weekly performance, shipments by month and by year-to-date, his profitability to date.

Raw Material Report: Receipts of all materials by color, pattern, and as relative to orders of materials. Source of raw material and total inventory value in dollars.

Monthly Style Report: Shows (1) sales for each style, (2) material in cutting and sewing, (3) shipments, and (4) sales by period.

Seasonal Report: A report showing two years' activity (four seasons) broken down by style and by customers and making seasonal sales projections.

Sales Projection Report: Use is made of a model based on past history to estimate demand by style group and fabric.

Other forms and types of reports are possible since all pertinent information is stored in the memory unit. When the need for such data arises, it can be readily obtained.

To what use is all this information put and how has the firm benefited? Purchasing problems in this industry require long range planning and the under-buying or over-buying of fabrics is a common occurrence. An accurate study of fabric movements, requirements, style planning, and raw material availability was made possible through the use of the reports mentioned above. Projections made through coordination of sales, fashion design and production activity have helped management make more intelligent purchases of raw materials. Complete up-to-date figures concerning inventory costs are available and aid still further in decision making.

The Company also believes that it has benefited from the use of "sales directed information." This is data which lets the salesmanager know where his abilities are most needed at any given time. An examination of the "Salesman's Booking Report" reveals each man's performance to date-not in the previous month but as of the moment. This report enables the salesmanager to observe style movements and to concentrate sales effort on the most profitable combination of the remaining lines. In addition, the sales manager is able to determine the quality and profitability of salesmen's calls. The figures reveal which customers are costing the firm more than their sales warrant and whatever action appears appropriate can be taken. A salesman's profit and lose report reveals to the sales manager those members of his selling force who require personal supervision. Advertising and sales promotion can be more accurately planned since reports on style movements, sales, fabric studies, and seasonal trends are available.

In short, electronic data processing has enabled the firm to increase its knowledge of all phases of the business. Previously, the sifting out of important facts posed a real problem and information could not be provided in time to influence company policies. In the words of the firm's president, "RAMAC 305 means better control of our entire operation. We have the information we need at our finger tips at the moment it is required." The effect of electronic data processing on the company can not be measured yet but the results appear so beneficial that a computer larger than the one now in operation has been ordered.

Historically, the airlines have striven to keep ground passenger service abreast of improvements in aircraft. As speed, comfort and convenience have progressed from the Condor and the Stinson A through the DC-3, DC-4, Convair 240, DC-6 and DC-7 to the 707 Astrojet and the Electra —and soon the 990 Astrojet—it has been a constant battle to maintain reservation service at the same level.

The increasing number of seats on each airplane have complicated the inventory-keeping problem. Faster airplanes require faster and faster communications to keep the inventory adjustments up with the progress of the airplanes from station to station. Each seat that flies empty on an airplane today is a far more expensive loss than on the airplanes of the past.

SABRE is American's electronic answer to the problem of keeping reservation service at Jet Age levels.

The SABRE system developed by American Airlines and International

AMERICAN AIRLINES' SABRE SYSTEM

FOR PROCESSING

TICKET RESERVATIONS

Business Machines Corporation for installation in late 1962 or 1963, is the largest electronic data processing system ever designed for business use. Eleven hundred reservation desks in 37 cities are linked by more than 35,000 miles of leased wires. SABRE (the title is taken from the code name assigned to the project when American Airlines and IBM began research on it) can process daily 85,000 telephone calls, 30,000 requests for fare quotations, 40,000 passenger reservations, 30,000 queries to and from other airlines, and 20,000 ticket sales. All of this processing for most individual interrogations takes less than three seconds.

The SABRE System incorporates two duplexed IBM 7090 computers, disk and drum storage devices of advanced design and much greater capacity than any now in use, and a specially designed on-line data communications network with remote input-output devices . . . all on a scale never before seen in commercial application. SABRE's main purpose is to handle on a nationwide basis the sale and control of air transportation from the customer's first call for information to arrival at destination. The functions to be performed can be grouped into three main areas: passenger sales, reservation record service, and management reporting. Each of these functions is discussed briefly in the following sections.

SABRE AS AN AID TO PASSENGER SALES

The primary role of reservation and ticket sales agents is to sell American Airlines' space and to provide the quality of customer service which will encourage passengers to turn to American for their air travel needs. The SABRE system was designed to help the agent provide this kind of customer service with increased speed and accuracy.

Suppose a customer telephones American Airlines Reservations in Boston, asking for a seat on a flight to Chicago on the following Friday. The reservations agent's desk is equipped with a console for communication with the Central Processing Center at Briarcliff Manor, N.Y. From a file near the flight selector unit of the console, the agent selects a card containing information on Boston-Chicago flights. The agent places this on the display rack of the flight selector where punched holes in the card will identify it to the computer. The agent then pushes buttons recording the date for the trip and the number of seats required.

Pushing the "availability" button on the console sends this information to the computer which scans its memory files to see which flights to Chicago have seats available and responds by activating lights alongside open flights on the card. After the customer selects the preferred flight, the agent presses a button beside it on the console and another marked "sell". This tells the computer to record a sale and subtract the seat or seats from inventory.

A record of the sale now is spelled out by the center on the agent's console printer showing the flight number, date, action taken, number of passengers involved, origin and destination city and departure time. The same information is stored in the computer. The agent then uses the console keyboard to enter such items as the passenger's name, home and business telephone numbers and any special requirements, such as a rental car. This information is printed on the console printer and also transmitted to the central processing unit. The agent signals the computer that the transaction is ended by pressing the "end transaction" button. The computer, if it finds no omissions, prints out "O.K." on the console printer and stores all information in the central disk files.

SABRE AS A RESERVATIONS RECORD SERVICE

SABRE provides immediate access to up-to-the-second records of all seats available on American Airlines and selected off-line flights as communicated by other airlines. The system automatically maintains a complete inventory of American Airlines seats. The complete record of any individual reservation is stored electronically where previously such parts of it as the passenger's name and other variable information were maintained by hand. This record can be retrieved by agents in the system for confirmation, alteration or cancellation. The agent can query the center through his console for information on the arrival or departure of any current flight for any of its stops. In addition, changes in flight forecast or flight progress information will cause the center to advise an agent if some action, such as calling a passenger, is required. The system can send teletype messages to other airlines requesting space, follow up if no reply is received and answer requests for seats from other airlines.

With the console and reference material on his desk, the agent can handle all reservations transactions. Each agent can prepare an itinerary and enter it with necessary passenger data directly into the electronic records. Also, he can retrieve previous records, cancel reservations in whole or part, rebook, or add additional space. About half the action is performed by pushing a few special function buttons. The remainder is done with the console keyboard.

The electronic center will compile a waiting list for fully booked flights, selecting passengers in a priority order if space becomes available and notifying the proper agent so the passenger can be contacted. The center makes an automatic check for expired ticket time limits on specific flights at critical booking levels and on all flights at a fixed time before departure so that the airline can regain space not likely to be used. The center makes a count of passengers expected to be on board a flight and notifies a provisioning city so meals can be planned. Before the departure of each flight from each of its stops, the center transmits to the boarding station a list of all passengers to board there, plus other information. After departure, the station transmits to the center the number of standby passengers boarded and the number of "no shows".

Such a reservations record system has many beneficial effects. Customer requests are processed more speedily and accurately with timely information that reflects the actual status of seats available. Aircraft are more efficiently and fully loaded, since cancellations, "no shows" and waiting lists are processed immediately and accurately. Also, with more timely and accurate information, it is not necessary to maintain a "cushion" of unsold seats to handle sales in the communications "pipeline" or to cover clerical errors.

SABRE AS AN AID TO MANAGEMENT REPORTING

The SABRE system, while basically devoted to the processing of reservations, is to be extremely useful in supplying management with information on day-to-day operations. In addition, SABRE is able to pinpoint critical items from a vast amount of data and "flag" such information to the appropriate executive. The possible management reports are of three kinds: information that is to be supplied SABRE management; routine information which must be given to outside agencies such as the Civil Aeronautics Board; information required by other divisions of American Airlines. The first type of report has already been discussed at some length. The second requires no elaboration, and the third type of management report is mentioned briefly in the following paragraph:

SABRE is able to retrieve, on command, existing records from the historical files to satisfy the needs of American Airlines' executives not directly connected with the system. The basic purpose of such reports is to illustrate past performances and to predict future goals. They can be of a regular or of a special nature. As an example of regularly recurring reports, SABRE is able to compute daily load factors (ratio of passengers boarded to total seats authorized) per flight for each airport. Management can also periodically receive information on such factors as the breakdown of sales by station, activity, sales account and sales agent; the reservation-making habits of customers for a particular period of time; the percentage of business obtained from other airlines, individual commuters, and conventions; passenger preferences for certain types of meals. For "one-time" analyses, the SABRE system will provide such information as the effect on bookings of specific advertising campaigns and measure the extent to which American Airlines is requested to make reservations for passengers on other airlines.

NCR Data Processing Centers sell computer time to individuals and organizations which cannot justify the purchase or lease of a computer, yet have a need for the specialized service a computer can provide. This method distributes the cost of the computer among each center's many customers.

But even with the cost of the computer reduced in this fashion, a great many potential users of the centers' facilities would still not be able to justify the cost of developing computer programs. For these organizations, the NCR centers have developed packaged programs—programs which satisfy the general needs of groups of potential customers. By this method, the cost of developing a program is also distributed among many users.

Generally, packaged programs are prepared for groups whose members for one reason or another use almost identical accounting procedures. For otherwise, the development of a program that would satisfy a large proportion of the members would be almost impossible.

NATIONAL CASH REGISTER PACKAGED

DATA PROCESSING PROGRAMS FOR

RETAILERS

Retailers form one group for which the packaged program plan is very practical. Here are the major reasons:

1. There are very many retailers, but only a small percentage are sufficiently large to support their own data processing systems.

2. The need for current sales analysis and inventory information is very great. The sooner a buyer knows which items are moving fast and what his inventory is, the better he can satisfy the desires of the customers, and the greater are the profits of the store.

3. Three influences—keen competition, long-term development, and tax requirements—have caused most retailers to use essentially the same accounting procedures.

While retail accounting procedures are practically the same everywhere, there are vast differences between retailers, particularly in size and lines merchandise. The need for detail in accounting records varies accordingly.

However, the number of retailers is large enough to support several packaged programs which differ from each other primarily in the amount of detail provided. Two of these are described below—one designed for the small-to-medium size specialty store and the other designed for the medium-to-large check-out discount house. Either service has associated with it the following benefits:

1. The final report is completed within 48 hours, while the information is fresh and timely. Store management can detect and take action on trends as the trends develop.

2. The system is extremely accurate. Information contained in the final report can be traced with certainty to the input register.

3. The computer checks all input data for reasonableness and accuracy. The final report also reveals errors made on the selling floor.

4. The system relieves a store of the tedious detail of bookkeeping, frees personnel for the basic store function—merchandising.

5. The system reduces the amount of office space needed at the store, so more space is available for merchandise display.

THE SPECIALTY STORE PROGRAM

The store using this program develops a punched-tape record of its sales by listing sales tickets on a tape-punching adding machine. At regular intervals of a week or a month, depending upon the needs of the merchant, the store sends the encoded paper tape to the data processing center for analysis. Within 48 hours, the center returns a sales analysis report; a complete breakdown of sales by department number, by price-line, and by salesperson.

PUNCHING THE TAPE

At the store, a paper tape recorder is connected to a 2-total adding machine to develop the punched paper tape which is the input medium to the processing equipment. The paper tape recorder selects information entered into the adding machine and punches the information in code into paper tape. The tape recorder is completely automatic and requires no attention from the operator. The actual punching of the paper tape is a by-product of an adding machine audit of the sales tickets written up at the time of the sale by the salespeople.

Each day, all sales tickets for the previous day, already grouped according to salesperson, are forwarded to the store office. There, the tickets are turned over to the adding machine operator who checks the individual ticket totals and determines each salesperson's sales total for the day. During this process, each salesperson's number, the number of each item sold and the price are punched in paper tape along with symbols which identify the type of entry. To record returns or correct errors, the operator simply makes reverse (subtract) entries. At the end of the period, all the accumulated tapes are forwarded to the processing center where they are spliced together and fed into the computer.

THE REPORT

The sales analysis report returned by the center has two sections. The first section of the report breaks down all sales by department number (class number) which identifies a type of merchandise such as women's hosiery. Under this department number, the report lists the number of items sold at each price, the unit price, and the total of sales at that price. The second section of the report lists the total of sales by each salesperson during the period.

One merchant who uses this program transfers the information from the first section of the report to price-line ledgers. One ledger is maintained under each department number. This record quickly identifies slow-moving or seasonal items for the buyers.

THE DISCOUNT HOUSE PROGRAM

Under this program, the subscribing merchant receives comprehensive and timely reports on the movement of merchandise derived from the store's sales registers. As in the previous system, punched paper tape is the link between the store and the processing center. The tape is punched automatically as a by-product of recording the sale in the regular way.

In the store, all items on sale are tagged with a class number and a price. As the customer goes through the checkout counter, the operator enters the number and price of each item in the register. As the register operates, the item number and price are punched in paper tape. Since the number of the register is punched in the tape at the beginning of the operation, all sales are traceable to a particular register.

The punched tapes are collected and forwarded to the processing center at regular intervals, usually daily or weekly. From the tapes, the center develops three reports; the sales report, the price-line report and the inventory control report.

THE SALES REPORT

The sales report provides store management with a detailed analysis of daily or weekly sales. This report breaks down sales by class and by register, records totals at five levels, checks register totals and shows sales returns.

CUSTOMER NO. 1234	TRANSACTION DATE 12/25		STORE NUMBER 099		PAGE 1					
CLASS		**SALES TODAY**		**SALES THIS WEEK**		**SALES THIS MONTH**		**SALES THIS YEAR**		**RET. THIS MONTH**
101	COATS A	1	12.34	8	98.72	25	308.50	41	505.94	1	12.34
102	COATS B	3	70.35	10	234.50	27	633.15	56	1313.20	1	23.45
103	COATS C	2	69.12	6	207.36	18	622.08	39	1347.84	1	34.56
1031	COATS	6	151.81	24	540.58	70	1563.73	136	3166.98	3	70.35
111	BETTER SUITS A	1	56.78	3	170.34	5	283.90	7	397.46	1	56.78
112	BETTER SUITS B	2	135.78	4	271.56	4	271.56	5	339.45	1	67.89
113	BETTER SUITS C	1	78.90	2	157.80	3	236.70	4	315.60	1	78.90
1131	BETTER SUITS	4	271.46	9	599.70	12	792.16	16	1052.51	3	203.57
121	SLACKS	1	20.12	1	20.12	2	40.24	3	60.36		
122	SLACKS	1	11.23	3	33.69	4	44.92	5	56.15		
126	SLACKS	1	32.10	3	96.30	4	128.40	5	160.51	1	32.10
127	SLACKS	1	21.09	2	42.18	2	42.18	3	63.27	1	21.09
1271	SLACKS	4	84.54	9	192.29	12	255.74	16	340.28	2	53.19
1272	WOMENS WEAR	14	507.81	41	1332.57	94	2611.63	168	4559.77	8	327.11

Fig. 1. Sales Report–Discount Store.

Examination of Figure 1 reveals that the first part of the report, the sales breakdown by class, contains the following information:

Class Number—The system accepts up to 995 class numbers. In this report, the class numbers are listed in numerical order. The class numbers may be divided into four separate sequences at the option of the store management.

Description—This description may use up to 15 alphanumeric characters, including spaces.

Number of Unit Sales—This column lists the number of unit sales up to 10,000 with totals up to 10 million.

Amount of Sales—This column lists the dollar amount of sales for each class up to $10,000 with totals up to $100 million.

The second part of this report, the register distribution, carries this information:

Register Number—The number of the register which recorded the sale.

Description of Illegal Entry—A listing of unassigned class numbers entered in error.

Register Total—Dollar total of sales accumulated by the register and punched into tape at the end of the period.

Register Returns Total—Total dollar returns (if any) accumulated by register and punched into tape at the end of the period.

Processor Total—Dollar total of sales distributed by the processor for each register. This provides a direct check against the register total.

Processor Returns Total—Dollar total of returns distributed by the processor for each register. This provides a direct check against the register returns total.

Sales Error—This indicates the difference between the register total and the processor total on sales, if any.

Returns Error—This indicates the difference between the register returns total and the processor returns total, if any.

The third part of the report, the recapitulation of totals, is extracted from the breakdown by class and is printed in the same format.

THE PRICE-LINE REPORT

The price-line report shown in Figure 2 is actually a breakdown of sales within the item classification. This report provides as detailed an analysis

		CLASS	PRICE LINE	UNITS	EXTENSIONS
CUSTOMER NO. 1234		PERIOD ENDING 12/25	STORE NUMBER 099		PAGE 1
		SUMMARY OF SALES BY PRICE LINES—WOMENS AND CHILDRENS DEPTS			
	101	COATS A	12.34	1	12.34
	102	COATS B	23.45	3	70.35
	103	COATS C	34.56	2	69.12
	1031	COATS		6	151.81

Fig. 2. Price-Line Report–Discount Store.

DOCU	SOURCE	PURCH COST	PURCH RET	% MK ON	TRANSFERS	PRICE CHG	% OF SLS	ADJUST	SALES	END INV
CUSTOMER NO.1234	WEEK ENDING DATE 12/25			STORE NUMBER 099					PAGE 1	
93471	RUBEN & CO.	1200.00	1600.00	33.33						
CLASS NO.701	DSHWSHR A		SALES-		PRIOR WEEK	984.00	2ND PRIOR WEEK	932.00		
WEEK-		1200.00	1600.00	33.33	·00	·00	·00	.00	1014.00	17,216.00
M-T-D		3000.00	4000.00	33.33	.00	.00	.00	.00	1998.00	
Y-T-D		7008.00	9344.00	33.33	.00	.00	.00	.00	9028.00	
FREIGHT	WEEK-	100.00	6.25%	M-T-D 400.00	10.00%	Y-T-D 800.00	8.86%			

Fig. 3. Inventory Control Report–Discount Store.

as the user's pricing structure permits. It also reveals errors made in entering prices into the register. The price-line report may be provided daily or weekly or once a day, cumulative for the week.

THE INVENTORY CONTROL REPORT

The inventory control report (Figure 3) records current inventory and also enables management to consider current sales in relation to profits and prior sales. Because the report is available less than **48** hours after the end of the base period, it permits management to spot inventory trends as they develop. The report also permits a buyer to base his buying decisions on up-to-date information.

Fig. 4. Data Processing Center.

Development of the inventory control report requires that information on purchases be punched in paper tape and introduced into the processing system. This is in addition to the information punched in tape at the sales register. The information on purchases is usually captured as a by-product of an accounts payable routine on an adding machine or an accounting machine in the store office.

For each class of merchandise in stock, the inventory control report carries the following information:

1. Acquisitions
    a. Document number (purchase order, transfer order, etc.)
    b. Source (by name)
    c. Purchase cost (to store)

    d. Purchase retail (intended selling price)

    e. Mark-on percentage

    f. Transfer (intended selling price of goods transferred from other store or warehouse)

    g. Price change (change due to bargain sales)

    h. Adjustments (price change due to competition or error)

    i. Date (of purchase or transfer)

2. Prior Sales

    a. Class number

    b. Class description

    c. Dollar amount of sales in prior week

    d. Dollar amount of sales in second prior week

3. Sales Summary

    a. Summary period (sales for three periods are listed on separate lines —this week, month to date, and year to date)

    b. Purchase cost (to store)

    c. Purchase retail (intended selling price)

    d. Mark-on percentage

    e. Transfer (intended selling price of goods transferred)

    f. Price change (change due to bargain sales)

    g. Percent of sales (percent of items sold at bargain sale prices)

    h. Adjustments (price change due to competition or error)

    i. Sales (total dollar amount for week)

    j. Ending inventory (dollar amount)

The inventory report also provides the sales summary information at five total levels—item group sales, department sales, department group sales, department class sales, and total sales.

At the department level and above, the inventory report also provides totals of freight costs and discounts in absolute terms and as a per cent of profits. Freight costs include all costs of shipping merchandise to a store. Discounts include discounts for prompt payment of invoices, claims against vendors for shortages or against shipping lines for damaged goods, and other such entries. This information is provided in a single line in the report.

The case history presented in the following pages deals with the successful computer control of five major problem areas encountered by an Aviation Logistics Control Center. The aviation industry was chosen for this discussion because it is particularly sensitive to market planning and inventory control problems. However, similar situations are encountered in many other industrial lines—retailing, trucking, supermarket operations, etc.

The following are the five major areas of computer usage developed to aid management in its parts requirement forecasting and parts procurement and distribution:

1. *Parts Application*
2. *Usage Data*
3. *Engineering Data*
4. *Aircraft Overhaul Scheduling Related to Available Facilities*
5. *Inventory Reporting and Control*

THE COMPUTER AND THE PROBLEMS

OF AN AVIATION LOGISTICS

CONTROL CENTER

PARTS APPLICATION

A central magnetic tape file of parts data was established, using the aircraft (or the engine, or the major end assembly) as the key, and relating all parts to their end usage. Control difficulties had been encountered earlier because the same part has application to many assemblies, and many sub-assemblies are used in various locations throughout the airframe.

Each part was identified by number and was related to its end application by means of a six-digit numeric code. The number of times the part was used on that particular assembly was also indicated. Thus a record was established which showed the end use of each part, together with the number of times it was required in the end application.

While standardization of parts manufacture has, of course, lowered production costs, the central magnetic tape file established for this air command succeeded in effecting significant savings in determining and scheduling its parts requirements. It was also found accurate forecasting of requirements aided the home office in dealing with the problem of the relatively long procurement lead time from the parts manufacturer.

USAGE DATA

The nucleus of the EDP program for determining parts requirements was the accumulation of data concerning past usage of the some 250,000 parts carried in the system. This data was related to their application, to the routine maintenance cycles through which an aircraft passed, and to the aircraft's overhaul schedule.

As parts and/or assembly replacements were made (either during the maintenance cycle or the overhaul period), a report of the number and type of parts being replaced was submitted by the field installation to the home office. The computer collation and summary of these reports from the air terminals, supply centers, and overhaul points provide extremely valuable data on the percentage replacement of each part on each aircraft during the overhaul period for that aircraft.

Prior to the development of this integrated magnetic tape file system, many individual files of various types and varying degrees of reliability were maintained both in the field and in the home office. Thus accurate data concerning parts usage was immediately available with far less expenditure of time and effort.

ENGINEERING DATA

In order to provide a current and uniform source of information throughout the entire supply system, a source which could be used to develop each aspect of the supply and market planning functions, the inclusion of engineering and technical information in the central magnetic tape file was deemed essential.

Accordingly, the several files maintained by each department were eliminated, and the central magnetic tape file (described in a preceding section) was established for each part carried in the supply system. This central file was maintained in current status by processing all changes, additions, supersedures, modifications, etc., on a cycle basis.

This central file can be considered as technically oriented. It is intended to show all information on a part that will uniquely identify it. This would include each part's use in aircraft modification, its particular relationship with one or more assemblies in which it may be substituted for another part, and other similar vital technical and engineering information.

The following items were felt to be essential for each part carried in such a file:

Stock number or part number
Nomenclature
Unit of issue
Unit price
Shelf life
Technical data (equivalent number, supersedure, modification, etc.)
Model of aircraft or assembly on which used
Units per application
Maintenance replacement percentage per model on which used
Overhaul percentage replacement per model on which used
Maintenance factor (units x percentage replacement)
Overhaul factor (units x percentage replacement)
Fiscal program number for procurement and budget control
Code identifying the source of the part (purchase, make, local purchase, etc.)
Accountability code (repairable, expendable, etc.)
Manufacturer's part number
Procurement lead time

With this minimum information for each part carried in the supply system, the engineering data from the master file on magnetic tape enables the home office to compute and distribute the planned requirements by line item to support any given aircraft program and movement.

All items in the entire system can be rapidly reviewed and a procurement analysis made. A budget justification can be made for every commodity, showing the cost of an overhaul and the cost for any aircraft program. The home office can also furnish accurate and up-to-date catalogs to field installations for their use in parts identification and requisitioning.

AIRCRAFT OVERHAUL SCHEDULING RELATED TO AVAILABLE FACILITIES

The problem of balancing requirements with available facilities in order to prevent the overloading or any particular overhaul point was successfully handled by the EDP system. The assimilation of overhaul scheduling into the management planning picture and the use of this data in parts requirement became an integral part of the system.

Accordingly, the necessary channels were established which furnished the supply center with information on planned aircraft flight hours, aircraft movement from terminal to terminal, and future planned overhauls by individual aircraft at the various overhaul activities.

With this information, significant savings were realized, financially as well as in time and effort, both in the home office and in the field.

INVENTORY REPORTING AND CONTROL

The inventory reporting function was one which had always been in effect, and little modification of existing reporting procedures was necessary.

Field installations submitted quarterly reports of stock movements, as well as "on hand" and "on order" figures for all items that were active during the month. Summary inventory figures were then updated at the home office and action taken to replenish or redistribute material, based on EDP information.

With the development of these five separate but interrelated procedures for the Logistics Command, the electronic data processing system could be used in projecting future market requirements and in furnishing management with meaningful reports upon which to make decisions.

BASIC INPUT DATA NECESSARY FOR THE EDP SYSTEM

A detailed analysis of the overall management plant reveals that the computer requires the following basic input data:

    a. *Inventory Reports*

       These reports on active items are received quarterly from the various installations. They are used to update the inventory records of stock maintained at each activity. On hand and on order figures are compared with figures in the home office inventory record and adjustments made as required.

    b. *Planned Aircraft Movement Reports*

       These data are used to project the number of flight hours and actual movement of individual aircraft in order to arrive at the number of maintenance cycles and overhauls that must be supported in any given future period, at any given terminal, or for any given aircraft model.

    c. *Parts Usage Data*

       Reports on the issuance of parts by appropriate agencies are collated with existing data of the usage of these parts. The percentage replacement factor at maintenance and at overhaul is adjusted accordingly. This results in a currently accurate figure of individual parts replacement on each aircraft, engine, or accessory.

    d. *File Data Additions and Changes*

These data are received from various sources, including manufacturers, purchasing agents, technical representatives, etc., and are used to update the technical and logistic elements of the Master File.

e. *Purchase Orders*
Purchasing personnel furnish these data on vendor's name, quantity of parts ordered, date ordered, expected delivery date, and delivery point.

f. *Budgetary Figures*
Fiscal data on budgetary limitations for various elements of the aircraft programs are furnished by appropriate accounting personnel.

The function of the computer, given the above basic input data, is to analyze the factors involved, to update and keep current the various elements of the central magnetic tape file, and to produce significant output data.

BASIC OUTPUT DATA PROVIDED BY THE COMPUTER
PROCUREMENT AND DISTRIBUTION SCHEDULE

An overhaul schedule may be ascertained and the number of aircraft, engine, and accessories overhauls suitable for each installation determined by an analysis of aircraft movement and location, and projected flying hours per aircraft. This will determine the number of maintenance periods for each aircraft at each air terminal.

The central magnetic tape file will then reveal the percentage replacement factor for each part on each assembly at both maintenance cycles and overhauls. This factor multiplied by the total projected maintenance cycles and overhauls for each terminal will produce a gross requirements figure for each stock item necessary to support future operations.

Next, an analysis of the latest "on hand" and "on order" figures in the inventory record for each terminal will reveal a net requirement of the same parts for the future.

The actual formula might be stated as:

$$(A \times B \times C) + (E \times F \times C) = H$$

$$H - I + J = K \qquad \text{Where}$$

A = Number of overhauls to be performed on equipment at terminal.

B = Percentage replacement of a part in the equipment to be overhauled.

C = Units per part per equipment.

E = Number of maintenance cycles on equipment at a terminal.

F = Percentage replacement of a part per maintenance cycle.

H = Gross requirements of a part.

I = Terminal "on hand" quantity of the required part.

J = Terminal "on order" quantity of the required part.

K = Net requirements of the part at the terminal.

K, of course, can be a positive or a negative figure.

If the analysis of the inventory record in the central file indicates a positive requirement, the computer can be used to further analyze data to determine the most economic method of meeting the need.

Computer analysis will provide the basis for sound decision when management is confronted with questions such as the following:

Is there available stock at some other location close enough to enable redistribution cost to be less than procurement?

Is the required part available for local purchase by the terminal at less cost than purchase and distribution centrally?

Is there a possibility of manufacture of the required part by mechanics at the terminal at less cost than purchase from the manufacturer?

Is there a substitute part available in sufficient quantities at the terminal?

The computer can produce a schedule showing net requirements for the part at each terminal, a total system requirement for the part, and recommended procurement or disposal action in each case. Obviously, major savings can be effected with intelligent action in each of these areas.

BUDGET ESTIMATION AND JUSTIFICATION

The integration of all relevant factors into a single central magnetic tape file has enabled the EDP system to furnish management with firm facts and figures concerning future budget requirements and with justification for budget increases or reductions.

A program of cost estimation for each type of aircraft may be easily obtained from data generated by scanning and analyzing parts requirements for future maintenance and overhaul periods of that aircraft. (The total parts to be expended in this program plus new parts procurement plus distribution costs equal the program cost for each type of aircraft.) The system can also develop similar figures for all programs. These data may then be collated, sorted by individual class of material (electronic, engine, airframe, accessory, etc.) to arrive at a projected future budgetary requirement figure for each individual type of material to be procured. Thus, costs for any particular aircraft program or material are accurately projected and available for a sound decision.

Budgetary estimates in the past have frequently been hard to justify because of the lack of sufficient data with which to support them. Due to the high speed data processing techniques available only through electronics, guesswork is eliminated. Management has furnished a projected budget figure which is based on future operations and future parts requirements for each aircraft type at each terminal and related to the procurement and distribution cost for each commodity class.

The value of and the savings to be effected by using accurate budget estimates is noteworthy, as may be revealed by a comparison of EDP figures with the results of past budget estimates.

CATALOGS

Much of the data listed in the central magnetic tape file is of great value to field installations in their daily routine. Item descriptions, substitution data, application, parts supersedure, etc., are of importance to the mechanics, storekeepers, and warehousemen at each terminal. Accordingly, on a cycled basis, the EDP system edits and prints out a complete technical and supply-oriented catalog of material. Wide dissemination enables completely uniform information on the various stock items available to all employees.

ALLOWANCE LISTS

Many of the installations supported by the home office supply system do not possess the facilities to perform anything more than the most rudimentary type of maintenance work. Consequently, these installations need not stock many of the thousands of parts required at an overhaul point.

The electronic data processing system, through analysis of parts costs, parts usage, aircraft movement, and other factors, is able to furnish management with a list of recommended spare parts to be stocked by these non-overhaul terminals.

This list is prepared for each type of aircraft in use. It is therefore a simple matter to furnish the terminal with the parts needed when a particular type of aircraft is to be serviced by that terminal. Such a procedure reduces the overall inventory stock requirement for the system, reduces the workload at the terminal itself, reduces pipeline inventories, cuts budget requirements, and still permits the optimum in flight operating safety.

CONCLUDING REMARKS

1. The preceding paragraphs indicate the policies being followed by one particular supply agency and the striking role being played by the electronic data processing system in assisting management.

2. Substantial difficulties were encountered in developing and refining the system now in use.

3. Much advanced systems planning effort was expended, and the computer programming was fairly complex.

4. In return for the time and money invested, however, the computer has become a useful management tool.

5. A significant saving is already evident in stock procurement and distribution costs, in the elimination of critical shortages, in the development of purchase requirements within the stated manufacturers' lead times, and in the ability to furnish personnel with a "management by exception" philosophy.

The company is a completely integrated manufacturing organization geared for volume production of precision equipment. Manufacturing and product distribution facilities recently underwent an extensive modernization program. The firm markets over 500 end products and several thousand service or after-market parts through direct contact with customers, warehouses, and distributors.

For many years, it had utilized a very successful punched card system for manufacturing control. Management felt, however, that even though the system was producing excellent results, certain refinements should be made to the data processing procedures to keep pace with increasing customer demand and the factory modernization program.

With the punched card system, a new production schedule for 10,000 end products and manufactured parts, represented by 40,000 bill of material cards, had been produced monthly. This schedule reflected all changes in orders. The planned refinement was to reflect changes as they

MANUFACTURING AND INVENTORY CONTROL

occur, thus eliminating critical situations requiring crash conferences of key personnel. Also, if more current inventory records were available, items necessary to build an end product or subassembly, but currently unavailable, could be scheduled for production just prior to the data required.

Under the punched card method, shop orders had been issued up to 40 days in advance of the start date so that the shop could determine what was not available in inventory. When orders were changed before the production start date, all the paperwork affecting these orders had to be traced back and changed.

Finally, it was felt that if additional usage and historical data could be accumulated, it would be possible to produce items in more economical quantities, thus reducing ordering and shop setup costs.

With these refinements in mind, this company undertook a complete study of its data processing system in an attempt to eliminate the problem areas. They first determined that their system should be able to process effectively, with little outside intervention, varying types of input including all material transactions, engineering changes, service require- ments and production schedules by time period. Second, these input docu- ments must be processed against internally stored records to:

1. Convert product schedules to requirements by time period.
2. Measure requirements against on-hand, on-order, and reorder points for each inventory item to determine the time period when shop orders and purchase orders must be prepared.
3. Revise economical order quantities and reorder points by constant evaluation of the factors involved in their calculation.
4. Cancel and/or re-schedule unreleased manufacturing or purchase orders.

Finally, the system must rapidly select from storage the data required to prepare:

1. Status reports for all released manufacturing orders.
2. Shop orders to manufacture in economical size lots by time period, indicating standards costs for all components.
3. Stock planning status for any part on request.
4. Evaluation of optimum inventory based on economical order quan- tities and reorder points.
5. Immediate answers to questions concerning any part in inventory.

When the study was completed, the application requirements were compared against available equipment. On the basis of this analysis, an IBM RAMAC 305 was placed on order. Many features of the 305 made it ideal for the application in question. For example, the storage capacity of the system, ten million characters, was more than adequate to maintain inventory records for the finished goods, assemblies and parts; a bill of material for every manufactured item; and the quantities of each part needed to satisfy orders and forecasts by time period. The random access storage principle would allow the updating of inventory records on a cur- rent basis and would also provide the most direct method of breaking the production down to its individual requirements. This would be accom- plished in a single pass through the system. Through the inquiry feature, up-to-date facts on any part would be available as needed. In addition, the cost of the RAMAC could easily be justified by the potential savings.

ADVANTAGES GAINED FROM USE OF THE IBM RAMAC 305

Now that the system is installed, management is able to evaluate the performance of the RAMAC against previously determined requirements.

They have found that the following results and benefits have been derived from the system:

1. Reduction of the number of shop and purchase orders processed.
2. Reduction of inspection, ordering and setup costs by cutting the number of manufacturing lots processed through the shop.
3. Leveling of production through the use of economical order quantities, with consequent reduction in unemployment insurance payments.
4. Reduction of paperwork handling, resulting in a corresponding reduction in clerical costs.
5. Indications of inventory shortages in time to take corrective action.
6. Increased accessibility to accurate, up-to-date production control records.
7. Balanced inventories through the use of historical and usage data, by investing dollars in active, salable items.
8. Isolation of inactive or obsolete items to reduce record keeping and inventory handling.
9. Restandardization of costs, done quickly at comparatively low expense.
10. Ability to control the availability and maintenance of perishable tools.

These combined advantages have already resulted in savings which are in excess of $100,000 per year over and above data processing equipment costs. The company estimates these savings will be tripled. Other applications using data already stored in the system should provide the further savings.

THE DEVELOPMENT AND USE OF ECONOMICAL ORDER QUANTITIES

A large portion of the savings in the new manufacturing control system is based on the ability to reduce not only the number of orders issued to the plant but also the setup costs associated with these orders. The key to reducing order and setup costs is establishment of realistic economical order quantities and reorder points based on certain base factors and accumulative statistics.

Before deciding which items should be reordered on an EOQ basis, all units and subassemblies were analyzed and divided into three categories. The first category consisted of 2,000 items which were either expensive or were produced for irregular sales volumes (indeterminate forecast). The company did not wish to stock these items and so established no reorder point or EOQ here. One thousand common parts were inexpensive enough and in sufficient demand to decontrol to a minimum-maximum bin card basis. The remaining items could be practically controlled on an EOQ and reorder point basis.

Using historical data, all elements of cost which affect the manufacture and warehousing of inventory items were then studied. The results of their study can best be indicated by the accompanying Figure.

The line labeled "Working Stock Carrying Charges" indicates the cost of carrying inventory, which, of course, increases at a constant rate as the amount in inventory increases. The line labeled "Order and Setup Costs" indicates the order and setup costs involved in issuing and producing

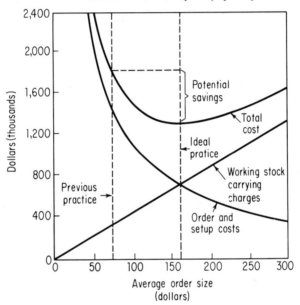

Fig. 1. Manufacturing and inventory control.

orders. This, of course, decreases as the size of the order increases (i.e., fewer orders and less setup). The line labeled "Total Cost" is the combined cost or total of order cost, setup cost and inventory carrying charges. As indicated, there is a high total cost involved in issuing many orders and carrying a small inventory. This cost decreases if more inventory is carried and fewer orders in larger quantities are issued—but it decreases only to a point; then the cost climbs again because too much inventory is being carried.

The "Previous Practice" line indicates the company's practice before ordering RAMAC. Lacking historical and usage data that could be constantly and currently reviewed, the company had been issuing many orders and carrying relatively small inventory. The "Ideal Practice" line, drawn through to the point of intersection of carrying charges and order costs, indicates what the constantly reviewed EOQ within the system is approximating. In other words, there has been a controlled buildup of inventories by producing larger lot sizes (i.e., less order and setup cost) based on constantly reviewed usage and historical data. The "Potential Savings" area is bracketed and indicates the difference between ideal and previous practice.

CONCLUSION

In speaking of their IBM RAMAC production control system, the company said that the entire process of determining level-by-level net inventory requirements was completed without human intervention. This included the automatic preparation of purchase requisitions and shop fabrication orders.

Further, with planned extension of Management Operating System techniques to the four remaining basic manufacturing functions of forecasting, scheduling, dispatching, and operations evaluation, the company expects to more than triple its current annual savings.

On July 1, 1961, American Cyanamid Company put into operation an automatic inventory control system for its Surgical Products Division. The system involves a computer (IBM RAMAC 305) and the use of punched cards.

Cyanamid is a chemical company and, in many of its divisions, supplies a small number of customers with bulk products in carload lots. However, the Surgical Products Division at Danbury, Connecticut, presents a much different inventory and distribution problem. The division's products are small in size. They require widespread distribution and their nature is such that a customer *must* have them when he wants them, not later.

Surgical Products manufactures several different types of surgical sutures, each delicate suture packaged in a separate sterile pack ready for use in the operating room. Other products include hypodermic syringes, needles, foam bandages, and ring dispensers.

Many of the products, particularly sutures, require a lengthy produc-

AN AUTOMATIC INVENTORY CONTROL

SYSTEM FOR A SURGICAL

PRODUCTS DIVISION

tion time. Preparation of the raw material, animal gut, cannot be hurried. Moreover, the products must be subjected throughout to the most rigid quality control procedures.

Inventories are maintained at the division's warehouse in Danbury, in eleven Cyanamid branch warehouses around the country, and at approximately thirty contract agencies which sell the products on a consignment basis.

Before the introduction of Ramac, inventory control was handled by a Distribution Manager who had the assistance of a clerical staff of four. The divisional agencies and branch warehouses reported sales information weekly to the manager in Danbury. Basing his computations on this data and established inventory levels, the distribution manager would initiate new shipments to the warehouses. He also advised the production department of estimated product requirements based on manually-recorded sales trends.

Even with the greatest care and the most efficient operations, this clerical department found it difficult to keep the various warehouses adequately stocked with the right products. The division occasionally found itself with numerous back orders running into hundreds of thousands of dollars.

"The firm often failed to have the right materials in the right place at the right time. It would be forced, on occasion, to tell a customer that his order could not be filled for a number of weeks. Such sales were lost since hospitals do not re-schedule their operations while waiting for a shipment of sutures. Frequent out-of-stock conditions were jeopardizing customer relations.

RAMAC has gone a long way in solving these problems. The computer system has taken the guesswork out of inventory control. It is up-to-the-minute in its information of the products available in each location. And it uses statistical principles to forecast what products should be made and *sent* to the various locations.

The method employed is this: Each of some forty-three field locations has a "master stock list" which is kept up to date by RAMAC with periodic additions and deletions. The master stock list contains products to be stocked at each location. Usually, these are products that sell above a stipulated minimum quantity per week. Products selling less than the minimum quantity are stocked centrally at Danbury reducing their total inventory as well as reducing the problem of obsolescence.

The inventory at each of the stock locations is maintained on punched cards. The field locations send in their sales information each day on punched cards, but a smaller clerical staff now prepares this data. The computer does most of the rest of the work.

RAMAC computes the reduction in inventory as a result of each day's sales. It produces accurate information on exactly what is in each field location and in the plant warehouse. Moreover, it can supply the complete inventory status for each of the 1400 different product types. The field warehouses need not calculate inventory themselves, nor need they re-order from Danbury when stocks are running low. The Danbury warehouse knows automatically from RAMAC when and where to ship goods to the field. The division can thus maintain the right amount of inventory at each location—enough stock to remain above the order point, not too much stock to involve waste and oversupply.

The computer keeps a close watch on sales trends and product demand. It is thus able to forecast sales for each product and for the division as a whole. It calls attention to products that have had little movement and which might be considered for deletion from the product line. Conversely, the computer RAMAC notes when the demand for a product is such that further production is required.

In the case of production, the computer can test the availability of raw materials, allocate the quantity of raw materials needed, make up production schedules, and test the hourly work load of each manufacturing department against capacity.

In addition to all this, RAMAC is used for computing bills and writing up invoices.

Perhaps the most advantageous aspect of this system is its ability to cut lead time, the time between the decision to place an order and the arrival of the goods where they are needed, in three different ways. The speed of the computer completes the many steps necessary in processing an order in less time than a manual system. By calculating the quantities necessary to replenish field stocks as they are being depleted, the computer eliminates stock orders from field warehouse locations. The computer also integrates sales forecasts and production plans to make finished products available in stock with minimum delay.

During the months in which the computer system has been in operation, the division has been able to cut down investment tied up in back orders to less than $10,000. Even further improvement is expected as the system is refined. Perhaps most important, Surgical Products Field representatives report that they are now placed in a vastly improved position for customer relations. They can give hospitals the products they want, when they are needed. The monetary value of such good relations is incalculable.

chapter eleven | ***Purnell H. Benson***

Before spending money for improving product quality, for consumer and trade promotion, or for advertising, management should consider the following: Does the profit from increased share of the market sufficiently to justify the cost? What outlay in advertising and promotion is required to hold share of the market? Needed to answer these questions is information on the numerical relationships between money spent in various ways and the numbers of consumers gained from or lost to competing brands.

Similarly, if one of the competing brands raises its advertising outlay or initiates a wave of consumer promotion, what change in share of the market can be anticipated? How can the threatened change most effectively be met by counter-strategy? Answers to such questions require that market behavior be understood in terms of the quantitative changes in share of the market which occur when market conditions of competing brands are altered.

Knowledge of the numerical relationships between variables has long

ANALYSIS OF RELATIONSHIPS

BETWEEN MARKET CONDITIONS

AND GAIN OR LOSS IN BRAND SHARE

OF THE MARKET

been recognized as a valuable aid in understanding, predicting and controlling market behavior. But the actual discovery of the numerical relationships has posed formidable tasks of data collection and analysis.

In the past several years, comprehensive data concerning brand share, price, advertising, promotion and product quality have for the first time become available in sufficient amount for successful analysis. Numerical relationships in the marketplace cannot be satisfactorily defined unless all or most of the influencing factors are reckoned with together. These factors fall under the several headings of price, advertising, promotion and product quality. If one or more of these variables is ignored in the market analysis, that variable has the effect of blurring or obscuring the influences of the other variables. For example, market operator A drops his price to increase volume. Meanwhile, competitor B steps up his advertising campaign to meet A's threat. Competitor C responds by improving product quality while holding his price line. If advertising effort and product merit are left out of consideration, how can the net effect of price change on brand share be determined? The answer, of course, is that all of the relevant variables must simultaneously be considered in the analysis. The simultaneous inclusion of key variables is made possible by the kinds and amounts of market data now available, such as Nielsen and MRCA data services and agency auditing of advertising.

DEVELOPMENT OF THE PROJECT

Recognizing these possibilities for progress, the marketing research division of a major grocery products manufacturer authorized a program for an attack upon the problem of defining the numerical relationships between gain or loss in brand share and the market influences playing upon or in behalf of the brand. The program is one in which each staff member has contributed from his special competence in market research and in which frequent group discussions and conferences have illuminated the confused and complex picture which market behavior presents to those investigating it. Sufficient progress has now been made in achieving correlation relationships to justify describing the rationale followed. When introducing 17 independent variables, 11 are found to have regression coefficients three or more times the size of their probable errors. The coefficients of correlation range from .5 to .8 for numbers of observations of brand behavior ranging from 100 to 300.

RELATIONSHIP OF CHANGE IN BRAND SHARE TO BRAND SWITCHING

One of the components of the rationale is provided by recognition that the gain or loss in market share for a given brand over a specified period of time is equal to the sum of its separate gains or losses from each of the competing brands. Letting ΔS_A refer to the gain or loss in percentage share for brand A, ΔS_{AB} refer to A's gain from or loss to brand B, ΔS_{AC} refer to A's gain from or loss to brand C, and ΔS_{AA} refer to advanced or retarded buying of brand A by regular A buyers who change their buying under the influence of promotion, we have the following accounting relationship:

$$\Delta S_A = \Delta S_{AB} + \Delta S_{AC} + \Delta S_{AA}. \tag{1}$$

The usefulness of this relationship is that it directs attention to what goes on between each pair of brands or within a brand's buyers.

RELATIONSHIP OF BRAND SWITCHING TO BRAND INFLUENCES

If we commence market analysis at a point of equilibrium, it seems reasonable that the brand switch which occurs during the subsequent interval of time due to price changes of the two brands is roughly dependent upon the difference between the price changes which occur. If both brands behave similarly, no brand switch would be anticipated. If one brand raises its price more than a competitor does, a switch to the less costly brand may be expected. Similar hypotheses can be stated for differences in increments in advertising, special promotions, store distribution, or brand quality. Letting these variables for brand A be represented by $X_{1A}, X_{2A}, \ldots$, and the corresponding regression coefficients by $B_1, B_2, \ldots$, then the following functional relationship is assumed to connect brand switching with differences in increments in brand influences:

$$\Delta S_{AB} = B_1[\Delta X_{1A} - \Delta X_{1B}] + B_2[\Delta X_{2A} - \Delta X_{2B}] + \ldots \qquad (2)$$
$$\Delta S_{AC} = B_1[\Delta X_{1A} - \Delta X_{1C}] + B_2[\Delta X_{2A} - \Delta X_{2C}] + \ldots .$$

THEORY OF COMPARATIVE JUDGMENT

How much of a switch occurs between two brands manifestly depends upon whether they are similar or not. A given difference in advertising may induce little switch between Fords and Cadillacs but a substantial switch between Fords and Chevrolets. It is necessary to consider how many consumers regard brands A and B as a live option, and of these, how many are on the margin of choice between A and B so that they can readily be swung one way or the other.

The percentage of consumers for whom A and B are the active option is represented by those who either buy A as first choice and would buy B as second choice, or are buying B as first choice and would buy A as second choice. We represent the percentage of those for whom A and B are the live option by L_{AB}. This quantity should be used as a multiplying moderator of all the market influences involving brands A and B, and a similar quantity L_{AC} is to be used with numerical terms for brands A and C.

Of those consumers for whom brands A and B are the live option, we next ask what fraction of them are on the margin of choosing between A and B. At this point, the theory of comparative judgment is useful. The law of comparative judgment formulated by L. L. Thurstone incorporates the theory of comparative judgment, and he advocated that principles of comparative judgment be used in the analysis of consumer choice and market share.

If consumers for whom A and B are the live option are asked to rate each of the brands on a one-to-ten scale, some will rate A higher than B, and some will rate B higher than A. From their reports, a frequency distribution of the numbers of consumers who have different degrees of preference difference for one brand over the other can be constructed. Studies performed with consumer survey data show that these frequency distributions are hump-shaped, approximately normal, tailing off at the extremes of preference difference. The accompanying figure shows such a distribution to which a smooth curve is fitted.

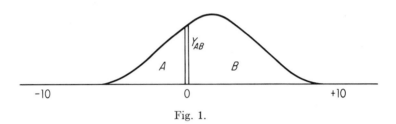

Fig. 1.

If we inquire as to the number of consumers who have a given preference difference, plus or minus, for buying brand A relative to brand B, the answer is given by the height of the frequency distribution curve at the point along the horizontal axis for that preference difference. The consumers who are on the margin of indifference between choosing brand A and choosing brand B are represented by the vertical column Y_{AB} at zero preference difference. The relative number of consumers among those for whom A and B are the live option who can be switched from brand A to brand B is given by the quantity Y_{AB}. This is the height of a normal probability curve at the point defined by the separate proportions preferring brand A and brand B. This height can be obtained from probability tables by normal translation of the proportions into the ordinate.

The height at the zero point of indifference is determined not only by Y_{AB}, the ordinate of the normal curve at the zero point of preference difference along the horizontal axis, but it is also determined by peakedness or flatness of the distribution curve. If two brands are much alike, consumers tend to rate them about equally, and the resulting preference difference curve is high and narrow. For two such brands, a switch from one to the other is more readily induced than for two brands which are dissimilar. If two brands are unlike in nature, few persons will rate them the same in level of preference. Depending upon their personal tastes, consumers will rate one brand more highly than the other. The resulting preference difference curve is wide and flat. The measure of the flatness or narrowness of the preference difference curve is provided by the standard deviation for the distribution curve. The relative number of consumers who can be switched from one brand to the other by a given difference in marketing conditions is given by the reciprocal of the standard deviation for the preference difference curve. For brands A and B this would be $1/SD_{AB}$.

These psychometric considerations require that, in expression (2) for ΔS_{AB}, the terms involving brands A and B be multiplied by L_{AB}, Y_{AB}, and $1/SD_{AB}$, and the terms involving A and C be multiplied by L_{AC}, Y_{AC}, and $1/SD_{AC}$.

$$\Delta S_{AB} = \frac{L_{AB}Y_{AB}}{SD_{AB}} [B_1(\Delta X_{1A} - \Delta X_{1B}) + B_2(\Delta X_{2A} - \Delta X_{2B}) + \ldots] \qquad (3)$$

$$+ \frac{L_{AC}Y_{AC}}{SD_{AC}} [B_1(\Delta X_{1A} - \Delta X_{1C}) + B_2(\Delta X_{2A} - \Delta X_{2C}) + \ldots]$$

The quantities L_{AB}, Y_{AB} and $1/SD_{AB}$ etc., can be learned from consumer surveys which ask respondents for their first and second choice brands for purchase and their preference ratings on a one-to-ten scale for these brands. The acquisition of this information with the required degree of accuracy for pairs of brands which are live options for few consumers may be relatively expensive. Also, the question arises as to the accuracy with which the choices and preference ratings involved are given by consumers.

As an alternative procedure, solution can be made for the psychometric quantities as unknown moderator coefficients in the correlation analysis. Investigation of these psychometric quantities has disclosed a useful relationship which facilitates the solution.

When L_{AB}, the percentage of consumers for whom brands A and B are a live option, is related to S_A and S_B, the percentage shares for brands A and B in the market, the following form of functional dependence is found empirically to exist:

$$L_{AB} = K_{AB}(S_AS_B)\left(\frac{1}{1-S_A} + \frac{1}{1-S_B}\right) \qquad (4)$$

The rationale for this relationship can be seen as follows. The percentage of consumers for whom brands A and B constitute the live option is equal to the sum of those choosing brand A first and brand B second plus those choosing brand B first and brand A second. The first of these two subgroups is proportionate to S_A, the brand share for A, which is the number of those for whom brand A is the first choice. Of those making up the brand share of first choice for A, the fraction choosing B second can be presumed to be proportionate to the brand share which B occupies relative to the other brands in the market besides brand A, that is, $S_B/1 - S_A$. Writing out these relationships for brands A and B and collecting terms gives the functional relationship in (4).

Our studies indicate that the quantities K_{AB}, Y_{AB} and $1/SD_{AB}$ are relatively stable for brands A and B from one market area to another and from one time period to another. Therefore the product of these three quantities can be replaced by a single unknown quantity, Z_{AB}, for which solution is made. The functional relationship for DS_{AB} is then given by:

$$DS_{AB} = Z_{AB}(S_A S_B)(1/1 - S_A + 1/1 - S_B)[B_1(DX_{1A} - DX_{1B}) + \ldots] \quad (5)$$

$$DS_{AC} = Z_{AC}(S_A S_C)(1/1 - S_A + 1/1 - S_C)[B_1(DX_{1A} - DX_{1C}) + \ldots].$$

In work of initial approximation, the Z's may be assumed to be invariant. This would be the case for brands having similar qualities.

RELATIONSHIP OF ADVANCED OR RETARDED BUYING TO BRAND INFLUENCES

The inducement to users of brand A to increase or decrease their consumption, or to increase or decrease their inventory, is occasioned by a change in brand A's price, advertising, product availability or consumer promotion. This may be formulated as follows:

$$DS_{AA} = C_1[DX_{1A}] + C_2[DX_{2A}] + \ldots \quad (6)$$

COMBINING FUNCTIONAL RELATIONSHIPS

The functional system for DS_A, the change in sales or percentage share of the market for brand A, is spelled out by expanding the terms DS_{AB}, etc., in relationship (1) by means of the terms on the right hand side of (3) or (5), and in the case of DS_{AA}, the terms from relationship (6). Similar functional relationships are written out for each of the brands A, B, C, etc.

The independent variables are introduced for the current bimonth of audit, for the previous bimonth, and for the bimonth lagged twice. This incorporates delayed influences. The use of lagged variables also helps to isolate relationships of cause and effect. Additional data from test markets would increase the range in the variables observed and would improve the definition of cause and effect relationships. The playback of results from changes in marketing policies would also yield information of this kind.

The dependent variable lagged once and the dependent variable lagged twice are also introduced as independent variables in the correlation system. This has the effect upon the correlation analysis of making allowance for long-range changes in market conditions not included among the other independent variables. Furthermore, some of the variance in the dependent variable due to sampling error of market audit procedures is removed.

ROLE OF AUTOMATIC COMPUTATION

The foregoing ideas describe the system of numerical relationships used as a model for investigating the influences playing upon or in behalf of each brand in relation to each of the other brands in the market. Each brand in each of sixteen market areas for each period of time included in the analysis provides a separate set of observed quantities for price, promotion, advertising, distribution, etc., and for the resulting change in share or sales which occurs during the period of time.

Automatic computing is needed to process the large amounts of data in the detailed numerical relationships utilized. The computations have been programmed for carrying out the arithmetic prior to the correlation analysis. One program, which we call "Alpha," prepares data to compute the primary regression coefficients B_1, B_2, etc., which tell how much brand share changes for given differences between brands for price, advertising, promotion, distribution, etc. A second program, called "Beta," performs the arithmetic preparatory to solving for the moderator coefficients Z_{AB}, Z_{AC}, etc. After market audit data is processed by the Alpha or Beta programs, then multiple correlation analysis is carried out to define the regression coefficients. The two sets of coefficients are defined by progressive approximation, each set being used as trial values to improve the least squares fit with the other set.

The Alpha and Beta programs are general multi-purpose programs which can be utilized to investigate a wide variety of moderator variables. Three different moderator variables can be multiplied together. Nine competing brands and ten types of market influence can be considered simultaneously. Time lags or leads, as well as curvilinear or cross product terms can be introduced into the sequence of computations at the discretion of the market analyst. The programs have been prepared for the IBM 7040 machine. These computational procedures provide research tools for a comprehensive program of market analysis being pursued to gain improved understanding of the parts played by different market influences.

PART V

APPENDICES

INTRODUCTION

In the truest sense, a computer is only a computer by virtue of the programs which govern its operations. In the absence of a program or a program library, the computer is only a piece of complex electronic hardware as incapable of computations as a bin of electronic parts. It is little wonder, then, that the short-run usefulness of a computer depends more on its "education" than on its "anatomy."

In the past five to ten years, vast strides have been made in software. As late as 1954, programming costs could easily be a thousand times as high as the costs incurred in setting up worksheets and instructions for clerks operating desk calculators and adding machines. At that time, the writer received programming cost estimates from computer service bureaus of from one to two thousand dollars for very simple computations which could be set up in work sheets in five to ten minutes.

ON STANDARD COMPUTER PROGRAMS

FOR STATISTICAL TECHNIQUES

In the intervening years, the accumulation of vast libraries of specific routines has greatly reduced programming costs. Of increasing importance in this cost reduction has been the recent development of automatic programming systems which permit computers to write their own programs on the basis of instructions expressed in a rigid English or algebraic programming language which is structurally similar to a conventional language. In the long run, the development of these generalized automatic programming systems or "compilers" will be a much more powerful force for the reduction of programming costs than the continued accumulation of specific programs or routines. As program libraries grow into the tens of thousands of routines, it may be easier and cheaper to create a new program than to search existing libraries for that routine with just the characteristics desired for a specific problem. The compilers have the further advantage that they are not associated with an individual machine and therefore not obsolete when a machine becomes obsolete.

Yet, ready-made programs are (1962) still an important factor in reducing programming costs in spite of the existence of English language and algebraic language compilers. The cost quotations of computer service bureaus will be markedly influenced by the amount of programming that is necessary (or felt to be necessary) for a specific job. Because programming talent and facilities are still scarce resources, service bureaus are prone to make the first client bear the full cost of programming even though that program may be useful to the bureau at a later date. Quotations on the same specifications can vary as much as six to one according to the amount of programming that each service bureau feels is necessary in the given application.

In a recent mail-survey tabulation with which the writer is familiar, the task was to locate questionnaires having one or more specific punches in columns ranging over a sixty column field. Service bureau bids ran from approximately $2,000 to over $12,000 and differed widely as between service bureaus having the same make of equipment. Conversations with the bidding organizations indicated that the main reason for the widely ranging quotations was differences in the amount of programming felt to be necessary. This experience points up the relevance of "canned" programs in total computation costs, and, therefore, the desirability of shopping for quotations when purchasing computational service.

The word "on" in the title of this paper is positively essential, for the subject itself is far too vast to be covered in a single work of limited scope. This paper, therefore, is a commentary on the subject of standard programs for statistical techniques rather than a definitive survey and description of programs and their characteristics. Its purpose is to acquaint the prospective occasional user of computer service with the existing situation, so that he may more intelligently decide whether it will be worthwhile to approach computer installations when the occasion arises. We will not attempt to present a handbook or listing of programs, for such would be rapidly out of date.

DIVERSITY OF EQUIPMENT

Inasmuch as programs for statistical techniques are specific to a machine area for a particular manufacturer, the subject in a sense is as broad as is the equipment. Some fifteen or sixteen manufacturers of computers can be listed readily at this writing: IBM, Remington Rand, Univac, RCA, Burroughs, Philco, General Electric, Royal McBee, National Cash Register, Honeywell, Bendix, Control Data, Packard Bell, Digital Equipment Corp., El-Tronics, Monroe, Ramo-Wooldridge, and Sylvania. Thus, when we talk about computer programs, we are conceivably talking about some

40 different computers ranging in monthly rent from less than $1,000 to $200,000. Obviously, a list of machines themselves and the briefest comment about the state of programming of statistical techniques for each machine would occupy more space than is available. This range of subject matter makes it necessary for my remarks to be illustrative rather than exhaustive. Attention will be focussed on two machines produced by a single manufacturer.

IBM 650 PROGRAM LIBRARY

For the IBM 650, the manufacturer has assembled a library of programs generated by users of this equipment. The library contains several hundred programs and each program is described by a single page abstract. The collection of abstracts requires two or more rather thick binders. In fact, the library of programs for the 650 has become so voluminus that IBM intends to be selective henceforth in the additions that it makes to the library. Depending on what one classifies as statistical, there are some sixty to eighty statistical programs in the IBM 650 library.

This program library contains approximately 25 programs on multiple regression and correlation analysis and 12 programs each on least square polynomial curve fitting and on analysis of variances and covariance. Three subject areas thus account for some five-sixths of the statistical programs in the library. Other techniques treated are auto correlation and cross correlation, chi-square computation for contingency tables, factor analysis, time series analysis and seasonal index computations, and present value and rate of return calculations.

It should be mentioned that there is a substantial number of programs in the management science areas for the 650. Among some 20 management science program abstracts, there are seven linear program routines, one transportation problem routine, and several production scheduling and balancing line routines.

IBM 704-7090 PROGRAM LIBRARY

For its 704-709-7090 users, IBM has what it calls its Share Organization. This is a program whereby the routines developed by each user can be shared with all. Abstracts for the program are printed from punch cards. Each machine user has a card deck which can be used to generate printed abstracts in whatever order is most convenient for review. The program library as of August 1961 involved 14,000 cards in which the average abstract required some 10 cards. At present, the Share Organization

Library contains approximately a dozen statistical programs. The distribution of these programs across subject matter areas resembles that of the 650 library.

GENERAL OBSERVATIONS ON USE OF CANNED PROGRAMS

With the development of the compilers, it is entirely feasible for a statistician to become his own programmer. An analyst who has a command of one or more of these languages may more often than not prefer to machine-develop a program rather than to take a program from a user Share Organization library. Typically, a canned program does not exactly suit his needs and may not be thoroughly debugged. Therefore, considerable time is often required to learn the characteristics of a program so that it may be appropriately modified. Since the machine manufacturer takes no responsibility for the accuracy of efficiency of the program, its quality depends entirely on the skill of the author of the program and the amount of testing in use that this program has received.

PROGNOSIS

The private program libraries of individual computer installations and service bureaus are also growing rapidly. Consequently, a steady decline in service bureau programming costs is to be expected. It will become increasingly feasible and economical to use a computer for one-time jobs or tasks that would take man weeks as well as man months if traditional punch card equipment or desk calculators were used. In the processing of opinion survey data from questionnaires, one may look forward to marked progress with the growth of programs which permit the use of traditional punch card language in computer programming.

Since the first electronic computer for processing business-type data was installed in 1951 by the United States Bureau of the Census, there has been a fantastic growth in *business* computer applications. It is estimated that 12,000 computers were in operation or on order in the Spring of 1962, and that a new computer installation is sold every 30 minutes. Design and engineering changes have increased computer speeds from seconds to microseconds and have brought into existence computer models that can be afforded and profitably used by virtually all medium-sized companies and many smaller ones. New computers and related equipment are being announced almost weekly, and the body of computer literature, programming techniques, and operating "know-how" is being expanded at an even more rapid rate. It is really no exaggeration to say that—par-

THE NATURE AND EXTENT OF COMPUTER USAGE IN MARKETING OPERATIONS AND DECISION MAKING

ticularly during the past five years—American industry and government have been going through a computer revolution.

But, back of these overall statistics, another and perhaps more meaningful set of facts has to do with the specific ways in which the computer has been used to date and the extent to which it has been applied in the various functional segments of the business.

My associates and I find that wherever computers have been installed, they are working extensively for the accounting and financial executives. In almost as great a degree, they also work for the production executive. And they are even working in many companies for the engineering executive or director of research. But, the plain fact is that computers have not yet been put to work in any such measure by the man in charge of marketing. In none of the major functions of American business has the impact of the computer been so lightly felt as in marketing. Yet, in none of the major functions is its *potential* contribution so great. The promise cannot become a reality quickly or easily, but it is clearly worth the time and effort that will be needed.

In further elaboration of the above points, I propose to attempt the following in the remainder of this paper:

1. To spell out the basic reasons why the computer has thus far been less widely used in marketing than in other functional segments of American business. An understanding of these reasons is important because they, in turn, suggest the specific steps that the marketing executive must take to capitalize on the growing potential of the computer and related analytical techniques.

2. To describe some of the specific marketing applications on which the computer *is being* used today. This material will be based on a research study which my associates and I have just completed and which indicates the extent to which the computer has been applied to date across the whole range of potential marketing applications—that is, the extent to which it is being used in each of the data-processing and decision-making areas comprising the typical marketing operation.

3. To suggest a course of action for the marketing executive to follow in capitalizing on the full potential of this rapidly evolving technology.

REASONS WHY THE COMPUTER HAS NOT BEEN AS WIDELY USED IN MARKETING

There are three major types of potential computer applications in marketing (or, for that matter, in any other functional area). These three types of application, moving from the least important to the most important, are (1) processing individual transactions, (2) producing sales statistics or marketing information of the conventional type, and (3) facilitating the management decision-making process through advanced mathematical or operations research type analyses.

In the course of reviewing where the computer is actually being used in marketing today, we will look at some specific applications of each of these three basic types. But, at this point, let us limit our attention to the third of these application categories—that is, the more advanced decision-making use of the computer. The difficulties in this type of application are the reason why the computer has not yet come to play the dynamic, profit-making role in marketing that it does in other areas.

The most useful way of bringing out these difficulties is by drawing a contrast between management decision making in production and physical distribution activities, on the one hand, and decision making in marketing, on the other. In both of these functional areas—production and marketing —operating executives are continuously confronted with a vast number of alternative courses of action on which decisions must be made and with widely varying kinds and amounts of information to assist in making these decisions.

As an example, a given company that distributes its products nationally may have (1) several plants spread across the country; (2) many different products—not all of which are made in any one plant; and (3) significantly different mixes of equipment, unit production costs, and break-even points among its plants.

In face of these circumstances, the production executive is confronted with an enormously large number of variables and alternative courses of action to be weighed in reaching decisions on such questions as (1) from which plant should a given customer's order be shipped; (2) on which piece of equipment should a given part be made when alternative manufacturing methods are available; (3) what, when, and how much should be produced for inventory; (4) when should a given plant work overtime; and (5) when should equipment be added or dropped at a given plant.

In the same company, the marketing executive is also confronted with an endless array of variables, alternative courses of action, and bodies of marketing information. Out of these ingredients, he, too, is almost continuously engaged in reaching and evaluating the effects of decisions— decisions involving salesmen and how they spend their time, advertising and promotion expenditures, pricing and competitive pricing strategy, distributor and dealer relations, product line changes, and so on.

But—while there is admittedly a high decision-making content in both the marketing and production management jobs, the critical question to be weighed here is: How do the decision-making processes in these two functional areas differ, and what implications does this difference have on computer usage in each area?

In coming to grips with this question, we all recognize, of course, that production involves a series of physical operations that are readily observable and measurable, and the relationships among which are known fairly precisely. For example, a factory bottleneck and its impact can usually be seen by the naked eye. In addition, there are quality control and cost accounting records that show significant cause and effect relationships. For example, it is clear that if machine speeds are increased by X percent, scrap losses will increase by Y percent. Moreover, in the factory, scientific analysis and quantification have been going on for many years. As an example, so-called inventory models have been available for a long time. To be sure, many of these models today are much more sophisticated, now that they have been programmed on a computer. But these improvements are essentially refinements of inventory decision-making techniques that have been in existence for a long time.

On virtually all of these points, the circumstances that exist today in the marketing world are different—sometimes very much different.

The one common element is the existence of as great a fund of quantitative information in marketing as there is in production. There are enormous amounts of industry wide marketing information (such as that provided by the Department of Commerce and by Nielsen and similar market research reports) as well as company information on sales results by product, by territory, by salesman, and so on.

But beyond that point, the differences are marked.

Specifically, much less is known in marketing about the relationship between cause and effect—such as the impact of different levels of selling effort on sales results or the impact of different prices on demand for a product. Secondly, in marketing—notwithstanding the enormous volume of statistical information—a good many of the important variables are difficult to quantify. An example is the problem of quantifying the relative attractiveness of several different advertising media.

Finally, in marketing—unlike production—one must deal with a number of *external* factors that are often not readily observable and are also subject to considerable uncertainty. An example of this type of external factor is the moves of a company's competitors. In a production decision-making model, one does not ordinarily need to make allowance for the possibility that a strike will take place or that the supply of a critical raw material will be shut off. The reason is that these contingencies—though uncertain—are also so unlikely to happen that for all practical purposes they can be fully disregarded. In contrast, the moves of a company's competitors have such continuing and significant, if uncertain, effect that they must be taken into account in marketing decision making.

And so, in summary, there are three factors that have slowed down application of the computer to high payout decisions in the marketing area. These are:

1. The high degree of uncertainty or unpredictability that prevails
2. The difficulty of quantifying some of the key variables
3. The problem of measuring cause and effect relationships.

Although computer usage in marketing lags behind that in other functional areas, this does not mean that no progress is being made. On the contrary, the very difficulty is also some measure of the high payout potential that lies in finding ways of successfully using the computer to facilitate marketing decision making. And, in recognition of the high stakes that are involved, more and more companies are making a real effort to find some breakthrough answers in this area of marketing and the computer. To underscore the fact that it is just a matter of time before such breakthroughs are achieved, a subsequent section contains a description of how one company is using the computer to improve advertising decision making.

PRESENT USES OF THE COMPUTER IN MARKETING

Against this background of difficulty and opportunity, let us now consider the specific ways in which the computer is being used in marketing today. To develop a more definitive answer to this question, some of my McKinsey associates and I have recently completed a survey covering three elements:

1. An extensive search of the literature on computer usage
2. Interviews with a substantial number of companies known to be leaders in computer usage
3. Depth discussions with knowledgeable persons in the various computer manufacturing companies.

The results of this survey are summarized in highly condensed form on Chart 1, "Use of the Computer in Marketing Operations and Decision Making."

The results of this survey are broken down among three major types of business—retailing, consumer product manufacturers, and industrial goods manufacturers. For each of these three categories, the chart shows the extent of the present applications of computer to each of eight major operating and decision-making areas comprising the marketing function. These are:

> Order Processing
> Physical Distribution Planning
> Sales Forecasting
> Sales Force Management
> Product-Line Planning
> Pricing
> Advertising
> Total Planning and Control Systems.

Finally, for each of these eight marketing elements in each type of business, the chart shows one of three different degrees of computer usage. These are indicated by the legend:

1. Substantial usage—which is symbolized by a dark square
2. Moderate usage—symbolized by a lightly shaded triangle
3. Rare usage—symbolized by an unshaded circle

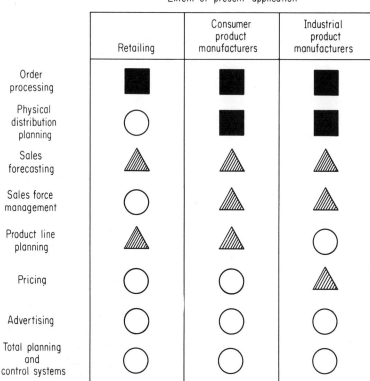

Fig. 1. Use of the computer in marketing operations and decision making.

ORDER PROCESSING

The first of the eight elements to be dealt with is that of order processing. Here, as one might imagine, a fairly substantial number of applications exist among computer users in all three types of business. But the management significance of this use is minimized by the fact that it is a routine, operating application—the processing of sales orders and the preparation of invoices to customers. As such, it does not contribute to marketing decision making except indirectly as the individual transactions being processed represent the raw data inputs for some of the subsequent uses —such as preparation of sales statistics for field sales control. In substance, however, this application simply represents the use of advanced hardware to perform more quickly and, in some instances, more efficiently the same operations that have always been performed.

PHYSICAL DISTRIBUTION PLANNING

The next area is that of physical distribution planning, to which the computer has been applied fairly extensively in industrial as well as consumer product manufacturing. Two types of decision making have been improved by this sort of computer application. The first might be called an investment or facilities planning decision. For example, how many warehouses should the company have and where should they be located? How much inventory should be carried in each warehouse and how much should be shipped directly to customers from the company's plants as opposed to being shipped from its warehouses?

This type of computer application is well illustrated by the following experience of a major food company, the marketing leader in the product lines that it manufactures. This company was faced with the fact that its distribution costs were increasing significantly and eating into profit margins. Management had defined the problem question as this: Do we need every one of our 39 branch warehouses or could we eliminate some of them?

Management turned this problem over to a study team which redefined the key question as this: What should our distribution set up be so as to meet customer demand at lowest total distribution cost?

In taking the first cut at this question, the team developed information on the variable costs incurred in shipping from three factory sites and 39 field warehouses to 1,200 customer destinations. Then the team developed a statistical model—known as a trans-shipment model—and used a computer to determine the optimum methods of shipment given the existing system of facilities. This produced what might be called an operating decision-making technique. That is, given our present facilities setup, how can we operate it at lowest cost and still meet minimum customer-service requirements?

As a second and more fundamental cut at the problem, the study team then developed a second computer model that included the *fixed* costs of each field warehouse as well as the variable costs. This produced a basis for overall facilities planning—that is, for deciding which warehouses, if any, should be given up, since the so-called "fixed costs" of a warehouse become variable and are eliminated when that warehouse is dropped from the system.

Use of the computer in this instance demonstrated that over $1 million per year could be saved by reducing the number of field warehouses from 39 to 17 and planning a larger number of shipments direct from factory to customers. The computer was also used to identify opportunities for additional savings by building warehouses in new locations and changing the size of existing ones.

Finally, the study team developed a computer-based inventory control setup for the replenishment of inventories in the planned new distribution system. This company now anticipates that application of the computer to this additional activity will result in inventory reductions of approximately 30 percent.

Somewhat similar computer-based techniques of facilities planning are being used by some oil companies in service station site selection and by retail chains in locating their retail outlets. The added dimension in these applications, however, is that of predicting demand or traffic in the location or neighborhood under consideration.

SALES FORECASTING

Our survey showed that the computer is being used for sales forecasting in a fair number of instances in all three types of business. These forecasting applications vary widely in degree of sophistication. Some involve fairly elementary analyses and extrapolation of a company's own past sales. Others employ much more advanced techniques designed, for example, to forecast prices and demand on the basis of an analysis of the relationship among business cycle factors, and industry wide inventories, turnover rates, and sales.

One of the computer-based methods that is being used extensively to increase the accuracy of sales forecasting is a technique called exponential smoothing—which is simply a method of weighting past sales results and seasonal factors in a way that produces minimum forecasting error. A number of the computer manufacturing companies have developed general purpose or standard computer programs for readily applying this technique to the past sales results of most any company. In addition, work is being done to further improve machine-based sales forecasting techniques by giving weight to cyclical fluctuations and to the effect of past and proposed promotional campaigns.

These advanced sales forecasting techniques have been used to the greatest advantage in a number of companies where they are integrated on the computer with inventory and production control programs in such a way that replenishment of inventories—both at the factory and in the field—is provided for automatically by the machine-based system of information and control.

SALES FORCE MANAGEMENT

The fourth major element of marketing operations and decision making shown on Fig. 1 is that of managing the field sales force. Here, there are two potential types of computer applications. First is the preparation of the traditional sales volume and profit reports as a means of measuring performance of the sales force against some target or previous period's results. The scope of this sort of sales-results reporting is symbolized by the schematic diagram appearing in Fig. 2, which shows how one company identified the key financial variables around which it then built its structure of conventional sales reports.

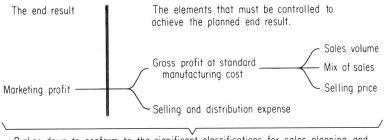

Fig. 2. Key financial factors in marketing performance.

As one example of the way in which the computer can facilitate sales management through this sort of reporting, one of the major liquor companies prepares on its large-scale computer a weekly summary of the sales volume of each of its independent distributors on each of the company's different brands. Local sales management then uses these up-to-the-minute reports to plan the activities of the company's field representatives, whose main function is to help pull sales through the independent distributors by calling on the retail stores that are the distributors' customers.

Wherever computers have been installed in business organizations, we find that the machine installation is being used extensively to turn out this sort of conventional sales report. Nevertheless, on Fig. 1 we have used the symbol indicating *moderate* use rather than indicating substantial use because the computer is not yet regularly employed in the second major aspect of sales force management, the planning of how the sales force *should* spend its time (as opposed simply to reporting how it *did* spend its time).

This second and more dynamic use of the computer in sales force management is aimed at helping marketing managers reach better decisions on such problems as:

1. Determining the overall size of the sales force
2. Allocating salesmen's time to territories, customer types and sizes, individual customers, and products. For example, one manufacturer of style goods has used computer-based techniques to determine much more scientifically than before just how much salesmen's time should be concentrated on sales development work among noncustomer companies and new customer companies to continuously offset the inevitable attrition of business from old, established customers. This is the kind of computer-aided decision making that enables this company to focus adequate effort on the things that must be done well today to maintain or improve the company's share-of-market position two, three or five years into the future.

In summary, although the computer is used extensively on reporting sales force performance after-the-fact, it is only beginning to be used to reach better decisions in advance on the best way of deploying the sales force among markets, customers, and products. Hence, in the aggregate, computer applications in this area of sales force management net out to moderate use.

PRODUCT-LINE PLANNING

The next area of decision making that involves the marketing function is that of product-line planning. As shown on Fig. 1, the computer is being used to a moderate extent for this purpose in retailing and consumer products manufacturing, but very little in industrial goods manufacturing.

As an example of this application, some retail chains are beginning to install punched-tape point-of-sale recorders in their stores to produce a much more detailed record of merchandise moving through each of their outlets. These tapes are then fed into a centralized computer to give store managers and buyers much faster and more complete information on which to place replenishment orders, to plan promotions and sales markdowns, and so on. One of the first chains to adopt the technique states that, as a result of this computer application, it has realized a significant improvement in turnover and dollar volume on investment in floor space.

As another example, a manufacturer producing style goods has developed a computer-based approach to deciding what is the optimum balance between the number of style and color varieties in its product line and the increased production, inventory, and related costs resulting from offering a larger number of items.

PRICING

Next we move to the critical decision-making area of pricing where the computer to date has been used only sporadically. The principal exception lies in the industrial products field where the computer is being used to a moderate extent to pull together engineering estimates as a basis for bidding, and to develop more detailed and extensive cost information in support of cost plus settlements.

Beyond these sorts of fairly straightforward data-processing applications to the pricing function, another more dynamic use can be found in the application of the computer to development of bidding strategies. Some of the oil companies have employed this methodology in determining how much to bid for individual oil leases. Another dramatic and widely publicized application was the recent use that a small investment underwriting firm made of a computer in pricing its successful competitive bid for the purchase of $100 million of State of California bonds.

Both these latter two examples are admittedly purchasing bids, but they do nevertheless represent applications of the computer to a pricing decision.

ADVERTISING

Finally, we come to the two major marketing areas in which the computer has seen very little usage to date—although signs of real promise are evident in both.

In the first of these—the area of advertising decision making—one of the well known advertising agencies has recently announced development of a computer program for facilitating the selection of advertising media to meet any given advertising objective. This is a fairly simple and straightforward application of computers and operations research techniques to a process that marketing executives and agencies have been carrying out in the past by less precise methods. The key to this newer computer-aided approach lies in assigning a quantitative value to each specific media for every potential audience group or class of potential customer that that media might reach. The computer then makes possible the rapid manipulation of hundreds or thousands of these quantitative values in a way that helps select the optimum combination of media to meet a predetermined advertising objective.

A much more far reaching and sophisticated approach to advertising decision making has just been developed by one large company in a processing industry after four years of intensive research.

The approach used in developing this advanced technique is too complex to describe in detail here. Basically, however, this company, through carefully controlled consumer surveys and field testing, has developed a precise picture of the degree of brand switching that takes place—that is, switching from its brand to a competitive brand—as the level of advertising on the company's brand in a given market is changed but all other conditions in that market remain the same. To develop a useful model, this research had to be complete enough to provide a picture of brand switching behavior for each of a large number of different sets of market conditions such as share-of-market, price, distribution facilities, selling and promotional effort, and the like.

Through the use of these data, plus a prediction of the market conditions in each major area in which it sells, this company is able to identify the markets in which an increase in advertising expenditure would bring them the largest increase in sales volume and profits.

Somewhat more specifically, this advanced analytical approach has enabled the company, with the aid of a large scale computer, to do the following four things:

1. Predict, given the level of advertising, their market share for each sales territory within an accuracy of one percent
2. Predict the profit from any given level of advertising budget
3. Determine the optimum level of advertising both in total and by market
4. Determine the minimum advertising budget, nationally and by market, needed to reach a planned profit goal.

TOTAL PLANNING AND CONTROL SYSTEMS

The eighth and final area on our grid is that involving development of a total, integrated marketing planning and control system. Very little in the way of end-result accomplishment can be shown to date in this area. Nevertheless, it is an area of particular importance to this discussion because it represents the ultimate goal toward which the improvement efforts in all of the other seven areas are targeted or toward which they should be targeted. That is, the continuing pressure on computer-based decision-making systems is to encompass larger and larger aggregations of decisions—until all the related subsystems are tied together into a single master system in which all the pieces fit together with jig saw puzzle precision.

It is easy to see why this sort of a total, all-embracing system should be the ultimate goal because there is obviously a high degree of relationship between many of the subelements that are now handled by separate decision systems. For example, physical-distribution planning is affected by product line decisions; advertising campaigns need to be taken into account in planning sales force deployment; sales forecasting underlies most of the other elements, and so on.

Development of this sort of total planning and control system is one of those goals that we might call "simple but not easy." That is, it is simple in concept but very, very difficult to implement. The reason is, of course, that it represents a complex and massive job—one that for many companies substantially exceeds the capacity of even the largest computer.

Yet despite these difficulties, the pressure to move in that direction is very great. And from responding imaginatively to this pressure, one company, at least, is—today—close to achieving the ultimate goal. After three years of work on developing decision systems for most of the individual elements on Fig. 1 as well as related elements in manufacturing, this company has just completed the process of tying all these developments into a single integrated system on which most (but not all the elements) are computer based. This master system includes sales-forecasting and sales inventory and production planning models that give management a rigorous, analytical basis for reaching decisions on:

Adding or dropping products

Determining style and color varieties to be offered

Scheduling the company's plants (in terms of overall level of operations as well as amount of capacity to be allocated to each product)

Producing inventories in advance of the selling season

Purchasing raw materials

Allocating selling effort

Altering manufacturing facilities by eliminating or adding equipment.

In concluding this overall assessment of the "state of the art," so to speak, we can summarize by saying that the computer is being used extensively on routine, pedestrian applications but—because of the difficulties already pointed out—the great marketing problems of most companies have not yet been helped much by the computer and the high payoff applications have not yet been well exploited.

A COURSE OF ACTION FOR THE MARKETING EXECUTIVE

In face of these "facts of life," what course of action should today's marketing executive follow? That is, confronted with difficulties, risks of failure, and high costs, should he try at all to push ahead in the application of the computer to marketing operations and decision making? Or should he wait until other companies have done the pioneering job needed to find breakthrough answers which he could then adapt to his own situation?

As comfortable as the wait-and-see strategy sounds, it simply will not work in the circumstances under consideration. The need cannot be met simply by planning to get a computer "at the right time," so to speak, for the mere acquisition of a computer will not, by itself, result in better information or improved decisions. Nor can the need be met simply by pulling the right general purpose computer program off the shelf and using it to convert your company's mass of raw marketing data into a finished set of decision-making tools.

In short, the wait-and-see strategy will not work because there is no possibility of "buying one's way" into advanced, computer-based management methods at the last moment. The reason is that the effectiveness of the computer as a tool of management depends almost completely on the relevance, completeness, and reliability of the basic data that are fed into it. For a computer application to a decision-making problem to be of real value, new data that adequately relate cause and effect in the marketplace of that company and that give new insight into the criteria to be used in making that company's marketing decisions must be developed.

Development of these sorts of "inputs" for the computer can require, at the very least, a great deal of effort in routine data gathering. And at the opposite end of the range, it may even require field experiments or pilot runs to test alternative marketing strategies. But regardless of the range of data to be developed, the job—in all instances—requires ingenuity, creativity, practical judgment, and a deep understanding of the basic economics of the particular business. In summary, installation of a computer does not obviate in any way the need for thinking through the real decision-making process of the company involved and then identifying the data needed to facilitate that process.

Long and difficult though this task may be, there can be little doubt that for many companies it is clearly "worth the candle." The reason is that although marketing is a world in which uncertainties are high, so is it also one in which the stakes are high. This suggests that even the crudest of computer-based aids to marketing decision making—one capable of producing only a relatively small edge in timing or impact—could make a large difference in market franchise and profitability. This potential stands out in sharp contrast to the well structured problems of inventory and production control where a number of the computer applications that have been developed are rigorous and elaborate—indeed, even "elegant"—but unfortunately have produced only a trivial payoff.

The significance of this greater profit-making leverage in the marketing area is represented in Fig. 3 which shows the relative advertising effectiveness of two major competing companies with similar product lines. Over a long period of years, Company B has consistently surpassed Company A in sales volume generated per dollar of advertising. With this fact in mind, one can realize why the large processing company mentioned earlier in this paper invested four years of intensive research in developing a computer-based advertising decision model. It is clear from that case example and from Fig. 3 that the stakes are great enough to warrant almost any effort at improving advertising effectiveness.

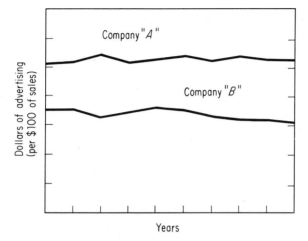

Fig. 3. Comparison of advertising effectiveness.

Given the enormous effect of improved marketing decisions, marketing executives in most companies simply cannot afford to let the difficulty of computer-based approaches stand in their way. A beginning needs to be made now. One of the most effective ways of organizing to meet this challenge would be to create a joint study team or task force consisting of members of the company's line sales management force and market research staff as well as its operations researchers and EDP systems analysts. This sort of composite attack would help see to it that the computer applications ultimately developed were not only technically sound but also sufficiently well understood by *sales executives* to be used consistently and wisely in running the company's marketing operations.

In launching such a computer-application-development program in the marketing area, marketing executives must understand that dramatic results will not be achieved overnight. The development and testing of computer-based information systems for improved decision making and control is a long, hard process. This is so not because the techniques themselves are so complex, but principally because of the great mass of data that usually needs to be gathered, evaluated, and put to intelligent use.

Regardless of the nature of the improved decision-making tools that should ultimately result from this effort, the very process of carrying out such a project should, by itself, produce great benefit. It should arm the sales executive with much greater insight into the key marketing variables and how they interact upon each other. In this way, the search for better decision-making tools produces greater understanding and sharper perceptions that—by themselves—are a force for profit improvement. Clearly these are potential gains that few companies can afford not to pursue.

chapter three | *William F. Massy, Gerald B. Tallman*
and Arnold E. Amstutz

During the past three years the authors have been engaged in developing a complex marketing game for use in the M.I.T. School of Industrial Management. Use of this game in undergraduate, graduate and executive programs has provided the opportunity to make a preliminary evaluation of the potentialities and limitations of complex gaming as an aid in attaining established teaching goals. This article examines the place of complex games in the overall development of management games and discusses the present status and future potential of complex games as assessed by the authors on the basis of their experience.

The M.I.T. Marketing Game has been used successfully in courses at each of the three levels mentioned above. We are convinced that the concepts to be discussed apply to all three although the details of administration and integration differ somewhat—especially at the executive development level.

THE COMPLEX MARKETING GAME[1]

ACCOMPLISHMENT AND OPPORTUNITY

In addition to their value as educational and training devices, it also appears that games of the type discussed may be useful as operational tools for executive planning and decision making. This conjecture is based both upon our experience with complex marketing games and upon the military's extensive utilization of war games and their close cousins, map maneuvers, for operational planning.[2] This hypothesis has yet to be verified by empirical research, however, and will not receive specific treatment in this paper.

[1] The work reported represents the joint efforts of the authors, and of Professor Peter S. King, formerly of the School of Industrial Management and now in India. It was made possible through a generous grant of computer time made by the M.I.T. Computation Center, Cambridge, Mass.

[2] A. M. Mood, *War Gaming as a Technique of Analysis,* The RAND Corporation, Santa Monica, California, #P-899 (September 3, 1954).

A BRIEF HISTORY OF BUSINESS GAMING

This discussion of the M.I.T. Marketing Game can best be understood within the context of the historical development of business gaming.

One of the most widely known early treatments of business games appeared during the spring of 1958, when G. R. Andlinger surveyed the field and described his non-computer executive game in the *Harvard Business Review*.[1] In describing how the business game aims at learning rather than entertainment, he cited the following points:

1) The game must approach reality
2) The players' experience, judgment, and skill—as opposed to luck —must influence the outcome.

These points are still valid today.

His game was quite remarkable in that it considered a variety of important business variables in a fair degree of detail (e.g., the hiring, training, and attrition of men in the sales force, urban vs. rural differences in attainable call frequencies, etc.). Since Andlinger did not wish the play of his game to be limited by computer availability he was unable to incorporate as rich and realistic a simulation model as would appear desirable in light of recent developments. Nevertheless, Andlinger's work and writings provided valuable publicity and exerted an important influence on subsequent developments.

With the aid of hindsight, it seems safe to say that the American Management Association's pioneering efforts in the development of a computerized executive decision simulation represent the turning point in the history of business gaming.[2] This work was done concurrently with that of Andlinger and while the AMA game did not provide as rich a set of decision variables as his did, the procedures for determining each team's sales, costs, and profits were considerably more sophisticated. Moreover, the AMA experience showed that digital computers could be used to compute the results of players' decisions, and that properly integrated machine processing did not disrupt the normal flow of game play.

---

[1] G. R. Andlinger, "Business Games—Play One," *Harvard Business Review*, **36:2** (March-April, 1958), p. 115; G. R. Andlinger, "Looking Around—What Can Business Games Do?" *Harvard Business Review*, **36:4** (July-August, 1958), p. 147.

[2] R. Bellman, C. E. Clark, D. G. Malcomb, C. J. Craft, and F. M. Ricciardi, "On the Construction of a Multi-state, Multi-person Business Game," *Operations Research*, 5:4 (August, 1957), p. 469.

The original AMA game was played by five teams of three to five men each competing in a single market. Decisions covering a calendar quarter of simulated time were submitted every twenty to thirty minutes, with twenty to forty "moves" being made before play was terminated. Participants attempted to influence the sales of their product, together with their company's profit position, by adjusting selling price, marketing (promotional) expenditures, and research and development outlays. Production commitments had to be made in advance of sales, and contracts for additional plant capacity let if necessary. Information about competitors' behavior could be obtained by paying a market research fee. All inputs were punched on cards and fed into an IBM 650 digital computer, which in turn produced sales and accounting results for distribution to the team. Processing time was in the order of a few minutes.

The AMA game was played at the Association's seminars at Saranac Lake, New York. Its successful reception there, together with a growing recognition by both the business and academic communities of the new tool's potential, led to the development and use of a wide variety of business games.[1] It has been estimated that more than one hundred different games are in use in the United States at the present time.

At least three deviations from the AMA's "top management decision" orientation occurred early in the general development of business games. First, "functional area games" were built. The Remington-Rand game for marketing executives, which is a good example of this kind of effort, provides a detailed representation of marketing areas while deemphasizing problems of production and finance.[2] In this game, promotional expenditures must be divided between advertising and selling programs, for example, with the latter being complicated by problems of hiring, training, and compensating salesmen. Experienced salesmen can be hired away from a competitor if the offer is right!

An important group of what might be called "problem oriented games" comprises a second deviation from the original AMA form. In these, emphasis is placed on training lower echelon personnel or beginning students to make specific kinds of business decisions. The inventory management simulation described in Greene and Sisson's book on non-computer business games, for instance, is designed to promote the use of the square

---

[1] The most widely known of these games are the IBM game and the UCLA Executive Decision Games (models 1, 2, and 3); c.f. Publications by the IBM Management Decision-Making Laboratory, International Business Machines Corporation, New York; J. R. Jackson, "UCLA Executive Decision Games" (Processed), University of California, Los Angeles, Research Report No. 58, December 9, 1958.

[2] "Marketing Management Simulation," Remington Rand Univac, A Division of Sperry Rand Corporation, New York City.

root rule in inventory control.[1] In addition to providing practice in applying the rule in a realistic situation, differences in performance attributable
to its application can be a convincing demonstration for those who do
not believe in the management science concept. A number of problem
oriented games have been developed in a variety of contexts (using manual and computerized computation), and more may be expected to emerge.
In keeping with their very specific purposes, they are relatively simple
to design and administer.

A third line of approach has evolved more recently. While acknowledg-
ing their debt to Andlinger and the original AMA designers, the builders
of "complex" management games have pushed the state of the art far
beyond the scope of those pioneering works. INTOP, the international
business operations game developed at the University of Chicago and
described by Professor Thorelli in this volume, is an excellent example
of this kind of effort. The Carnegie Tech Management Game was the first
and is perhaps the best known work in the field.[2] Our own M.I.T.
Marketing Game was evolved from the same line of thought.

THE M.I.T. MARKETING GAME [1]

The M.I.T. Marketing Game, developed as a major and integrating element in advanced marketing management courses, is a good example of
what has been called a "complex game." From two to four student teams
operate simulated competing companies which produce a product and sell
it in a national market. In its present form the game is based upon the
marketing of electric floor polishers for household use. Response to a
mix of marketing activities at both trade and consumer levels is programmed in models designed for the IBM 709 computer available for
educational use at M.I.T. Student decisions concerning volume of production, plant investment, product and process development, inventory policy
and financial management influence the success of company operations.
Major attention, and the most detailed elaboration of plans and decisions,
is devoted to basic marketing questions. In seeking profit growth for
their companies, the student managers may manipulate the following
variables: product quality, retail and factory price, dealer margins, chan-

---

[1] J. R. Greene and R. L. Sisson, *Dynamic Management Decision Games* (New
York: John Wiley and Sons, Co., 1959), Ch. 4.

[2] K. J. Cohen, et al., "The Carnegie Tech Management Game," *Journal of Business* (University of Chicago), XXXIII:4 (October, 1960), p. 303.

[3] Portions of this and the following section are based upon:

P. S. King, W. F. Massy, A. E. Amstutz, and G. B. Tallman, "The M.I.T. Marketing
Game," *Marketing, A Maturing Discipline* (Proceedings of the Winter Meeting,
1960), American Marketing Association, Chicago, 1961.

nels of distribution (including the number and type of retail outlets), geographic market area, advertising expenditures, advertising media and appeals, the number of disposition of salesmen, and promotion within the retail store.

THE CONTROL TEAM

In contrast with the business games discussed above, the M.I.T. Marketing Game requires the planning of marketing program content as well as of expenditures and price levels. In making an advertising decision, for example, students generally plan media schedules, promotional appeals, copy, illustration, layout, and point of purchase tie-ins, as well as deciding upon the dollar budget. While dollar allocations are charged directly to expense, functions influencing sales in the market model are modified by a "control team" appraisal of the quality and appropriateness of the plans for spending these dollars. Thus one dollar of expenditure may buy 80¢ or $1.20 worth of results. The control team is made up of the instructors teaching the marketing course in which the game is being played, sometimes supplemented with other members of the marketing faculty. They react to the less quantifiable elements in the company's market plans in a dual role—as consumers and as marketing professionals. The interposition of the control team between the student managers and the computer is accepted by the students as a fact of life—probably as reasonable as the consumers and dealers which the control group attempt to represent.

The use of the control team to handle market responses not programmed in the game model offers three major advantages. (1) It removes constraints on the range of marketing actions that may be used. (2) It allows consideration of the content as well as the budget for marketing plans. (3) It tends to remove the check list effect inherent in the play of many business games—where the fact that particular blanks have been provided on the input form serves to focus student attention on a particular set of decisions. In the qualitative areas of the M.I.T. Marketing Game, the players themselves must determine which variables are worth manipulating.

OVERVIEW OF TEACHING OBJECTIVES

The fact that the M.I.T. Marketing Game was developed for use in an advanced marketing course is significant. This frame of reference requires that the success of game play be evaluated in the light of well defined teaching objectives. The game serves as the laboratory of the marketing curriculum, wherein students who have been exposed to a wide range of important marketing concepts in basic courses are given the opportunity to try their wings—to gain experience in solving real-world marketing problems.

We have found that the management of a game company provides a continuing purpose and point of reference against which students can test the subject matter learned elsewhere for relevancy and usefulness in particular problem situations. They do not attempt to "beat the model" in the sense of trying to solve some artificial puzzle formulation (they are warned that it is too complex). Rather they accept the game world market as a real one to be probed by market research, which they can buy, and by successive variations in carefully developed marketing activities.

To be successful, moreover, this probing must not be blind. Rather, it must be based upon established marketing concepts, supplemented with liberal doses of insight obtained from studying equivalent real-world situations and written case materials. We feel that our approach is successful in large part because students find market response in the game world reasonably consistent with the concepts presented in assigned readings or developed from case discussions.

The students are, of course, carefully advised that the game market place is an artificial one. We are careful to avoid giving the impression that a specific elasticity of demand to price or to advertising or to other sales effort found in the game environment will be encountered when marketing a similar product in the real world. On the other hand, the students are assured that the game world is based on the same kinds of considerations which shape responses in real world markets.

They are aided in assuming a real world perspective by receiving descriptive and quantitative information in advance of play (e.g., a history of the industry, the past marketing programs pursued by their own firms, the structure of the trade, and a brief report on relevant consumer behavior patterns). Of equal importance are the competitive market reports, market research information, and detailed verbal feedback given by the instructors and the game administrator on a regular schedule throughout the duration of the game. Provision of detailed data is possible both because of the complex subjective factors introduced by the control team and as the result of the richness of the market simulation model itself. The latter operates at a level of disaggregation sufficient to provide the answers for many market research questions. Intermediate outputs describing detailed activity within the simulated market are readily available to the game administrator for interpretation and distribution to the teams.

To put it another way, the students begin the game by analyzing what is in effect a detailed and realistic business case. Then the teams are given the reins of company management and a responsibility that continues over a period of business years. They are placed in a position where they must correct or live with past mistakes in planning, as in the real world, and in addition consider the question of consistency in dealing with consumers and the trade. Thus, the student can discover the necessity for integrating specific decisions into a long-run policy framework, rather than operating in a time vacuum or singling out specific areas for action without regard for related questions.

We have had no difficulty in getting students to accept the marketing executive's role enthusiastically.

INTEGRATION OF THE GAME INTO A COURSE STRUCTURE

The game is used regularly in advanced marketing management courses at the School of Industrial Management. Students taking the game course have credit for at least a one semester course in marketing principles and often for marketing research as well. Graduate and undergraduate courses are taught separately, but the subject matter and techniques used are similar.

Our normal course plan is based on ten weeks of active game play beginning in the third week of a fifteen week semester. Plays are made at the rate of one per week, and involve one or sometimes two calendar quarters of simulated time. During the weeks preceding the opening play the students work out their team's organization and become familiar with the operational requirements of the game and with the history of their company's activities prior to the time when they took over responsibility for management. After game play terminates, the students prepare an analytical review of their own operations which, in turn, forms the basis for class discussions and for debriefing by the instructors.

With a course enrollment of 25-35 students, we have found it desirable to operate two games with two companies competing in each game. Thus we have a team A and team B in game I, and game II. The two A teams form one class group under one instructor while the two B teams are placed under a second instructor. The two teams in a class do not compete directly with each other but rather with teams in the other class. Though both games are based on the same model and initial conditions, operating results quickly diverge because of differences in individual team decisions. The members of team AI find themselves faced with competitive situations quite different from those encountered by their classmates on team AII. With larger enrollment we would add additional games or class sections, creating groups III and IV or companies C and D. The number of companies per game should not exceed the number of course sections. The model has been constructed to permit up to four company teams to operate in one game.

The course organization outlined above permits company strategies to be freely discussed in the classroom without fear of divulging competitive secrets. Since the situations prevailing in the two games are different each student finds himself involved with a wider range of questions than would be the case if only a single game were involved.

In addition to providing a vehicle for class discussion, the game gives the student a need to know—right now—more about marketing management and marketing decision-making processes. Here is where the teacher gets his opportunity. In the marketing management course at M.I.T. the teacher is a consultant to the managers of firms. These managers are very inexperienced. Very soon after the game begins they develop an intense awareness of their lack of knowledge; but they are encouraged and not overpowered by their assignment since they are competing with their peers. In addition to the considerable amount of work involved in the game itself, they read without much coaxing texts on marketing management and advertising, and search the periodical literature for articles on promotion, pricing, channels, and dealer aid policies. They also analyze ten to fifteen cases describing the activities of companies with problems similar (or dissimilar) to their own. Most importantly, they read and analyze with a new insight which comes from a more responsible and broader view of the marketing manager's world.

DESCRIPTION OF THE M.I.T. GAME MODEL

The mathematical model developed for use in the M.I.T. Marketing Game is an example of the application of computer simulation techniques to problems of marketing interest. It is no accident that each of the complex business games cited in this article was developed by persons familiar with the techniques of digital computer simulation. While the marketing game model does not make extensive use of explicit formulations developed in connection with the marketing systems research currently in progress at M.I.T.,[1] the methods of approach and experience gained from that project permeated the design and programming stages of game development. The research activities have also benefited from game developments. We expect that empirical studies initiated in order to improve certain sectors of the marketing game will feed back and be of value in research.

The mathematical model for the M.I.T. Marketing Game is divided into two sections. The first, or market simulation model, determines industry sales and market shares for each competing company in each of three geographic regions. Treatment of companies by the market simulation model is entirely symmetrical, given the same initial conditions and in-

---

[1] A. E. Amstutz and G. B. Tallman, "Dynamic Simulation Applied to Marketing," *Marketing Keys to Profits in the 1960's* (Proceedings of the 42nd National Conference), American Marketing Association, June, 1959, pp. 78-95.

puts. Section two of the game model accepts information on the number and price of units sold by each company and produces a profit and loss statement based on assigned fixed and variable operating costs and expenditures by the teams. The accounting model is based on a simplification of generally accepted practices, and offers no particular conceptual difficulties. Primary attention is, therefore, focused on the market simulation model.

The simulation program operates to produce sales data on a basic time increment of one month, although financial documents are prepared quarterly. This time base allows market responses to promotional decisions and external factors to be lagged or spaced-out in varying proportions over several months. Thus, in advertising, for instance, an immediate action (price appeal) placement in newspapers or television can provoke an immediate sales response while an image building appeal placed in magazines can have a slow growth and decay of effect.

The market simulation model determines: (1) primary demand or industry sales; and (2) the market share of each competitor. Both are computed separately for each of the three geographic regions making up the national markets, cumulated over the three months within a quarter, and then added together for transmission to the accounting model in which financial documents for each company are prepared. The monthly sales figures by region, for each company are plotted on a graph and presented to the players along with financial reports. The form of data presentation facilitates evaluation of market trends as well as current position.

DETERMINING INDUSTRY SALES

A normal industry sales trend based on the percent of families that may be expected to purchase this type of product in each year following its introduction is built into the game model. This pattern reflects slow initial acceptance of floor polishers as a new appliance, then more rapid sales as the majority of consumers become potential buyers, followed in turn by the effects of market saturation. The several regions in the market differ as to the time when the product was introduced and the level of ownership at which saturation is likely to occur. This smooth trend is displaced by seasonal and cyclical factors which may be introduced by the game administrators as desired. The actual level of industry sales will deviate above or below this trend as the pricing and promotional policies of the student managers differ from those we have specified as "typical" or normal for the industry.[1]

---

[1] We do not imply that these preprogrammed normal promotional levels are optimum in any sense of the word.

Actual industry sales depend on programmed normal sales as influenced by: 1) an elasticity function based on the lowest price for each quality of product offered by any competitor, 2) a promotion elasticity function based on the aggregate of advertising and sales aids provided by *all* competitors, and 3) an aggregate retail margin elasticity function. Each of these functions has essentially an "S" shape made piecewise linear to facilitate computation. Thus, expenditures above and below certain levels are less effective than expenditures falling within the "normal" range. An "adequacy of distribution" function is also used to reduce sales if retail distribution is inadequate to reach the number of families otherwise expected to purchase the product. Function coefficients are built into the model, but, as stated earlier, a control team appraisal is used to modify the quantitative values of student inputs which are applied against the coefficients.

DETERMINING MARKET SHARE

Each company's sales are computed by multiplying actual industry sales by the market share achieved as the result of its pricing and promotional decisions, taken in relation to those made by its competitors.

Market share depends basically upon prices, advertising, and distribution policies. The general approach can be seen through an analysis of the computation for "effect of retail distribution." This function involves an interaction between the number of sales calls made on a particular store, trade advertising, the amount of point-of-purchase advertising accepted by the retailer for use in his store, retail margins, advertising allowances, and a "dealer enthusiasm function" which depends on sales in that outlet during the previous period. In addition, the marginal effect of adding sales calls responds favorably to increases in company media advertising. The allocation of sales effort among different styles and sizes of retail stores must be specified by the firm whether sales to stores are direct or through distributors. Since sales call effectiveness varies with the type of retail outlets and wholesale channel utilized, the policy chosen is of considerable importance.

The distribution effect on market share is computed separately for each type and size of retail outlet. The results are aggregated, and combined with the direct effects of prices and advertising to produce an overall market share figure. The firm's total sales for each region are then apportioned to the appropriate classes of retail outlets on the basis of each outlet's contribution to the total share of the market. The resultant sales breakdowns are fed back to the company teams.

Six types and three size classes of retailers—a total of eighteen separate groups in each of the three geographic regions—are recognized by the game model. Each of the groups is characterized as including a different number of outlets, and accounts for a different fraction of aggregate industry potential. The teams must allocate their available pool of sales calls, as determined by their sales force expenditures, among the various groups of stores, specifying the number of stores to be called upon in each case. Estimates of store census and market potential figures are given to the teams, but since the cost of providing salesmen to call upon all the stores in every class with a reasonable frequency is prohibitive, the resulting allocation problem is by no means trivial. In addition, if store types which appear to be incompatible with one another are included in the same channel of distribution, the control team will reduce its rating accordingly.

EFFECTIVENESS FUNCTIONS

The number of sales calls allocated by each company is transformed to an index of selling effectiveness according to a function approximating the one shown in Figure 1. For the example discussed above, the argument (x) is computed by multiplying the number of calls on a given type and size of retail outlet by the control team rating of the company's sales program and dividing the product by the number of stores to be covered. The dimension of this resultant is "net number of calls per store per quarter."

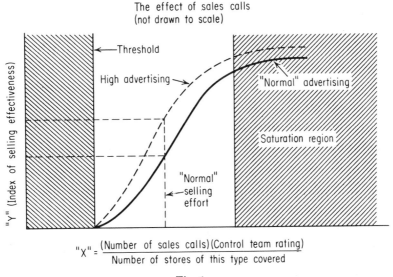

$$"X" = \frac{(\text{Number of sales calls})(\text{Control team rating})}{\text{Number of stores of this type covered}}$$

Fig. 1.

The index of selling effectiveness (Y) for a given value of (X) can be read off the solid curve, provided a "normal" amount of media advertising is being employed by the company. If advertising is increased the selling effectiveness curve will be rotated upward, as shown by the dotted curve. If advertising is cut, so is selling effectiveness. It can be seen that advertising changes both the height and the slope of the effectiveness function, with the greatest effect taking place at high (but not saturating) call frequencies—good promotion must be supported by adequate sales coverage.

Threshold and saturation effects exert a strong influence in the behavior of the selling effectiveness index, as well as in other parts of the market simulation model. The use of these particular characteristics is consistent with common sense and empirical evidence in marketing.[1] In addition, the saturation effects provide boundary conditions and constrain the operation of the system at its limits, thus introducing an important element of stability.

In summary, we believe that the following are the most important features of the M.I.T. Marketing Game simulation model.

1) The richness of marketing alternatives offered in the model, including the various kinds of promotional activities, different advertising functions, and distribution policy alternatives available at both the wholesale and retail level.

2) The incorporation of ratings of subjective factors in the marketing program, and the availability of feedback describing the control team's decisions.

3) A sufficient degree of complexity and disaggregation in the model formulations to allow feedback of detailed information to students and to guide the control team in performing its various tasks.

4) Representative interactions between the effects of different promotional policies, e.g., of advertising and selling expenditures.

5) The high degree of operational control enjoyed by the game administrator through the existence of a normal industry sales function and its associated exogenous inputs which permit booms, recessions, entry of competitors and competitive products and other external events to be easily effected.

6) The high degree of stability inherent in a model employing "S-shaped" effectiveness functions.

WHY A COMPLEX MARKETING GAME?

Our current high level of interest in gaming at M.I.T. stems from a degree of dissatisfaction with the more traditional methods of teaching advanced

---

[1] c.f. John A. Howard, *Marketing Management—Analysis and Decision* (Homewood, Ill.: Richard D. Irwin Co., 1957), p. 70.

courses in marketing policy and administration.[1] While we believe that textbook discussion and case approaches are valuable elements in the teacher's kit of tools, the advanced student can most fruitfully bring his newly acquired powers of analysis to bear in exercises that involve: 1) a wide range of relevant marketing problems and alternative solutions; 2) the presence of feedback of results; 3) a dynamic setting; and 4) a continuity of situation.

SPECIFIC ADVANTAGES OF GAMING IN MARKETING

The kind of exercises which we envision can clearly be built around an appropriate marketing game. The game provides each of the above advantages in the following manner:

1) It generates a variety of marketing problems and possibilities—important and miniscule, obvious and difficult to recognize, easy to cope with by standard techniques and completely intractable. The student must learn to search the environment, evaluate critical pieces of information, and take action where necessary. Moreover, he must exercise discretion in choosing problems to consider and the type and extent of analysis to be undertaken, or he will be overwhelmed by non-essential details. He must learn to recognize the important aspects of marketing situations and to match appropriate means and ends.

2) Since feedback of results is provided after every play, the student is given the opportunity to discover and remedy his mistakes—to learn from experience. Critical review of his forecasts, assumptions, and decisions in the harsh light of results can be a most valuable part of the learning process.

3) Games can be constructed so that players must make and carry out intermediate or long range plans. If firm advertising contracts must be let for several periods into the future the span of the planning period must be lengthened accordingly. This, in turn, might require an extended sales forecast, projection of requirements for salesmen, warehouse capacity, etc. The same condition holds where the full results of current advertising expenditures are not achieved until some months have passed, as is the case in the M.I.T. Marketing Game. It should be apparent that awareness of the problem of advanced planning and its relation to current decision making is important in marketing education.

---

[1] W. F. Massy, P. S. King, and C. D. Fogg, "The Place of a Business Game in the Marketing Curriculum," *Industrial Management Review* (M.I.T.), **II:2** (May, 1961), p. 43.

4) Continuity of situation is another byproduct of the sequential nature of game play. It implies three things as far as the student player is concerned. First, he is allowed more time to gain familiarity with the problem environment than would be possible in a "one-shot" exercise. Coupled with the feedback attribute discussed above, this usually results in a fair degree of intimacy with the environment once a few plays have been completed. ("Intimacy" is used in the sense of being "steeped" in a situation—one can handle the obvious details without effort, even though the more subtle considerations may still be out of reach.) Second, the student can be encouraged to develop and use routines for handling the simple repetitive tasks connected with each play. This skill is worthwhile for its own sake and, in addition, allows an increased amount of time to be spent on exceptional situations or special studies. Third, he must work in an environment which is at least partially of his own making. His own past decisions must be evaluated dispassionately, and he must learn to live with mistakes as well as success.

COMPARISON WITH THE CARNEGIE TECH HYPOTHESES

These four advantages of game play in marketing have been evolved from our experience in designing and using the M.I.T. Marketing Game. It may be interesting to compare them briefly with a set of strengths hypothesized for general management games.

By far the most comprehensive treatment has been that presented by Cohen and Rhenman.[1] They stress the following features of game play:

(1) the inter-relations between functional specialties; (2) the dynamics of play and the feedback of results; (3) the treatment of risk and uncertainty; (4) the necessity for systematic collection of information; (5) the provision of a field for systematic analysis; (6) the illustration of organizational problems; (7) the teaching of institutional facts; and (8) the focus of attention on planning and policy making. Except for points (6) and (7) the elements of this set are reasonably compatible with our marketing-oriented considerations discussed above. With respect to (6), the illustration of organizational problems, we frankly have not looked into its relation to the more substantive marketing questions described elsewhere.

As for point (7), we are quite emphatic in stating that we are *not* trying to teach institutional facts by having the students infer them from the structure of the game model. Two reasons for this view can be advanced. First, we agree with Cohen and Rhenman that such inference

---

[1] Kalman J. Cohen and Eric Rhenman, "The Role of Management Games in Education and Research," *Management Science,* **7:2** (January, 1961), p. 147.

becomes exceedingly difficult as the game becomes more complex—as more variables and stronger interactions between variables are introduced. Yet if the game is simplified to the point where effective inference becomes easy, the "facts" obtained are apt to be unrealistic. Second, the teaching of institutional facts by inference alone involves a substantial opportunity cost. We believe that to the extent that such facts are indeed known they can be taught better by other means. Textbooks or journal articles are excellent vehicles for communicating substantive materials or, if the subject matter is better expressed in the form of a computer or simulation model,[1] why not "open up the black box" and let the student examine the contents? This latter point of view corresponds to that of Forrester, expressed in his chapter in critique of business games.[2] While this article expresses a view that is generally contrary to the one presented there, we do agree with this aspect of his argument.

With respect to areas of agreement with Cohen and Rhenman, we find, first of all, that marketing games generally include at least rudimentary finance and production sectors, which insures that students will have the opportunity to observe interactions between functional specialties. Of even greater importance, perhaps, is the presence of interactions between the sub-specialties within marketing itself (e.g., advertising and sales management, line and research or planning functions, etc.). Second, the importance of game dynamics and feedback of results are well recognized and have already been discussed in several contexts.

It is our feeling that points (3) through (5) are of extreme importance, though they tend to run together in the marketing context. Our students are generally well aware of the presence of risk and uncertainty, and indeed of the influence of a complex competitive environment. As already stated, their problem is to (a) select appropriate long-range goals and immediate objectives, (b) choose those problems which are worthy of systematic study, (c) select and effectively process relevant kinds of information, and (d) apply the right decision-making criteria, based on the right models of the game "reality." Furthermore, this should be done in the context of multi-period plans and considered policies (8).

It should be noted that our goals with respect to gaming in marketing appear to go beyond those specifically discussed by Cohen and Rhenman in connection with points (3) through (5). Our game is, of course, intended to provide a field (or problem set) in which formal techniques for information processing and decision making can be invoked, *so far as they are applicable* given the current state of the art. We wish to go as far

---

[1] K. J. Cohen and R. M. Cyert, "Computer Models in Dynamic Economics," *Quarterly Journal of Economics,* LXXV (February, 1961), p. 112.

[2] Jay Forrester, *Industrial Dynamics,* M.I.T. Press (New York: John Wiley and Sons, Inc., 1961), pp. 357-360.

as possible in assisting students to find and utilize such techniques, but we would be over-optimistic to imply that their use can, by itself, lead to viable solutions for the bulk of marketing problems.

Quantitative and other formal marketing management techniques are growing rapidly in importance. The main *managerial problem,* however, lies not in learning their mechanics (though we do our best to teach these as well—in an earlier course) but in interpreting their results in terms of a reality that is much more complex than the models upon which the techniques are based. Linear programming might be utilized to provide a first approximation to a good selection of advertising media,[1] or simulation used to gain insight into the relative costs of various field warehouse configurations given existing demand patterns,[2] for example, but it would be amiss for marketing management to accept their findings *as given.* A careful analysis of assumptions made, with appropriate modification of results to fit the more complex real environment is clearly necessary in each case.

In our view, a comprehensive marketing game can be valuable in that students are given the opportunity to (a) apply systematic techniques, (b) interpret their results in the light of a "real" situation, and (c) compare the effects of using them, as modified, with those deriving from a purely intuitive approach. The real payoff is obtained if students not only develop some sense of judgment in the interpretive stage but also learn to appreciate the power, and practicality, of the combined "systematic procedure—intuitive" approach. We will go out on a limb and submit that to instill this attitude or frame of reference should be a major long-run goal for professional education in marketing management.[1] It seems clear that a comprehensive game is ideally suited to provide this kind of marketing education.

SUMMARY AND CONCLUSION

The purpose of this paper has been to describe the M.I.T. Marketing Game and—even more important—to make clear the premises upon which its design and utilization are based. The game is not simple to play, nor is it inexpensive to administer. Between one third and one half of the

---

[1] W. J. Baumol, "Mathematical Models and Thinking in Marketing," *Marketing, a Maturing Discipline* (Proceedings of the Winter Meeting, December, 1960), American Marketing Association, Chicago, 1961.

[2] R. B. Maffei and H. N. Shycon, "Simulation—Tool for Better Distribution," *Harvard Business Review,* **38:6** (November-December, 1960), pp. 65-76.

[3] We make a distinction between education for marketing management, and education for research or operations research, in the field of marketing. The latter should be oriented more towards methodology and technical competence.

available resources in our one semester advanced marketing courses, and approximately one fourth of the available class and study time in our executive seminars in marketing planning have had to be devoted to playing the game. The opportunity costs of allocations like these are high, as are the direct costs of personnel (one half time research assistant and considerable faculty time) and of machine time (approximately ten minutes of 709 time per quarter of play). These costs have required that the potential payoffs of gaming be considered carefully. We feel that use of the game is more than justified.

It should be clear that in our opinion not all games, nor even all marketing games, are suitable vehicles for attaining the teaching goals we have in mind. We have used the term "complex" gaming to indicate a type of game that provides a rich environment which will be sensitive to student decisions. We have stressed the use of human referees to handle decision problems for which no computer program can currently be written. The game as a whole must be built around the material to be taught, rather than around the capabilities of a particular piece of hardware, such as a computer.

In summary, it may be useful to quote from the set of guidelines we developed in connection with the design and use of our complex Marketing Game:[1]

(1) Reality of situation, freedom of student action, sensitivity to decision, and general plausibility of results are the most important characteristics of the complex marketing game. A particular real industry must be simulated with sufficient accuracy so that empirical data on product characteristics, known consumer preferences, media advertising rates and coverage, available types of outlets and their characteristics, and economic considerations can be open for student research. Once convinced that arbitrariness and artificiality have been largely removed, students can be encouraged to place themselves in the role of marketing executives of real firms. Achieving this frame of mind is, of course, one of the central objectives of the game. Students come to feel responsible for the fortunes of their firms. They are competing with their peers, not, as in a case analysis, attempting to improve on the decisions of experienced businessmen. They are made to feel that they have realistic freedom to respond to market vicissitudes and that operating results are meaningful and fair. The instructor becomes a consultant to men with pressing and difficult problems. In these circumstances student identification with the role of the marketing executive comes readily and easily.

---

[1] W. F. Massy, P. S. King, C. D. Fogg, *op. cit.*, pp. 48-49.

(2) In view of the richness of decision alternatives necessary for the effective teaching of marketing management, the game should follow the model of "Free Kriegspiel" rather than of "Rigid Kriegspiel," the two types of war gaming that grew up in Prussia during the nineteenth century.[2] In the free variety of war game, the experienced judgment of human referees played an important role. In developing a complex marketing game, one must similarly make provision for referees to rate variables such as advertising copy and appeals. Use of referees avoids the need to design an impossibly elaborate model and simultaneously the need to restrict the freedom of action of the players. Referees are thus an essential feature of a complex marketing game.

(3) In formulating detailed, realistic programs the student must have access to information equivalent to that which would be available in the real world. Most games include provision for market research and experimentation. When referees are used they, too, provide exceedingly valuable feedback data. They are particularly needed in providing feedback of qualitative information and are the source of all quantitative feedback not generated by the computer. We believe, in addition, that the student should be encouraged to reason by considering marketing principles and analogies from the real world. If the student views the game as realistic, supplementary readings become aids in solving *immediate* problems and not merely problems he may encounter ten years hence. Thus the student, because he is playing the game, may become more—rather than less—interested in supplementary readings and cases. The use of real world information need not diminish the significant aspects of the structure of the environment simulation. But how different this is from the blind probing which would result from students being forced to assume that the real world offers few lessons for the game player.

(4) Even though one is attempting to construct a realistic game in the sense described above, it will be necessary to abstract and simplify, especially within the mathematical model. The abstractions should be performed so that it is worthwhile for the student to apply systematic techniques and valid marketing principles. It may be practical, for example, to construct an advertising effectiveness function in a way such that a team which intelligently uses linear programming to find a media plan which maximizes exposure among a certain population, *ceteris paribus* does better than a competitor who does not.

---

[2] J. P. Young, *A Survey of Historical Developments in War Games,* Staff Paper ORO-SP-98, Operations Research Office, the John Hopkins University, 1959.

(5) The comprehensive marketing game is a vehicle through which the use of marketing tool variables can be taught. The game itself cannot do the job, as the simulation is not completely accurate and the outputs are often as difficult to interpret as events in the real world itself. In the last analysis, the actual learning and teaching responsibilities lie where they always have—with the student as he studies and interacts with his fellows and with the instructor as he guides the students' efforts and helps interpret their experience. The game merely provides a focal point for these efforts.

While the M.I.T. Marketing Game does not at present meet all of our desired specifications, we believe that we have moved in the right direction and, indeed, have proved the feasibility of the approach we advocate. We are at present working on a refined version of the game model and supplementary materials. When this project is completed, we shall welcome the opportunity to share the results with others who have a parallel interest.